AWN

In Search of Muhammad

In Search of Muhammad

Clinton Bennett

CASSELL
London and New York

Cassell

Wellington House, 125 Strand, London WC2R 0BB
370 Lexington Avenue, New York, NY 10017-6550

First published 1998

British Library Cataloguing-in-Publication Data
A catalogue record for this book is available from the British Library

ISBN   0-304-33700-5 (Hardback)
       0-304-70401-6 (Paperback)

Library of Congress Cataloging-in-Publication Data

Bennett, Clinton.
   In Search of Muhammad / Clinton Bennett.
      p.   cm.
   Includes bibliographical references (p.   ) and index.
   ISBN 0-304-33700-5 (hardcover). — ISBN 0-304-70401-6 (pbk.)
   1. Muhammad, Prophet, d 632—Biography—History and criticism.
   I. Title.
   BP75.3.B46 1998
   297.6'3—dc21
   [B]   98–12243
                                                       CIP

Typeset by Ben Cracknell Studios
Printed and bound in Great Britain by Biddles Ltd, Guildford and King's Lynn

Contents

Acknowledgements   vii

Introduction   1

Part One

1 Muhammad of History: the Primary Sources   17
2 The Sources: a Critical Evaluation   37

Part Two

3 Non-Muslim Lives of Muhammad: from the 7th
  to the 16th Centuries   69
4 Non-Muslim Lives: from the Renaissance to Today   93

Part Three

5 Muhammad's Significance in Muslim Life
  and Thought   139
6 Conversations Islamic   194

Conclusion: Towards a Postmodern Theology
of Religions   205

Appendix One: Time-Line of Main Events   245
Appendix Two: Muhammad's Marriages   249
Appendix Three: Questionnaire   253
References   257
Index   271
Index of Qu'ranic References   275
Index of Hadith References   276

Acknowledgements

The idea of writing a book about Muhammad dates back to 1989, when I attended a Christian–Muslim colloquium in Toronto, Canada. Professor David Kerr, then of Hartford Seminary (now at Edinburgh University), presented a paper on 'Divine Revelation and the Person of the Prophet', and Professor Mahmoud Ayoub of Temple University a paper on 'Divine Revelation and the Person of Jesus Christ'. These attempts, by a Christian scholar (who supervised my own doctoral work) to appreciate the Prophet Muhammad, and by a Muslim to appreciate Jesus, were stimulating and provocative. I would like to acknowledge David Kerr's passionate concern for a proper Christian approach to Muhammad as a major source of inspiration behind the writing of this book. At that time, however, I was just completing my doctoral research, followed by work on the published version, *Victorian Images of Islam* (1992), so a detailed study of the Prophet had to wait.

During 1993, I tentatively floated the possibility of working on what I called a 'theology of Muhammad' at a research seminar here at Westminster College. My colleagues expressed interest in the proposal, which subsequently found its way on to a list of future staff research projects! Some material which now forms part of Chapters 3 and 4 was originally presented at a gathering of Islamicists in the Selly Oak Colleges, Birmingham and also in the summer of 1994 at the Henry Martyn Institute of Islamic Studies in Hyderabad, India. The gathering of Islamicists is a group which has met annually, in the peaceful setting of Leasow House, Crowther Hall, for more than a decade. We read papers, exchange research, and offer mutual support and encouragement. Most of us are professional academics, many of us work in secular institutions. However, we share a concern to reflect theologically, as Christians, on what we study. We initially met under the auspices of the former British Council of Churches, and with the financial support of the Church Missionary (now Mission) Society. Not a few of us have served as missionaries.

Over the years, members of the annual gathering have contributed considerably to my thinking about Islam and the Prophet, indeed, to my knowledge of Islam – hence my references to books or chapters by members of the group in this study. I especially want to thank Bishop Michael Nazir Ali (who first directed me to the writings of Muhammad Iqbal), Dr George Bebawi, Dr Hugh Goddard, Professor A. K. S. Lambton, Dr Christopher Lamb, Dr Philip Lewis, Dr Neil Robinson, Dr Sigvard von Sicard (who examined my doctoral thesis) and Dr David Thomas. It was through the annual gathering, too, that I first met Dr Martin Forward, now Senior Tutor at Wesley House, Cambridge, who over the years has become a valued friend. His *Muhammad: A Short Biography* (1997), like this book, underlines the importance of Muhammad for all aspects of Islam. Martin explores Muhammad's role in such contemporary debates as *jihad*, apostasy, the status of women and men, and the Salman Rushdie affair, some of which I discuss, some I do not consider in any detail. 'Who is Muhammad for today's world?', he asks, 'And how may we find him?' (p. 97). Martin is somewhat less convinced than I am by the attempts of Kenneth Cragg, W. M. Watt and others 'to deem Muhammad a prophet' (p. 120). Nor does he think that the person of Jesus, about whom 'Christian and Muslim beliefs ... are so different' can 'ever be other than a divisive figure' (p. 72). This is at odds with my own conclusion to this book. Latterly, the members of the annual gathering were joined by Muslim partners; amongst others, by Dr Farid Esack whose *Qu'ran, Liberation and Pluralism* (1997) has stimulated my concluding reflections to this study.

Other projects, addressing methodological issues within Religious Studies' research, and what I call the 'outsider–insider polarity', intervened before I could begin this book. This work, however, helped to clarify my agenda: I would not attempt a critical biography of the Prophet as such, nor would my main focus be problematical issues *per se*. Rather, I would explore differences and similarities between insider and outsider accounts of the Prophet and, in concluding, suggest a possible Christian response. This addresses what I believe to be a relatively neglected area, and takes us to the interface between theology, history, fieldwork research and religious studies where I am most happily located; hence my concept of 'anthropological theology'. Like my last book, this one arises directly out of my teaching and research interests at Westminster College, Oxford, and has been made possible by a generous allocation of research hours. I particularly wish to record my gratitude to Dr Bernard Farr, formerly Director of Academic Programmes and Research, now a Fellow Emeritus, and to Dr Richard Ralph, Principal. I am also grateful to the Faculty of the Department of Religion at Baylor University, Texas, for electing me to an associate professorship. I hope that this book, which wrestles with the tension between my Christian faith and my encounter with Islam, will be read as an open-ended search for theological possibilities and not as a final, complete, no-questions-left-unanswered text. I fear that I may sometimes have fallen into a gulf – between my personal faith on one side, and my desire to respond to Islam on the other! However, if God's nature is made known to us through the biblical record, then it is right for us to inquire whether God is speaking to us through what we encounter in other world-views – as long as this does not contradict what we know of God in Christ, who is the touchstone for all Christians.

I gladly acknowledge academic indebtedness to all whose work I have referenced in this book; some – including Wilfred Cantwell Smith, Paul Knitter, John Hick – I have met; at least one, Lesslie Newbigin (who died earlier this year), once taught me; C. E. Bosworth was my external PhD examiner; Geertz, Lindholm, Zakaria, amongst others, I know only from their writing. However, I take full responsibility for any errors, misrepresentation or inadequacy in what follows. I can properly attribute this to nobody but myself. I hope, though, that despite any sins of omission and of commisison, this book will contribute something towards a better understanding, by outsiders especially, of the Prophet of Islam. 'The Red Menace is Gone. But Here's Islam', proclaimed headlines in the *New York Times* (21 January 1996; see Said, 1997: xix). In this book, I argue that 'Islam equals the Prophet'; thus, the view that 'Islam' equals 'everything-we-must-now-fight-against', which such headlines promote and which Said critiques, underscores the importance of trying to understand the Prophet.

As usual, the staff of Cassell Academic deserve praise for all they have done to produce this book. A word here about the cover illustration might be appropriate. The design team, after consultation, sent me a large choice of material. This included several artistic representations of the Prophet. My initial instinct had been to go for a mosaic, or calligraphic cover. However, when I saw these beautiful illustrations, I decided to choose the Prophet's Ascent. This incident is typical of how insiders and outsiders have interpreted Muhammad's story in radically different ways. For Muslims, Muhammad's Ascent is a real, if mystical, event. From it, they derive the five daily prayers, which lie at the heart of Muslim practice. Outsiders have ridiculed the event, dismissing it as pious fraud, as simply absurd, thereby also denying any historical link between Muhammad and Islam's third most sacred city, Jerusalem. Islamic art, too, has not infrequently depicted the Prophet – despite what is often said about Islam's lack of representational art.

The research offered in this book was conducted in libraries, on the World Wide Web, and in the field. Several Muslim friends assisted me with this project by arranging interviews and also by reading and commenting on the draft text. Libraries used were the University of Cambridge Library, the India Institute Library, Oxford, the Central Library of the Selly Oak Colleges, Birmingham, and the Learning Resource Centre of Westminster College, Oxford. I have also drawn on earlier research carried out in the British Library, the India Office Library, London, the Birmingham University Library and Birmingham Central Library and the Library of the Harford Seminary Foundation, Connecticut, USA. Over Easter 1997, the Taizé Community, near Cluny, France, gave me space on retreat to proof-read my draft MS. I am very grateful to the brothers for providing this facility. In the crypt of the Church of the Reconciliation, where I had the privilege of presiding at an Easter-morning Eucharist for our small group of Westminster College pilgrims, there is a beautiful icon of the Holy Trinity. I bought a replica of this, which now adorns our lounge at No 2 House, Westminster College; as I attempted to ground my conclusion in Trinitarian thought, I found myself contemplating this icon – somehow, it has come to represent for me the inclusiveness of God's love, the breadth of God's embrace. My field research took place during visits to Bangladesh in the summers of 1996 and 1997, and amongst my Muslim students here on campus. (I also draw on sustained encounters with Muslims, in various contexts, over the last two decades.) I am grateful to my brother-in-law and to Tushar Kona Khandker (a family friend) for assisting me during my stays in Bangladesh, to all who returned my questionnaire (see Appendix 3) and to all who, wittingly or unwittingly, have given me 'insider' responses.

Qu'ranic quotations in this book are derived from Muhammad Marmaduke Pickthall's English rendering, *The Meaning of the Glorious Koran*, first published in 1930. However, I have also consulted the Arabic. Thus, I sometimes take liberties with Pickthall, either stylistically or to help to interpret the meaning of the text. References to the biographical work of Ibn Ishaq are all from Alfred Guillaume's 1955 translation and is referenced thus, I.I. plus page number, unless given as rendered in another source. When I have managed to trace a saying of the Prophet, a *hadith*, to one of the classical collections, I have used standard referencing, namely B for Bukhari, M for Muslim, and Tir for Tirmidhi; thus, for example, B 3:37 refers to book 3, chapter 37, of Bukhari's *sahih*. To help readers locate references to particular *hadith* from some of the longer chapters of Bukhari, I also cite the number of the *hadith* following the Khan (1987) English (with Arabic) edition. Because of the frequency of citations from James Robson's translation of the *Mishkat-al-Masabih* (1990 edition) I have simplified my references to the *Mishkat*; here I identify the volume and the page number (e.g. MM, vol. 1, p. 3). Occasionally, I have been unable to trace a commonly cited *hadith* to any recognized collection; thus no reference has been given. As I hope to reach a general as well as a specialist readership, I have, rightly or wrongly – who knows? – decided not to use diacritical markings in this text. Some will no doubt find this deplorable in what aspires to be a work of scholarship; others may thank me for sparing them a lesson in linguistics, if not in orthography. I have, however, included in transliterations the Arabic *hamza* (') and *ayn* ('), and have also used my preferred rendition of such Arabic words as Makkah rather than Mecca, Madinah rather than Medina, Qu'ran rather than Koran, and so on.

Finally, I dedicate this book to my wife, Rekha Bennett, and in memory of my father, Howard Bennett, who died on 10 June 1997. Not only has Rekha put up with my long absences in the study, but she daily renews my commitment to pluralism by challenging me to move between two cultural worlds. It was my father's love of travel, I think, which (in part at least) inspired my own. My interest in cultures, religions, and in 'others' followed from this wanderlust. Without my father's help, too, I would not have been able to support myself through my initial theology degree at Manchester University – study on which I continue to draw in all my writing and teaching. Sadly, my father died without meeting my wife. It thus seems right to me to bring them together, as it were, in this dedication, since I (and in different ways, this book) owe them both huge debts of gratitude.

Clinton Bennett
The Vestry Study
Westminster College, Oxford
Hilary Term, 1998.

To
Rekha Bennett
and
Howard Bennett
(1922–1997)

Introduction

Why Muhammad?

Why did I choose the Prophet Muhammad as the focus of this study? First, whilst writing my earlier book (Bennett, 1992) which examined attitudes to Islam generally, I discovered that scholars' views of the Prophet inevitably colour their overall evaluation of Islam. Second, in dialogue with Muslims, the question, 'What do you think of Muhammad?' has repeatedly surfaced; as Cragg (1984) points out, 'There is an issue that disturbs Muslims more than any other in their approach to Christians ... It is ... the silence and reserve of Christians regarding Muhammad' (p. ix, citing a Muslim participant at a seminar in Tripoli, Libya). Cragg's *Muhammad and the Christian: A Question of Response* was 'at least one Christian's' attempt to fill this silence (*ibid.*). Third, my Muslim friend and colleague, Jabal Buaben (1996), has called for a scholarly *jihad* by Muslims and non-Muslims towards a fair and just portrait of the Prophet; 'effort', he says, 'to arrive at a dispassionate and more judicious application of the ubiquitous "scientific method" [*vis-à-vis* Muhammad] is a form of *jihad* for all scholars, be they Muslims or not' (p. 330). This, then, is my *jihad*.

'Muhammad is dead. But he is dead only in the least significant sense. For he is ideologically alive – and well', writes Shabbir Akhtar (1992: 28). Muhammad's memory, example and name are universally revered by Muslims, for whom he represents the highest human ideal. To vilify Muhammad, as many Muslims believe Salman Rushdie's novel *The Satanic Verses* (1988) did, constitutes – where Islamic Law is established – a punishable offence. The Salman Rushdie affair, with its call for Rushdie's execution, has newly alerted non-Muslims to Muhammad's ongoing significance in Muslim life and in the faith and practice of Islam, the world's second largest religion. This raises interesting questions, for non-Muslims especially, about who Muhammad was. What can be historically verified – as it were 'known' – about this figure, born, as one writer puts it, 'within the full light of history' (Hitti, 1961: 111; as I shall indicate, this historicity is challenged by some scholars)? On the one hand, any cursory glance through standard biographies of Muhammad such as those of Rodinson (1961) or Watt (1953, 1956, 1961), to cite some easily available works by non-Muslim academics, shows that we know a great deal about his life. On the other hand, these texts also reveal gaps in our information. For example, we know relatively little about Muhammad's childhood. Indeed, Henri Lammens

(1862–1937) went so far as to 'almost completely reject ... accounts of the Meccan period' (Watt, 1953: xiii). Perhaps, before he became a significant figure within the affairs of his community and on the stage of world history, nobody took much notice of him. Therefore, nobody could remember much about him from this early period. Also, stories associated with Muhammad's early life recount miracles; this, for some readers, raises the issue of what role myth-making might have played in their telling. Were these miracles invented after Muhammad had become significant, to indicate his future greatness (by investing his early life with suitable signs and wonders), or did they really happen? Of course, once Muhammad had become the Prophet of his people, the supernatural did play (or is said to have played) a crucial role in his story. This is especially true of the relationship between the Prophet and Islam's scripture, the Qu'ran, which, according to Muslims, Muhammad received word-for-word from God during a series of revelatory trances.

When history and theology meet

What we have here, perhaps, is the problematic of dealing not only with a man who undisputably did live but also of dealing with a man to whom spiritual qualities and significance are ascribed. Whilst Muslims quickly point out that Muhammad was only a man, that his biological makeup was the same as that of any reader of this book, they also point out that Muhammad was spiritually unique. It is interesting, in passing, to note that we know much less about Jesus than we do about Muhammad. In the famous quest of the historical Jesus, once Gospel accounts of miracles (including those associated with Jesus' birth and death) are subtracted, we are left with very few hard facts about his life. This is not the case with Muhammad. Although miracles are narrated in the biographical traditions, once these are subtracted we still have substantial material with which to reconstruct his biography. Thus, although I shall have cause to discuss some pessimistic views about the value and reliability of this reconstruction, it is possible to argue that through historical–critical study we can gain access to the flesh-and-blood man. However, what I argue in this book is that historical reconstruction of Muhammad's biography is not enough. It simply does not, in and of itself, explain why Muhammad has remained so important in the life of Muslims, individually and corporately. We can only begin to understand this phenomenon when we add to our historical reconstruction an investigation of what Muslims believe *theologically* about Muhammad. Inevitably, this takes us out of the arena of pure history into the arena of faith, of belief in supernatural things. If we are not prepared to explore the Muhammad of Muslim faith as well as the historical Muhammad, we shall fail to understand his continued significance. Muslims were not angered and upset by Rushdie's treatment of Muhammad (assuming that the character in the book should be identified with Muhammad; see my discussion in Chapter 7) because he was an important person in the seventh century. They were, and remain, upset because he is still an important person in their lives today;

Muhammad is reported to have said, 'None of you will have faith till he loves me more than his father, his children and all mankind' (B 2:8).

The theological dimension

Historical reconstruction leaves us (setting aside for now debates about whether we can accurately reconstruct Muhammad's life) with a man, perhaps like Caesar, Alexander the Great, or Napoleon, who made a permanent mark on history, and who left the world a different place for having lived and achieved greatness. It does not leave us with a man whose name or reputation, if vilified today, might result in imprisonment or even death. Nor would it leave us with a man whose example millions follow – for whom the highest ideal is to imitate Muhammad. Non-Muslims, secular women and men, humanists, or followers of a religious tradition which has difficulty accepting the truth of Muslim claims about Muhammad, may not believe in Muhammad's link with the supernatural; yet only by discussing what Muslims believe about this can they begin to understand his significance. The question of miracles has been debated by Muslims as well as non-Muslims, but for Muslims the significance of Muhammad's success cannot be separated from the one miracle which no Muslim doubts – the Qu'ranic revelation. No one can begin, I believe, to understand what Muhammad means to Muslims without exploring the relationship between Muhammad and the book he recited. For those who do not believe in the possibility of supernatural revelation, this exploration will be problematic. However, even if our own world-view compels us to explain the Qu'ran away as Muhammad's own creation, unless we attempt to appreciate what Muslims believe about its revelation Muslim belief about Muhammad will also remain beyond our grasp.

What this book sets out to do, then, is to explore different understandings of Muhammad – what can be said about the Muhammad of history by Muslims and non-Muslims, what can be said about the Muhammad of faith by Muslims and non-Muslims, and what similarities and differences arise as a result of our different (insider or outsider) starting points. This book is written by a non-Muslim scholar of Islam and addresses itself, primarily, to non-Muslims who wish to understand more about Muhammad's significance, or to appreciate his importance for Muslim faith and practice. However, as I shall indicate below, this book will try to treat its subject-matter in a way which I hope Muslims will find sober, scholarly and sympathetic. I also hope that a book about Muhammad by a non-Muslim who wants to engage seriously with Muslim convictions will attract some interest from Muslims themselves. Indeed, I hope that what follows may be of some value to Muslims as they engage in the process of interpreting their faith for today. Wilfred Cantwell Smith (1959) says, 'It is possible, both in theory and in practice for an outside scholar to break new ground in stating the meaning of a faith in, say, modern terms more successfully than a believer' (p. 43).

This, of course, begs huge questions: questions about methodology, epistemology, the role of subjectivity, as well as about the difference between insider and outsider knowledge. If we do not share Muslim belief about Muhammad, can we actually understand his significance? Can an outsider ever really understand another faith's significance, from an insider's point of view, or does it 'take one to know one'? This is a question which students of religions, anthropologists and others have long debated. Too often, anthropologists assumed an almost god-like ability to construct other people's cultural stories, believing that they understood more about others than the others did about themselves. Similarly, non-Muslim scholars of Islam have reduced Islam to a construct of their own making, often to justify their own preconceived fears or prejudices, if not their own notion of European or Christian superiority. Recognition of this has led to what Clifford Geertz, an anthropologist who has researched in and written about Muslim societies, calls an 'epistemological hypochondria, concerning how one can know that anything one says about other forms of life is as a matter of fact so' (1988: 71). Some go so far as to say that we can only ever understand ourselves or members of our own group. If it does, indeed, take one to know one, then the best that a non-native or outsider-scholar can achieve is a form of autobiography. This view would preclude any non-Muslim from understanding Muhammad's significance, any non-Christian from understanding Christ's. This usefully introduces discussion about the methodological assumptions which inform the writing of this book.

My methodology

Throughout, this book adopts a multi-disciplinary approach to its subject-matter. It draws on historiography, theology, anthropology – all tools with which I have worked, as a scholar, at various stages of my career. I began as a theologian, moved into Islamic Studies and, more recently, into anthropology and the use of ethnography in educational research. An underlying concern will be a focus on how, by whom and why images, histories, concepts, are constructed. Who tells the story? Do different people tell a different story and, if so, why? Modern historiography, as well as anthropology, recognizes that historical discourses result from selective processes of choosing particular 'strands of thought' instead of others. Michel Foucault (1926–84), for example, in *The Archaeology of Knowledge* (1972) and other writings has drawn our attention to the relationship between power and knowledge; knowledge, he says, is 'constructed' by those who exercise power. Histories can be made to tell selective stories to justify the political or social privileges enjoyed by the élite or powerful, or to justify present-day ideological dogmas.

Edward Said (1978) draws our attention to how self-serving images of the 'other' have often been created to confirm one's own sense of racial or cultural superiority, or to justify one's acquisition of other people's territory. He characterizes Western scholarship of the non-Western world, or 'Orientalism', as the West's corporate institution for dealing with the Orient – dealing with it by making statements about it, authorising views of it, describing it, by teaching it, settling it, ruling over it; in short, Orientalism is a Western style for dominating, restructuring, and having authority over the Orient. (1978: 3)

However, says Said, this 'construct' bore little relationship to the Oriental reality; there was but little correspondence between the Orientalist construct and the external reality it purported to describe. 'Knowledge of the Orient, because generated out of strength, in a sense creates the Orient, the Oriental and his world' (1978: 40). Norman Daniel's classic, *Islam and the West: The Making of an Image* (1993), also shows how Europeans constructed a self-serving image of Muslims as the 'other', as the exact counterpoise of their own self-image. They were good, their religion was true and God-given; therefore Muslims were evil and Islam, their religion, was false and Satanic. They were civilized, therefore Muslims were barbaric. In this process the 'others' became 'objects', defined not by their own discourses, but by a discourse which was imposed on them from outside. At its worst, this approach to scholarship of the other was, as indicated above, self-serving, grossly biased, a travesty of any claim to objectivity and truthfulness. I do not subscribe to the view that everything produced by Western scholars must be rejected (nor do I think that their motives were always suspect); much of the data collected and analysed remains of use today. Hourani (1979) was right to criticize Said for constructing 'an ideal type of 'Orientalist''; 'ideal types must be used with care' (p. 29). 'There is ... running through the work of the great Islamic scholars', Hourani continued (p. 29),

one central strand of concern ... which attempted to articulate what Muslims believed to be the revelation given to mankind through the Prophet Muhammad: tradition, law, theology, mystical thought. A hundred years of study of these matters have produced a body of work which cannot be regarded as badly done.

However, I do not agree with Lewis (1982) that Said's 'Orientalism' is nothing but a straw man invented in order to be knocked down; post-Said, we cannot accept any claim to be an 'authority' but must interrogate all texts to unmask the hidden assumptions which inform and shape them.

At its best, the Orientalist approach to scholarship of the other was descriptive and classificatory; sometimes, too, it was 'rather dull' (Hourani, 1979: 30). Hourani suggests that Said left the German contribution 'on religious and intellectual history', which he deems to have been 'painstaking and solid', out of his book because it 'lacked that spark which would excite Mr Said's mind'! Or perhaps, as Wilfred Cantwell Smith put it in his seminal 1959 essay on methodology within the Study of Religions (already cited above), 'The traditional form of Western scholarship in the study of other men's religions was that of an impersonal presentation of an "it"' (1959: 34).

Earlier, in his inaugural lecture at McGill University, Smith compared these scholars with 'flies crawling on the surface of a goldfish bowl, making accurate observations ... on the fish inside ... but never asking themselves, and never finding out, how it feels to be a goldfish' (1950: 2). Smith goes on to call for a new, personalized approach to the study of religion, in which, instead of Muslims being viewed as 'objects', they become partners and co-subjects:

The first great innovation in recent times has been the personalization of the faiths observed, so that one finds a discussion of a 'they'. Presently, the observer becomes personally involved, so that the situation is one of a 'we' talking about a 'they'. The next step is a 'dialogue', where 'we' talk to 'you'. If there is listening and mutuality, this may become that 'we' talk with you. The culmination of this process is when 'we all' are talking with each other about 'us'. (1959: 35)

According to Said, the real failure of the Orientalists' enterprise was their insistence on treating the people they studied as if they were inalienably different, occupying a different world from their own:

I consider Orientalism's failure to be a human as much as an intellectual one; for in having to take up a position of irreducible opposition to a region of the world it considered alien to its own, Orientalism failed to identify with human experience, failed also to see it as human experience. (1978: 328)

Smith's approach, I believe, serves as an antidote to the mistakes of Orientalism. In his view, anything said by a non-Muslim scholar about Islam is only 'valid' if it 'can be acknowledged by that religion's believers' (1959: 42). Here, we are dealing not only with a religion's 'externals', its texts, artefacts, observed practices, but with 'a personal thing, in the lives of men'. Smith wrote:

The externals of religion ... can be examined separately ... but these are not in themselves religion, which lies rather in the area of what these mean to those who are involved. The student is making effective progress when he recognises that he has to do not with religious systems basically but with religious persons; or at least with something interior to persons. (1959: 35)

This is exactly what this book aims to achieve – an understanding of what Muhammad means to those for whom he is Prophet, and of what he might, can or does mean for those for whom he is not a Prophet. I do investigate and describe 'externals' but my fundamental aim is to hear Muslim voices. When I examine textual and historical material, my aim is both to uncover voices which can be found within the texts, and to listen to other Muslim voices which have commented on and interpreted these texts. Since 1978, when I began my Islamic Studies as a post-graduate student at Birmingham University, my engagement with Islam has been dialogical as well as textual; I have discoursed with Muslims in Bangladesh, Britain, India, Turkey and Egypt. I have visited North Africa, Indonesia and Malaysia. I have encountered Sunni and Shi'a, women and men, converts and cradle-Muslims, Sufi and anti-Sufi Muslims, conservative and radical Muslims. Recently, members of the Oxford Centre for Islamic Studies have shared my teaching on Islam at Westminster, and have attended some of my lectures. In writing this book, I attempt to bring all these Muslim voices into dialogue with my textual sources.

I first encountered Smith's dictum, that the aim of an outside scholar writing about Islam is to elicit Muslim approval, towards the very beginning of my study of Islam, and have tried ever since to make it my motto. I have also tried to bring my study of Islam into constant discourse with Muslims themselves. This, I believe, has been (and remains) a profoundly anthropological exercise, similar to the 'historical anthropology' which Charles Lindholm has offered in his 1996 study, *The Islamic Middle East: An Historical Anthropology*. Lindholm is trying to bridge the gulf between history and anthropology, which, he says, 'have, unfortunately, grown too far apart' (p. xiv; see Bennett, 1996a: 125f). Like his, my primary concern is not with historical reconstruction but with 'developing, applying and re-thinking theory' (*ibid.*).

Phenomenology of religion

This century, both anthropology and Religious Studies have been influenced by phenomenology. This methodology or approach, as applied within these disciplines, seeks to enable a truer seeing of the 'other'. As a philosophical concept, phenomenology was pioneered by Edmund Husserl (1859–1938). In the academic study of religions, it was further developed by the Dutch scholar Gerardus van der Leeuw (1890–1950). Husserl's aim was to 'get back to things' – that is, to 'phenomena' – 'in themselves'. To do this, he said, we first need to free ourselves of preconceived theories and interpretive frameworks into which, if we are not careful, we will try to squeeze our data. We can all too easily mould our material, whether textual or anthropologically observed, to fulfil our preconceived theories. Historians, reconstructing the past, have often found there the evidence they need to justify their current ideological assumptions – Marxists find justification for Marxism, anarchists for anarchy, and so on. Anthropologists, too, have 'seen' what they have wanted to see. Husserl's method, then, was designed to filter out the distortions and prejudices which, according to Foucault, Said and Daniel, have too often 'created' an 'image' of the 'object studied' which bears no relationship to the 'reality' of the object. Such 'constructs' actually tell us more about the observers than they do about the observed. To filter out our a priori assumptions, Husserl proposed five stages of what he called '*epoche*', a process of 'bracketing out' values, presuppositions, judgements and prejudices, thus suspending our judgement until the phenomena have manifested their 'own essence'.

First, this process requires us to 'bracket out' our own likes and dislikes, including our emotions. Next, we must similarly 'bracket out' our theories and ideas in order to 'get back to things in themselves'. Third, we must 'bracket out' all philosophical assumptions so that the 'phenomena' in and of themselves can be isolated for study and scrutiny. Frank Whaling (1984) explains the next stages thus:

fourth, having performed this three fold *epoche*, there was the further step of getting behind the externals of phenomena in order to get through to their inwardness, the technical term for this process being the exercise of *Einfuhlung* (empathy); fifthly, there was the final step of getting behind the accidents of phenomena in order to unfold their essence (*eidos*), the technical term for this process being 'eidetic vision'. (p. 211)

This is not a clinical process, but involves the observer moving 'close enough to the subject of study so that the religious pulse makes itself felt against, or even within, his own skin' (Arthur, 1986: 81). However, having penetrated to the 'phenomena', and described them, scholars will want to incorporate their findings within a broader theoretical or interpretive framework; anthropologists study particular groups because they want to make sense of human life generally. As Geertz (1983) has put it, the anthropologist will always oscillate 'between looking particularly at particular views and defining globally the attitude that permeates them' (p. 11). Thus, a further stage in phenomenology has been advanced which involves stepping back into one's own world-view and accounting for one's 'new experience' in the light of that world-view.

Virtual insidership

Before turning to the subject-matter of this study, a final attempt at answering the question, 'Can an outsider understand another religion or culture from the insider's perspective?' would not be out of place. First, common sense tells us that we can learn a great deal about cultures which are not our own, and that we can move easily within them – either as a periodical visitor or as a permanent guest. People who choose to live as expatriates sometimes deliberately maintain a persona and lifestyle which belongs to their homeland (the British often did this in their colonies). Others, though, choose to 'go native'; they develop a love and appreciation of their adopted culture which rivals that of many who were born and brought up within that culture. Indeed, many of us today live in bicultural and bilingual homes, and freely move from language to language and from culture to culture. Salman Rushdie has explored this theme in much of his writing; despite the controversy which (for some) devalues all his writing he has, I believe, made an important contribution to our understanding of postmodern pluralism. I return to Rushdie in my final chapter. My own home is bicultural – English and Bengali – and I feel at home in either medium. Bengalis have sometimes said that I am 'half Bengali'. In an ethnic sense, I am not, and cannot be, either half or fully Bengali, yet I am accepted by Bengalis as someone who has at least one foot in the door of their culture, and world-view. My engagement with Islam cannot make me 'half a Muslim'. I could, of course, convert; Reat (1983) demands what he calls 'temporary conversion' as a precondition for seeing the 'others' from their perspective. Whilst conversion would turn me into an 'insider' and (presumably) bridge once and for all the insider–outsider polarity, I have not chosen to convert, even though some of my Muslim friends have said that they cannot understand why someone who knows so much about Islam can remain a non-Muslim.

Yet, just as Bengali friends recognize my ability to move within their culture even though I am not Bengali, so Muslim friends recognize my ability to handle Islamic concepts in a manner which does not seem completely alien to their own handling of them. In stating this I am not merely trying to 'show off', but to suggest that it is possible for us to gain proficiency in another world-view without actually identifying ourselves with it in any absolute sense. I believe that if we do not choose to *become the other*, it is possible to *almost become* the other. A year or two ago, I took students to visit a Hindu Temple in Leicester. After spending some time in the main shrine room, we retired to the meeting-room where the President invited questions from the floor. He also invited a Christian scholar of Hinduism, Dr Eric Lott, to join him on the platform. He sometimes deferred to Dr Lott's opinion, which he obviously respected. Eric Lott is a Methodist minister and remains rooted in his own faith. He writes:

though I have been powerfully drawn to certain key features of Hindu theology, especially its body-talk, and even though I have come to admire and love many Hindu people ... there was never any question of my leaving the faith community of my upbringing. (1995: 184)

Instead, Lott continues, 'The choice for me ... has been about what my vision is of the kind of Christian faith that has most potent meaning for the world I live in. What, within that faith, as it encounters and interacts with other faiths, provides a compelling new vision for our time' (*ibid.*). Here, the dialogian Lott becomes the theologian Lott. As my colleague Philip Meadows (1996) says, 'inter-religious dialogue is a means and not an end in itself. It is the responsibility of dialogians to account for their new experiences in terms of their own worldview: a step in which the dialogian becomes a theologian' (p. 39).

Of course, not all students of religion who use dialogue to gain insight into other traditions are at all concerned with theology. Many will instead want to integrate their dialogically gained data into a broader 'study of religions' perspective, perhaps, as James Cox (1992) suggests, through inquiry into 'the meaning of religion' generally (p. 56). In his 1996 article, Meadows draws on his background in information technology and computing, and his encounter with Hinduism, to explore the metaphor of 'virtual insidership' and argues that, 'Through immersion in, and interaction with, the thought world of the Hindu, made possible through interreligious dialogue, one may attain to an understanding which approximates, really-but-not-fully, that of the "full" insider' (p. 35). This wearing of the other's clothes does not turn us into the other, nor do we necessarily experience exactly what insiders experience, yet there may well be a 'genuine correspondence between' their experience and our own.

Meadows also identifies a weakness in the phenomenological schema: it assumes (or appears to) that we can, once and for all, 'bracket out' our own ideological bias. I doubt if we can. I think that this continues to influence our seeing, and that in order to see as others see we need to return again and again to our ideological premises, to check that they are not obscuring our vision. In a sense, instead of leaving our beliefs behind, we take them with us – not to impose them on the other but as hermeneutical tools to help us understand what we see; as Tracy (1981) says, 'each of us understands the other through analogies to our own experience or not at all' (p. 451). What we 'bracket out', says Meadows, are the 'evaluative and judgmental functions of [our] own belief system' and not our 'beliefs themselves' (p. 38). Thus, what Meadows has usefully called 'virtual insidership', construed as a dialogical process of under-standing, 'recognizes that we are inextricably involved in our research encounters and acknowledges the indissoluble necessity of one's existing worldview, or conceptual scheme' (p. 38). World-views, of course, may be modified, changed or even exchanged, yet they are much more than sets of clothes which can be taken off and then put on again. They are existential and reach into the deepest psychological recesses of our sense of self and of our place in the scheme of life. We fool ourselves if we think that these do not impinge on our efforts to see as others see.

Perhaps I have asked the wrong question. The right question may not be, 'Can I understand the other as they understand themselves?', but 'Can I get close to', or 'approximate', an insider view? (see Meadows, p. 38). Meadows suggests that the 'virtual insider view' is actually somewhere 'betwixt and between' that of the interlocutors, conforming *per se* to neither (p. 37). Elsewhere, I have suggested that the aim of an outside scholar, in conversation, partnership and dialogue with insiders, is to render an account of this exchange which will move all participants forward in their self-understanding (Bennett, 1996a: 176). Thus, rather than 'betwixt and between', the account will move beyond the interlocutor's particularities. There is much that is tacit and not explicit, in our culture; we take quite a lot for granted. The outsider, I suggest, may help us understand ourselves better by making the implicit explicit. Similarly, as the outsider encounters us, he or she may discover aspects of their own character, personality or world-view of which they were either partially, or totally, unaware. Neuman (1994) gives the example of a researcher visiting a nudist colony who in the process discovered much more about his or her own attitude to, and assumptions about, nudity! (p. 341). Whatever emerges from such encounters by way of an account, or a report, is in a real sense, as Geertz (1973) says, a 'fiction'; 'anthropological writings are ... "fictions", fictions in the sense that they are "something made", "something fashioned" – the original meaning of *fictio* – not that they are false' (p. 15). In *After The Fact* (1996), Geertz associates the hermeneutical task with that of finding the right metaphors. Accounts thus rendered are 'new creations', and by bringing together a range of insider perspectives and setting these alongside outsider perceptions, they may very well move us beyond any single view. What tests this account's scientific value is whether those involved in collaborating with the research are prepared to accept it as useful, fair and just. This does not mean that everyone will endorse the whole account. Indeed, the whole account may not command anyone's complete assent (apart from the author's!). Perhaps the real test is less the 'assent' of 'insiders', or even of collaborators, than people's willingness to concede that the perspective offered has a validity and an authenticity of its own, that it represents a voice worth listening to.

Anthropological theology

This introduction has deliberately included my personal voice in the text, because I believe that no research can be 'carried out in some autonomous realm that is insulated from the wider society' or from 'the particular biography of the researcher' (Hammersley and Atkinson, 1995: 16). A technical term for the type of constant revisiting of our a priori assumptions and ideological premisses which I have described above, is 'reflexivity'. Reflexivity is 'continued self-reflection and analyses' which aims to make 'explicit those subjective structures which implicitly condition all our understandings of the world' (Meadows, 1996: 38). When such reflection is included in an account, readers can follow and evaluate the writer's interpretive process for themselves. This is the style which I have chosen for this book. My world-view is Christian. Ultimately, I see the Trinity as the key to decoding the universe. My encounter with Islam has led to respect for the faith, many friendships with Muslims, and the conviction that Islam is indeed a 'misunderstood religion'; my allusion here is to the title of a popular, and amongst Muslims widely read, book *Islam: The Misunderstood Religion* (1954) by Muhammad Qutb, which set out to 'refute the age-old vile charges levelled by our detractors and antagonists against Islam'. This last conviction stems at least in part from my awareness that the Islam about which I often read in texts does not seem to resemble the Islam which my Muslim friends know, love and cherish. As Buaben (1996) observes, 'The human touch, the personal experience of Muslims and Muslim societies, is what most Western scholars miss to their cost' (p. 16). With Smith's dictum as my motto, in exploring Islam I have attempted (1) to see what Muslims see in Islam; (2) to understand why others have seen Islam differently, and, last but not least, (3) to ask whether what anybody sees in Islam can be justified, given the texts, voices and data which are available to us. To pursue this study, I have tried to become a 'virtual Muslim', and, over recent years, have increasingly regarded myself as an anthropologist of Islam within a Religious Studies perspective.

There are, of course, other ways of studying religion – sociology of religion, psychology of religion, history of religion, for example – all represent alternative ways of exploring the phenomena. I am not claiming that the 'insider', or 'virtual insider' view is the best, only that it is one way of studying or 'seeing' religion. However, as a religious person, my personal preference for 'phenomenology', or an 'insidership' which 'endeavours to understand religion in its own terms', reserving 'for religious people the right to define what their religion means ... from within' (J. Cox, 1992: 160) may not be accidental. I may well find other methods, which explain religion primarily as a social or a psychological construct, less appealing. Finally, because I am a Christian (and theologically trained), I have also tried to 'understand' how Islam can fit into my Christian world-view. This is not unproblematical.

Some Christian scholars of Islam, such as Kenneth Cragg, have been accused of 'Christianizing Islam' (see Buaben, 1996: 149). I may be guilty of the same charge, especially as Cragg has been a major influence on my own work. However, my agenda in this book is to ask, 'What, within my Christian faith, as it encounters and interacts with Islam, "provides a compelling new vision for our time"?' (adapted from Lott, 1995: 184). In the end, then, my anthropology becomes anthropological theology because, in trying to make sense of Islam, I am open to Muslim belief in Islam's divine origin. Some anthropologists have expressed the view that a 'non-empirical' category like 'divine reality' can have 'no place in anthropology'; 'anthropology', we are told, 'cannot answer theological questions ... but perhaps it can be used by theologians to help in framing the questions well' (Dietrich, 1992: 121). 'Anthropology is', says Benthall (1995), 'and is likely to remain Darwinian and methodologically agnostic – that is, an intellectual game in which no doctrinal trump cards are recognised' (p. 2).

However, if anthropology's aim is to understand what life is like for its subjects, to see the world through their eyes, 'To discover... [their] essential, deepest way of thinking' (Malinowski, 1967: 115), then it can be argued that it ought to take people's religious convictions as seriously as it takes their politics or their ethics. Next, if anthropologists want to integrate these particular religious beliefs into a general scheme of theological ways of thinking, they will find themselves engaged in theological discourse. This is what has been traditionally called 'theological anthropology', which, says Anthony Dyson in *A New Dictionary of Christian Theology* (1983), began by applying 'dogmas about human beings' derived from what was believed to be revealed scripture to empirically observed data, but is 'now more a case of setting what we know about humankind from many sources in a theological perspective which seeks to provide it with final meaning and depth' (p. 24). Theological anthropology, however, has tended to be 'so dominated by the doctrine of God as to lose its own proper content and qualities' (p. 26), which I take to mean that the 'anthropology' has suffered from too many theological presuppositions.

This is why I prefer the term, 'anthropological theology', which implies that the theology must be grounded in, and derived from, the anthropological data. I am aware, though, that some anthropologists dislike 'practitioners from other disciplines' appropriating the term 'anthropological' when describing their own approach or perspective – 'however tenuously anthropological these may be' (Shore, 1996: 3). I am also well aware that my own anthropological *bona fides* will not satisfy everyone. Nevertheless, what I set out to do in researching this book was an exercise in 'cosmopolitan anthropology' (with a theological gloss!); as advocated by Kuper (1994), this sees 'ethnography as conversation ... implicating ethnographers, informants [I prefer to talk about consultants] and the ancestral voices they evoke' (p. 551; see Bennett, 1996a: 173).

Our subject-matter

In exploring Muhammad's significance, this interpretive survey divides into three parts. The first surveys what can be historically reconstructed of Muhammad's life. Chapter 1 examines primary sources. This aims to be broadly descriptive: that is, to describe the origins and scope of our biographical sources. I have drawn quite unashamedly on English renderings of the primary material, although I have consulted Arabic texts to check certain words or phrases. I have tried to trace citations to the classical sources and, where possible, I give traditional references. Chapter 2 proceeds to a discussion of the sources' historicity and reliability. This discussion attempts to bring insider and outsider appraisals into dialogue and conversation. I try to deal fairly with views which express scepticism about the value of the historical material, and with those which see the sources as broadly reliable. I fully recognize that much traffic has already travelled along this particular road and that perhaps the best I can hope for is clarity of expression, rather than originality. I also visit the contribution of feminist scholars, such as Fatima Mernissi (1991) and Leila Ahmed (1992).

My own bias towards authenticity is made explicit. Indeed, the subject-matter of this section raises the problem of dealing historiographically with what a people considers to be *sacred history*. The application to sacred history of historiographical tools of critical analysis may treat the material in a manner which believers consider disrespectful, inappropriate or ill-founded. Muslims have, in the past, accused non-Muslim scholars of disrespect for the genre they are studying. This is also their charge against Rushdie – he 'enters the Mosque', says Akhtar, 'but tactlessly refuses to take off his shoes' (1992: 30). However, recognizing the theological nature of much of the material, I try to avoid using interpretive tools drawn exclusively from secular historiography.

Part Two reviews non-Muslim (mainly Christian) accounts of Muhammad – Chapter 3 surveys the period from the origins of Islam to the European Renaissance, Chapter 4 from the Renaissance until today. This two-chapter survey is ambitious and somewhat limited in scope, mainly to material published in English. My aim is (1) to offer representative evaluations of the Prophet; and (2) to identify particular views or problematical areas which have tended to attract discussion, censure, or praise.

Part Three discusses the 'Muhammad of Faith'; Chapter 5, drawing on textual and historical scholarship, examines the ongoing significance of the Prophet in Muslim life, piety and spirituality, and in the development of Islamic theology and philosophy. This is where historical anthropology features prominently. Much of my material is textual, but in reading and interpreting these texts I constantly (even when this is not made explicit) make mental reference to my encounter with Islam and with Muslims. What I have not included in this section is a survey of recent Muslim biographies of the Prophet. Although such a survey would very properly supplement my exploration of what Muhammad means to Muslims, I decided instead to substitute for this an attempt at some field anthropology – Chapter 6. My idea for Chapter 6 was to conduct a series of interviews with Muslims from a variety of backgrounds and various schools of thought, about their views of the Prophet. I wanted to explore with them those issues which, identified from my earlier chapters, have tended to divide Muslim from non-Muslim opinion. I realised that my sample would have to be opportunistic. I could not visit every Muslim state or interview Muslims from every conceivable school, movement or group. In the end, I contented myself with (1) conversations during visits to Bangladesh in the summers of 1996 and 1997; (2) discussions with my own Muslim students at Westminster College and other Muslim friends; and (3) a questionnaire distributed to my Muslim students and to staff at the Oxford Centre for Islamic Studies. I also sent my manuscript to a Muslim colleague who has himself written about 'images' of the Prophet, so that he could critique my text. As my 'picture' of the Prophet emerged, I wanted to know: 'Does it do justice to their understanding of who the Prophet is?' 'Are they offended by anything I say?' 'Do they think that, as an outsider, I am beginning to approach their insider view?' Chapter 6 is an impressionistic and reflective account of my first-hand data-collecting research, which aims to create a dialogue between this aspect of my study and my textual and historical analysis. I have tried to find the right metaphors.

Chapter 7 is my conclusion to this study. Here I explore how what Muhammad means, and has meant, to Muslims compares with what can be historically said about him. Christians, doubting the integrity of the compilers of the primary sources, have made moral judgements about Muhammad which have been unacceptable to Muslims. Is Muhammad inevitably viewed differently from without Islam? How much of the Islamic view of Muhammad can Christians share, whilst remaining Christian? Can outsiders be expected to treat Muhammad with the same reverence as Muslims do? If they do not believe in any possibility of a link between Muhammad, or any other religious leader, and the supernatural, are they inevitably going to find themselves at odds with the Muslim viewpoint? This, I shall argue, lies at the root of the Salman Rushdie affair, which I discuss in some detail. In my conclusion, I try to integrate my research findings into my own Christian world-view. Since I am not writing exclusively for Christians, I hope that this section will not detract too much from the book's value; it represents one outsider's attempt to engage sympathetically but rigorously with the contribution and achievements of another tradition's seminal personality.

Part One

1 Muhammad of History: the Primary Sources

In this chapter, my aim is to identify and describe the historical sources available for reconstructing Muhammad's biography. I shall also investigate how these sources were compiled. Information about the Prophet of Islam abounds, although not all of it helps very much with the task of biographical reconstruction: there are, for example, quite long lists of Muhammad's mules, camels, swords, shields, bows and lances (see Poonawala, 1990: 148); we know that Muhammad loved to eat honey, hated bad smells, and favoured his right hand. This information is all found in the *hadith* (accounts of Muhammad's words and acts). In this book, I follow Guillaume (1924) who, whilst noting that, strictly speaking, the word *hadith* refers to a single tradition, comments that, 'the constant employment of the Arabic broken plural *ahadith* is hardly to be desired' (p. 11). For the chronology of Muhammad and for information about particular events in his life, we are mainly dependent on a genre of literature known as *sira*. In the next chapter, I describe many of the criticisms which have been made about the authenticity and reliability of the *sira* and *hadith* literature (for convenience, I shall sometimes refer to this as the *sira–hadith* literature). Broadly, these fall into two sets of critical assessment: those which (with some reservations) accept their historicity; and those which see *sira* and *hadith* as almost wholly reflective of the biases, agenda, and reshaping of the early Muslim community.

Muhammad: three biographical phases

Before proceeding to describe the sources, a few significant facts may help us through the material under scrutiny. A useful schema is to divide Muhammad's life into three main periods or phases. The first is from his birth in the Year of the Elephant, 570 of the Common Era, until his first revelatory experience in 610 CE. The second is the period between 610 and the *hijrah* or migration from Makkah to Madinah, in the year 622 CE. The Muslim calendar begins with this event. The third period is Muhammad's rise to power at Madinah, through to his final sermon and death in 632. Some traditional accounts follow this schema: phase one covers the time before Muhammad became a public figure; phase two his early years as a religious reformer; phase three his rise to success. A more detailed outline of the most important events in Muhammad's life is reproduced at Appendix 1. This also includes a chronology of subsequent

Muslim dynasties to help readers locate my references to these periods. Appendix 2 details Muhammad's marriages and discusses some issues related to this controversial aspect of his life.

We should note at this point that 570 CE is by no means considered 'safe' as the date of Muhammad's birth. As Andrae (1936) commented, 'we do not know definitely when Mohammed was born' since 'the statement that [he] was born in the "Year of the Elephant" does not agree with other chronological facts in the prophet's life' (pp. 39–41). Amongst these, suggests F.E. Peters (1994a), is the fact that Khadijah appears to have borne Muhammad eight children 'after she had passed the age of 40' (p. 103). Reports about Muhammad's age at death also vary. He may have been 'anywhere from 60 to 65 years-old when he died' (ibid.: 102; B 59:83 says, 'Allah's Messenger was 63 when he died'). However, the date of the hijrah (and of Muhammad's death 10 years later) are generally accepted as accurate. Thus, the traditional birth date of 570 may be the result of a back-projection which has the Prophet aged 40 when his revelatory experiences began – presumably because 40 was considered to be theologically appropriate (see ibid.). B 58:27 gives us the standard chronology: 'Allah's Messenger was divinely inspired at the age of 40. Then he stayed in Mecca for thirteen years, and then was ordered to migrate … to Medina, and stayed there for ten years and then died'. Biruni (d. 1048 CE), however, in his account of Islamic history, commented that there was 'such a divergency of opinion' about 'the time of the birth of the Prophet' and 'when he was entrusted with his divine mission' that neither could become 'the basis of something which must be agreed upon universally' (cited in Peters, 1994b: 98).

The Qu'ran as biographical source

What, then, are our sources? The Qur'an, Islam's scripture, which (according to Islamic doctrine) Muhammad received, portion by portion, from 610 CE onwards, contains some information about its recipient. This material, however, relates to Muhammad's theological significance and provides little assistance in the task of biographical reconstruction; indeed, Peters (1994a) says that 'The Qur'an … is of no use whatsoever as an *independent* source for reconstructing the life of Muhammad' (p. 261). Typical of Qur'anic verses which refer directly to Muhammad are the following:

verily in the messenger of Allah ye have a good (*hasan*: noble, or beautiful) example. (33:21)

And whatever the messenger gives you, take it, and whatever he forbids you, abstain from it. (59:7)

Obey God, and obey the messenger and those who are in charge of affairs among you. Should you happen to dispute over something, then refer it to God and to his messenger. (4:59)

Thus the Qur'an does not, as it were, tell Muhammad's story – we cannot deduce from it when he was born or when he began to preach. On the other hand, all three of the verses cited above indicate why Muhammad's example, or *sunnah* (literally 'beaten track', i.e. 'custom', 'wont', 'usage') became so important to the early Muslim community. During phase two of his life – the Makkah period – the Qur'anic message which he received and preached was predominantly a message against idolatry and immorality. Ethical content revealed in this period does distinguish 'right' from 'wrong' behaviour, but mainly in broad brush-strokes such as 'oppress not the orphan nor drive the beggar away' (Q 93:9–10). This reflects the context; Muhammad was leader of a small, relatively poor, persecuted group, opposed by the wealthiest and most powerful tribal chiefs of the day. Many Qur'anic verses in this phase rebuke the Makkans for rejecting Muhammad's message and failing to recognize his mission. At this stage, Muhammad's message, whilst certainly directed at the rich and powerful, and social in intent as well as content, was in another sense aimed at converting *individuals* to his cause. After the *hijrah* the context changed. No longer was Muhammad leader of a persecuted group; now he headed an organized community which sought to order its whole common life according to God's will. Muhammad, as it were, was no longer concerned primarily with individual response but with establishing a social order according to God's will. He was concerned with corporate conduct. Significantly, it is in this phase that Muhammad's followers are first called an *'ummah'* (community, people) – see Q 2:143; 'Islam' is revealed as the proper name for the religion (at Q 5:3), whilst the corporate duty of this *ummah* is made explicit: 'And there may spring from you a nation who invite to goodness, and enjoin right conduct and forbid indecency'(Q 3:104). Later, under Khalif 'Umar (although the practice is said to have begun with Muhammad himself), the Islamic calendar took its starting point from the *hijrah*.

In summary, whilst the message at Makkah had revealed the nature of God (as One, just, merciful, and so on), the message at Madinah translated the consequences of this into social and religious norms. The *ummah* must reflect God's inherent qualities: as God is 'one' (*tawhid*; Q 112), so must the *ummah* be one; differences of wealth and poverty must be minimized and justice must be administered equitably; all aspects of life must be regarded as sacred. Nothing is to be left outside the scope of Islam. The *ummah* is not merely a religious congregation which comes together from time to time, to worship; it is a social, economic, religious unit. Reflecting this context, we now find more detailed legal material in the Qur'an, including rules about what is *halal* (permitted) and *haram* (prohibited). Indeed, it is now that Islam begins to adopt many of the practices which continue to this day: the five daily prayers, the dietary rules, and so on. There is some evidence that prior to the *hijrah* Jewish food laws were maintained. Now, as with the change in the *qiblah* (direction of prayer, see Q 2:142) from Jerusalem to Makkah, distinctive Islamic dietary rules replace Judaic ones (see Q 5:3–5). Ibn Ishaq notes that, 'When the apostle was firmly settled in Medina … Islam became firmly established. Prayer was instituted, the alms tax and fasting were prescribed, and Islam took up its abode with them'.

These rules, though, had to be applied to particular situations and, as Bosworth (1977) comments, 'many' such situations were 'highly specific' to 'which a work of universal appeal like the Qur'an could not be expected to have an answer' (p. vi). Thus, dating from the same period, we find the verses, cited above, which invest Muhammad with peculiar authority; all disputes, criminal, civil, religious, are to be adjudicated by him. Q 59:7 implies that his extra-Qur'anic judgements – applying Qur'anic principles to contexts not specifically referred to in the Qur'an – are to be regarded as binding. These judgements and Muhammad's saying and doings generally were later afforded 'semi-divine' status. The accounts (*ahadith*), which I discuss below, once recorded, came to represent what have been called 'uninspired records of inspired sayings'. Muhammad himself refers to the Madinah period as the time of his *sunnah* (B 58:4,5 *hadith* no. 265). Given that only 300 Qur'anic verses out of 6,666 contain what might be called 'law', the importance of the *hadith* can hardly be overstated (Zakaria, 1988: 33).

Here theology begins to merge with history; in other words, when Muhammad was adjudicating, he did not merely offer his personal opinion, but was 'inspired'. Such *hadith* as these testify to this very special, unique authority:

That which the prophet of God hath made lawful is like that which God himself has made. (MM, 1, p. 43)¶

I have left you two things, and from them you will not stray as long as you hold them fast. The one is the Book of God, the other is the law of his prophet. (MM, 1, p. 48)

He who loves my *sunnah*, loves me (*man ahabba sunnati faqad ahabbani*). (cited in Troll, 1978: 45 and see MM, 1, p. 46)

and, addressing Annas b Malik,

O my son, the one who has cherished my sunnah without doubt he has cherished me, and he who cherishes me will be with me in paradise. (*ibid.*)

As my discussion of the development of what might be called a 'theology of Muhammad' in Chapter 5 will show, belief developed in his 'sinlessness'. This is said to be a characteristic of the prophetic office generally, as Shahrastani (d. 1153) explains;

By my life, the prophet's soul and temperament must possess all natural perfections, excellent character, truthfulness and honesty in speech and deed before his appointment for office, because it is by virtue of these that he has deserved prophetic mission and has come into contact with angels. (cited in Glasse, 1991: 318)

Thus the many *hadith* which testify to Muhammad's honesty, piety and goodness are taken as 'proofs of his prophethood'. Abul Ala Maududi (1903–79), one of this century's most influential Muslim scholars, writes:

His life and thought, his truth and straightforwardness, his piety and goodness, his character and morals, his ideology and achievements – all stand as unimpreachable proof of his prophethood. (1960: 60)

Muslims believe that all prophets were honest, intelligent, monotheistic, sinless and chosen (*mustafa*). The Qur'an, of course, also affirms that Muhammad is 'but a messsenger' (Q 3:144); this is one of only four verses which explicitly names Muhammad. However, this should probably be interpreted as a warning against repeating the Christian error of deifying Christ, not as a belittling of the prophetic office. Rather, as the last, or 'seal' (*khatm*) of the prophets (33:40) his message and example take on a universal significance. Earlier prophets – according to the Qur'an, prophets have been sent to all peoples or tribes (Q10:48) – were for particular people at particular moments. Muhammad is prophet for all people, and until God's final judgement. I revisit this developing theology of the Prophet in Chapter 5. The doctrine of sinlessness does not mean that prophets never made mistakes but that they are incapable of committing any major error or sin. Perhaps another way of expressing this is to say that they do not share with other human beings the propensity towards 'forgetfulness' (*nisyan*) which made it necessary for God to send prophets.

Islamic doctrine also says that all prophets received in essence the same message, even if some were limited in scope, 'suited to a certain time and people', or primarily intended gradually to 'prepare a world intellectually and morally not yet fully developed for the coming of a teaching more universal, more exhaustive ... the teaching of Islam' (Asad, 1981: 3). In passing, it should be noted that Muslims believe the Qur'an to be, word for word, God's speech; Muhammad 'received' it – but contributed nothing to its content. Indeed, according to the traditions, Muhammad was unable to read or write. This has been a subject of considerable discussion by non-Muslims who find it inconsistent with the fact that he had managed Khadijah's business (see Watt and Bell, 1970: 36). Muslims, however, have never subjected the Qur'an to the type of redaction and source criticism that others have applied to the Bible. For their part, non-Muslim scholars have attempted to deconstruct the Qur'an by tracing material to various 'sources', such as the Talmud and rehashed biblical stories current, in a somewhat Arabized form, during Muhammad's lifetime (see, for example, Tisdall (1901); Bell (1945); Crone and Cook (1977); Cook (1983); Ibn Warraq (1995)). Wansbrough (1977) dates the standard version of the Qur'an as late as two centuries after Muhammad's death. In this view, much of its text was produced at a later date, reflecting sectarian interests. Goddard (1995) tells us that Wansbrough 'received a death threat for his efforts [at reconstructing] the process by which the Qur'an was assembled and interpreted ... as a result ... he moved his field ... to the comparatively tranquil pastures of the treaties worked out between Crusaders and Muslims in the twelfth and thirteenth centuries' (p. 8).

From the Muslim point of view, similarity with earlier 'sources', firstly, does not prove indebtedness; secondly, as such 'sources' are themselves believed to be 'revelatory' in origin, any similarity is due to their having the same 'author'. Indeed, the Muslim view that earlier scriptures were 'corrupted' (or 'altered') by unfaithful recipients (see for example, Q 2:59), and that the Qur'an was sent to 'confirm' them (Q3:3), offers adequate explanation for any discrepencies between Qur'anic and earlier accounts – in the Qur'an's favour. See I.I pp. 272–3 for a description of the context in which some of these criticisms were revealed – during a visit of Christians from Najran; 'they follow what ... they have invented and introduced anew that they may have ... a plausible reason for their doctrine' but the Qur'an is 'a plain ... book'. However, there is debate about the meaning of the word translated as 'corrupt' and 'alter' (*yuharrifuna*): does this mean textual corruption, or refer to how the text is interpreted? (see discussion in Chapter 3 below). There is also debate about which scriptures are said to have been altered. Based on several Qur'anic verses which appear to refer to its own pre-existence (that is, before its Revelation to Muhammad, see Q 85:22), Islamic theology has developed the doctrine of its 'uncreatedness'. It had always existed within God's essential 'self'. This doctrine, as I indicate in Chapter 5, also influences how some Muslims interpret the role and status of the Qur'an's recipient. Parts of the Qur'an were recorded during Muhammad's life-time by various scribes. These are referred to at Q 80:15–16 as 'noble and righteous'. During 'Uthman's Khalifate (643–56; see Chapter 5 below) an official recension of the Qur'an was produced under the direction of the surviving 'noble scribes'; this version of Islamic history, recorded in B 61:3, is rejected by Wansbrough, Crone *et al*. Variant editions were then destroyed. Revealed to Muhammad in Arabic (which Muslims often call the tongue of heaven), the Qur'an is believed to be the most exquisite text that has ever been written in that language. Robinson (1996) tells us that the Qur'an is less a book to be read than one to be recited and heard; 'listening, and learning to recite from memory', he says, 'precede the effort to understand' (p. 1). *Hadith* assure those who become expert in recitation that they will be counted 'with the Noble Righteous Scribes', whilst those who experience difficulty yet persevere 'shall receive double awards' (B 60: 332). Because it is a 'revelation in Arabic' (see Q 12:2; 13:37) the text of the Qur'an can, properly speaking, be read only in Arabic; any rendering into another tongue is an interpretation, not the Qur'an *per se*.

Muhammad himself appears to have recognized limits to his authority: 'My sayings do not abrogate the word of God, but the word of God can abrogate my sayings' (MM, 1, p. 49). There is also an oft repeated *hadith* about the Prophet offering advice on palm-grafting. Later, when he discovered that his advice had resulted in a decreased yield, he said:

I am a mere human being. When I command you to do anything about religion in the name of God, accept it, but when I give you my personal opinion about worldly things, bear in mind that I am a human being, and no more. (V 4:1259).

In other words, Muhammad's prophetic office did not make him an expert on everything, only on matters germane to his mission. The distinction here is important but quite subtle. Muhammad's office did enable him to offer general advice about 'cultivation' – there are *hadith* on this topic in the collections (see B 39). His concern, however, was ethical rather than practical. Thus, for example, these *hadith* forbid cultivating land to which you have no title (B 43:14; cultivating unclaimed land gives you title; see B 39:15) and praise farming as a 'charity' (B 39:1), but they do not pretend to offer expert advice on how to farm. We also know, however, of one 'Abdallah ibn-Abi Sarh who, whilst acting as a scribe, had inserted slight changes to the Prophet's 'dictation ... to see whether he would notice'. When Muhammad apparently did not, 'Abdallah found himself doubting the Prophet's sincerity, and deserted Islam. At first proscribed by Muhammad, he was later pardoned (Andrae, 1936: 233–4; see also Watt and Bell, 1970: 37). Salman Rushdie (see my Conclusion) has one of his characters engaging in a similar exercise. Here, Muhammad may possibly be regarded as making an error with respect to his mission (the text of the Qur'an).

Muslims give more weight to some *hadith* than to others. For example, explicit rulings on matters of criminal, civil, or religious law are regarded as 'general legislation (*tashri' 'amm*) whose validity is not restricted to the limitations of time and circumstance' (Kamali, 1991: 53). These form an integral part of the *Shari'ah* – the legal code which evolved in the tenth century to help administer the ever-expanding Islamic Empire (*shari'ah* is literally 'a path leading to a watering hole', thus guidance is a better translation than 'law'). Material on 'the manner in which he ate, slept, dressed ...', however, 'only indicate the permissibility (*ibahah*) of the acts in question' (*ibid.*). These *hadith* are not considered to be part of the *Shari'ah*'s legal corpus, although (known as *adab*) they have considerable impact on everyday Muslim life, as Nasr (1994) puts it;

[Muhammad's *sunnah*] is the vital integrating factor in Muslim society, for the daily lives of millions of Muslims the world over have been modelled upon the prophetic Sunnah and hadith. For nearly fourteen hundred years Muslims have tried to awaken in the morning as the Prophet awakened, to eat as he ate, to wash as he washed, even to cut their nails as he did. (p. 82)

Men may choose to wear their hair after Muhammad's style and to imitate his dress; green is the colour of Islam because the Prophet loved green, and so on. Handbooks are available which advise Muslims how they should conduct themselves; *adab* can be understood as 'good manners', 'the equivalent of the Latin *urbanitas*, civility, courtesy'. Such advice is derived directly from the *sunnah* of the Prophet (see, for example, al-Kaysi, 1986). Muslim customs surrounding birth, marriage and funerals are all derived from these non-legal *hadith*.

Acts or sayings related to particular historical circumstances are regarded as 'too situational' to be universally (that is, legally) valid. Jurists also attempt to deduce from the sources whether the Prophet had *intended* to establish a legal precedent. Thus, some importance was attached to the context of *hadith*, although collections do not usually record when events occurred. Jurists are less interested in the particularity of the situations described than in discovering and applying any universal principles. Acts are divided into the following categories: *fard* (obligatory), *Mandub* (recommended), *Mubah* (permitted but not recommended), *Makruh* (disliked but carries no legal penalty) and *Haram* (forbidden and can attract legal penalty). Muhammad's silence about 'something said or done in his presence' is usually taken as approval (B 92:23).

Some *hadith* carry the designation *hadith qudsi*; these, possibly about 800 in number, were 'revealed' to Muhammad directly from God, and consequently carry more weight (see Robson, 1986a). The significance of the *sunnah* within Islam can be further illustrated by pointing out that, in addition to offering guidance in the mundane areas already mentioned, much of what is crucial to Islamic faith and practice is derived from this source, not directly from the Qur'an. Whilst the Qur'an enjoins prayer, fasting and payment of the poor tax, the details of these *fard* (obligatory) practices are all in the *sunnah*. At Q 24:58 and 11:114, for example, three prayer times appear to be mentioned; the five are stipulated in the *sunnah*. Also in the *sunnah*, not the Qur'an, is the popular image of the '*fard*' duties of Islam as its 'pillars':

Islam is built on five things, the bearing of witness that there is no God but Allah and that Muhammad is the messenger of Allah and the keeping of prayer and the payment of *zakat* and the pilgrimage and fasting in Ramadan. (B 2:1 *hadith* no. 7)

The famous phrase, 'God has 99 Names' is also from the *hadith* (B 93:12) not from the Qur'an (thus 99 names have been derived from the text of the Qur'an).

Sources for Muhammad's life

What I have established above (setting aside for now the issues of historical reliability and *post eventum* fabrication) is the importance of the *hadith* for every aspect of Islamic faith and practice. Ibn Hanbal (d. 855), whose followers form the most conservative of the four recognized legal schools in Sunni Islam, is said to have refrained from eating watermelons because there was no record of Muhammad eating them! (Coulson, 1994: 71). Ibn Hanbal compiled his own collection of *hadith*, the *Musnad*, which contains quite a lot of material not found elsewhere (see Guillaume, 1924: 24 and Margoliouth, 1905: v; the *Musnad* records 80,000 *hadith*). What I examine now, however, is how these sayings and doings of Muhammad were gathered and recorded into officially recognized 'accounts', and what canons of criticism were employed to ensure their authenticity.

Clearly, as those who had known the Prophet died and the Islamic Empire expanded, it became impossible for those in charge of its affairs to fulfil their responsibilities without written sources. If they were to rule the vast Islamic Empire according to Islamic principles, they needed access to material containing precedents, prohibitions and proprieties. Of course, early extra-Qur'anic sources did exist – letters sent by Muhammad to various rulers; treaties between the Prophet and other tribes such as the treaty between Muhammad and the Christians of Najran, which guaranteed protection of their priests and buildings (see Ibn Sa'd, 1967, 1:149); and the Constitution of Madinah, which includes the words, 'The Jews of … are of one community with the believers' (I.I., 233). Patricia Crone (1995) thinks it problematical that none of these early written sources now exist in their original form:

all surviving versions have lost their starting point in as much as not a single *hadith* remembers the context in which the document was issued … many add extraneous material; and such clauses as they do remember are either summarized too briefly to be informative or else given in paraphrases so far removed from the original wording that their meaning has changed. (p. 271)

The weakness of Crone's view is that if the original versions have 'lost their starting point', she cannot prove or disprove her claim that 'surviving versions' have strayed from the original. They may just as easily be accurate, if summary, renderings. Some scholars argue, as I explore more fully in Chapter 2, that the *sunnah* (as a written source or, more radically, in any form) did not begin to play a significant part in legal proceedings until the very end of the first century AH, and that it did not gain real authority until the third century. If true, this may be because most of those occupying positions of power or responsibility could recall the Prophet's example from their own first-hand experience rather than, as these scholars argue, because the rulers regarded their own authority as equal to that of the Prophet. They may well, though, have exercised their own judgement when they lacked any guidance from Muhammad and, given their own position as guardians of Islamic tradition, their rulings may then have taken on something of the status of *sunnah* as it became the recognized custom or practice of the Muslim community. Indeed, this is how the scope of *shari'ah* was extended – *qiyas* (analogy), and *ijma* (the consensus of the community on a matter of Islamic practice) were used to deduce the Islamic position whenever direct or explicit rules or guidance could not be found in Qur'an or *hadith*.

As fewer could remember the words of the Prophet, a more scientific, indeed systematic, approach was required. There is some evidence that Muhammad encouraged his closest Companions, or *sahaba*, to memorize his sayings, and that they realized the importance of preserving these during the Prophet's own lifetime. Siddiqi (1993) tells us that, 'Abu Hurayra kept his [Muhammad's] constant company for three years, sacrificing all worldly pursuits, in order to see and hear what the prophet did and said, and regularly devoted a period of time to fixing in his memory the words he heard' (p. 4). Muhammad's companions, we are told, would enquire from each other whether, in their absence, any new *hadith* had been witnessed. As it happens, Abu Hurayra may not be the best example to cite; *hadith* attributed to him are perhaps especially vulnerable to criticism. 'Umar (Companion and Khalif) called him 'the worst liar among the *muhaddithun* [narrators of *hadith*]' (cited by Forward, 1994: 105). Al-Bukhari (d. 870) actually reports Abu Hurayra as saying (as a boast?):

'There was no one from among the contempories of the Prophet who reported more *hadith* from him than myself, but 'Abd Allah ibn 'Amre used to write while I did not' (B 3:40 *hadith* no.113). In contrast, 'Umar was reluctant to narrate *hadith*, conscious that in doing so he might inadvertently add to or detract from the facts (see Muir, 1894: i). On the other hand, Hurayra was aware that 'people [said] that [he] narrated "too many Hadith"' and responded by claiming that whilst others were busy trading or farming, he 'used to attend to Allah's messenger' memorizing 'that which they used not to memorize' (B 3:43 *hadith* no. 118).

Were records kept?

This introduces debate about whether Muhammad did or did not permit the Companions to keep written records of his sayings. Guillaume (1924) says that the literature 'probably presents us with more contradictory statements on the question as to whether it was permissible to write down traditions of the Prophet in the early days of Islam than on any other question' (p. 16). On the one hand, there are traditions which prohibit the writing down of non-scriptural material, whilst on the other hand, others have Muhammad encouraging, or at least permitting, this activity. For example:

For: A man from among the Ansar [Madinan supporters] said, O Messenger ... I hear from thee a *hadith* which pleases me very much but I cannot retain it in my memory. The messenger of Allah said, 'seek the help of thy right hand'. And he made a sign with his hand for writing. (Tir 39:12).

Against: Do not write from me anything except the Qur'an and whoever has written anything from me other than the Qur'an should erase it (Abu Sa'id al-Khudri, cited by Azami, 1978: 22–3).

Ibn Thabit acted as Muhammad's amenuensis in recording the verses of the Qur'an, and wrote letters for him. He also read to Muhammad letters sent him by others. Al-Tabari lists, amongst others, the following as having served Muhammad as scribes, at various stages in his career: Ali b Abi Talib, Khalid b Sa'id, Aban b Sa'id and Zayd Ibn Thabit (Poonawala, 1990: 147–8).

Siddiqi (1993) summarizes the arguments 'for' and 'against' 'the written perpetuation of *hadiths*', and concludes:

that the sayings of the Prophet which discourage the writing of *hadith*, being fewer and weaker than those which encourage it, must have been based either on the generally unfavourable public opinion prevailing in Arabia at the beginning of his career as a prophet, or on fears that written *hadith* might become confused with the text of the Qur'an ... But as soon as he discerned that these hazards were at an end, he permitted the written recording of *hadith*. (p. 27; see Azami, 1978: 23–4 for a similar view)

It is also argued that, just as some later Qur'anic verses abrogate some earlier ones, so the later *hadith* which permit writing abrogate the earlier ones which prohibit writing (see MM, 1, p. 49 for the abrogation of *hadith*). Thus, some *hadith* probably did exist in written form during the Prophet's lifetime. It was, however, in the second century after the *hijrah* that Muslims began to record *hadith* in book format. Some travelled far and wide in pursuit of this very special type of knowledge, and appear to have regarded this as following Muhammad's advice, 'He who goes forth in the search for knowledge is in the way of Allah' (Tir 39:2; see B 3:20). These collections form the earliest genre of *hadith* literature. Usually they ordered the sayings under the name of their initial source, almost always a Companion. Known as *musnad* (I have already referred to the *Musnad* of Ahmed Hanbal), these began to develop the rules by which authenticity would be judged. Already, scholars were aware that some dubious traditions were being cited, either to justify heretical views or regional or personal claims to special status. Other *hadith* in circulation were simply too bizarre or contrary to what was widely accepted about the Prophet. These usually much embellished tales about supernatural doings had become the stock-in-trade of itinerant storytellers (*kussas*), whose aim was to astonish their audience in return for payment. They were not necessarily dishonest but nor were they even pretending to be scholars. Early writers thus openly admit that many fraudulent traditions were circulating and that a primary aim of the collectors was not only to collect but also to authenticate traditions. Al-Bukhari, perhaps the most renowned of all *hadith*-collectors, is said to have dreamt that he was 'driving flies' off the Prophet. Inquiring of an interpreter what this meant, he was told to 'drive away lies' from Muhammad and thus commenced his prodigious task of authenticating legitimate *hadith* (Muir, 1894: xxxviii). That reverence for Muhammad was an early rather than a late development is suggested by the fact that as well as collecting *hadith*, some collected anything that Muhammad had touched, and used it 'as a miracle cure for disease'. One Companion collected Muhammad's perspiration and 'stipulated in his will that it should be sprinkled on his body before it was put into the grave' (Siddiqi, 1993: 4).

Early collections

Some early collections were made at the request of the Umayyad Khalif, 'Umar ibn 'abd al-'Aziz (717–19), who 'wrote a circular letter asking the *hadith* scholars living in various parts of his country to collect in the form of books as many *hadith* as were available' (Siddiqi, 1993: 6; see also B 3:35). These early collections made little systematic effort to sort the *hadith* into topics and thus it was difficult to locate relevant material. Soon the genre known as '*musannaf*' evolved, which classified *hadith* under topics, including, classically:

- belief
- law and rulings
- piety
- manners (e.g. eating, drinking)
- *tafsir* – comment on the text of the Qur'an

- *tarikh* and *siyar* – historical and biographical material, including pre-Islamic history and lives of Muhammad and his Companions.

Clearly, this made it much easier for rulers and judges to locate *hadith* relevant to the particular issues they were adjudicating. In passing (although this discussion belongs more properly to the following chapter), it seems to me that the view that the *hadith* did not gain authority in legal matters until the time of Iman Shafi'i (d. 819) – who, according to Schacht, 'was the first "lawyer" consistently to define *Sunna* as "the model behaviour of the Prophet"' (J. Burton, 1994: xx; see Schacht, 1964: 47) – fails to explain why *hadith* collection began well before the time of Shafi'i. Schacht's thesis seems to beg the questions: Why was effort invested in collecting material which carried little, if any, significance for Muslim obedience? And why would anyone take much notice of decisions based upon such material if it lacked authority for them? We have, however, evidence of collections by scholars who pre-date Shafi'i, such as those by al-Zuhri (d. 742) and Abu Qilaba (d. 722) which, although not extant, are described for us in some detail in a bookseller's catalogue, the *Fihrist*, written by Ibn al-Nadim (see Siddiqi, 1993: 7).

The biographical (*sira*) material

Some collectors limited their scope to material on a single topic. These collections were called *Risalah*; amongst these we find 'the *sira*' – literature almost exclusively concerned with reconstructing Muhammad's biography. The earliest *sira* was compiled by Ibn Ishaq (704–767). Compiled whilst the science of *hadith* criticism was still in its infancy (for which see below), it made, arguably, little attempt to distinguish 'fact' from 'fiction'. Guillaume (1955), in his English rendering, says that phase one of Muhammad's life is 'filled out with legends and stories of miraculous events which inevitably undermine the modern reader's confidence in the history of this period as a whole' (p. xiv). On the other hand, when Ibn Ishaq was himself unconvinced by the material, he prefixed his text with the statement 'it is alleged' (or, sometimes, 'only God knows the truth') which, comments Guillaume, 'carries with it more than a hint that the statement may not be true, though on the other hand it may be sound'. Ibn Ishaq also frequently employed the phrase, 'that only God knows whether a particular statement is true or not' (*ibid.*, xix).

Watt (1953) says that Ibn Ishaq succeeded in moulding his material 'into a coherent story' (p. xii). The third phase of Muhammad's life is generally accepted as being 'much better vouched for than the earlier' phases, not 'merely because it was less romantic, but because it was witnessed by many more people' (Baker, 1980: 71). Ibn Ishaq's original *sira* is not extant. What we have is the edited version of Ibn Hisham (d. 833), and a section of al-Tabari's account of the Makkah period, which also uses Ibn Ishaq. The latter ceases with the siege of Madinah five years before the Prophet's death. This volume of al-Tabari has been rendered into English by Ismail K. Poonawala (1990). Ibn Hisham, says Muir (1894), was 'celebrated for his

learning, and possessed superior information in genealogy and grammar'
(p. lxix). Ibn Saʿd, Ibn Hisham and other *sira*-related material is also available
on computer disc, *WinSeera*, through the Islamic Computing Centre, London.

Ibn Ishaq

Scholars have redacted Ibn Ishaq from these works, and are confident that
the original has been faithfully reconstructed. Ibn Hisham's notes sometimes
offer variant readings, cite alternative sources or additional material, and for
the most part resemble modern day historical annotations. If 'feelings' are
allowed a part in scholarly scrutiny, the text conveys the 'feeling' that it has
been produced by a very careful and serious scholar indeed. As well as
Guillaume's 1955 English rendering (which includes Ibn Hisham's notes)
F. E. Peters has usefully reproduced substantial extracts in his *A Reader on
Classical Islam* (1994b). Ibn Ishaq relates quite a lot of poetic material, songs
as it were in honour of battles or of people, which gives the narrative a 'first-
hand feel' despite the process of editing which produced the text as we have
it today.

Ibn Ishaq begins with a lengthy section detailing what we might call Islam's
pre-history (pp. 3–69). This contains Muhammad's genealogy, interspersed
with such stories as the beginning of Christianity in Najran (pp. 14–18);
Abraha the Abyssinian's rise to power in the Yemen (pp. 20–30; he led the
elephant-mounted attack on Makkah in 570); and an account of idol worship
amongst the Arabs (pp. 35–40). This section establishes Muhammad's link
with Abraham and Ishmael, and ancient Makkah as a centre of monotheistic
worship. Some scholars think that Abraham only became an 'important
personality' during the Makkah period; thus this material must be apocryphal
(see Buaben, 1996: 266). The account of Muhammad's birth, infancy and
youth begins on p. 69. Incidentally, my reading of this section leads me to
conclude that Guillaume was exaggerating when he said that the story of
Muhammad's early years is 'filled out with legends and miraculous events'.
There are, I suggest, surprisingly few; on p. 69, his mother Aminah relates a
dream voice which said, 'You are pregnant with the lord of this people' and a
light shone 'forth from her by which she could see the castles of Busra'. On
p. 70 a Jew sights a star 'under which Ahmed is to be born' (but note the
similarity between these, and the biblical 'annunciation' stories). On p. 71 an
old she-camel's udders become full and Muhammad's nurse's sheep always
had milk whilst he was being weaned; p. 72 narrates the 'opening of the breast'
incident.

I may have omitted material which others might think miraculous but which
appear to me to be natural occurrences. In this section, we also have the stories
of how Christians and Jews 'recognized' Muhammad, including the Bahira-
account (pp. 79–82). We learn that Muhammad was briefly a shepherd,
because 'there is no prophet but who has shepherded the flock'. Some take
this to be an example of after-the-fact invention – to stress similarity, say, with
Moses in the land of Midian (Genesis 2 and 3). On p. 82 Khadijah, the

wealthy widow for whom Muhammad worked, proposes marriage. Between pp. 84 and 87, Muhammad, renowned for his honesty, acts as 'umpire' during the rebuilding of the Ka'abah. (Critics find it difficult to suppose that Muhammad was not somehow implicated in the worship of the idols around the Ka'abah which assured its commercial significance.) Muhammad was known as '*al-Amin*' – the trustworthy. His first revelation is described on pp. 104–7. The *hijrah* begins on p. 222; the battle of Badr is described at considerable length on pp. 289–360, with many lists and much poetry. The defeat at Uhud takes us from p. 370 to p. 426, again with lists and poetry. The building of the Trench is from p. 450 to p. 460, with several examples of 'God's justifying His apostle and confirming his prophetic office'. Makkah's occupation begins on p. 540; the events surrounding the Prophet's death on p. 678 (to 690, the last page of Guillaume's translation).

Later biographies

Two other *sira*, those by al-Waqidi (d. 822) and his secretary, Ibn Sa'd (English rendering by S. Moinul Haq, 1967), and the biographical sections of other *hadith* literature (to which reference will be made below) represent the most reliable sources for Muhammad's biography. Muir especially praises al-Waqidi: 'I do not hesitate to designate the complilation as the fruit of an honest endeavour to bring together the most credible authorities current at the end of the second century', he wrote (1894: lxxiii). Al-Waqidi may have had Shi'a sympathies. His work appears to have used some independent sources which therefore help us to corroborate Ibn Ishaq. These accounts do not agree in all details, and I examine some of these differences in Chapter 2. In compiling his biography, Ibn Ishaq attempted to acknowledge his sources, that is to establish an *isnad* or chain of narrators, tracing the incident, or saying, back to a first-hand authority. He did not, however, always supply a complete *isnad*, and the reliability of some of his 'links' has been queried. Like al-Waqidi, he may also have had Shi'a sympathies because of his claim that 'Ali, not Abu Bakr, was the first male Muslim convert (see p. 114). If this is so, we may have in this early biography an example of political reshaping of the material. The Shi'a text, *Nahjul Balaaghah*, has 'Ali claiming, 'I am the first ... who responded to the call of Islam' (1996: 95).

Thus, whilst the historical value of Ibn Ishaq's work is generally recognized, other *hadith* scholars tended not to rely on his material. Bukhari, though, is cited thus: 'Whoever wishes to obtain acquaintance with the early Moslem conquests, must borrow his information from Ibn Ishac' (in Muir, 1894: lxviii–lxix). I explore Muir's analysis more fully in Chapter 4 but I shall also have cause to return to his contribution in Chapter 2, when I discuss in more detail the issues of reliability and historicity. Other material, regarded as less reliable and of later authorship, also contains *sira*, such as the *Mukhtasar tarikh al-Bashar* (*Concise History of Man*) of Abu'l Fida (1273–1331), which devotes 13,000 words or so to the life of the Prophet. This was amongst the first Muslim accounts of the Prophet's biography to be rendered into European languages (see Chapter 4). More recently, Martin Lings (Abu Bakr Siraj ad Din) has produced a biography (1983) which draws on the early *sira*, on the historical sections of the *siha sita* (see below) and on some later *hadith* collections, to produce a coherent, composite account. This work was 'declared the best work on Sirah in the English language at the national Sirah conference, Islamabad, 1983' (inside cover, 1983 edition). Not all scholars, including Muslim academics, think that Lings paid sufficient attention to issues of historicity and reliability, as Syed Vahiduddin (1986) comments:

it is not a critical account and addressed as it is to the international audience of a sceptical age, it is not properly balanced. The aspects which deserve most attention are relegated to the background whereas incidents of dubious authenticity are given prominence. (pp. 233–4)

Nevertheless, it represents a useful compilation. Readers will find citations from Lings in this text. Guillaume's rendering of Ibn Ishaq, too, has not met with universal praise, especially from Muslim critics; for a summary of Muslim response, see Buaben, 1996: 144–6. Whilst aware of this criticism, I have made considerable use of Guillaume in this study, although I have generally tried to consult a range of sources when discussing particular incidents or issues.

The *hadith* literature

Six collections, compiled by al-Bukhari (810–70), Muslim (817–74), Abu Daud (817–88), al-Tirmidhi (821–92), al-Nasai (d. 915), al-Darimi (797–868) and Ibn Maja (824–86) became so highly regarded by Sunni Muslims that they were afforded a type of canonical status. They are known as the six *sahih* (sound) collections. There is in Sunni Islam (as will be seen in Chapter Five) no 'authority' to confer such recognition apart from the consensus (*ijma*) of the *ummah*. This itself derives from a *hadith*, 'my community will not agree in error' (MM, 1. pp. 45–6). Shi'a Islam developed its own authoritative collections, the *al-kutub al-arb'ah*, or Four Books; however, 'the content of most of the hadiths in the two collections, Sunni and Shi'ite, are basically the same. It is the chain of transmission which differs in many cases' (Nasr, 1993: 19). All six of the Sunni scholars were active after Ibn Ishaq's death, when *hadith* criticism had developed into a more systematic science. The size of this material can be grasped by describing what is probably the most popular and critically acclaimed *sahih*, Bukhari's: it is divided into 97 'books' (*kutub*), subdivided into 3,450 'chapters' (*abwab*). Each book deals with a different topic, although the relationship between title and content is not always obvious. To indicate the range of topics covered, here are some of the 'books': revelation (1), faith (2), knowledge (3), prayer (8), fasting (31), renting (34), *adab* (72), *hudud* punishments (81; Khan's numbering, he has 93 books). Bukhari actually left some chapters blank, demonstrating that he did not know of any sound *hadith* on that particular subject. In these areas, Muslims might exercise *ijtihad* (mental effort) to deduce the Islamic position.

The historical material in Bukhari has been translated into English by Muhammad Asad (d. 1992) as 'The Early Years of Islam' (1981), which has three sections, 'How the Revelation began', 'The Merits of the Prophet's Companions', 'The Beginnings of Islam' (this chapter was untitled in the original) and 'The Book of Campaigns'. This representes *sira* within Bukhari's *ahadith* although, unlike Ibn Ishaq, there is no attempt to tell a coherent story or offer a complete chronology of events. Nevertheless, there is a great deal of useful material. Altogether, Bukhari records 7,275 *hadith* (although 2,762 of these are repeated more than once) and is said to have scrutinized a total of 600,000 before singling these out for inclusion. He is also said to have interviewed 1,080 persons and to have performed two *rakahs* of prayer before 'inserting a tradition in the book' (Robson, 1986b: 1297). Similarly, Abu Daud is said to have thrown aside 495,200 out of the 500,000 traditions he amassed, thus judging only 4,800 as trustworthy. Bukhari's 'books' were arranged after the already established sub-divisions of *fiqh*, or jurisprudence, which shows how inter-related the two disciplines had already become. Gibb (1969) observes;

Viewed as a whole, the *sahih* is a work of immense interest and scrupulous scholarship. Variants are carefully noted, doubtful or difficult points in the *isnads* or texts are glossed. On any careful student the book produces a remarkable impression of honesty combined with piety. (p. 54)

Similarly, Guillaume (1924) tells us that 'Bukhari published the results of his researches into the content of what he believed to be genuine traditions with all the painstaking accuracy of a modern editor' (p. 29). Robson comments: 'the criticism of traditions was very detailed, showing how seriously the work was undertaken and one recognises the genuine effort made to clear what was false' (1986c: 26). The *Sahih-al-Bukhari* has been translated into English by Muhammad Muhsin Khan (1987); this translation is also available on computer disc, *WinBukhari* (with search facilities) through the Islamic Computing Centre, London; home-page http://www.ummah.org/icc /index.htm. Khan tells us that, 'It has been unanimously agreed that Imam Bukhari's work is the most authentic of all the other works in Hadith literature put together' (p. xvi). His nine-volume translation is itself an impressive accomplishment.

Not all traditions included in these collection have equal status; those classed as '*sahih*' passed all the tests (see below). Most scholars accept the whole of Bukhari as '*sahih*', although even he does not always supply a complete *isnad*. Many also accept the whole of Muslim. *Hadith* classed as *hasan* (good) fulfil most, but not all, conditions (*shurut*). Those classed *da'if* (weak) are suspect for a variety of reasons including: gaps in the *isnad*; they are traced back to a Companion, not directly to the Prophet; they contradict other traditions; some narrators are thought less reliable, being 'weak' links in the chain.

Only the soundest of traditions could be used for legal purposes (and, as already noted, only those believed to be universally applicable). Weak *hadith* could only be used for purposes of exhortation, to encourage piety or good conduct. Some *hadith* (which many non-Muslim scholars take to be apocryphal) solemnly warn against the transmission of false ones, such as:

Convey to other persons none of my words, except those you know of a surety. Verily he who represents my words wrongly shall find a place for himself in the fire. (cited in Hughes, 1888: 639 and attributed to Ibn Abbas, for whom see below)

If anyone relates a tradition from me thinking that it is false, he is one of the liars. (MM, 1. p. 50, attributed to Samura b Jundub and al-Mughira b Shuba and transmitted by Muslim)

Others appear to license invention:

After my death more and more sayings will be attributed to me, just as many sayings have been ascribed to previous prophets. When a saying is reported and attributed to me, compare it with God's book. Whatever is in accordance with God's book is from me, whether I really said it or not. (cited in Goldziher, 1981 pp. 43–4)

Other categories were also applied; a *murfu hadith* traces its *isnad* directly to the Prophet, a *maktu* to a Companion. A *mutawatir* is traced back to numerous sources, and has widespead support for its authenticity. Many scholars, however, think that only the text of the Qur'an and possibly as few as five *hadith* fall into this category (see Troll, 1978: 138). A *mashhur hadith* has more than two chains of narration – which must include some notable authorities. A *gharib hadith* is traced to a single source, that is, to only one Companion of the Prophet. A *muttasil hadith* has an unbroken chain right back to the original source, whether a Companion (*muttasil-marfu'*) or the Prophet (*muttasil-mawkuf*). A *mursal* has some break in the chain, usually at the beginning (i.e. citing a successor rather than a Companion as the original source). Al-Hakim (d. 1014) developed 52 different categories (*naw*) of *hadith*; Ibn al-Salah (d. 1245) developed 65. In his important work on *hadith* science, he set down rules governing 'methods of learning and transmitting traditions', 'rules about writing ... and methods of making necessary corrections in one's manuscript' (Robson, 1986c: 27). For example, a tradition should be 'heard' (*sama*) from a recognized master; a written record should only be accepted as authentic if 'the man who receives is familiar with the handwriting'. The transmitter should also record when, where, and how he or she (women are included in the *isnads*) received the tradition. Discussion also ensued about minimum and maximum ages for receiving and passing on a *hadith*. Was five too young, eighty too old? Bukhari is said to have started memorizing *hadith* at the age of ten. Conventions also governed the actual wording of *hadith*, which ought to begin thus: 'he reported', 'he announced', 'on the authority of ... '.

The chain of narration

As I have already indicated, much value was attached to the *isnad*. This relied, primarily, upon establishing that every link in the chain could be 'trusted', and that the original link was as close as possible to Muhammad, preferably a Companion. The logic of this is that if the honesty of the original source, and of each subsequent link in the chain, is beyond doubt, the validity of the *hadith* follows. No honest Muslim would transmit something the Prophet did not really say. There is much discussion about who qualifies for the status of Companion. Asad (1981) argues that just to have seen Muhammad, or to be a contemporary, was insufficient, 'Companionship can be attributed only to those personalities from among the earliest Muslims who were on intimate terms with him and shared his daily life and, in varying degrees, also his thoughts; that is, to those who could be called friends in the deepest meaning of this word' (p. 14). Others attach significance to presence at the Battle of Badr, and name 314 as having been 'with the Prophet' (see I.I. pp. 327–36). Bukhari devoted a whole section to the 'Companions', establishing their closeness to, and friendship with, the Prophet, who attributed a special collective authority to them; 'my companions are even as the stars – whichever of them you follow, you shall be rightly guided' (MM, 2, 29, p. 1320). Ten were singled out for special praise when Muhammad predicted that they would all find a place in Paradise (Watt, 1994b: 31, 55).

The Mishkat

The collecting of *hadith* did not stop with the work of the famous six. Other important collections followed, such as the very popular *Mishkat-al-Masabih* (Niche of Lights) by al-Tabrizi, an edited version of an earlier work by al-Baghawi (d. 1122). The *Mishkat* was one of the earliest collections to be comprehensively rendered into English; an edition by Captain A. N. Mathews appeared in 1809. James Robson's new and critically acclaimed translation appeared between 1960 and 1965. Guillaume (1924) considers the *Mishkat* to be an especially valuable

synopsis of the *hadith* literature. The author has ... ranged almost the whole of the literature, and ... given a representative selection of the traditions free from the constant repetitions occurring in almost all the original translations. (p. 6)

Whilst writing this book, I found my edition of the *Mishkat* very useful for checking references and searching for *hadith* on particular topics. Also useful, although much shorter, is Muhammad Ali's *A Manual of Hadith* (1977) to which Professor C. E. Bosworth has written a 'preface'. Unlike the 1990 Lahore printed edition of the *Mishkat*, this uses traditional referencing to the standard versions of the *siha sita*, thus enabling readers to trace traditions to their original source.

The importance of biography

Later, biographical works were compiled on all the 'links' in the *'isnad'* – Ibn Sa'd, in addition to his material on Muhammad, includes biographies of 4,000 'traditionalists'. Bukhari's own *Tarikh* 'deals with 42,000'. Whilst doubt has been cast on the accuracy of these dictionaries, there is evidence that genealogy was a well established science in Arabia well before the Islamic period began, as Siddiqi argues, citing David Margoliouth (1858–1940):

The biographical literature of the Arabs was exceedinlgy rich; indeed it would appear that in Baghdad when an eminent man died there was a market for biographies of him, as is the case in the capitals of Europe in our time. (p. 95; for a detailed analysis of Margoliouth, see Buaben, 1996: ch. 3)

Whilst links in the *isnad* chain are not usually created by blood, there is clearly some similarity between authenticating family descent and a chain of narration. For example, you need to establish when people lived, where they lived or travelled, to ascertain whether they might have met the people to whom the traditions they narrate are ascribed. It was also vital to establish their honesty and piety. Within the Arabic-speaking world biography has benefited from the impetus given it by *hadith* science, and vice versa. Muir, who did not have very much positive to say about *isnad*-criticism, wrote:

These could not be feigned names, but were the names of real characters, many of them personages of note. The traditional collections were openly published, and the credit of the compilers would have been endangered by the fabrication of such evidence. (1894: xxxixf)

Muhammad and Islamic art

Veneration of and devotion towards Muhammad, which I describe in Chapter 5, for some Muslims, borders on worship of him, which is anathema. In Chapter 5, I note how some aspects of Muhammad's developing role within the Islamic world have not met with universal Muslim approval. However, before I conclude this survey of our sources for Muhammad's biography, a brief word about his place within Islamic art seems appropriate at this stage of our study. To avoid the danger of idolatry, Islamic art has often favoured the abstract: geometric shapes, arabesques, mosaics and patterns which have no logical end adorn mosques and public and private buildings throughout the Muslim world. All these symbolize the harmony of creation and of its infinite Maker. Calligraphy, too, plays a very important part within Islamic art, mediating the 'divine word' within the workaday world. However, Islam has also developed a rich tradition of representational art; many historical works, including lives of the Prophet, are beautifully illustrated (for some superb examples, see the Channel 4 *Rear Window* programme 'The Khalili Collection: Dispersed By Time', broadcast 15 June 1993). However much some Muslims may frown upon this, a numer of paintings and engravings exist which depict Muhammad, sometimes, but by no means always, with his facial features left blank. Museums display such pictures in various parts of the Muslim world. Artistic representation of the Prophet may suggest how his life and deeds have been regarded and interpreted by Muslims at different times, and a study of this art might prove to be of considerable interest. Human figures, however, are usually stylized in Islamic art, so artists may not have made much, if any, effort to picture Muhammad as he is described in the texts.

The Prophet's physical appearance, however, can be reconstructed. What follows is a description of what he probably looked like in the 'prime of manhood'; he was slightly above middle height, with a broad chest and a well-built, strong body. His neck was long, and 'finely moulded'. Descriptions usually comment on the size of his head, which was large with a broad brow; his eyelashes were long and dark. His jet black, not-quite-curly hair fell down over his ears. His beard was long and bushy, whilst his moustache was clipped; one day someone said to him, 'You ought to clip your beard and allow your moustache to grow' and he replied, 'My Lord has commanded me to clip my moustache and allow the beard to grow' (but did he command all Muslims to do the same?). His eyes were black and piercing. He had a long, aquiline nose with 'an attenuated end'. His teeth were well spaced; he never travelled without a toothpick made from green palm wood, which he used every morning. His face, we are told, 'beamed with intelligence'. His skin was clear, although a line of hair ran from his neck towards his navel. He walked quickly, with purposive strides, but with his back slightly bent.

On his back was the 'seal of prophecy' – a lump about the size of a pigeon's egg. It is said that few could keep pace with him. He enunciated his speech very clearly. His Companions noted when he paused during Qur'anic recitation, and Muslims still imitate this today. He loved to sniff simsim and eat sweetmeats and honey (which is used as a cure-all throughout the Muslim world). Often, however, he survived on dates and water. B 59:84 relates that when Muhammad died 'his armour was mortgaged to a Jew for 30 Sa'as of barley'. He hated bad smells. He did not like wearing silk; he did like wearing a black turban and long woollen robes, always with an undergarment which hung to just below his knee. The *Bismi-Llahi-r-Rahmani-r-Rahim* (in the name of God, the compassionate, the merciful; all chapters of the Qur'an except Chapter 9 begin with this formula) was never far from his lips; he conveyed to all the impression of nearness to the God whose word he recited. And so on. Not all, but much of this, continues to inform how Muslims today choose to dress and go about their daily lives (based on Muir, 1894: 24–5; 508–19; various *hadith* also consulted).

The aim of this chapter was to describe the sources available for reconstructing Muhammad's biography, although I found it difficult to refrain from some analysis and interpretation. However, my next chapter explores in much more detail how scholars have evaluated the historicity and reliability of this material, and those issues which have been found problematical.

2 The Sources: a Critical Evaluation

At the beginning of our previous chapter, I stated that scholars advocate two approaches towards the historical reliability of the sources. Some, whilst expressing reservations, accept as genuine the broad outline and main events of Muhammad's life; others regard the sources as almost purely reflecting the interests and agendas of later generations, and reject the standard life of Muhammad as a largely fictitious fabrication. The pessimistic approach, with reference primarily to the *sira* literature, was pioneered by Henri Lammens (1862–1937), a Jesuit scholar; and with reference to the *hadith* by a Jewish scholar, Ignaz Goldziher (1850–1921). Lammens expressed extreme pessimism about the historicity of the standard biography of Muhammad, which he saw as almost wholly the product of back-projection and myth-making by later Muslim generations.

Rodinson (1981) describes Lammens as 'filled with a holy contempt for Islam' (p. 26). Buaben (1996) comments that even 'Christian writers expressed disquiet about the impact of his methodology', which only gave credence to material 'that reflected unfavourably on Muhammad and his family' (p. 134). Lammens' view of the *hadith*, too, was that they reflected the personal and party interests of their compilers rather than telling us anything very much about Muhammad: 'Each party, each sect, each school, strives to possess the traditions which are most favourable to its claims or doctrines. The *hadith* is even made to subserve personal grudges' (1968: 71).

Goldziher, similarly, viewed the *hadith* as 'outright forgeries from the late 8th and 9th centuries' (Humphreys, 1991: 83). According to Goldziher, these forgeries were produced as a 'result of the religious, historical and social development of Islam during the first two centuries' (Goldziher, 1967–71, V2: 19). Scepticism about the historicity of the sources we possess for reconstructing Muhammad's life has also been expressed by such scholars as Patricia Crone and Michael Cook (1977). In their view, the traditional Muslim version relies on material that is simply too unreliable and from too late a period to be of any real historical value. They use some Syriac, Greek and Armenian texts to construct an alternative version. This argues that the story found in the *sira* is an idealized myth created by later generations. Crone's Muhammad was relatively unimportant within the life of the expanding Khalifate, died after the Muslim conquest of Palestine, and probably originated not from Makkah (which she says was not a major centre anyway) but from north-west Arabia (Crone and Cook, 1977). The early Khalifs had regarded themselves as lawgivers, religio-political leaders in succession to the Prophet but in no sense inferior to him. Thus, 'it was the caliph who was charged with the definition of Islamic law; the very core of the religion, and without allegiance to a caliph no Muslim could achieve salvation' (Crone and Hinds, 1986: 1).

In this view, Muhammad's authority developed posthumously, invented by the religious scholars as a device to wrestle power out of the hands of the Khalif. Crone argues, then (*ibid.*, p. 2), that the classical view, found in 'practically all the literature', that on the Prophet's death 'there ceased to be a single representative in religious matters', whilst political power passed to the Khalif, was invented at a later period – usually identified with the early Abbasids. It was Muhammad's 'escalation into a fully-fledged founder-prophet' which undermined 'the position of the Caliphs in the long run' (*ibid.*, p. 26). The *hadith* tell a different story: Muhamamd's successors lack any authority of their own but are exhorted to rule according to the Qur'an and *sunnah*, and to consult before reaching 'personal opinions' (see, for example, B 92:2 and 92:13).

Cook's 1983 contribution to the popular Oxford University Press 'Past Masters' series elicited this Muslim response: 'Michael Cook exhibits great hostility and prejudice for the man Muhammad ... This is surely a very biased, atheist-tinted vision of Islam' (A. S. Boase, cited in Buaben, 1996: 154). Cook's Muhammad had 'created' Islam. However, he had 'found much that to us is distinctively Islamic already present in his Arabian environment' (Cook, 1983: 77), including Jewish and Christian stories and ideas; for example, 'Jewish apocalytic thought' was 'a point of departure for his political idea' (p. 82). It has been argued that not only do we know very little about the life of the man called Muhammad but that even some of the most characteristic features of Islam, such as the five pillars, evolved sometime during the second Muslim century (see Rippin, 1990: 86). The writings of Crone and Cook invite readers to reject the Muslim version of events. Whilst I endorse Robinson's conclusion that 'Not only is Crone's and Cook's reconstruction of early Islamic history implausible, it also makes less sense of the Qur'anic data than an account based on the Islamic tradition' (1996: 56), I would commend Crone's and Cook's writing to readers of this book; it represents a negative appraisal of the traditional accounts of Muhammad and of the rise of Islam which, set alongside the standard account, may enable you to judge for yourselves between these radically different approaches (see Robinson on Crone *et al.*, 1996: 47–59). I return to Cook and Crone in Chapter 4.

However, other scholars argue that by a careful and critical scrutiny of the sources we can distinguish dubious from reliable material and reconstruct with reasonable accuracy the broad outline of Muhammad's life. These scholars do not reject altogether the idea that material has been shaped to reflect personal or political interests, or even that some of it was fabricated, but nor do they totally reject its reliability. Andrew Rippin, a scholar who is by no means inclined to accept Muslim sources at face value, and whose opinion about the five pillars as 'posthumous' has been cited above, comments:

In broad outline all [the] sources present the same story but matters of chronology and detail are always problematical. ... The account of the events during Muhammad's life is fairly standardized, despite the multiplicity of sources available and the numerous disagreements among scholars of Islam as to how to interpret the material in a meaningful way. (1990: 31)

Watt (1953) affirms the 'general soundness' of the 'material'. He comments:

Once the modern student is aware of the tendencies of the early historians and their sources ... it ought to be possible for him to some extent to make allowances for the distortion and to present the data in an unbiased form; and the admission of 'tendential shaping' should have as its corollary the acceptance of the general soundness of the material. (p. xiii)

Forward (1997) notes that the earlier consensus 'of Muslims and non-Muslims' which had accepted 'the basic reliability' of the early sources for 'accessing the historical Muhammad ... has broken down' but he also adopts 'a conservative, traditional approach to them' (p. 3; but see his critique of Crone *et al.*, pp. 99–100). Where many accounts of Muhammad differ is less in their historical reconstruction of Muhammad's biography, than in their estimate of his personality, moral conduct or prophetic status. There is general agreement about the outline of Muhammad's life, but disagreement about how his life is to be understood. This will become significant in Chapters 3 and 4, when I discuss non-Muslim views of Muhammad. Nevertheless, lives of Muhammad by such non-Muslim writers as Watt (1953, 1956, 1961) and Maxime Rodinson (1961), which distil detailed and critical scholarship of the sources, offer biographies which, arguably, are as reliable as those of any other historical figure. Rodinson states that he has 'never rejected – explicitly or implicitly – any accepted version of the facts without compelling reasons' (1961: xii–xiii). As a Marxist, Rodinson had no obvious vested interest in producing a coherent and generally sympathetic account of Muhammad, but this is exactly what he does, arguing that 'through the unreliable tales and one-sided traditions' we may yet 'glimpse ... something that is the echo of a remarkable personality' (p. 313). Rodinson recognizes what he calls a 'power' in Muhammad, 'which, with the help of circumstances [made] him one of the rare men who have turned the world upside down'. On the one hand, says Rodinson, the atheist must conclude that the extra-human origin of such a power remains unproven; yet on the other, he 'may be forced to admit that it may be rooted in functions of the human mind that we do not yet understand' (p xiii). His Marxist ideology, however, inclines him towards a 'historiography freed from the chains of theology' (1981: 51). Buaben (1996) draws our attention to Rodinson's portrayal of 'the Jews as innocent people who happened to be at the wrong place at the wrong time' which he suggests shows us 'where Rodinson's sympathies lie' (p. 152; and see especially ch. 5 of Rodinson's *Muhammad*. Rodinson's family was Jewish).

In William C. Chitick's opinion, too, F. E. Peters' *Muhammad and the Origins of Islam* (1994a) 'puts down what can be known with any certainty about the career of Muhammad from the point of view of the contemporary secular historian' (from the back cover). As Crone comments, Peters' account is remarkably 'traditional' despite his expressed pessimism about the possibility of historical reconstruction (see Peters, 1991). In my own examination of the sources I shall incline towards the position of Watt and Rodinson rather than that of Cook and Crone. Three problematical areas will be highlighted: first, that of divergent material in the sources; secondly, that of miracles; thirdly, of *post eventum* fabrication or tendentious shaping of the material.

The problem of divergent material

Turning to a critical investigation of the sources for reconstructing Muhammad's biography, I begin by noting some divergent material within the the *sira* and *hadith*. There is, for example, dispute about the number of campaigns which Muhammad personally led, after the *hijrah*. There is (as noted above) dispute about the identity of his first male convert; Ibn Ishaq has 'Ali (see I.I., p. 114), al-Tabari names 'Ali, Abu Bakr and Zayd b Harithan as early converts but leaves the issue open as to who was the first. Preference for 'Ali as the first male convert may, as I have already suggested, have had a political motive. In fact, traditions which Shi'a interpret as supportive of 'Ali's claims are found in both the Shi'a and Sunni collections. It is the Sunni interpretation which differs. There is dispute about which Companions were with Muhammad at various stages, which obviously effects the reliability of *hadith* traced to them at such times. There are two accounts (one in Ibn Ishaq, one in Ibn Sa'd) of the order of the expeditions sent by Muhammad before the Battle of Badr, and a difference of opinion about when some of these took place. There are various lists of who was present at Badr (I.I. lists 314; B 59:6 says 'over 310'), which may bear on whether certain people qualify as Companions or not. This dispute, however, covers a comparatively short period of time. No one suggests that the expeditions did not take place and their order is not of major import. Alluding to dispute about the exact date of Badr itself, Rodinson comments that 'such disputes can only take place because everyone agrees that the battle did take place' (1961: xii).

There is conjecture about the number of times, and for how long, Muhammad used to visit Mt Hira, where he received the first Qur'anic Revelation (Q 96), and about the period of time between Muhammad's first and second experiences of revelation. I have read suggestions ranging from a six-month (see Ali, 1977: 9, n. 12), to a seven-year (see Hughes, 1888: 392) 'revelatory break' (*al-fatra*). Whilst this difference of opinion may seem remarkable, even this has relatively little impact on our ability to piece together the most significant events of Muhammad's career. There is also discussion about which *surah* (chapter) was the second to be revealed; some sources have 74, which begins, 'O Thou wrapped in thy cloak, arise and warn' (which some think was the first revelation). Most sources take this to be Muhammad's summons to preach publicly, which is almost unanimously dated three years after the first revelation. Ibn Ishaq writes; 'Three years elapsed from the time that the apostle concealed his estate, until God commanded him to publish his religion according to information which has come to me' (I.I. 117). Bukhari also takes 74 as the second revelation (see B. 1, *hadith* no. 3). However, Q 68 has strong claims to be the 'second revelation', reassuring Muhammad that he was not, as he thought, 'mad', and that he really had experienced what he thought: 'Nun. By the pen and that which they write. Thou art not, for thy Lord's favour unto thee, a madman.' This may then have been followed by Q 93, which also offered the Prophet reassurance and is taken by some to call Muhammad to preach to his close family and friends: 'By the morning hours, and by the night when it is stillest, the Lord hath not forsaken thee.' Others date this later, during the early period of Muhammad's public preaching, after another brief break in revelation (for a detailed discussion about the chronological order of the Qur'an see Robinson, 1996: 60–96).

Relationship between the Qur'an and the traditions

Generally, however, information contained within the *sira* helps us enormously in our interpretation of the Qur'an, as Nasr (1994) says: 'Without *Hadith* much of the Qur'an would be a closed book' (p. 83; Bukhari Book 60 is entitled 'Commentary of the Holy Qur'an'). Even with confusion about the order of the revelations cited above, the *sira* still help us understand their content; for example, without the *sira–hadith* we would not know why Muhammad was told that he was not mad, or why he needed reassurance, or the significance of the reference to his 'cloak'. However, the *sira–hadith* tell us that Muhammad used to 'wrap himself in his cloak' whilst receiving revelations (see B 1:1, *hadith* no. 3B). Later this became a symbol of his prophetic office. Later still, the jurists regarded the legal content of any Qur'anic verse which addressed Muhammad as 'O you folded-up in garments' as applying exclusively to him, rather as universal legislation (for example, permission to marry above the limit of four was granted exclusively to Muhammad, not generally to all Muslim men). More often than not, the *sira* help us identify when verses and incidents took place. Because the chapters of the Qur'an are arranged according to their length, not according to when they were revealed, it is impossible, without the aid of extra-Qura'nic material, to know when verses were revealed in the context of Muhammad's life. Many *hadith*, too, about Muhammad's experiences of revelation tell us much more about this important phenomenon than we could ever glean from reading the Qur'an. It is, then, from the *sira* (and *hadith*) that we know that Muhammad was sometimes left 'dripping with sweat' even on bitterly cold nights (B 1:1 *hadith* no. 2); that at times he was forewarned by hearing 'a bell ring'; that although he often 'saw' and 'heard' the angelic messenger, at other times the 'words' seemed to 'burn themselves' into his heart. Q 75:16 says, 'stir not thy tongue herewith to hasten it'; it would be difficult to interpret this without the accompanying *hadith*, which tells us:

Ibn 'Abbas said, 'The messenger of Allah used to exert himself hard in receiving Divine Revelation and would on this account move his lips ... so Allah revealed: "Move not thy tongue with it to make haste with it. Surely on Us devolves the collecting of it and the reciting of it" ... so after this when Gabriel came to him the Messenger of Allah would listen attentively, and when Gabriel departed, the Prophet recited as he, Gabriel, recited it.' (B 1:1 *hadith* no. 4 and B 93:43)

Many other examples of how the *sira* shed light on the Qur'an could be cited. Suffice one more: Q 9:40 reads:

Allah helped him when those who disbelieve drove him forth, the second of the two; when they were in the cave, when he said to his comrade: Grieve not, Lo! Allah is with us.

This refers to an incident during the *hijrah* when Muhammad and his Companion, Abu Bakr, asleep in a cave, were almost caught by five or six of their enemies:

The voices were not far off – five or six at least – and they were still approaching. The Prophet looked at Abu Bakr, and said: 'Grieve not, for verily God is with us.' And then he said, 'What thinkest thou of the two when God is their third?' They could now hear the sound of steps, which drew nearer and then stopped: the men were standing outside the cave. They spoke decisively, all in agreement there was no need to enter the cave, since no one could possibly be there. Then they turned and went away. When the sound of retreating steps and voices had died away, the Prophet and Abu Bakr went to the mouth of the cave. There ... almost covering the entrance, was an acacia tree ... which had not been there in the morning ... and over the gap that was left ... a spider had woven its web. (Lings, 1983: 119)

Some, of course, will find the 'miraculous' aspect of this story suspect. I discuss the problematic presented by the miracle material in my next section. Readers interested in exploring further the relationship between Muhammad's life and the Qur'an, will find Rafiq Zakaria's *Muhammad and the Quran* (1991) a very useful study; 'it is impossible', says Zakaria, 'for even Muslims, let alone non-Muslims, to understand the Quran without an acquaintance with the circumstances in which each revelation descended on Muhammad' (p. xi).

But did Muhammad wear a ring?

Other differences include details about what is, and is not, *halal* and *haram*. For example, is all sea food edible, or only fish? Did Muhammad eat lizard flesh or not? Sir William Muir seems to have attached some import to the dispute about which finger Muhammad had worn his ring on, and about what was inscribed upon it, as an example of how untrustworthy the *hadith* are. He wrote: 'it is repeatedly added that after Mahomet's death, it was worn by Abu Bakr, by Omar and by Othman, and was lost by the latter ... There is yet another tradition that neither the Prophet nor any of his immediate successors ever wore a ring at all' (1894: lx).

Muir's point is probably this: whilst the actual subject matter of these disputed *hadith* might not be all that serious, if the compilers could not get this one right they should not be trusted on more weighty matters either. In the legal sphere, there is dispute about which penalty should be imposed for adultery; Q 24:2 mentions '100' lashes, but the *hadith* record Muhammad as 'stoning' adulterers/adultresses to death. Thus we indeed have dispute about a weightier issue than Muhammad's ring! The argument in favour of stoning, which seems to 'abrogate' the Qur'an, was that this is an example of Muhammad 'elucidating', and not contradicting, its text. The commentators take the Qur'anic passage as referring only to the unmarried partners of an adulterous relationship, which left the Prophet free to decide what penalty should apply to married partners; see J. Burton (1994: 86) and MM, 1, p. 762 for several examples. These include the stoning of a rapist; in one *hadith*, Muhammad first ordered lashes, then 'on being told ... that the man was married he commanded that he should be stoned to death'. Q 24:6–8, however, sets rules of procedure for finding anyone guilty of adultery which, in practice, makes a successful prosecution extremely difficult (see also Phipps, 1996: 139).

Schacht (1964) characteristically has it that the traditions concerning the stoning of adulterers were posthumously created during the 'first three generations after the death of the Prophet'. The ruling, he says, 'was obviously borrowed from Mosaic law' (p. 15). Bukhari, in fact, recorded a *hadith* which has Muhammad quite openly adopting the Mosaic penalty (B 82:24, *hadith* no. 825). Why did Schacht suppose that this must post-date Muhammad? Similarly, he dates *hadith* which prescribe penalties for drinking wine from at least the Umayyad period, since in his view this 'was still unsettled under the Umayyads' (p. 16). Here, Schacht may be confusing debate about the penalty which the Prophet prescribed (Q 2:219, 4:43 and 5:90 proscribe consumption but give no penalty) with debate about what had been proscribed; was only *khamr* (grape wine) *haram*, or all intoxicating beverages? (See Goldziher, 1981: 60.) In fact, if the *hadith* on this topic was invented to lend support to a posthumous ban on all alcohol by vesting the 80 lashes penalty with the Prophet's authority, the inventers did not do a very thorough job. The relevant section in the *Mishkat-al-Masabih* (vol. 2, 16, 4), for example, has the Prophet replying with laughter to one reported case of drunkenness, giving 'no command regarding him'. Another reports the Prophet thus, 'I am not one to have any feelings about a man who dies when I inflict a prescribed punishment on him, with the exception of one who has drunk wine, for if he were to die I would pay bloodwit for him' (MM, 1, p. 772; and B 81:5). The subject of B 81:6 is 'cursing is disliked against the drunkard and the fact that he is not regarded as a non-Muslim'. This may be why, as Halliday (1996) points out, 'One may recommend the wines of Shiraz, the arak of Turkey and Lebanon, the brandies of Baku and much else besides' as evidence of the importance which alcohol 'has always held, and continues to hold, in the life of Muslim peoples' (1996: 247, n. 17; 203).

Exploring variant traditions

The traditionalists were perfectly well aware that their collections contained contradictory accounts. Often, these were followed by the phrase 'But God knows more than we do' (see Rodinson, 1961: xii) or, as Muir puts it, 'The Lord knoweth whether this be false or true' (1894: xl). Sometimes the biographers even added 'an expression of their own opinion' as to which version of a narrative is 'preferable' (*ibid.*). Two concluding remarks may be offered, in my view, about the problematic of divergent and contradictory material. First, as I have already noted, the *hadith* do not always set Muhammad's rulings in context. Thus different traditions may relate to different contexts. One important aspect of Islamic thought is often neglected by non-Muslim writers in their attempts to evaluate the traditional material, namely, the scope allowed for local custom. Within the Islamic legal code, there is room for what is termed "*urf*' (custom). This refers to any practice which, current during the time of Muhammad, was not overruled by him. Thus, 'the Companions ... often referred to it through such statements as, "we used to do such-and-such while the prophet was alive"' (Kamali, 1991: 291). Generally, *'urf* must be accepted as Islamically sound by the majority of Muslims but there is also a type of *'urf* known as 'special custom', 'which is prevalent in a particular locality, profession or trade' (*ibid.*: 290). Muhammad, too, may have allowed for such regional variation in practice, provided that this did not run directly counter to the text, clear intent, or spirit of the Qur'an. Once in circulation, such *hadith* could well suggest confusion or even lack of clarity on Muhammad's part concerning whatever issue they address. As I have had cause to note, *hadith* often became divorced from their specific context. It is also a well-known fact that many *hadith* which contain variant rulings on the same subject were extant in different regions; thus they may well represent not confusion or lack of precision but a tolerance of regional practices not thought to contradict the principles of *shari'ah*. This may also suggest that Islamic law is not meant to be rigidly applied to every situation, notwithstanding context, but may be adjusted in the light of particular circumstances or differing contexts.

Secondly, the fact that different, even contradictory, material has been preserved invites Muslims to examine such traditions for themselves and to make their own decisions about it. I disagree with Coulson (1994) when he claims that, because 'Muhammad's decisions were recognized as divinely inspired, the substance itself of a Tradition could no more be challenged by objective criticism than the text of the Qur'an itself' (p. 63). Muslims are under no obligation whatsoever to accept the content of a saying merely because it purports to be from Muhammad! This does not mean that it *is* from him. They are quite free to examine any *hadith* critically to see if it conforms to Islamic values; 'Muslims', writes Ahmad (1990), 'have every right to reject any normative tradition the authenticity of which is not absolutely beyond doubt' (p. 148).

The Qur'an is the Qur'an, and will remain so eternally: *hadith* have always been subject to scrutiny; and, as Mernissi (1991) comments, 'debate in Islamic religious literature is never closed' (p. 147). Similarly, Sayyid Ahmed Khan (1817–98) points out that, as the 'narrative of *hadith*s is not a literal report (*bi'l-lafz*), but rather gives only the meaning (*bi'l-mani*) of the words of the Prophet, [there is] ... no reason why the contents (*madamin*) of *hadith*s should not be examined critically' by Muslims in any generation (Troll, 1978: 139–40). Indeed, only the very few *mutawatir hadith* are to be accepted 'without criticism of their content'; the vast majority of *hadith*, even in 'the great collections' should only be accepted as reliable after their content has been critically assessed, and 'rationally analysed' (*dirayatan*). Our critical faculties are given us by God; we dishonour God when we fail to exercise 'the precious gift of reason' (see Troll 1978: 112). The easy availability of *hadith* in English translation, too, as well as through interactive electronic media, makes their scrutiny more accessible to Muslims today than at any previous period of history. To cite words attributed to the Prophet:

Things are of three categories: a matter whose right guidance is clear, which you must follow; a matter whose error is clear, which you must avoid; and a matter about which there is a difference of opinion, which you must entrust to God. (MM, 1, p. 47)

The problem of the miraculous

Non-Muslim scholars are especially critical of the many references to miracles contained in the collections, which they suggest discredits their historicity. This, of course, is equally true of much religious literature – of the miracles surrounding the birth of the Buddha, and of the Gospel narratives. However, whilst Jesus never appears to have disclaimed the ability to perform miracles, Muhammad's alleged miracles are said to contradict the Qur'an. Some of the miracle *hadith* are not considered *sahih*, and can thus be discounted as historically weak even in terms of classical *hadith* criticism. However, miracle stories which are found in the *sahih* collections cannot be easily dismissed as 'weak'. For example, the 'splitting asunder of the moon' tradition: 'The people of Mecca asked the Apostle of God to show them a miracle, thereupon he made them see the moon split in twain so that they could see Mt Hira between two pieces' (B 58:35 *hadith* no. 208; and B 56:26).

This is often contrasted with Q 2:23, which appears to assert that the Qur'an itself was the only 'miracle' to which Muhammad could point (as confirmation of his mission and claims). Similarly, 29:50 says, 'And they say: "Why are portents not sent down upon him from his Lord?" Say: Portents are with Allah only, I am a plain warner.'

Muir comments that 'there is no position more satisfactorilly established by the Coran than that Mahomet did not in any part of his career perform miracles ... Yet tradition abounds with miraculous acts' (1894: xlii). John Burton (1994) cites ten Qur'anic references which deny, or appear to deny, that Muhammad wrought miracles (see pp. 97–8). On the other hand, Asad (1981) identifies the 'splitting of the moon' with Q 54:1; 'the hour drew near and the moon was rent in twain', which he dates as having taken place five years before the *hijrah*. In his rendering of Bukhari, Asad includes four versions of the 'splitting of the moon' tradition, each with different *isnads*, and comments 'although we cannot explain it in terms of our every-day experience, its occurrence is amply established by the evidence not only of the Qur'an, but also by that of several Companions' (p. 172). Clearly, Asad does not regard the tradition as contradicting the Qur'an. In fact, only the version cited above actually refers to the miracle occurring as a result of Muhammad's initiative; the other three simply state, 'The moon was split asunder in the time of the Apostle of God' (B 58:35 *hadith* nos. 209–11). Robinson (1996) surmises that the 'story of Muhammad splitting the moon' may be 'merely an exegetical fable invented to explain an otherwise puzzling' Qur'anic text (p. 46).

Witness reliability

Others point out that many of the miracle *hadith* are traced to two transmitters, Ibn 'Abbas (a cousin of the Prophet) and Anas Ibn Malik, whose youth at Muhammad's death (they were 13 and 19 respectively) may cast doubt on their testimony, and to Abu Hurayra, to whom reference was made above. As it happens, of the four *hadith* in Bukhari, one is attributed to Anas Ibn Malik (58:35 *hadith* no. 208) and one to Ibn 'Abbas (58:35 *hadith* no. 210) and thus Asad (1981) comments on the weakness of both *hadith*. 'Anas', he says, 'was not present at Mecca at the time in question' whilst Ibn 'Abbas 'was not yet born'! 'Abbas indeed appears to have narrated not a few incidents which he could not possibly have witnessed. Commenting on another *hadith* attributed to 'Abbas, Asad writes, 'as to Abbas having heard these words from his father … this is impossible, for Ibn Abbas was born ten years after the beginning of the Prophet's mission (p. 151). If 'Abbas was a source of false *hadith*, he may have coined the warning about false transmission (cited above) to protect himself; Anas narrates a similar tradition: 'the Prophet said, "Whoever tells a lie against me intentionally, surely let him occupy his seat in hell fire"' (B 3:39). People would hardly suspect these sources of fraud! On the other hand, 'Abbas was renowned, amongst his contemporaries, both for his Qur'anic *tafsir* (exegesis; see his *Majimu'ah min al-Tafasir*) and for knowledge of the *hadith*, and is said to have kept written records.

Other 'miracle' stories have also attracted criticism – as contrary both to reason and to the Qur'anic verses cited above. These include some incidents from Muhammad's first phase, such as the 'opening of the breast' narrated thus:

There came unto me two men, clothed in white, with a gold basin full of snow. Then they laid hold upon me, and splitting open my breast they brought forth my heart. This likewise they split open and took from it a black clot which they cast away. Then they washed my heart and my breast with the snow. (Ibn Sa'd, 1: 96 cited in Lings, 1983: 26).

Muhammad's Night Journey and Ascension

The incident known as the 'Night Journey and Ascension' (*isra'* and *mi'raj*) has also been subject to much criticism. This is an interesting and important *hadith* since it contains the instigation of the 'five daily prayers', and its rich symbolism was later incorporated, especially by the mystics, into Islam's philosophical system. It also sheds light on the somewhat scanty Qur'anic reference to this event, at Q 17:1: 'Glorified be He who carried his servant by night from the Inviolable Place of Worship to the Far Distant Place of Worship'.

The *sira–hadith* record, in contrast, runs for several pages (see Khan, 1987, 1: 211–14 and 5: 142–8; I.I. 181–7), and tells how Muhammad, accompanied by Gabriel, was taken on a white steed, Buraq, first to Jerusalem, where 'he found Abraham the friend of God, Moses and Jesus assembled with a company of the prophets' (I.I., 182), then upwards through six heavens: into the seventh heaven, where he saw Paradise (some think that Q 53:1–12 refers to the same event). There, the obligatory prayers were 'laid upon him' (I.I., 186). Some non-Muslim scholars have dismissed the whole account as a Muslim adaptation of Zoroastrian myth (see Tisdall, 1901). Others dismiss it as incredible. In fact, Ibn Ishaq records that when Muhammad first confided this experience to Umm Hani (who narrated the tradition), she responded thus: 'O Prophet of God, don't talk to the people about it for they will give you the lie and insult you' (p. 184). Lings (1983) reads, 'His enemies were immediately triumphant, for they now felt they had an irrefutable cause for mockery' (p. 103). We might also note that whilst some have disputed the identification of the 'Inviolable Place' referred to in the Qur'anic text with Jerusalem, since Jerusalem is not specifically named; this 'seems to be borne out by a painstaking analysis of Surah 17 as a whole' (Robinson, 1996: 29). Themselves convinced that Muhammad did visit Jerusalem, Muslims regard that city as their third most holy (and refer to it as al-Quds, the Holy); its loss to Israel in 1967 'constituted a devastating blow to Arab/Muslim pride, identity, and self-esteem' (Esposito, 1992: 12). The Palestinian desire to recover Jerusalem as their capital stems from this historical, indeed theological, legacy.

However, Muslims have also long discussed whether the story should be understood as a literal account of a physical journey, or as a psychological or spiritual experience. Asad (1981), for example, citing classic sources to support his view, suggests that:

By assuming that the Night Journey and the Ascension were 'spiritual', we do not diminish the extraordinary value attaching to this experience of the Prophet. On the contrary, it appears that the fact of his having had such an experience by far transcends any miracle of bodily ascension, for it presupposes a personality of tremendous spiritual perfection – the very thing we expect from a true prophet of God. (p. 187)

He comments similarly on the 'cleaning of the heart' incident (see above). Ibn Ishaq's account of the Night Journey and Ascension includes the comment; 'I have heard that the Apostle used to say, "My eyes sleep while my heart is wake".

47

Only God knows how revelation came and he saw what he saw. But either he was awake or asleep, it was all true and it actually happened' (I.I., 183). Lings' rendering also invites a spiritual interpretation; 'he now saw with the eyes of the Spirit' (1983: 102). Those who deny that Muhammad could have enjoyed any genuine spiritual experience (either because they do not believe in a spiritual dimension at all, or because they restrict genuine spiritual experience to their own tradition) will need to find an alternative explanation for this story; they will probably explain it as delusion, madness, or an invention. I discuss some such explanations in Chapters 3 and 4; I also revisit the impasse between believers (insiders) and sceptics (outsiders) in Chapter 7. Muir, for example, had no difficulty accepting biblical accounts of miraculous happenings literally, but rejected Muslim accounts as fraudulent. The Night Journey and Ascension was an example of what he called 'pious fraud' (1894: 117).

A Muslim response

Sir Sayyid Ahmed Khan, responding to missionary apologetic, or rather polemic, also argued for a metaphorical interpretation of the miracle stories, arguing that Islam was in 'total harmony with the laws of nature'. Although he stressed the primacy of reason, he did not reject miracles because they were 'against reason but because the Qur'an does not support the happening of events or occurrences that are against the laws of nature' (Esposito, 1991: 134). However, Sir Sayyid could accept as 'miracles' events which, although 'unusual and unexplained', yet remain 'within the confines of the law of nature' (Troll, 1978: 178). Thus, neither the Night Journey nor the splitting open of the Prophet's breast, interpreted as spiritual happenings, need be rejected. However, Sir Sayyid went further than most Muslims in 'refusing to exempt even early Islamic history from the laws of the rise and growth of legends' (*ibid.*: 143) and readily accepted, for example, that the stories surrounding Muhammad's birth represent 'poetic creations fabricated after the astonishing success of Islam, and predated in poetic manner to the time of the birth of the Prophet' (*ibid.*: 177). By surrounding Muhammad's entry into the world with extraordinary happenings, for example, poetry is not necessarily saying that these events literally occurred. Rather, poetry makes use of such 'miracles' as a type of metaphor – to underline the fact that Muhammad's birth was a moment of profound significance.

'Allah speaks in allegories'

The Qur'an itself appears to allow for 'allegorical' interpretation; for example, in a chapter describing in great detail the felicities of Paradise, we read: 'A similitude of the Garden ... is promised' (Q 47:15). In another chapter, the beautiful *Al-Nur*, or 'light' – much beloved within Islam's mystical tradition – we read: 'and Allah speaketh to mankind in allegories' (24:35). Later, discussing how to understand such verses as Q 57:4 which refers to God 'sitting on a throne', and Q 75:23 which speaks about seeing God's face on the Day of Reckoning, Muslim scholars decided that it is humanly impossible to know 'in what sense God sits', or 'in what sense we shall see his face'. Rather, we should accept that God does sit, that we shall see God's face, and so on, 'without asking how' (*bila kayfa*). In fact, the scholars concluded that when the Qur'an uses anthropomorphic language of God it is really saying something more like 'it is as if God sits on a throne' than that God literally sits. Thus, what we may have in the Night Journey is an account of a real, but spiritual rather than physical, journey, told allegorically. Not all Muslims, however, have accepted allegorical interpretations – the *Zahiri* (literalist) school insisted on a literal interpretation of the Qur'an (citing Q 3:7 and 25:33 in support) and *sunnah*, rejecting the use of *qiyas* (analogy), but this school died out in the tenth century. Allegory, on the other hand, was defended by Ibn Rushd (1126–98), who distinguished between different 'modes' of truth. Kurtz (1996) explains that

there is unity of truth [but] there are several modes of access to it: (1) rhetoric, which was easily available to ordinary people by means of teachers; (2) dialectics, which involves arguments in defence of revelation and scripture; and (3) demonstration, which involved the rational inference of conclusions from indubitable premises. (p. 31)

This latter 'mode' is accessible only to a 'qualified group of philosophers and not to the masses' (p. 32). If there is any apparent contradiction between philosophy and scripture, 'Scripture should be given an allegorical interpretation and is not to be taken in a strict literal sense' (p. 32).

Problem miracles

Some 'miracles' are less easy to interpret allegorically. For example, we are told that before the start of Battle of Badr (623 or 4) in which, though vastly outnumbered by about 310 men against 1,000, the Muslims won a victory over the Makkans, Muhammad threw pebbles at the enemy: 'the prophet took up a handful of pebbles and shouting at Quraysh: "Defaced be those faces!" he hurled the pebbles at them, conscious that he was hurling disaster' (Lings, 1983: 148). At Q 8:17 we read: 'Ye [Muslims] slew them not, but Allah slew them. And thou [Muhammad] threwest not when thou didst throw, but Allah threw.' Q 3:124 also tells us that God sent 3,000 invisible angels to reinforce the Muslim army. Apart from the possible inconsistency between the *hadith* account and the Qur'anic reference, how are we to interpret this incident? Without venturing overmuch into *tafsir* (Qur'anic exegesis), one explanation, quite consistent with Islamic dogma, is this: inasmuch as God was responsible for the Muslim victory, thus demonstrating his favour towards the Muslims (later Muslim dogma upheld God's 'determination of all events'), Muhammad only threw the pebbles as his human instrument, just as Moses' 'miracles' were 'tokens' from Allah (see Q 26:15 and 63). However, if the Muslim army was also God's instrument, were the 3,000 angels necessary?

In considering the question of miracles, it is worth reminding ourselves that the seventh century is far removed from our own. People loved fairytales, and tales of the extraordinary. That an extraordinary man was surrounded by extraordinary happenings would hardly have stretched their imagination. Indeed, the possibility that Muhammad had not performed miracles was probably harder for people to grasp than stories that he had. At about the same time, too, the wonderful *Thousand and One Nights* (with its magic lamp and wish-fulfilling genii) was gaining popularity and, although pre-Islamic in origin, its contents and settings were being adapted to the Islamic context; it begins, 'In the Name of Allah, the Compassionate ... and grace and blessings be upon Our Lord Mohammed, Prince of the Apostles' (Burton, 1997: 1; the *shahada* is found on p. 67; see also Foreword, 1994: 102). Many miracles recorded in the *sira–hadith* may perhaps best be explained as the product of zealous but misplaced adoration of the Prophet. Book 24 of the *Mishkat* (vol. 2, pp. 1271–98) is devoted to miracles – feeding and healing stories, amongst others. Hughes's dated but still useful *Dictionary of Islam* (1885) lists 12 miracles, taken from Bukhari and Muslim (p. 351):

(1) On the flight from Makkah, Suraqah being cursed by the Prophet, his horse sank up to his belly in the hard ground.
(2) The prophet marked out at Badr the exact spot on which each of the idolaters should be slain, and Anas says not one of them passed alive beyond the spot marked by the Prophet.
(3) He cured the broken leg of 'Abdu 'Illah ibn Atiq by a touch.
(4) He converted hard ground into a heap of sand by one stroke of an axe.
(5) He fed a thousand people upon one kid and a sa'a of barley.
(6) He gave a miraculous supply of water at the Battle of al-Hudaibayiyah.
(7) Two trees miraculously moved to form a shade for the Prophet.
(8) He made Jabir a good horseman by his prayers.
(9) A wooded pillar wept to such an extent that it nearly rent in two parts, because the Prophet desisted from leaning against it (see B 56:24, *hadith* nos 783 and 784).
(10) A sluggish horse became swift from being ridden by the Prophet.
(11) Seventy or eighty people miraculously fed on a few barley loaves and a little butter.
(12) Three hundred men fed from a single cake.

Khan (1987) begins his translation of Bukhari thus: 'At this point I would like to bring to the notice of the reader that the Prophet was granted many miracles by Allah, and some of them are as follows' (p. vii). His list includes: Muhammad's meals were heard glorifying Allah; the dates in Jabir's garden increased after Muhammad had blessed them; stones would greet the Prophet 'whenever he passed by through the lanes of Mecca'; a Companion heard a wolf speak of 'Allah's Messenger ... inviting people to Allah' (p. viii). At B 56:24, *hadith* no. 782, Muhammad caused rain to fall during a drought. Ibn

Ishaq has a tree moving towards Muhammad at his command, then returning to its place (see I.I., 178–9), whilst Abu Jahl's hand withers around the stone with which he intended to strike Muhammad (*ibid.*: 135). Lings adds a club which turned into a sword before the Battle of Badr (1983: 148). Often (although not always) Ibn Ishaq prefixes his reports of miracles with his famous phrase 'it is alleged'. Some of these miracle *hadith*, such as the rock being reduced to sand and crowd-feeding (all of which took place during the building of the Trench; see Lings, 1983: 218–19; I.I. 452–3), could be explained by prodigious, seemingly miraculous efforts being inspired by Muhammad's example, or the Companions simply forgetting that they were hungry or being shamed into producing their own food when Muhammad produced the little he had. Indeed, the following description of Muhammad's deeds might well support this explanation: 'He worked now with the Emigrants, and now with the Helpers, sometimes with a pickaxe, sometimes with a shovel, and sometimes as a carrier' (Lings, p. 217). Muhammad Ali (1948), describing Muhammad as 'an indefatigable worker' tells us that, 'when a ditch was dug round Medina ... he was seen at work amongst the rank and file' (p. 114; Muhammad Ali (1875–1951) was leader of the Lahori Ahmadis; see Bennett, 1992: 147–9).

Watt's 'iconic truth'

This type of explanation, of course, is often used to explain the somewhat similar crowd-feeding miracles of Jesus (see, for example, Watt, 1995a: 55). In this useful study, Watt suggests that religious truth and religious narrative should not be confused with historical or scientific description. He writes:

A distinction is often made between the primary and secondary use of language, the secondary uses also being described as metaphorical, symbolic or analogical ... The language used to express religious truth is largely of a secondary character, and so it becomes important to show that, despite the use of language in this way, religious statements are dealing with reality. (p. 9)

According to Watt, the question we should ask of miracle or creation stories is not 'Did the writers believe that the event happened literally as described?', but 'What truths or faith convictions are they attempting to express?'. Thus, in an 'iconic sense', the stories about Abraham and Ishmael restoring the Ka'abah at Makkah may be theologically true (affirming the universal significance of Abraham's faith) even if they are not literally true. He is close here, I think, to what Sir Sayyid Ahmed Khan meant when he describes the 'miraculous events around the birth of the Prophet as poetical creations' (Troll, 1978: 177). Believing that Muhammad's birth represented a moment of immense import for all the world, it seemed appropriate to greet it with fabulous happenings. This explanation could be applied to other miracle stories; for example, believing that Muhammad enjoyed a very special relationship with animals, perhaps the *fitrah* relationship which all humans were originally intended to enjoy, his followers may have expressed this through such miracle stories as (9) and (10) in Hughes's list above. Indeed, Muhammad was renowned for his love of the natural world (see Masri, 1987). Muir expressed outright scepticism about the miracle *hadiths*, which he regarded as examples of 'pious fabrication', yet suggests that they may still 'adorn' ... 'well-founded facts' (1894: liii).

Miracles 'by Allah's leave'

It is my view that non-Muslim scholars may have overstressed contradiction between the Qur'an and the miracle stories. The Qur'an clearly wants people to accept its message by rationally appraising its content, not because its recipient could do exceptional things. Muhammad is himself described as commissioned to invite people to accept Islam 'with wise counsel and good admonition' (Q 16:125; Zakaria translates 'with wisdom and persuasion', 1991: 27). Muhammad was a 'plain warner', not a magician. However, a verse such as Q 13:38 does not actually deny that Muhammad could perform miracles, only that he could not do so 'other than by God's permission' (*bi-idhni-'Llah*; see Schuon, 1976: 90). On the other hand, there is some evidence that miracles may have been introduced into the early *sira* in order to 'demonstrate the authenticity of the Prophet's calling' in debate with Christians and Jews, as Peters (1994a) comments:

there is a consistent, though low-key, attempt to demonstrate the authenticity of the Prophet's calling by the introduction of miracles, a motif that was almost certainly a by-product of the eighth century biographer's contact with Jews and particularly with Christians. (p. 263)

This may explain the similarity of style between Ibn Ishaq and the Christian Gospels: 'it begins, much the same way Mark's Gospel does, with a declaration that "This is the book of the biography of the Apostle of God", and provides, like Matthew and Luke, a brief "infancy narrative"' (*ibid.*).

The story of Aminah (Muhammad's mother) hearing a voice saying 'You are pregnant with the lord of this people', also resembles the various pre-birth announcements of Jesus in the Gospels. We also have a genealogy tracing Muhammad to Abraham through Ishmael which somewhat resembles the Gospels' effort to trace Jesus' Davidic and Abrahamic descent (B 58:27 only traces Muhammad's descent to Adnan). Certainly, in eighth-century apologia, Muslims frequently did refer to the miracle stories as found in the *sira* when challenged by Christians whether 'there [was] any record of miracles performed by Muhammad'. The Christian apologists advanced miracles as proof of divine calling, and cited Q 29:50 against Muhammad. Thus, as Guillaume suggests,

Not content with the picture of a courteous, kindly and able man, famed as the possessor of all human virtues, the idol of his race, if he was to compare with the Messiah they must represent him as a worker of miracles. (1924: 135)

Nevertheless, even if we concede that a process of myth-making did take place around the memory of the Prophet, it remains true that in responding with miracle stories the Muslim scholars do not appear to have thought that these contradicted the text of the Qur'an – at least as they understood it (see Sweetman, 1945: 69–70). That an apparent contradiction would have concerned the compilers is probable rather than improbable, given that, as Muir commented,

We find ... that in its main historical outlines the Coran is at one with the received traditional collections. It notices, either directly or indirectly, those topics which, from time to time, most interested Mahomet; and with these salient points, tradition is found upon the whole to tally. (1894: xiii)

Indeed, Muslim scholars have long believed that God grants 'evidentiary miracles (mu'jizat) to his prophets, which 'confirm that those claiming prophethood are genuinely receiving revelations from him' (Watt, 1994b: 19). Thus we have, in a tenth-century creed, the words 'we believe in the wonder-miracles that have come to our knowledge and have been soundly reported by trustworthy persons' (ibid.: 55; the creed of al-Tahawi, d. 933). Al Farabi (870–950), amongst the most distinguished Muslim philosophers,

believed that prophets have prophetic dreams – which tell about the future as their source is Active Intellect – and can perform miracles, which though incomprehensible to human intellect because of its limitations, nevertheless have their causes in the realm of intellects and heavens. (Qadir, 1988: 83)

Muhammad's spiritual heirs, the Sufi shaikhs, also have miracles attributed to them. However, as Margaret Smith (1994) observes, they themselves appear to have placed 'little value upon the exercise of ... miraculous powers'. She cites al-Bistami (d. 874):

The saints do not rejoice at the answers to prayers which are the essence of miracles ... since the prayers of unbelievers receive an answer, and the earth contains both Satans and men ... Let not anyone who is perplexed by such things, put any faith in this trickery. (p. 53)

Watt, I think, is right to say that religious or sacred literature is not to be confused with scientific or even with historical description. Thus, instead of reading the miracle hadith as literal descriptions of actual events, we need to decode what they tell, or intend to tell us, about Muhammad whilst still bearing in mind that they may indeed serve to 'adorn' or 'account for well-founded facts' (Muir, 1984: liii). The fact that Muslims chose to recount miracle stories in a literary style that resembled the Gospels does not of itself prove that they also invented the material. That there is stylistic resemblance between the Gospels and the sira may rather suggest that Muhammad's biographers knew they were dealing with sacred biography and utilized what seemed to be the most appropriate literary format for the Life they were writing, which, given their cultural context, included poetic description. However, in the telling of Muhammad's biography their aim was as much theological as historical. To a degree, I agree with Crone's view that the 'process whereby information was reshaped is more akin to the growth of rumours than the fabrication of documents, and the simplistic choice between authenticity and forgery [albeit a dichotomy I have tended to uphold] gets us nowhere' (1995: 271). However, admitting that 'myths' were created, I am interested in why. Was it to surround Muhammad with a mystique he neither had nor deserved, or was it to depict metaphorically (and in the idiom of the day) a mystique he really had? If the former, we may impute insincerity to the compilers; if the latter, this seems to be an inappropriate judgement, however far-fetched (by today's standards) the myths seem to be.

Political shaping

In this section, I address the criticism that *hadith* so reflect the interests and agendas of particular people, or groups, that more often than not they represent *post eventum* fabrication of material rather than historically reliable accounts of actual events. Guillaume comments that '*Post eventum* prophecies dealing with conquests, the geographical advantages of certain cities, and royal personages are the clearest examples of this development' (1924: 24). Ignaz Goldziher (1967), Joseph Schacht (1950, 1964), N. J. Coulson (1964) all argue that the majority of *hadith* were fabricated for various ulterior motives. Coulson writes:

We take the view that the thesis of Joseph Schacht is irrefutable in its broad essentials and that the vast majority of the legal dicta attributed to the Prophet are apocryphal and the result of the process of 'back projection'... (p. 64).

Shafiʿi - sunnah's creator?

Schacht (1964) suggests that the concept that the *sunnah* of the Prophet was binding, and that it was the *sunnah* which would interpret the Qurʾan, 'not vice versa', was developed by Imam Shafiʿi. Thus its authority dates from the late Umayyad period. Earlier, *sunnah* had been a much more elastic concept; 'it referred to the policy and administration of the caliph' (Schacht, p. 17). Shafiʿi identified it exclusively with 'the contents of formal traditions from the Prophet' (p. 47). This view might be thought to exempt historical data – even if legal dicta were constructed posthumously, why should the historical material also be of posthumous origin? However, as Ibn Warraq (1995) observes, 'in their formal structure, the *hadith* and historical traditions were very similar' and, since 'many Muslim scholars had worked on both kinds of texts', it is unlikely that their methods of reconstruction would have differed between the two types of materials; thus, in his opinion, 'the *hadith* is useless as a basis for any scientific history and can only serve as a "reflection of the tendencies" of the early Muslim community' (pp. 69–70). In this view, the *isnad*s were purely and simply forgeries. There is indeed considerable evidence that political pressure was exerted on the compilers. Muʿawiyah, the first Umayyad Khalif, instructed scholars and others to suppress all *hadith* favourable to the house of 'Ali and to extol instead 'the glories of the family of 'Uthman' (Guillaume, 1924: 7): 'Do not tire of abusing and insulting 'Ali, and calling for God's mercifulness for 'Uthman, defaming the companions of 'Ali, removing them ... praising in contrast the clan of 'Uthman' (cited in Ibn Warraq, p. 70). This effort at suppression, however, was only partially successful, since even in Sunni collections, there are many *hadith* which extol 'Ali; (e.g. *Mishkat*, vol. 2, ch. xxxv). Not surprisingly, even more survive in the Shi'a collections.

Some traditionalists may have shaped material according to their personal interests – Ibn Ishaq's and al-Waqidi's preference for 'Ali, for example, reflected probable Shi'a sympathies. Muir, in his early essay about 'Sources for the Biography of Muhammad', originally published in 1857 and described by Watt as 'still a useful introduction' (1953: xiii), wrote: 'We have undoubted evidence that the bias of PARTY effected a deep and binding impress upon tradition' (Muir, 1894: I). Goldziher (1981) thinks that it was under the 'Abbasids that the *hadith* gained real authority:

> The 'Abbasids derived their right to rule from the fact that they descended from the Prophet's family. In further justification, they proclaimed that upon the ruins of a government which the pious had denounced as ungodly, they, the 'Abbasids, were establishing a regime in harmony with the sunna of the Prophet and the requirements of divinely revealed religion ... Thus, they wished to be not merely kings, but primarily princes of the church. (p. 45)

'Abbasid influence?

Similarly, Muir maintained that most of the compilers worked 'within the circle of Abbaside influence, and some of them under the direct patronage of Ma'mun' (1894: xxxvi). The latter is actually highly unlikely, since Ma'mun favoured the Mu'tazalite rationalists, who were vehemently opposed by the tradition party. Ma'mun imprisoned the leading traditionalist, Imam Ahmed Hanbal. The Mu'tazalites gave more scope to human reason than they did to religious documents. Schacht (1964) calls them 'extreme opponents of the Traditionalists' and says that they 'used ... systematic reasoning in order to discredit the traditions' (p. 64). Muir also maintained that any dissent was silenced by the political masters, so that

> every rising doubt must be smothered, every question vanish. If doubts did arise the sword was unsheathed to dispel and silence them. The temporal power was so closely welded with the dogmas of Islam, that it had no option but to enforce with a stern and iron hand an implicit acquiescence ... To the combination, or rather unity, of the spiritual and political elements in the unvarying type of Mahometan government, must be attributed the absence of candid and free investigation into the origin and early incidents of Islam, which so painfully characterises the Moslem mind even to the present day. The faculty of criticism was annihilated by the sword. (1894: xxxviii–xxxix)

According to Goldziher,

the rulers succeeded in seducing a number of prominent scholars into defending their position and illegitimate policies by inventing *hadith*s in their favour, putting into the mouth of the Prophet statements condemning their enemies as unbelievers. (J. Burton, 1994: 51)

A *hadith* such as the following may well foreshadow the victory of the 'Abbasids (regarded as striving to reinstate true religion) over the Umayyads (regarded as paying Islam lip-service only):

There was no prophet whom God raised up among his people who did not have from among his people apostles and companions who held to his *sunnah* and followed what he commanded [the four rightly guided Khalifs]; then they were succeeded by people who said what they did not practice and did things they were not commanded to do [the Umayyads]. So he who strives against them [supporters of the 'Abbasid coup] … is a believer. (MM, 1, p. 42, attributed to Ibn Mas'ud and transmitted by Muslim)

Posthumous authority?

In this view, the *hadith* party resisted Umayyad claims to power and authority and succeeded, first by forging counter-traditions and then by supporting the 'Abbasid coup, in effectively wresting real power from the hands of both dynasties. As Muir put it, 'Perverted tradition was … the chief instrument employed to accomplish their ends … tradition was coloured, distorted and fabricated' and 'gradually acquired the character of prescriptive evidence' (1894: p. xxxiv). Muir held that 'pious fraud' was not in any way 'abhorrent from the axioms of Islam' since the Prophet himself had taught that 'deception, under certain circumstances, is allowable' (*ibid.*: lviii). What seem to emerge from this discussion are two contradictory scenarios: first, that it was either the Umayyads who created much of the *hadith* in order to justify their rule, or the 'Abbasids who did the same to justify their rebellion against the former (yet both parties may also have claimed an authority which overrode *hadith*); second, that *hadith* authority was a myth created by the religious scholars in order to assert their authority over and against that of all rulers. Underlying both assumptions there is the view that the *sunnah* did not carry very much authority before it was created in the second and third centuries to further the aspirations of the parties involved. Thus Rippin (1990) argues that the early Khalifs 'appeared to have combined religious and political power only to have the religious dimension removed from them in the third century' (p. 58). This follows Schacht (1964), who argued that the early 'Khalifs acted to a great extent as the lawgivers of the community' (p. 15). '*Sunnah*', he says, 'referred to the policy and administrative acts' of the rulers and of their representatives (p. 18).

As previously noted, Crone and Hinds (1986) advance a similar view of the Khalifs as more or less absolute rulers, in no way subject to the authority of the Prophet's legacy (see also Chapter 4 below). Were this in fact the case, it is difficult to understand why anybody should have taken any notice whatsoever of either party's claim to the Prophet's blessing. If the *hadith* and Muhammad's *sunnah* only gained authority posthumously, and as late as the third century, why and how did it do so? Where did this authority suddenly come from? Why did the Khalifs feel the need to justify their rule by calling *hadith* to their defence? Likewise, why did those who opposed the Khalif look to *hadith* to justify their actions? Rather, it could be argued that the *sunnah* always enjoyed authority but that some Khalifs attempted to manipulate its use, whilst others were happy to live according to its principles. It seems to me that the *hadith* could only have been used, or indeed misused, by either party if its authority was already popularly recognized by the Muslim community at large. Otherwise, that community would have been unlikely suddenly to recognize an authority about which they knew nothing, and had no reason to accept as legitimate. There is early evidence, too, that Abu Bakr, the first Khalif, regarded the *hadith* as second only to the Qur'an as the source of Islamic law: 'If he found no applicable judgement in the Qur'an he referred to the usage of the Prophet' (Siddiqi, 1993: 111 citing Darimi's *Sunan*; Darimi, the traditionalist and legal scholar, was also briefly and reluctantly a *qadi*, or state-appointed judge).

Political neutrality

Whilst admitting that political patronage and bias did influence the work of the *hadith* collectors, we also have evidence of the compilers working quite independently of the rulers, even resisting interference. We know that Bukhari, for example, refused to go to the local Amir of Bakhara's house to read portions of his collection, saying to the Amir's emissary, 'Go, tell your master that I hold knowledge in high esteem and I refuse to drag it into the antechambers of sultans' (Mernissi, 1991: 45). He also refused to give the Amir's children 'preferential treatment' by teaching them privately, and was subsequently sent into exile (Robson, 1986b: 1297). Imam Hanbal, too, refused to visit his son and uncle (or even to pray behind them) because they had accepted posts from the Khalif and, as I have indicated already, he was imprisoned for many years by Khalif Ma'mun al-Rashid. Ahmad's *Musnad* (mentioned briefly in Chapter 2) contains material which extols 'the virtues of the Banu Umayya' as well as '*hadith* which support the claims of the Shi'a' and thus demonstrates a quite remarkable political independence. As late a scholar as the great al-Ghazali (1058–1111) expressed unease with too close an association with the Sultan, writing: 'Woe to him who is forced to serve the sultan, for he knows neither friend, kinsman, nor children, neither respect nor reverence for other', and 'it is a religious obligation to avoid the authorities' (cited in Lindholm, 1996: 269). It would be naive to think that the compilers were never influenced by political considerations, but to suggest that they were always so influenced would, I believe, be equally mistaken.

Narrator versus content criticism

Non-Muslim critics have tended to suggest that too much attention was devoted to establishing the *isnad*, too little, or none at all, to the plausibility of content or *matn*, vide Muir: 'It was not the *subject-matter*, but simply the *names* responsible for it, which decided the credit of a tradition ... If these were unimpeachable, the tradition *must be received*' (1894: xxxviii). This may have been true in the earliest period when the quantity of material was so great that *matn* criticism had to take second place. However, at quite an early stage rules about *matn* did evolve; after all, the whole science of *hadith* criticism began because scholars were aware that traditions were being forged. Certainly, *hadith* placed in the *da'if* (weak) category were often so classified because of the implausibility of their *matn* (or because this contradicted better-authenticated traditions). Later, during what we might think of as the second round of *hadith* criticism, when the genre of literature known as *Mawdu'at* appeared (which deals with fabricated and forged *hadith*), including the work of Ibn al-Jawzi (d. 1200) and al-Shawkani (1427–97), more elaborate rules concerning *matn* were developed as follows:

(1) *Hadith* must not contradict any other, or the text of the Qur'an.
(2) *Hadith* must not be contrary to the dictates of reason.
(3) They must not guarantee false reward for insignificant good deeds, or punishment for insignificant bad deeds.
(4) They must not praise parts of the Qur'an over and against others.
(5) They must not attribute racial superiority to any groups.
(6) They must not contain dates of future events.
(7) They must not ascribe to the Prophet anything inconsistent with his office.
(8) They should conform to the rules of Arabic language and usage.
     (Paraphrase of Siddiqi, 1993: 114 who cites the *Al-Mawdu'at*, Madina, 1386–9.)

Similar rules of criticism were employed by Shah 'Abd al-'Aziz ibn Wali Allah al-Dihlawi (1746–1823) and by Sayyid Ahmed Khan, especially in their response to Muir (see Troll, 1978: 138–9). In my view, there are quite a few *hadith* in wide circulation which do not conform to the above criteria, which could easily be identified and disregarded. One example: Abu Hurayra recounted a *hadith* that Muhammad declared that a 'woman went to hell because she starved a little female cat' (B 55:46 *hadith* no. 689). This conforms neither to the first *matn* criterion (the Qur'an holds out the possibility of repentance and divine forgiveness even for very serious crimes, see Q 5:39, 3:135, 17:33; 42:40), nor to the third criterion, even if it does reflect Muhammad's well-known fondness for cats (which I happen to share). Indeed, Mernissi cites 'A'isha as saying, 'A believer is too valuable in the eyes of God for Him to torture that person because of a cat' (1991: 72). Similarly, *hadith* containing 'miracles' can easily be disregarded without detracting very much from Muhammad's story, although some of the explanations suggested above may be preferred to the option of dismissing them outright. At least one Muslim scholar has chosen the 'outright rejection' option: Sayyid Ameer Ali, in his *The Spirit of Islam* (1922), once a best-seller throughout the Muslim world, wrote: 'Disclaiming every power of wonder-working, the Prophet ... rests the truth of his divine commission entirely upon his teachings' (p. 32).

Many *hadith* have Muhammad predicting future events, which, whilst not contravening criterion (6) as such, resembles the type of 'soothsaying' (*kihana*) which Muhammad himself detested and forbade. I have in mind, for example, *hadith* which predict, or appear to predict, the order in which Abu Bakr and Umar would rule as Khalif and their respective accomplishments (see MM, 2, p. 1322). One *hadith* has Muhammad predicting the location of their and 'Uthman's graves. These *hadith* are remarkably similar to *kihana* in their use of ambiguous symbolism and, sometimes, rhyme. This may be thought inconsistent with Muhammad's straightforward personality, and thus to contravene criterion (7).

But were *isnad*s falsified?

It has also been suggested that *isnad*s were sometimes falsified in the name of 'elegancy'. As rules of *hadith* transmission developed, so did the convention, almost etiquette, that a short *isnad* (*isnad'ali*) was a better proof of its authenticity and your own calibre as a scholar. Short-cuts may therefore have been taken by, for example, omitting a 'link'. This could easily result in someone claiming to have received a tradition from a link whom they could not have met, at least without the aid of a time-machine! Or, surmises Cook (1981):

You transmit a saying of a certain authority from your teacher ... I like the saying, and wish to transmit it myself without acknowledgment to you [reducing one link in the chain – there is no prestige in receiving *hadith* from mere contemporaries]. But instead of claiming that I heard it from your teacher, I ascribe it to my own. (Perhaps it is well-known that I have never met your teacher, or he carries no weight in the circles I wish to impress, or I consider his politics objectionable.) Again, assuming that your transmission survives independently of mine [posterity inherits two rather than one *isnad*].

However, as Cook points out, surmising that such 'falsification' may have occurred is not the same as establishing that it did occur. (Careful research might reveal weaknesses, but this was just the type of biographical work in which *hadith* scientists engaged.) Cook continues: 'in the present state of our knowledge there may be no good reason to say that the documents are authentic ... it is something else to go beyond this and claim that there is good reason to consider them inauthentic' (p. 153). Also, even if *isnad*s were 'manufactured' in this way, this hardly established that the *matn* was also manufactured; as Azami (1978) writes, this 'only means that their *isnad*s are questioned while the subject itself may or may not be false' (p. 305).

Orientalist assumptions

We shall have cause to revisit this issue in subsequent chapters, because what lies behind much non-Muslim scepticism about the authenticity and historicity of the *hadith* is simply the suspicion that Muslims were self-serving, dishonest and not very interested in 'truth'. Thus, we have Muir's comment cited above and, amongst many others, the following: 'want of accuracy, which easily degenerates into untruthfulness, is ... the main characteristic of the Oriental mind (Lord Cromer, cited in Ahmed, 1988: 118f). Or, as Reynold Alleyne Nicholson puts it:

The beginning of wisdom, for European students of Oriental religion, lies in the discovery that incongruous beliefs – I mean, of course, beliefs which our minds cannot harmonise – dwell peacefully in the Oriental brain; that their owner is quite unconscious of their incongruity; and that, as a rule, he is absolutely sincere. Contradictions which seem glaring to us do not trouble him at all. (1963: 130)

Perhaps not surprisingly, the eminent Muslim scholar, Seyyed Hossein Nasr, adopts the opposite view. He argues:

As to the statements made by the critics of *hadith* that the forged sayings came into being in the second century ... The *Sunnah* of the Prophet and his sayings had left such a profound imprint upon the first generation and those who came immediately afterwards that a forging of new sayings, and therefore of new ways of action and procedure in religious questions that already possessed precedence, would have been immediately opposed by the community. (1994: 81)

Sayyid Ahmed Khan, responding to Muir, saw no reason to suspect that the 'early believers, men and women, should willfully lie and deceive' (Troll, 1978: 136). Furthermore, Muir had misinterpreted *hadith* as sanctioning 'deceit'; rather, Muslims had 'divine permission to deny the faith outwardly (in a situation of danger)', which is 'a practice called *taqiyah*' (*ibid.*: 137), but there was no justification to claim, as Muir did, that Islam encouraged untruthfulness. Instead, the transmitters of traditions were 'virtuous and pious, instilled with the fear of God and His Prophet's word' (see Chapter 5 for *taqiyah* in Shi'a Islam).

Isnad criticism, as I have noted, was based on the conviction that, if the transmitters were good, pious and honest, they would only have passed on what they had actually heard, and that a chain of such pious and honest Muslims must lead us back to the authentic voice of the Prophet himself. Indeed, in contrast to Muir's dictum that 'pious fraud is not abhorrent from the axioms of Islam', there is a tradition (curiously this is also cited by Muir) that Muhammad 'hated nothing more than lying; and whenever he knew that any of his followers had erred in this respect, he would hold himself aloof from them until he was assured of their repentence' (Muir, 1894: 509, citing al-Waqidi's secretary). Another *hadith* (which Muir would probably have classed as false – he characteristically associated Muhammad with violence) tells us that 'inscribed on the Prophet's sword' were the following words:

'Forgive him who wrongs you; join him who cuts you off; do good to him who does evil to you; and speak the truth even if it be against yourself' (source: 'Sayings of Muhammad', Internet, down-loaded 6 December 1996; http://www.webcom.com/threshld/society/hadith.html).

Feminist critique

Before drawing some conclusions from this survey, I turn to some recent feminist criticism of *hadith*. In passing, I commented above that women have been included as transmitters of *hadith*. Indeed, many are regarded as authentic because they are traced back to a female relative of Muhammad, especially 'A'isha, 'one of the most important figures in the whole history of *hadith* literature – not only as one of the earliest reporters of the largest number ... but also as one of their most careful interpreters' (Siddiqi, 1993: 117–18). A *hadith* tells us that 'God's messenger's companions never asked 'A'isha about a tradition regarding which [they] were in doubt without finding that she had some knowledge of it' (MM, 2, p. 1362). Later, too, the creeds would assert 'that after Khadijah, 'A'isha is the most excellent of the women of the world ... the mother of the believers' (Watt, 1994b: 60, citing Abu Hanifa). Who better to report on Muhammad's conduct in private as well as in public? Indeed Muhammad once said, 'inspiration does not come to me when I am beneath the cover of a wife, except that wife be 'A'isha (MM, 2, p. 1361).

Siddiqi (1993) has an appendix on 'Women Scholars of *hadith*' in which he states that 'Since its early days, women had been taking a prominent part in the preservation and cultivation of *hadith*, and this function continues down the centuries' (p. 117). However, some women scholars, especially Mernissi (1991) and Leila Ahmed (1992) are highly critical of what they call numerous misogynist *hadith* ascribed to Muhammad. B 72:43, for example, appears to condone wife-beating, as does 'a man will not be asked why he beats his wife' (MM, 1, p. 693). Another *hadith* records Muhammad saying that women are less intelligent than men (thus their testimony is worth only half of a man's). A wife, says another *hadith*, must satisfy her husband's desire whenever called to do so, 'even if she is occupied at the oven' (MM, 1, p. 691). Also included in Bukhari's *sahih* are: 'those who entrust their affairs to a woman will never know prosperity': 'three things bring bad luck; house, women, and horse'; 'The Prophet said that the dog, the ass, and women interrupt prayer if they pass in front of the believer, interposing themselves between him and the *qibla*' (Mernissi, 1991: 75); and, 'I looked into paradise, and saw that the majority of its people were the poor, and I looked into the Fire, and found that the majority of its people were women' (B 76:16 and 51).

Mernissi, from another source (Imam Zarkash's collection; see *ibid.*: 72), cites the following refutation by 'A'isha;

He [Abu Hurayra, Bukhari's source] came into the room when the Prophet was in the middle of this sentence. He only heard the end of it. What the prophet did say was, 'May Allah refute the Jews; they say three things bring bad luck: house, horse, and woman'. (p. 76)

I have already drawn attention to this narrator's dubious reputation, notwithstanding his inclusion in Bukhari's *sahih*. However, Bukhari does include at least two *hadith* narrated by 'A'isha which reject the saying cited above; 'You have made us [women] dogs [but] I saw the Prophet praying while I used to lie in my bed between him and the Qibla' (B 9:13). What Mernissi hints here, perhaps, is that Bukhari was himself misogynist. She also cites *hadith* which suggest that no love was lost between Hurayra and 'A'isha (see p. 72). In my view, however, *hadith* which depict Muhammad as possessing extraordinary sexual virility resemble the type of exaggeration of which his admirers, rather than Muhammad himself, may have been guilty (wishful thinking!); 'I asked Anas, "Had the Prophet the strength for it?" Anas replied, "We used to say that the Prophet was given the virility of thirty men"' (B 5:13). Interestingly, this *hadith* expresses confusion about the number of wives involved: 'Sa'id said on the authority of Qatada that Anas had told him about nine wives, not eleven'. This might impugn the accuracy of the whole tradition.

Other *hadith*, however, testify to Muhammad's fondness for women and appear to contradict the misogynist material cited above; these include the much quoted 'Three things have been especially dear to me in this world. I have loved women and pleasant odours, but the solace of my heart has been prayer' (MM, 2, p. 1091), and, 'After women, nothing was dearer to the Apostle of God than horses' (Guillaume, 1924: 154). We also have 'The whole of this world is an object of delight and the best object of delight in the world is a devout woman' (MM, 1, p. 658). 'Paradise', says another oft-cited *hadith*, 'lies at the feet of the mother.'

Leila Ahmed (1992) says that although women played an influential, even a crucial role in the early days of *hadith* collection, later, when Islam's authoritative texts were compiled, especially in the 'Abbasid age, male attitudes towards women had changed. This, she suggests, was due to numerous factors – not least to the easy availability of concubines (i.e. women for sexual use) which led to a 'blurring' of the 'notions "women" and "object"' (p. 85). She writes:

The men, creating the texts of the 'Abbasid age of whatever sort, literary, legal, grew up experiencing and internalizing the society's assumptions about gender and about women and the structures of power governing the relationships between the sexes ... Such assumptions ... in turn became enscribed into the texts the men wrote, in the form of prescriptive utterences about gender ... Women were not, in this age, creators of texts in the way that they were in the first Islamic age. (p. 82)

In Mernissi and Ahmed's view, many *hadith* which attribute misogynist attitudes to Muhammad contradict the ethical spirit of the Qur'an, as well as other traditions about the Prophet such as those I have cited above. Whilst the Qur'an does not grant women the same rights as men, Ahmed's argument is that it did, compared with their pre-Islamic status, improve their rights, and that had the Muslim legislators followed its spirit, not its letter,

a reading by a less androcentric and less misogynist society, one that gave greater ear to the ethical voice of the Qur'an, could have resulted in – could someday result in – the elaboration of laws that dealt equitably with women. (p. 91)

Conclusion

What, then, can we conclude about the historicity of Muhammad's life? Perhaps this: that phase one of his life is relatively obscure; phase two, in broad outline, is less obscure; whilst phase three, miracle and misogynist *hadith* aside, is almost wholly authentic. I refer here to the principal events, achievements and speeches rather than to the theological or religious aspects of Muslim conviction about Muhammad. This position is actually remarkably close to that of Sir William Muir, to whom I return in Chapter 4. Whilst his estimate of Muhammad's personal conduct was negative and he was critical of much of the material about Muhammad, he yet concluded that the investigator could

arrive at a fair approximation to historical fact. Many Gordian knots regarding the prophet of Arabia will remain unsolved, many paradoxes still vainly excite curiosity and baffle explanation. But the groundwork of his career will be laid down with confidence. (1894: lxxvi).

My personal view is that is it comparatively easy to subtract from the collections *hadith* which extol or condemn certain groups or individuals, without compromising the value of much of the legal and historical material, just as the subtraction of many miracle *hadith* leaves the outline of Muhammad's life similarly unimpaired. John Burton (1994) echoes the view of James Robson and other Western writers, that the 'wholesale rejection of the *hadith* as invention and fabrication' cannot be sustained, and that many take us back, if not to the Prophet himself, then to a period 'soon after' (p. 181). In other words, it is possible to recognize bias and fabrication where these exist, but because some of the compilers were arguably dishonest, there is no reason to suppose that they all were. All were human, and as such subject to human faults and failings. I fully accept that fabricated traditions, influenced by bias and party-interest, are to be found in the canonical collections, but nevertheless believe that much of the material is authentic and historically reliable. Although my own view on historicity is thus conservative, I have drawn attention to Crone's and Cook's alternative account.

Whether the mass of *hadith* about how Muhammad ate, washed and treated animals are or are not authentic, is another issue. On the whole, given that the vast bulk of this literature exhorts humane, exemplary behaviour, I am inclined to think that if Muhammad did not say or do what he is reported to have said and done, he indeed might have done! The *hadith*, 'Whatever is in accordance with God's book is from me, whether I really said it or not' may not be far from the mark. In my view, if we extract miracles from Muhammad's biography, including the Night Journey and Ascension, or interpret them metaphorically, and resist attributing to his lips *hadith* which seem to contradict his message (including those which extol or condemn people and places), we are left with a very credible account of a charismatic personality who, as a religious and social reformer, overcame great odds to achieve success and power without ever losing his personal humility and humaneness.

Interestingly, even Muir, who has much to say about the Prophet's moral culpability, includes hardly anything in his extracts from al-Waqidi on Muhammad's 'habits' which does not show Muhammad in a positive light, and this despite his expressed view that 'statements which ... reflect unfavourably on the Prophet' are more likely to be authentic than those which place a halo around him. Similarly, although he also cites *hadith* which, in his view, reflect negatively on Muhammad, Guillaume writes that

any estimate of his living influence must necessarily be one-sided unless it allows not only for the all-pervading authority and example of the prophet applied to every single detail of human life, but also for the consistent expression of a loving and affectionate concern for mankind. (1924: 99)

In similar vein, he remarks that 'A large section of the *hadith* is full of sayings inculcating the necessity of kindness and love' (*ibid.*: 104), and that

Trustworthy tradition depicts a man of amazing ability in winning men's hearts by persuasion and in coercing and disarming his opponents. If we ignore the legendary claims to miraculous powers – powers which he himself expressly disclaimed – he stands out as one of the great figures of history ... Far more worthy of credence [than the hagiographical *hadith*] are those stories which go far to explain, when taken with his generosity and kindness, why men such as Umar loved him. (1973: 53–4)

On a personal note, after hours spent reading Bukhari, the picture of Muhammad that stayed in my mind was of a man who was passionate about the welfare of the poor, who disliked ostentation and wealth, and whose often quite simple concept of justice stands the test of time. Thus, 'The rich who do not spend their money on good deeds are in fact the poor' (B 76:13); 'to feed others is a part of Islam' (B 2:6); 'It is illegal for one to sell a thing which has a defect' (B 34:17); 'May Allah's mercy be on him who is lenient in buying, selling and in demanding back his money' (*ibid.*); and 'wish for your brother believer what you like for yourself' (B 2:7) are among the *hadith* which, for me, communicate Muhammad's qualities best of all. Yes, there are *hadith* (on punishment, women, and so on) which I do not find appealing but I actually had a hard job tracing many references to these in other literature to their original source! There are also many *hadith* which remind me of Gospel injunctions, such as B 85:4, 'Allah is more pleased with the repentance of his slave than any one of you is pleased with finding his camel in the desert.'

My object in this chapter was to examine the Muhammad of history. However, as I wrote, theological convictions about Muhammad (that he was sinless, that his example is 'perfect', that he enjoyed a 'perfect' or harmonious relationship with the natural world, and so on) constantly mingled with the biographical material, making it all but impossible for me to untangle the two. For example, if we reject the view that he was inspired, then all the efforts devoted to authenticating his *sunnah* by Muslims ever since must be deemed wasted; the Qur'an, and other experiences, such as the *mi'raj*, must presumably be explained away as delusion or wilful contrivance. As noted above, and as I explore more fully later in this book, this is just how non-Muslims have explained away the Muhammad phenomenon. On the other hand, if you believe in Muhammad's inspiration, the evidence becomes self-authenticating; you will accept as authentic both those Qur'anic verses which affirm Muhammad's status and his own claims about that status. Each supports the other, and both support your theological conviction about Muhammad's unique status. This is why Crone calls the Qur'an 'a text without a context' (1995: 269), yet she bases her own arguments on non-Islamic sources. It is, however, because Muslims believe in Muhammad's unique status that they revere him today. Similarly, as stated in the introduction, it is not because he lived in the seventh century and indisputably achieved greatness that they continue to imitate him, but because they believe that he, and no one else, can guide them along God's 'straight path'. As Maududi (1960) says,

whosoever [would] be a seeker after truth and anxious to become an honest Muslim, a sincere follower of the way of God, it is incumbent upon him to have faith in God's last prophet, accept his teachings, and follow the way he has pointed out to man. This is the real road to success and salvation. (p. 60)

This is why Muhammad exercises what Shabbir Akhtar refers to as 'posthumous authority'. He does not mean, of course, that this authority began after Muhammad's death but that, for Muslims, it remains as important today as it was when he was alive. What I explore in Chapter 5, then, is the even more complex understanding of who Muhammad was which developed from the comparatively simple Qur'anic statements, cited above, that his '*sunnah* is the best example', and his life the last prophetic mission between 632 CE and judgement day. 'To love the Messenger', says B 3:8, 'is part of faith'. Arguably, as Muslim theology develops a view of Muhammad which goes beyond (some, including Muslims, say far too far beyond) what the Qur'an says about him, the need to possess sources which portray him as exemplary also increases. First, however, I turn in Chapters 3 and 4 to non-Muslim accounts of the Prophet, beginning with the period from Islam's origins to the sixteenth century.

Part Two

3 Non-Muslim Lives of Muhammad: from the 7th to the 16th Centuries

In examining the sources for Muhammad's biography and their critical assessment in Chapter 1, I anticipated some of the issues which will be encountered in this survey of how non-Muslim writers have interpreted Muhammad's life. The task of surveying non-Muslim attitudes to Muhammad is too ambitious for me to claim that what follows will be either very comprehensive or even perhaps very adequate. Within the various constraints that apply – the vastness of the subject, the variety of languages in which non-Muslims have written about Muhammad and the length of the chronological period involved – I attempt to focus on some of the different ways in which outsiders have tried to make sense of Muhammad. I highlight how different attitudes have sometimes answered different questions, since these often depend on what agenda has been set and how the sources used have influenced attitudes. Christians, for example, have sometimes written about Muhammad in order to inform fellow-Christians what they should think about him. Others have written mainly to tell Muslims what they ought to think.

Some have written about Muhammad to score points against other Christians; some have written about Muhammad for reasons that actually have very little at all to do with trying to make sense of who he was – for example, as an attack on all religious belief, or as a vindication of secular thought. Some have written about Muhammad from specifically religious perspectives, some as secular historians, others as 'free thinkers'. It has also been suggested that the context in which people write influences both their agenda and their attitude. Just as no social science research can be conducted in 'some autonomous realm that is insulated from the wider society and from the particular biography of the researcher' (Hammersley and Atkinson, 1995: 16), so no history, as I suggested in my Introduction, should be read without also 'reading' the historian.

In order to give realistic parameters to this survey, I concentrate on what Europeans have had to say about Muhammad. However, I also refer to some non-European accounts, especially during the initial period of encounter between Muslims and non-Muslims. Here, as in my chapter, 'Images in the Making' in *Victorian Images of Islam* (1992), I follow Robert Caspar (1987) in speaking about three different contexts: those non-Muslims (mainly Christians) writing within the Muslim world; those writing from within the Byzantine world; and those writing from Western Europe. I also ask what factors influence attitudes, such as encounter, or lack of encounter, with Muslims, the sources of information used, and whether it is possible to speak of a progression in understanding of Muhammad. This, of course, begs the question, what qualifies as progression in this instance? I draw unashamedly in this chapter on the work of scholars who have explored, and explored extensively, the material before us. I am especially indebted to Norman Daniel (1993), J. W Sweetman (1955), Maxime Rodinson (1974, 1988) and R. W. Southern (1962). Sweetman has, very usefully, rendered substantial extracts from the early writers into English in his detailed, but not easy, *Islam and Christian Theology* (1945, 1955).

These writers, however, address Western views of Islam, and whilst their work is replete with references to Muhammad, this was not their primary concern. In making liberal use of their scholarship, I have therefore sifted from it material relating specifically to views of the Prophet. Whilst this may not represent original inquiry, I hope that it does perform a useful indexing service. The Victorian period has also been explored by Philip Almond (1989), whose book (which does focus on the Prophet) I have found useful. Finally, my friend and colleague Jabal Buaben's *Image of the Prophet Muhammad in the West* (1996) has been invaluable, offering as it does a Muslim perspective on non-Muslim accounts of the Prophet. However, my debt to these scholars diminishes the closer we come to our own period. Thus my review from, say, the seventeenth century onwards claims a greater degree of originality. I have divided our survey into two chapters. In this chapter I explore accounts from the seventh century to the sixteenth. Chapter 4 explores from the end of the Renaissance until today.

Non-Muslims on Muhammad within the Muslim world

There is some logic in beginning with early responses to Muhammad within the Arab world. Non-Muslims there found themselves subject to Muslim rule, which invited them either to accept *dhimmi* status or to become Muslim (see Q 9:29). There is some evidence to suggest that those Christians who did not conform to Byzantine orthodoxy, especially the Alexandrian and Antiochene traditions (Nestorians, the Syrian churches, the Copts of Egypt), found Muslim rule neither more nor less congenial than they had found Byzantine or Persian rule. In fact, they may have experienced less interference from the Khalif than they had from either of their previous emperors. Here, the writing of a tenth-century bishop, Agapius, Mahbub Ibn Qustantin, Bishop of Hierapolis, can be cited. He appears to have stressed how Christians could come to terms with the Muslims by accepting *dhimmi* status. Several major cities were actually 'handed over' to the Muslims by Christian leaders (Jerusalem in 638 by Patriarch Sophronius, Alexandria by the Monophysite Patriarch Benjamin in 645) because favourable terms of surrender led to the preservation of 'their urban society and life' and 'cultural and educational institutions' (Sahas, 1991: 16). Agapius recorded how Christians and Jews had made peace with Muhammad and how he had 'written a document for them' (Sweetman, 1955: 9). The latter is presumably a reference to treaties between Muhammad and the Christians of Najran and the Jews of Khaibar, preserved in summary within the *sira*, which guaranteed them protection. Agapius also chronicled how the Christians of Edessa had been forced by the Persian emperor to change their allegiance from Byzantium to one of the Antiochene traditions, and then forced by the Byzantine emperor to revert back again. On the other hand, after the Muslim conquest, he records how Khalif Muʿawiyah 'gave orders that the ruined churches of Edessa should be restored and rebuilt' (*ibid.*: 10).

Agapius, Bishop of Hierapolis

Agapius also records, however, that Khalif Walid (705–15) began to destroy churches and ordered Christians to use Arabic instead of Greek. Agapius himself wrote in Arabic. Positively, this meant that Christians were subsequently able to play a fuller part in the intellectual life of the ʿAbbasid Khalifate, and contribute significantly to its cultural achievements. Sahas (1991) suggests that despite the 'controversial context' in which encounter occurred, Middle Eastern Christians and Muslims enjoyed an 'inherent cultural and religious affinity'. In part, this affinity resulted from the fact that Islam and the Byzantines shared a 'theocratic ethos' (p. 16).

In writing about Muhammad's rise to power, Agapius demonstrates accurate knowledge. Muhammad, he wrote,

commanded his community to believe in prophets and messengers and in what Allah had sent down upon them and that they should believe in Christ, the son of Mary – saying that He was the apostle of Allah, His Word and His Servant, and His Spirit – and in the Gospel, and in Paradise and the Fire, and in the Accounting at the Last Day. He told them that there was in paradise eating, drinking, marrying, streams of wine, milk and honey, the houris of the dark eyes who had not been touched by men or jinn. He also made obligatory for them fasting and worship and other things which for fear of prolixity I do not mention. (Sweetman, 1955: 7 and see Q 4:171 for references to Jesus)

Agapius's attitude seems to have been primarily pragmatic: Muslim ascendancy was a fact, but Christians could live with this reasonably well if they understood what their Muslim rulers demanded of them. How, though, did Agapius explain the loss of Christian power or the coming of a prophet after Christ, whom Christians hold to be God's absolute self-disclosure? As a bishop and theologian, his community might very well have looked to him for answers to these questions.

Emperor Heraclius of Byzantinium

The closest we have to an answer is his account of Heraclius's response to the initial advance of Muhammad's army. Agapius records Heraclius (610–41), the Byzantine emperor contemporaneous with Muhammad, writing to Egypt, Syria, Armenia and Mesopatamia, ordering his lieutenants

not to fight with the Arabs any longer and no more to oppose the will of God. He told them that the Great God had sent this misfortune upon men, who should not oppose the will of God when he had promised to Ishmael the son of Abraham that there would issue from his loins many kings (Sweetman, 1955: 9)

This may well be the earliest independent account, by a non-Muslim, of a response to the phenomenon of Islam. The statement suggests that Heraclius, and presumably Agapius in relating this tradition, regarded the cause of Muhammad's rise as in some sense divinely inspired, as fulfilling prophecy and a God-sent punishment (possibly against Christians for squabbling so much amongst themselves). Perhaps this seeing of God's hand behind Muhammad's rise means no more than that God is Lord of history and used Muhammad as he had once used Nebuchadnezzar. This, as such, does not imply that Muhammad was a good man, any more than the biblical account of Jerusalem's fall implies anything positive about Nebuchadnezzar's character. What it does represent, however, is the view that God's hand (as it were) rests on all human history and that Islam's existence, and the role of its Prophet, must somehow be interpreted and understood in relation to God's ultimate purposes. The reference to Ishmael, from whom Muhammad is said to be descended, is also interesting (see the genealogy at the beginning of Ibn Ishaq). This appears, to some degree, to concede that Muhammad was 'promised' (see Gen 17:20) and therefore anticipated within the Judaeo–Christian scriptural record. Not all who have found themselves writing about Muhammad share this understanding of the historical process. What can be said about this early response is that Agapius and the Muslims occupied the same world. He did not assume a total 'otherness' between how they and he experienced the world.

Another writer adds the following words to Heraclius' statement:

They [Muslims] are far from being in darkness, inasmuch as they have rejected the worship of idols and worship only one God. But they still lack the perfectly pure light ... because of the incomplete knowledge which they have of our Christian faith and our orthodox confession. (*ibid.*: 15)

Ibn Ishaq devotes two pages to Heraclius. According to him, Heraclius had a dream in which he saw 'the kingdom of a circumcised man victorious' (I.I., p. 654) and would have followed him but for his fear of the Romans; 'Alas, I know that your master is a prophet ... and that it is he whom we expect and find in our books, but I go in fear of my life from the Romans' (I.I., p. 656). Muslims believe that numerous biblical passages predict Muhammad's prophethood, and argue that Christian interpretation of these passages as pointing to Jesus is wrong. For example, ur-Rahman (1977) writes:

what else could be suggested by the description which Moses is supposed to give of the Messiah, when he said, Deuteronomy 18:18, 'I will raise them up a prophet, from among their brethren, like unto thee, and will put my words in his mouth, and he shall speak unto them all that I command him. (p. 174)

Ahmed Deedat has a lengthy and widely published lecture on 'What the Bible Says About Mohammed' (available on the Internet, http://www.wam.umd.edu/~ibrahim/Muhammad.in.Bible.htm, my copy down-loaded 16 December 1996). Citing Q 4:157, 'They slew [Jesus] not, but it appeared so unto them', Muslims traditionally deny the historicity of the crucifixion. Khan (1987) prefaces his translation of Bukhari with a chapter called 'Biblical Evidence of Jesus Being a Servant of God and Having No Share in Divinity' by M. T. Al-Hilali of Madinah University. This chapter has a section on 'Finality on Proofs of the Fabrication of the Story of the Cross' (vol. 1, pp. lix–lx), and cites Gospel as well as Qur'anic passages as evidence.

Abu'l Faraj, Bishop Bar Hebraeus

It was the thirteenth-century Jacobite bishop, Bar Hebraeus, (1226–86), otherwise known as Abu'l Faraj, who, in his *Chronicle of Universal History*, wrote the words cited above about Muslims being 'far from darkness'. Muhammad, he suggested, had been in some sense raised up by God; also, the religion which he had propagated was not to be regarded as altogether bad. This view of Muhammad could perhaps be characterized as a partial affirmation and a partial denial of his claims to be an apostle of a God-given faith. This resembles the Muslim estimate of Christianity; Christians share much in common with Muslims but do not possess the complete truth about God. What this view almost certainly does is reflect the political reality: being a Christian in the Muslim world was not altogether unpleasant. Robinson (1996) suggests that, for pragmatic reasons, Muslim rulers could adopt a conciliatory policy towards Christians by referring to early Qur'anic *ayah*s which 'evince a positive attitude' (pp. 54–5). B 52:174 cites 'Umar instructing his would-be successor to 'take care of those non-Muslims who are under the protection of Allah and His Messenger' and 'not over-tax them beyond their capability'. Living towards the end of the 'Abbasid Khalifate, Bar Hebraeus wrote about Muslim culture and civilization with considerable admiration, 'There rose among them philosophers and mathematicians and physicians excelling all the ancient sages ... Their architecture was great by reason of consummate style and skilful research', for example, 'but their law [was] cumbersome' (Sweetman, 1955: 15). This last statement may represent the beginning of a long tradition of contrasting Christianity as a religion of 'grace' with Islam as a legalistic religion. Like Agapius, however, Bar Hebraeus occupied the same, not a different, world from his Muslim neighbours and colleagues. He rendered Avicenna's *Kitab-al-Isharat* into Syriac. He did complain about 'tyranny and persecution' against Christians, but he did so 'boldly and freely without giving [the] impression that he [felt] himself to be in jeopardy for doing so' (*ibid.*: 14–15).

Minorities within the Muslim world

There has been much debate about the status of minorities within the Muslim world (a debate which continues to this day). This was probably subject to considerable flux, depending on circumstances. There is, however, evidence that Christians and Jews could move with ease in Umayyad and early 'Abbasid society (several Khalifs had Christian wives), and that many occupied responsible positions. As one commentator observes: 'key departments such as finance, taxation, commerce and trade were usually manned by either Jews or Christians. Even the royal physicians were, in several cases, non-Muslims' (Zakaria, 1988: 73).

We have, for example, a tenth-century description of the Exilarch or *Nasi*, who was recognized by the Khalif as head of the Jewish communities, and who oversaw a type of Sanhedrin council of elders which exercised responsibility for governing the internal affairs of the Jews. This description (cited in Johnson, 1987: 182) suggests that the Exilarch enjoyed considerable respect and freedom:

He has extensive dominion over all the Jewish communities by authority of the Commander of the Faithful [i.e. the Khalif]. Jews and Gentiles alike rise up before him and greet him ... Whenever he goes to have an audience with the caliph he is accompanied by Jewish and Moslem horsemen who ride in front of him, calling out in Arabic, 'Make way for our lord, the Son of David'. He himself is mounted, and wears an embroidered silk robe and a large turban Before the caliph, the *Nasi* prostrates himself ... Then the caliph makes a sign to his eunuchs to seat the *nasi* on a chair closest to him.

The Nestorian contribution

The Nestorian Catholicos, too, appears to have been recognized by the Khalif as head of the whole Christian community and to have enjoyed an almost peer relationship with the Khalif. The Nestorians flourished under Muslim rule. Their Catholicos, Mar Timothy (in office 780–823) debated with the Khalif, al-Mahdi (in office 775–85) about the claims of their respective religions. This conversation, translated and edited by Alphonse Mingana (1881–1937) as *Timothy's Apology for Christianity* (1928), gives us valuable insight into the issues, and agenda, of Christian–Muslim debate from this early period of encounter. Similarly, we have the fictitious dialogues (probably based on actual encounter) of Yuhanna Sargun, better known as John of Damascus (675–79), especially his *Disputatio Christiani et Saraceni* and his *Disputatio Saraceni et Christiani*. These documents show knowledge of the Qur'an, including references to Jesus, and stress the titles 'Word' and 'Spirit' (Q 4:171) already referred to in the citation from Agapius. There is much debate about the Trinity, and about how Jesus could be God whilst dying on the Cross:

'Why', asks the Caliph, 'did not all three become incarnate if they are not separable one from another? If Father and Spirit did not put on a human body with the Son how are they inseparable by distance and space?'

Timothy responded: that just as the whole of the taste and the whole of the scent is from the whole of the apple, and yet scent is not taste nor taste scent, so, too, the persons of the Trinity being uncircumscribed are not separate one from another and not mixed and confused with one another but 'separated in their person in a united way and united in their nature in a separate way'. (Mingana, pp. 25f)

Are the Christian scriptures corrupt?

There was debate about how literally scripture should be understood, which has bearing on contemporary Muslim discussion about the 'verses of likening' (which speak of God as sitting, seeing, etc) and those which prohibit comparison of God with any created object. The claims of the Qur'an versus the Bible were much debated. The Muslims accused the Christians of having corrupted the Bible (alluded to in Chapter 1) and asserted that 'the *Furqan* [Criterion, e.g. the Qur'an] has abrogated the *Injil* as the Gospel abrogated Moses' (see Sweetman, 1955: 80–1). For examples of verses charging the 'corruption' (*tahrif*) of scriptures, see Q 2:59, 75, 140; 3:63; 4:44. Debate continues, however, about whether all or some of the People of the Scriptures are so charged; see Q 2:121 and 3:113, 'They are not all alike. Of the Peoples of the Scriptures there is a staunch community.' Farid Esack (1997) discusses these verses in his chapter, 'The Qur'an and the Other' (pp. 146–78; see Chapter 7 below). Watt, in his 1957 article, 'Early Development of the Muslim Attitude to the Bible', concluded that the Qur'an 'does not put forward any general view of the corruption of the text' of the Bible but 'makes clear allegations of the concealment of passages' (p. 50). Sayyid Ahmed Khan, in his *The Mohammedan Commentary on the Bible* (1862, 1865), argued in favour of a corruption of meaning and interpretation, not of actual alteration of the written text. The discussion about Muhammad often centred on whether he was or was not predicted by Jewish and Christian scripture. This tended to end in stalemate, since the Muslims accused the Christians of having removed predictions from scripture, which they rejected:

Al Mahdi says that there were many prophecies of Muhammad in the Scriptures but these books have been corrupted. Timothy replies that if this is the case then where is the uncorrupted copy whereby it may be known that the books in the hands of the Christians have been corrupted? (Mingana, pp. 35f)

However, the Christians were able to swap Qur'anic texts with their Muslim protagonists just as freely as the Muslims made use of Judaeo-Christian scripture to claim that Muhammad's prophethood was predicted therein. The Christians and the Muslims still appear to see each other as occupying the same world. Neither views the other as irremediably different, even if they did view them as misguided or in error! Debate about free will versus predestination (which was equally prominent within intra-Muslim discussion) also featured prominently. The Christians were fully aware that they were 'associators' in Muslim eyes (guilty of associating a partner with God), and of Muslim belief about Jesus. John of Damascus wrote (summarizing Muslim belief) that 'the Jews unlawfully purposed to crucify Him, and, apprehending Him, they crucified Him only in appearance for Christ was really not crucified nor did He die, but God took Him to heaven for love of him' (Sweetman, 1945: 65 and see Q 4:157).

Interestingly, neither John nor Timothy appear to have had any knowledge of the miracle *hadith*. John argued that Muhammad could not be the Paraclete (as Muslims assert) because 'The Paraclete searches the deep things of God, but Muhammad confesses ignorance' (Sura vi. 50). 'The Paraclete wrought miracles through the disciples but Muhammad not a single miracle through his' (*ibid.*: 82). Reference to Muhammad as the 'paraclete' is found in Ibn Ishaq, who recorded that, 'Among the things which have reached me about what Jesus the Son of Mary said in the Gospel' was that 'Muhammad ... is the paraclete' (I.I., pp. 103–4; see also Khan, 1987: lxi). Timothy was careful not to impugn the integrity of Muhammad, whilst John of Damascus and the polemicist al-Kindi were much less circumspect. In his *De Haeresibus*, John calls Muslims 'Hagarites', thus, like Heraclius, giving some recognition to Muhammad's own belief that he stood in the Abrahamic tradition. Muhammad, however, is 'a pseudo-prophet'.

The polemicist, al-Kindi

Al-Kindi wrote about 830 in response to a letter from the Muslim polemicist al-Hashmi, dated 820, although the exact date and identity of al-Kindi has been much debated. He depicted Muhammad as a soldier of fortune; furthermore, he could point to no miracle to confirm his claims. For al-Kindi, the Qur'an's own reply – that it represents a 'miracle' – was spurious; the Qur'an was a rag-bag of discrepancies and garbled tales, 'a confused heap, with neither system nor order. The sense moreover consisteth not with itself; but throughout one passage is contradicted by another' (Muir's edition, 1882: 78–9), in it,

histories are all jumbled together and intermingled; an evidence that many different hands have been at work therein, and caused discrepancies, adding or cutting out whatever they liked or disliked. Are such, now, the conditions of a revelation sent down from heaven? (pp. 18–19, 26).

Al-Kindi 'condemns Holy War and the laws concerning women' (Sweetman, 1945: 69). Muhammad's chief 'object and concern', according to al-Kindi's *Risalah*, 'was to take beautiful women to wife, to attack surrounding tribes, slay and plunder them, and carry off their females for concubines' (Muir, 1882: 49–50). Unlike John, al-Kindi was familiar with many of the miracle *hadith*, thus demonstrating considerable knowledge of Muslim sources. These include: the shoulder of goat's flesh which warned Muhammad that it had been poisoned; the miraculous production of water; and the story of the healing of the leg of Salma after the battle of Khaiber (see Sweetman, 1945: 36).

John of Damascus

The 'goat's flesh' story was probably based on an authentic tradition in which Muhammad refused to eat a piece of roast beef when it told him that it had been poisoned (I.I. 516). The 'production of water' took place during the Affair of al-Hudaybiyyah (I.I. 501). John of Damascus also accused Muhammad of sexual licence and 'stimulating revelation', instancing the story of Zaid and Zainab (see Q 33:36–40) which later became 'a classic Christian theme' (Daniel, 1993: 14). He thought that 'Muhammad had made up his doctrines from the Old and New Testaments on the advice of an Arian monk who instructed him' – possibly building here on knowledge of traditions concerning Muhammad's early encounter with Christian monks, such as his meeting with Bahira (Daniel, *op. cit.*; see I.I., pp. 79–82 for Muhammad and Bahira). Muhammad's 'claim' 'to have received a book from Heaven' was therefore spurious. Here we have the beginning of the Christian view that Muhammad was, directly or indirectly, the author of the Qur'an, and Islam's 'founder' or 'inventor'. Many (see Chapter 1) have disputed that Muhammad could have been, as Muslims believe, the 'unlettered' (*ummi*) prophet. Watt takes this to mean that Muhammad was 'unscriptured' (not versed in the earlier sacred writings). However, whilst this may be viable from the non-Muslim perspective (see Buaben, 1996: 209) it arguably misses the point theologically. Nasr (1994) states:

The Prophet must be unlettered for the same reason that the virgin Mary must be virgin. The human vehicle of a divine message must be pure and untainted. The divine word can only be written on the pure and untouched tablet of human recep-tivity. (pp. 44–5; see Chapter 7 where I offer an opinion about this comparison)

Of course, it is possible for Christians to believe in the incarnation whilst also believing that God uses normal reproductive means to enter human life.

Popular themes emerge

Bar Hebraeus pointed to Muhammad's multiple marriages, his recourse to the sword, and the sensual nature of his promised paradise as evidence of Islam's this-worldly, human origin. The intention here is obviously to place a sword-wielding, womanizing, worldly man alongside a sword-spurning, celibate, ascetic Christ. These themes (Muhammad's sexuality and violence) become almost endemic in non-Muslim literature. What is significant, however, about the role played by these criticisms in much if not all of this early apologetic is that more was not made of them. Three reasons can be suggested: first, these Christians preferred, if they could, to try to win the intellectual argument rather than to resort to character assassination. They knew that the theological equivalent of Christ for Muslims was the Qur'an, not Muhammad, which may be why they tended to argue from Muslim belief in the uncreated *Kalam* to Christian belief in the eternal *logos* (see Chapter 5 for a more detailed discussion of this dogma); in other words, if an eternal, uncreated attribute of God could become book, so it could also become 'flesh'. However, I return to the appropriateness or otherwise of a Christ–Muhammad comparison in Chapter 7. Second, they knew that despite the relatively open intellectual climate, they could not afford to go too far in impugning the moral integrity of Muhammad. At times, severe penalties for speaking disrespectfully of Muhammad were enforced; they were fully aware of the role that devotion to Muhammad plays in Muslim life. Finally, they also knew that Muslims were quite familiar with the facts of Muhammad's life and with the Qur'an's physical accounts of Paradise. Therefore, they were not saying anything about Muhammad that Muslims would deny. What they did not seem to realize was that Muslims did not see these verses or incidents in a negative light; they did not give credence to Muslim interpretation of the verses or incidents they cited. On the whole, their writing was intended for Christians, who were free to draw their own conclusions from these references to Muhammad – perhaps that Muhammad could not compare with Christ but that this was *their* secret. To know that the founder of your minority faith is really a better fellow than the man to whom the majority look can be a comforting thought. It is probable, too, that these writers thought Islam would prove to be a temporary phenomenon.

Apocalyptic expectations

Later, when Islamic power showed no sign of decline, apocalyptic ideas began to provide an explanation for its existence, as Sahas (1991) surmises: 'When the force of Islam could no longer be contained and the notion that the Arab conquests were a temporary punishment had faded, an apocalyptic interpretation seemed to provide the most plausible explanation of this new reality' (p. 15). The rubric appears to have gone something like this: the more public the debate, the more circumspect the language; the more private, the less circumspect. It remains, however, quite remarkable that all this was written and said by Christians living within the Muslim world at the very height of its military success, and as it expanded geographically at what many outside the Khalifate must have regarded as an alarming rate. Muslims, for their part, readily pointed to their military success as a sign of divine blessing; 'since the armies of Islam had laid low a mighty empire God's blessing was upon Islam, and the truth of Islam was proved' (Sweetman, 1945: 83).

To summarize thus far: these early writers appear to be generally well-informed about Muslim beliefs and about Muhammad's life and teaching. They made some effort to enter creative discourse with Muslims, and even appear to have shared their world-view to a considerable degree. Nevertheless, the criticisms of the Prophet which we find in these early works (of his multiple-marriages, sexual indulgence, use of the sword, forging revelation) became the stock-in-trade of later anti-Muslim polemicists.

Attitudes within Byzantium

Not surprisingly, with territory, including Jerusalem, already lost, Islam was feared within the remnant of the Byzantine Empire as the enemy intent on destroying Eastern Christendom. Byzantium had been built as the Christian capital of a Christian empire; Chadwick (1967) writes:

When in obedience to a divinely granted dream [Constantine] decided to found a new capital for the eastern half of the empire at the magnificent strategic site of Byzantium on the Bosphorus, he intended it to be a 'New Rome', providing it with two noble churches dedicated to the Apostles and to Peace. (p. 127)

Given this heritage, the Byzantines could only look upon Muslims and their Prophet as inherently anti-Christian. John of Damascus, although domiciled within the Muslim world, won recognition as a Doctor of the Church. His writings, widely disseminated and studied throughout the Greek-speaking world, provided the basic material for subsequent Greek writing about Islam and Muhammad. On the one hand, this ensured some accuracy; on the other, it did not lend itself to a very positive view of the prophet. Had other Christian writing, for example, Mar Timothy's *Apology* with its statement that Muhammad 'had walked in the path of the prophets' (Mingana, 1928: 61) informed Greek attitudes, the result might have been different. This work, however, did not emerge until Mingana brought it with him to England in the 1920s with other precious manuscripts. Mingana established the tradition of Islamic Studies and concern for Christian–Muslim relations at the Selly Oak Colleges, Birmingham, where Sweetman – on whose work I have drawn in this chapter – was also professor (1946–1962). My own study of Islam began at Selly Oak.

Christians living within the Muslim world had to find some *modus vivendi* with Islam; those outside did not. Believing itself God's kingdom on earth and guardian of the Greek and Roman legacies, the logic of Byzantium was that the enemy without was also without God. Whilst the Damascene's references to Muhammad as a pseudo-prophet as such imply no more than self-deceit, the idea quickly took root amongst the Greeks that something more malevolent was at work, a satanic attack on the true faith. Usually, the term 'Antichrist' or the 'second Sennacherib' was used of Muhammad. As the prince of Christ's enemies, the Antichrist is either Satan himself, or Satan's servant. A monk (evidence here of direct borrowing from John) had helped Muhammad write the Qur'an (subsequently many Bahira stories passed into circulation), but was later murdered by him. Now imagination begins to fill out the story with a quite detailed account. Thus, a trained pigeon, posing as the Holy Spirit, had eaten grain out of Muhammad's ear and was passed off by Muhammad as a divine messenger bringing him the text of the Qur'an. Sometimes an ox brought him whole chapters. Muhammad's tomb could be seen suspended in the air (by magnets) at Makkah (see Gibbon, 1869: 113, citing Greek and Latin sources) The Damascene's references to Muhammad's marriages, his use of warfare and his self-delusion were much elaborated, whilst his accurate account of what Muhammad had actually taught was forgotten.

Calumny feeds calumny

Whilst John (a childhood friend and companion of Khalif Yazid) and other Christians writing within the Muslim world knew full well where Muhammad had been born and where he was buried, they did not always mention such details in their accounts. This enabled the growth of legend and myth around many aspects of Muhammad's biography (thus the magnet at Makkah). Another popular legend was that Muhammad had predicted his resurrection three days after his death but that instead his body was dug up and eaten by dogs (or pigs in some versions – presumably chosen because these were known to be considered unclean by Muslims). What passed into the Greek world, then, was a partial account of Muhammad's life (those events which John, al-Kindi and others chose to criticize) which lent itself to malicious and self-serving elaboration. It was these legends, together with copies of al-Kindi, to which early Latin writers had access.

Epilepsy

It is in this early Byzantine literature that Muhammad was first represented as an 'epileptic', which also emerges as an endemic theme. The intent is to find some alternative explanation for his 'revelatory trances'. Theophanes' *Chronographia*, which appeared in 810, depicted Muhammad as an epileptic; curiously, Theophanes also calls Muhammad a 'false abbot' (probably because Theophanes (758–817), himself a monk, presumably looked to an abbot as his authority-figure). Perhaps not surprisingly, Muhammad's enemies had also accused him of being victim to some sort of 'delirium', a charge which his Companions had rejected: 'you said he was possessed, but he is not, for we have seen the possessed, and he shows no signs of their grasping and whispering and delirium' (I.I., p. 136).

As I have suggested already, John and al-Kindi had probably written what they wrote primarily to give Christians a sense of their own value *vis-à-vis* their political overlords, whilst they themselves had still lived and moved within the Muslim world and shared much in common, intellectually and culturally, and probably socially too, with their Muslim neighbours. The Greeks occupied a different world and, from a comparatively safe distance, found it convenient to see Muslims and their Prophet as 'different', and evil. Sahas (1991) observes that whilst for Christians living within the Khalifate, 'there were plenty of characteristics in Islam, albeit "heretical", which they could recognize and identify with', Byzantium could only see its theocratic claims being 'subjugated and replaced' by another; thus, 'Ironically, it was theocracy, and their mutual affinity in this trait that shaped and determined ... relations between the Byzantine and Islamic societies and, by extension, between Christianity and Islam' (p. 17).

Spain

There is evidence of this picture of the Prophet surfacing in Spain, the first point of sustained contact between the Western and Muslim worlds after the halting of the Moors' northern advance at Tours (732). For example, a group of ninth-century Spanish Christians, who interpreted the Muslim onslaught as the beginning of the end, constructed a picture of Muhammad which Daniel describes thus (1993: 18–19):

Muhammad, a poor man employed by a widow, was active in business ventures, in the course of which he frequented meetings of Christians, and amongst the 'brutish Arabs' he came to pass for a learned man ... seized with sexual desire, he lived with his patroness *iure barbarico*. The spirit of error, in the beautiful form of the angel Gabriel, inspired him to prophecy ... he began to preach ... and persuaded his followers to give up the cult of idols and adore the incorporeal god of heaven ... he taught them to kill their enemies ... he composed 'psalms' which he put into the mouths of dumb animals ... falsified revelation to justify marrying the wife of his neighbour, Zayd ... foretold that he would rise from the dead.

Here, some gobbets of the *sira* story, probably derived from John of Damascus and which reflect some accurate facts about Muhammad's life, mingle with the stuff of which legend and, in this case, calumny are made. Muhammad was a trader, for example, and he did meet with Christian monks; Gabriel is correctly named (Theophanes also named Gabriel correctly), as is Zaid (or Zayd). Zaid, however, was not merely a 'neighbour' but Muhammad's adopted son (adoption was later proscribed, see Q 33:4–5. For Muhammad's marriage to Zainab, see Q 33:37). Also suggesting indebtedness to John, the Spanish Christians were aware that 'Muhammad recognised Christ as a great prophet, and as a Word and Spirit from God ... but [as] a man like Adam, not the equal of God' (Daniel, 1993: 19; see Q 3:59, 'the likeness of Jesus with Allah is as the likeness of Adam').

As far as this group of Christians was concerned, the rule of Islam was the rule of the Antichrist (a term already applied to Muhammad in Greek literature); thus, by publicly insulting Muhammad and incurring martyrdom, their deaths would hasten Christ's victorious return. They applied such texts as Daniel 7 to Muhammad and to Muhammad's religion, in the 'details' of which – 'and they knew very few' – they 'thought they saw ... that total negation of Christianity which would mark the contrivances of the Antichrist' (Southern, 1962: 25). Incidentally, at least two different usages of the term 'Antichrist' ought to be identified: some, like John of Damascus, used it to refer to Muhammad as a 'heretic' who had deviated from true Christian faith; whilst the martyrs of Cordoba used it of Muhammad as Satan's final weapon against the Kingdom of Christ. Lacking both interest in, and ability to comprehend more sophisticated material on Islamic theology, these Spanish Christian writers concentrated on what they could understand – moral defects in the character of Muhammad. Such material, comparing Muslim belief in Divine Attributes with the Trinity, or the pre-existing book with the pre-existing Christ (not lacking even in the *Risalah*, which uses the 99 Names of God to try to explain the Trinity), had entered Spain at a very early period.

The Spanish Christians especially seized on any hint of sexual immorality. Indeed, as Daniel observes, this appears to have become something of an obsession. For example, 'Alvarus harps on ludicrous accusations against Islam so much so as to suggest that he is less than sure of his own innocence' (*ibid.*: 18). An early idea was that Muhammad and Muslims worshipped Venus, the goddess of love. Interestingly, a *hadith* (which Daniel calls 'authentic', p. 18), that Muhammad had the virility of forty men, was equated with Jeremiah 5:8 which, paraphrased, means 'each neighs after another man's wife like a well fed and lusty stallion' (*ibid.*; B 5:13 has 'thirty men' and says that Muhammad 'used to visit all his wives' each day; but see my comment in Chapter 2). As already noted, criticism of Muhammad's sexuality and his militiary involvement represent two of the most persistent themes of anti-Islamic discourse. Forward (1997), although broadly sympathetic towards the Muslim view of Muhammad, expresses moral difficulty with the Zaid/Zainab affair; Muhammad, says Forward, 'seems to have married all the women he sexually desired' (pp. 85–6).

Latin takes priority

I have suggested that the early Christian writers on whose work the Spanish drew had not needed to write detailed biographies of Muhammad – their readers would already have been familiar with these details. Thus, references to supposed defects in his character were not set within the total story of his life. Incidents from Muhammad's life were used to disprove his prophetic claims (such as the Zaid/Zainab affair); incidents which might have lent credibility to his claims were naturally not included. Much was made of the defeat at Uhud, the victory of Badr was totally overlooked. Taken as they were quite out of context, these incidents could not but convey a biased, distorted picture of Muhammad. By the time this material reached Spain, even the year of Muhammad's birth could be conveniently dated at 666 (see Southern, 1962: 25). There also appears to have been a desire to equate Islam with paganism which Oriental Christians had never contemplated, although it was a view towards which Greek (Byzantine) writers had tended. The association of Islam with idol worship continued; Buaben (1996) notes that a 'story circulating in the twelfth century claimed that Archbishop Thiemo of Salzburg was martyred in AD 1104 because he destroyed a Muslim idol' (p. 7). At the end of the thirteenth century, Marco Polo has the Grand Khan stating that Christians have Jesus Christ, Muslims Mahomet, 'the Jews, Moses and the idolaters, Sogomombar-kan' as their 'divinity' (Polo, 1946: 158).

An interesting aspect of this early Spanish response to Islam is that those responsible for formulating it lived in the midst of Muslims. However, they appear to have derived few if any of their ideas about Muhammad or Islam from Muslims. They preferred, it seems, 'to know about Mahomet from … meagre Latin source[s] rather than from the fountainhead of the Koran or the great biographical compilations of their Moslem contemporaries' (Southern, 1962: 25), thus asserting their own 'sacred language' and the value of anything written in it, over the tongue of the Arabs. They preferred an 'authority' outside Islam. Although physically within the Muslim world, they (unlike John, Timothy, Agapius *et al.*) construed 'reality' quite differently from their Muslim neighbours.

European images

At this stage, it is unlikely that Christians elsewhere in Europe were even vaguely aware that Muhammad had existed. Europe was itself recovering from the collapse of the Roman Empire. The Holy Roman Empire was still struggling to emerge from the ruins. A historian such as the Venerable Bede could refer to the Arabs as Ishmaelites (which again shows some ability to link Islam with the biblical record) but there was little reason to develop interest in the details of Muhammad's life or the tenets of Islam. Other enemies were pressing on Europe from other directions; Islam (after its initial advance through Spain) probably seemed, then, to represent no greater threat than did the Vikings or the Slavs (see Southern, 1962: 14–15).

This changed. By the beginning of the eleventh century, the Vikings and the Slavs had embraced Christianity. Now the remaining threat to Europe's sense of security, if not superiority, was the apparently ever-expanding Khalifate. Since very little was actually known about Muhammad or Islam, it was easy for invention to become the mother of wisdom. What Europeans did know (or thought they knew, just as the Byzantines did) was that Christianity was true and they were civilized – the heirs to the legacy of Rome (which, of course, was also claimed by Byzantium); therefore anyone else's religion must be false and their culture inferior – if not less advanced, then at least debased and immoral. Given that only very scanty information about Muhammad was available, and that this was of the same genre as that used by the Spanish martyrs, the following represents a fairly accurate summary of the popular view: the Saracens were idolaters who worshipped Muhammad, who was either a magician or the devil incarnate. Mahound, the medieval corruption of Muhammad, was used as a synonym for the devil (Mahound is also the name of the Prophet in Salman Rushdie's *The Satanic Verses*). Muhammad's success had been due to a combination of magic and cunning. Sexual licence and promiscuity were sanctioned by his religion. Paradise is a brothel.

Muslim testimony goes unheeded

The charge that Muhammad's 'heaven' was designed (as it were) to attract men – whilst offering little or no incentive to women – is one which frequently features in polemical literature. Rarely if ever did anyone stop to listen to Muslim exegesis, or to cite a tradition such as: 'They [the heavenly maidens] are devout wives, and those who with grey hairs and watery eyes died in old age. After death, Allah re-makes them into virgins.' Andrae (1936) comments, 'That the wives and children of the believers share in the joys of paradise is self-evident for Mohamed, and is especially mentioned in several places' (p. 26). Much continued to be made of the fate of Muhammad's supposed collaborator in writing the Qur'an. Similarly, accounts of Muhammad's death vied with each other in portraying a disgusting end. In some accounts he was suffocated by pigs during an epileptic fit. Guibert, Abbot of Nugent (1053–1124), who gives one such account, admitted to having no written sources for his tale but wrote, 'it is safe to speak evil of one whose malignity exceeds whatever ill can be spoken' (Southern, 1962: 31). The 'outgrouping' of the Khalifate also relegated its religion into the 'outer darkness': all aboard the good ship 'Christendom' (the metaphor of Noah's Ark was often used) were safe. Muslims were outside and therefore perishing in the deluge of their sins.

Naming Muhammad

Interestingly, there was much confusion about Muhammad's name, hence the enormous variety of alternatives – Mahound, Maphomet, Bafum – and also (as I have already indicated) about when he had lived. Words derived from 'Muhammad' entered the English vocabulary and carried a range of negative connotations; these included 'mummery' (from 'Mahomerie', meaning superstition), and 'Mawmet' or 'Mammet' which was commonly used to mean 'idol' or even 'doll' (see R. B. Smith, 1876: 77). Even 'miscreant' has been traced to the same etymological root. Some wrote of Muhammad as if he was still alive. In one account, he was a cardinal who had founded Islam out of pique when his colleagues elected somebody else as pope (Daniel, 1993: 104). Some of these views of Muhammad passed into the legendary or mythical literature of the age, for at this time Europeans were busy inventing romantic stories of their own national origins: Arthur of Britain, Roland of France. In *The Song of Roland*, Muslims worship three Gods, Tervagan, Muhammad and Apollo (Southern, 1962: 32). Facing the Saracen hordes, Roland declares, '*Paien ont tort e Crestiien ant dreit*' ('Pagans are wrong and Christians right'; cited in Holt, 1972: 9). Sweetman surmises that when, in *Ivanhoe*, Sir Walter Scott (1771–1832) puts words into his jester's mouth referring to the Saracens as 'worshippers of Mahound and Termagant' he is 'exercising no licence ... but is a faithful reporter of what he had found in his wide mediaeval reading. It was indeed thought that Muhammad was worshipped' (1955: 63).

I cannot help speculating whether the problem of rendering Muhammad's name accurately into European languages was a genuine linguistic challenge or, as I suspect, symptomatic of assumptions about Muhammad's ethical and religious unacceptability. On the other hand, there was also the beginning of a tendency to represent the world of Islam as fabulously wealthy and condoning sexual indulgences condemned in Christendom. Whilst, as Daniel comments, many clerics thought that his sexual proclivities alone disqualified him from being a candidate for genuine prophethood (see Daniel, 1993: 124 for the many descriptions of Muhammad's sexuality), for others this actually appeared rather attractive. This represents the beginning of another Western trend – to romanticize about forbidden Eastern fruits. Muslims indeed occupied a different world – but in this version the 'other world' is like grass on the far side of the fence!

The Crusades

This dark and inaccurate view of Muhammad appears to change from the beginning of 'the Crusades' – the end of the eleventh century until the end of the thirteenth century. Whilst the Crusades were an attempt to defeat, even to annihilate Islam, and whilst popular images of Islam's evils may well have helped to attract support for the venture, they also brought Europeans into more intimate contact with the Muslim world. Latin writers who lived within the Muslim world (or, rather, in the crusader strongholds therein) such as William of Tyre (1130–86) and William of Tripoli (1220–73), were reasonably accurate in what they wrote about Islam. Indeed, Tripoli emphasized what he deemed to be consistent with Christianity and believed that evangelism should replace confrontation. He thought that Islam would soon yield to the true faith and saw no reason to malign it when he could stress points of similarity between the two faiths. He wrote: 'Though their beliefs are wrapped up in many lies and decorated with fiction, it now manifestly appears that they are near to the Christian faith and not far from the path of salvation' (cited in Southern, 1962: 62).

Sweetman credits William with 'one of the earliest informative treatises on the Muslim faith' and comments that he 'deserves commendation for accurate observation and faithful report' (1955: 86). Other Christians shared this confidence that Islam's end was nigh, especially after the Mongol sacking of Baghdad in 1258. Some cited a supposed saying of Muhammad that his empire would not survive the end of the 'Abbasids (see Southern, p. 62). Others, though, stressed fraternity rather than conflict; at times peace treaties were negotiated which resulted in commercial advantage to both sides – for example, with Saladin's successors, the Ayyubids, which restored Jerusalem to crusader control. Some crusaders adopted local dress and adapted local customs. Architectural styles, landscape gardening and medical knowledge were amongst the acquisitions which the crusaders took back to Europe. Constantine the African (1020–87), for example, translated many medical texts into Latin. Rules of chivalry were greatly valued by both sides; indeed, 'the tolerance of the Franks, noted by Arab visitors, often surprised and disturbed newcomers from the West' (Baldwin, 1984: 300). The great enemy Saladin, Sultan of Egypt (1137–93), was respected by his enemies and found his way into European myth as the epitome of chivalry; see Walter Scott's *The Talisman*. Legend has it that he visited Rome and France in disguise and the Queen of France is said to have fallen in love with him. Ahsan (1996) writes: 'the crusades helped, in a sense, in forging a variety of links between the two adversaries – ranging from an exchange of military techniques to food, dress and vocabulary' (p. xiii). This new genre of legend to which the Crusades gave birth did not lack magic, but this time its hue was attractive, not ugly. Thus we have 'Arab horsemen as savage hero, the seductiveness of beauties in the *harim*, the charm of the bazaar, the pathos of life continuing among the ruins of ancient splendour' (Hourani, 1991a: 300). In *The Thousand and One Nights* (which later reached European shores) women as well as men, for example, enjoy sexual encounters.

The Crusades reappraised

In my earlier book (1992) I stated that the Crusades embittered attitudes on both sides. I was following Guillaume (1954), who wrote that 'its [the Crusades] one lasting result was to embitter for ever, it would seem, the relations between Christians and Muslims' (p. 86). Similarly, Akbar Ahmed (1996) writes from the Muslim perspective: 'The memory of the Crusades lingers in the Middle East and colours Muslim perceptions of Europe. It is the memory of an aggressive, backward and religiously fanatic Europe' (p. 66). Attempting to reflect Muslim attitudes towards Christians, especially Christian missionaries, Pettifer and Bradley (1990) wrote of the Crusades, 'The Christians became the bloody aggressors. For many Muslims, that is how they have remained: the Christians will never be able to wash away those bloodstains' (p. 207). However, I now incline towards the somewhat different estimate of Watt (1972), who suggests that the Crusades' negative impact on Christian–Muslim relations has been overestimated:

In short, the Crusades had no more importance for the greater part of the Islamic world than the wars on the North-west Frontier of India had for the British in the nineteenth century, and probably made less impression on the general public consciousness. (p. 81)

'Muslims', he says, 'formed no new image of Christianity as a result of the Crusades.' This, he suggests, was partly because Islam already had a critique of Christianity and a strong 'belief in [its] own superiority' (p. 81). Nevertheless, it is difficult to see how the Crusades could have influenced Muslims towards a more positive view of Christians.

Spain revisited

Rejection of the sword, as advocated by William of Tripoli, also found support amongst a new generation of Christians living in Spain. There, early Christian opposition to Islam had yielded to positive scholarly exchange. As learning flowered in Muslim Spain, scholars came from Paris and elsewhere to study the thoughts of Ibn Rushd, Ibn Tufayl and Aristotle (whose work had been preserved by the Muslims but neglected in Europe), as well as medicine and astronomy. Learning Arabic in order to study significant texts, it was natural that some would also turn aside to peruse the Qur'an and other religious writings, and the realization soon dawned that a reasoned Christian apologetic was a more enlightened, rational approach than the *jihad* of the Crusades.

Peter the Venerable (1092–1156), initially attracted by what has been called the 'new learning', commissioned two such translators to render the Qur'an into Latin. Completed in July 1143, this work has been described as 'a landmark in Islamic Studies' (Southern, 1962: 37). Now, 'for the first time', the West 'had an instrument for the serious study of Islam' (*ibid.*). Peter also had al-Kindi's *Risalah* translated.

Some Christians, such as Peter himself, Roger Bacon (1220–92), Ramon Lull (1234–1316) and Ricoldo de Monte di Croce (1243–1320), not only were able to use the Qur'an in their apologetic writing, but advocated that the proper mode of contact with Islam was the use of reason and argument, not the sword. 'There is much here', observes Sweetman, 'which calls for criticism from the privileged position which we occupy today, but one should bear in mind always that these men were pioneers' (1955: 87). Peter the Venerable wrote that he aimed to assail Islam 'Not with weapons, as other Christians have often done, but by word, not by force, but with reason, not with hate but with love, by a love albeit such as a Christian can have towards the enemies of Christ' (*ibid.*: 79; Southern, p. 39). Unfortunately, observes Southern, it is doubtful if Muslims actually read these irenical words, since they were written in Latin. This irenic approach was commended as more Christlike, especially by St Francis (1128–1226), who is said to have travelled to the court of Saladin. Thus, some European Christians who wrote about Islam and Muhammad had direct personal contact with Muslims.

Ricoldo OP

Ricoldo, a Dominican missionary in Baghdad, could write with considerable, if grudging, respect of Muslim virtues. He mentioned Muslim devotion to prayer, pity for the poor, reverence for the names of God, sobriety of manner and hospitality to strangers, 'their harmony and love for each other' (Daniel, 1993: 221). His aim, though, was to demonstrate the inherent inadequacies of Islam, which represents 'all the offscourings of antiquity which the devil has spread broadcast' (Sweetman, 1955: 118) rather than to commend Christianity; thus, 'attack and defence are more prominently displayed' in his writing 'than appeal and persuasion' and there is much in his *Confutatio* which Muslims find offensive (*ibid.*: 159).

In chapter 13, for example, he asks who the author of the Qur'an was, and concludes that it was 'the Devil who, by his own malice and by the permission of God, has prevailed to initiate the work of the antichrist' (*ibid.*: 144). The Qur'an's 'incoherence and bad arrangement' compared with the Bible (which is well-ordered 'according to the order of history, or at least of subject matter') are 'a sure sign that it is not from God' (*ibid.*: 142). Something of Ricoldo's indebtedness to the *Risalah* can be detected here. Bahira, a Nestorian monk, becomes one of Muhammad's chief disciples. Nevertheless, Ricoldo knew not only the Qur'an but also some *hadith* and, says Sweetman, despite his inability to 'transcend the limitations of the time' we can 'discern a competent mind, a high degree of proficiency in Arabic' and 'a fairly wide knowledge of literature dealing with Islamic tradition' (*ibid.*: 159).

Roger Bacon: an English contribution

For Roger Bacon, 'preaching [was] the only way in which Christendom can be enlarged' (Southern, 1962: 57). He believed that philosophy, rather than scripture, provided the best evangelical tool, representing as it did common ground between thinking people. Bacon spent much of his life at the Franciscan study house in Paris. He is said to be buried at Oxford, where he may also have taught and studied. An encyclopedist, he was especially interested in the relationship between science, philosophy and theology. The cause of philosophy, he believed, had been ill-served in European thought. He may or may not have visited Spain, but his knowledge of Arabic texts, scientific and philosophical, was unrivalled. His premiss was that Christians and Muslims occupy similar, if not identical, worlds. He complained that, 'Louis X1 could not find a man in the University or at his court who could read and translate a letter from the sultan of Egypt' (Sweetman, 1955: 98). Anawati (1979) comments that Bacon was so 'influenced by Avicenna (and by al-Farabi) that his theory of the Sovereign Pontiff is in full agreement with the theories of the caliphate put forth by Avicenna' (p. 383). Sir Muhammad Iqbal (1876–1938) puts it like this: 'Roger Bacon was no more than one of the apostles of Muslim science and method ... and he never wearied of declaring that knowledge of Arabic and Arabic Science was for his contemporaries the only way to true knowledge' (1930: 123).

Ramon Lull

Lull, a wealthy Spanish knight, left royal service at the age of 30, following a religious vision of Christ and the Cross which led him to devote the rest of his life to evangelizing Muslims (after making provision for his family). Pragmatic as well as mystical, he wanted to establish colleges to train clergy and laity in Arabic and 'such other subjects as would most fit them for their task' of Christian witness. He did not share Bacon's admiration for Islamic philosophy but rather set out to rebut the arguments of Ibn Rushd (Averroes) especially, whose popularity in Europe was resulting in 'an insidious spirit of irreverence and rationalism' (Sweetman, 1955: 104). Against the doctrine that the 'All Soul is all the souls' (p. 110) he asserted Trinitarian orthodoxy. Invective is not absent, but his *Disputatio Raymundi et Hamar Sarraceni* (1308) depicts a Christian and a Muslim engaging in Socratic-type dialogue (about incarnation and Trinity) in a non-polemical style clearly aimed at winning an intellectual argument. Sweetman surmises that he may even have translated 'in a somewhat free style from the Arabic something actually written or said to him in the course of debate' (1955: 103). He could, however, stack the cards in Christianity's favour. For example, he has the Muslim conceding that Muhammad had 'worshipped idols' before he became a prophet in order to 'show that no such false worship could be attributed to Christ' (*ibid.*); Muslims believe that Muhammad was never anything but a monotheist and from childhood experienced discontent with the religious practices of his peers. Lull accurately reflects, though, Muslim belief about the divine origin of the Qur'an, as a 'perpetual miracle', the 'peak of perfection' (*ibid.*: 102) and relates the tradition that Muhammad was unlettered.

The idea that rational argument rather than the magisterium of the Church might be allowed to judge between right and wrong belief lacked universal appeal, as Sweetman comments: 'There were some who considered that this tide of free inquiry should be stemmed. Thus the Council of Tarragona forbade laymen [like Lull] to debate in public on the Catholic faith' (1955: 74).

Lull visited North Africa three times; twice he was deported, 'and on the third, in 1315 or 1316, when he was probably past eighty years of age, he was stoned so severely that he died' (Latourette, 1975, 2: 404). His view that reason and peaceful exchange of ideas ought to replace hostility may not have translated into practice as successfully as he hoped, but even unto death he did not swerve from this resolve.

Peter the Venerable

Peter the Venerable also had to defend his efforts against those who thought them misguided and possibly even dangerous, and did so (whether this was or was not his real opinion is open to speculation) on the grounds that he was 'forging weapons against heresy' (Southern, 1962: 39). As Sweetman points out, even his 'compassionate spirit' did not always 'constrain him from harsh utterance':

The fathers of the church would not have allowed a heresy to arise in their days without opposing to it all the forces of the faith and without exposing its direful tendency by writing and debate. The religion of Islam, the error of errors, the cesspool into which the majority of the heresies had poured and which had polluted half the world, demanded a work of proportionate measure (1955: 75).

There is very little evidence of what might be called progress in relations between Christians and Muslims as the result of all this activity. The same issues – Muhammad's moral character, trustworthiness of Christian scripture versus the Qur'an, Trinity versus Unity, and so on, all of which had featured in John, Timothy, al-Kindi *et al.* – are encountered again and again in writings from this period. What can be said about this period is that Europe was placed in Islam's intellectual debt; thus,

When Dante placed the Islamic philosophers Avicenna and Averroes, and the Islamic warrior Saladin, in Limbo as the only moderns among the sages and heroes of antiquity, he was acknowledging a debt of Christendom to Islam which went far beyond anything he could have expressed in words. (Southern, 1962: 55–6).

Thomas Aquinas

This debt is reflected, for example, in the work of Aquinas (1223–74) who 'made use of ... Islamic material to construct his systematic reflections on the Christian faith' (Berthrong, 1995: 24). Aquinas was familiar with Ibn Rushd's writing and always cited him with respect even when he disagreed with his view. Like Ibn Rushd, Aquinas wanted to harmonize faith and reason. It has even been suggested that Aquinas 'more or less plagiarized' Ibn Rushd (see Wild, 1996: 156). St Thomas responded to the challenge of Islam with his 'monumental piece of apologetic', the *Summa Contra Gentiles*, which, specifically intended for missionary use, was 'definitely designed to present Christian theological thought *vis-à-vis* Islam' (Sweetman, 1955: 114).

Like Bacon, Aquinas wanted to 'prove Christian theses by the sole light of reason' (Rodinson, 1974: 19). Sweetman points out, too, that Aquinas conceded that Muslims and Jews had 'certain rights'. Those who do not accept Christianity 'should not be compelled to it' and are not to be regarded as 'utterly outside the pale' (*ibid.*). I have already identified Bacon's indebtedness to Islamic philosophy. However, as I note in our next chapter, Europeans have not always readily recognized or acknowledged their debt to Muslim Spain. Writing in 1930, Sir Muhammad Iqbal pointed out that 'Europe has been rather slow to recognise the Islamic origin of her scientific method' (p. 123).

Of course, especially after the rise of the Ottomans, Islam remained Europe's principal enemy. These Christians, however, began to believe that whilst Islam's military advance must still be checked, the proper Christian response to Muslims was not to kill them but to convince them that Christianity was more godly, rational and moral. However, two significant factors still handicapped European writing about Islam generally and about Muhammad especially. First, possession of the Qur'an in Latin dress did not itself provide detailed information about Muhammad's life, and most Christian writers remained ignorant of even such important events as the *hijrah*, which Bar Hebraeus had accurately described: 'He fled that place and went to another town called Yathrib. People went forth to welcome him, offering him aid in all things, whereupon they were called ANSAR (helpers)' (Sweetman, 1955: 15). For Muhammad's life, their main sources remained disjointed references in such works as the *Risalah*. Second, confused about the relationship between the Qur'an and the *hadith*, they referred to all and sundry as 'Muhammad's words'. Also, the way in which they used the Qur'an *vis-à-vis* the Bible to prove its inaccuracy, unreliability or absurdity, was not calculated to win Muslim approval. Even a writer like Ricoldo, who did enjoy discourse with Muslims, does not appear to have interested himself in Muslim exegesis. Daniel says: 'If the Qur'an appeared to say a silly thing, it must really say it; Arabs could not be allowed to explain what the Arabic meant' (1993: 87).

Some popular themes

Ricoldo devoted a whole chapter to ridiculing the story of the Night Journey and Ascension; why did Muhammad need an ass? How was it 'possible for him to bear all the glory of the angels in heaven when we are told that when one angel appeared to him he collapsed, fell to the earth foaming and arching his body with his hands drawn up?' (Sweetman, 1955: 148). Humphrey Prideaux (1648–1724), writing at a comparatively late date and in English, calculated that the height of one of the angels as traditionally described in accounts of the *mi'raj* was four times that of all seven heavens, so the angel could hardly have stood within the heavens (see Ockley, 1848: 23).

Muhammad's *mi'raj* is also ridiculed as yet another example of Muslim belief in a carnal paradise, which remained a popular theme. This can be regarded as non-Muslims once again claiming authority to interpret Islam over Islam's self-understanding. Allegorical interpretations were disallowed. Their aim, though, was less to impugn Muhammad's character than to prove the unreasonableness of Muslim law. Yet, despite this, and despite some concessions to Muslim virtues, their portrait of Muhammad remained essentially identical to that inherited from the Byzantines. Muhammad's marriage with Zainab is still singled out: 'God commanded me to commit this adultery' is how Ricoldo puts it. Here we see echoes of John of Damascus's charge that Muhammad had manufactured revelation. Muhammad's use of violence is still stressed. The story of his death is still surrounded with absurdity – usually, his companions retain the body for weeks until they loose hope that Muhammad will be raised and, in disgust, bury the now rotten corpse – unceremoniously. The corpse is then eaten by animals.

The 'Satanic verses' affair (see below, and also the Chapter 7 discussion of Salman Rushdie's novel) was instanced by at least one polemicist, Pedro de Alfonso (1062–1111) as an example of Muhammad's hypocrisy. Alfonso, a convert from Judaism, was hugely influential on 'medieval scholars' thinking on Muhammad' (Buaben, 1996: 9). On the other hand, Muhammad is no longer generally pictured as a magician, although the pigeon trained to eat grain from Muhammad's ear still features in Hugo Grotius's *De Veritate Religionis Christianae* (1627). Edward Pocock (1604–91), Oxford's first Professor of Arabic, omitted this as unfounded in his Arabic translation (see Gibbon, 1869: 114). The idea that Muhammad dreamt up his religion in league with Nestorian monks remained popular (see references in sixteenth- and seventeenth-century French writing reviewed by Jane Smith, 1996) Reference to the giant magnet at Makkah suggests where these writers found their information (see J. Smith p. 52).

The supposed link with renegade monks ensured that Muhammad was sometimes dubbed 'the heresiarch'; thus he was the 'first born of Satan' who had 'seduced' the Orient with his 'pestilent doctrine' (Daniel, 1993: 210). Ricoldo heaps upon Muhammad such names as 'tyrant', 'blasphemer' and 'hypocrite'. Such a picture of Muhammad was unlikely to commend itself to Muslims, but it would have reassured Christian readers that Muhammad could not have been a genuine prophet. According to the history of ideas, this survey has now reached the brink of the European Renaissance, itself the backdrop to the Enlightenment, when reason is said to have replaced dogmatism. What impact the beginning of the age of reason had on non-Muslim attitudes towards Muhammad and on evaluation of his legacy will be addressed in the second part of this survey.

4 Non-Muslim Lives: from the Renaissance to Today

The birth of serious scholarship

It may not be accidental that the birth of serious non-Muslim scholarship of Islam begins with the Renaissance, since, as I have already indicated, Europe's rediscovery of its classical legacy, including that of the ancient philosophers, was largely mediated by the Muslims of Spain. Thus, if only to access this material in its Arabic dress, scholars turned to the study of that language. Inevitably, however, some also took an interest in what the Arab world had to offer, which led to texts about Islam as well as Arabic translations of the Greek masters reaching the hands of European scholars. The creation of Chairs in Arabic at leading European universities also helped to make the task of writing a history of the Arabs as academically respectable as writing the history of the rise and fall of the Romans. So, Arabic histories were translated into Latin. Amongst historical texts that found their way into Europe were those by Abu'l Fida (1273–1331) and Ibn Athir (1160–1233), whilst Edward Pocock brought back to Oxford (from his time at Aleppo) Bar Hebraeus's *Chronicle* and other Arabic texts. He rendered these into Latin in his classic *Specimen Historiae Arabum.*

Scholars such as John Gagnier (1670–1740) and Johan Jakob Reiske (1716–74) also worked on translations. Gagnier's *Abu'l Fida* appeared in 1723. This offers a romantic and highly stylized portrait of Muhammad. He is depicted as the 'last and greatest of the prophets'; 'all the details transmitted by Arab tradition about the life, acts, and sayings of the Prophet ... were all undoubtedly true' (Patai, 1989: xxi). Thus Gagnier tells us that at Muhammad's birth the Tigris burst its banks, whilst the sacred Zoroastrian fire ceased to burn after a thousand years. On the other hand, Abu'l Fida's *sira* does faithfully narrate many fundamental Muslim beliefs about Muhammad, for example, that he did not compose the Qur'an but received it from God 'through the intermediacy of the Angel Gabriel'. Other events in the Prophet's life, described in the *sira* in some detail (such as his calling, his early preaching, the *hijrah*) all added considerably to what Europeans knew about Muhammad. As a result of Gagnier's translation and Pocock's work, a new genre of European literature starts to emerge, a genre which begins to make exclusive use of Islamic sources.

In 1705 Adrian Reland (1676–1718) was able to produce a Life of Muhammad devoid of myth, calumny or fiction. Reland suggested that Christians had been less than honest in rendering justice to Muhammad: 'If ever any religion was perverted by adversary's [sic] it was this religion.' Too often, he said, writers had relied on the old authorities instead of listening to 'Mahomet speak in his own tongue' (cited in Daniel, 1993: 318). Here is serious scholarly interest in Islamic history and the biography of Muhammad, which begins to give priority to Islamic sources (on which Reland's account drew exclusively; see Rodinson, 1974: 37).

Henry Stubbe

Earlier, less scholarly but equally significant as an example of this new approach (indeed, it has been called a new 'pro-Muhammad approach' – see Patai, 1989: xx) was Henry Stubbe's *An Account of the Rise and Progress of Mahometanism: With the Life of Mahomet and a vindication of him and his religion from the calumnies of the Christians*. This was probably written in the 1670s (see Bosworth, 1976: 7). The source for this quite remarkable book, a genuine effort to do justice to the Muslim point of view (see Daniel, 1993: 309), was Pocock's rendering of Bar Hebraeus. Although it circulated in manuscript form only until printed this century, it became a very influential text. Stubbe (1632–76) discussed and refuted some of the traditional charges made against Muhammad; for example, that he spread his religion by the sword. He did this by distinguishing between Muhammad's territorial conquests and how Islam spread as a religious movement. Aware of 'fabulous inventions' about Muhammad, Stubbe also refutes, amongst others, the following as 'myths':

the legend that Muhammad was indoctrinated by a Nestorian monk and a Jew, that a tame pigeon was feigned to be the Holy Ghost, that his tomb was suspended between two loadstones, and the rest of the trivia bred by religious hatred and political apprehension. (Holt, 1972: 22)

This shows how many ninth- or tenth-century myths survived even into the seventeenth century. On the other hand, the Night Journey and Ascension might, he says, 'be explained as a vision or ecstasy, just as St Paul was transported up to the third heaven' (Bosworth, 1976: 9). Like Reland, Stubbe deliberately set out to correct what he believed was an ill-informed and erroneous view of Muhammad – apparently because he thought that not to do so would leave an injustice unredeemed. With Gagnier and Sale (for whom see below) he also rejected the idea that Muhammad's trances had been caused by epilepsy. His Muhammad, though, was the successful leader of an emergent power rather than a divinely guided prophet of God. Stubbe's book, observes Bosworth (1976),

is a remarkable one for its time, both in its underlying plea for a rational consideration of the Islamic faith and recognition of its favourable aspects, and for its interesting stress on the place of historical causality in human history. (p. 19)

Bosworth also points out another remarkable aspect of Stubbe's book,

[his] insistence that the Prophet should be called by the proper form of his name, Muhammad, as it is pronounced in Arabic, and not by the mediaeval European perversions like 'Magmed' or 'Macholet'. Not till the 19th century did Orientalists and writers on eastern topics start using the proper form, and that of 'Mahomet' still remains in use today, especially in France. (One might mention at this point, although it has no direct connection with Stubbe, that the erroneous description of the religion of Islam as 'Muhammadanism' is equally reprehensible, and likewise that the designation of God in an Islamic context as 'Allah' insinuates that the God of say Christianity and Judaism and the God of Islam are two separate deities.) (p. 8)

Le Comte de Boulainvilliers

Another example of a 'pro-Muhammad' work appeared in 1731, the Comte de Boulainvilliers' *Vie de Mahomet,* which also celebrated Muhammad's human achievement and Islam's contribution to European civilization. Henri Boulainvilliers (1658–1722) portrays Muhammad as a great statesman and legislator, unequalled in the ancient world. Daniel describes the book as a work of 'considerable charm' (1993: 310) albeit one which depended solely on secondary sources. Ibn Warraq (1995) thinks it 'impossible to exaggerate the importance of this book in shaping Europe's view of Islam and its founder, Muhammad' (p. 19). Muhammad, said the Count, had 'invented' Islam, but only in order to better his people and to govern them well:

He did not more enslave his country; on the contrary, he only desir'd to govern it, in order to make it mistress of the world, and its various riches; of which, both he and his first successors made so disinterested a use, that in this respect they much compel the admiration of their greatest enemies. (p. 244)

Boulainvilliers' Muhammad was a *rational* man (was he creating a Muhammad in his own Enlightenment image?) who had had no need of the miraculous; he had 'constantly declared and protested that he had no power other than to persuade those who would calmly listen unto him, or to conquer those ... who resisted the force of his reasons' (pp. 249–50). Boulainvilliers' Islam was a successful human movement ... 'all that [Mahomet] laid down is true', he suggested, 'but he has not laid down all that is true, and that is the whole difference between our religion and his' (p. 294). Curiously, and perhaps inconsistently, Boulainvilliers still refers to Muhammad as 'the impostor' yet 'credits him with the best of intentions in trying to render to God his true glory'. Where Muhammad failed, in the Comte's view, was in not recognizing 'that the sanctification of Jesus was necessary to cleanse humans from the taint of original sin' (J. Smith, 1996: 56). Boulainvilliers' appraisal of Muhammad, then, moved towards a Muslim view in its estimate of Muhammad's motives and human achievement, but not in its removal of God's hand from his biography.

Voltaire

Almond (1989) has suggested that at this time in the development of European thought, the progressive 'decline of Christian "sacred history" made possible shifts in attitudes to Muhammad and his religion' (p. 5). Voltaire (1694–1778), for example, a writer who had no time for religion in any shape or form, also addressed Muhammad in his play, *La Fanatisme ou Mahomet le Prophet* (1742). Voltaire, who knew and made use of Boulainvilliers and Sale (for Sale, see below) and criticized them both, appears to have used Islam as a broom to sweep away all religious delusion; Muhammad deceived both himself, and others:

violently moved by his own ideas like all enthusiasts [he] first recited his ideas in good faith, confirmed them with visions, deceived himself in the deceiving of others, and finally supported with necessary deceits a doctrine which he believed was good. (Voltaire, 1826, XV: 314–15)

Voltaire stressed Muhammad's sensuality, lust and worldly ambition, 'Lust and Ambition, Mirvan, are the Springs of all his Actions' (Miller, 1744: 12). On the other hand, he also seems to have admired what Muhammad actually achieved and vacillated between

putting forward an apologia for the profound-thinking politique, founder of a rational religion and on the other hand taking advantage of the official faith of his country to denounce this selfsame Muhammad as the prototype of all the impostors who had enslaved people's souls by religious fables. (Rodinson, 1974: 39)

In his later *Essai sur les moeurs*, Voltaire appears to have modified his verdict; he acknowledges Muhammad's 'greatness and his abilities' but censures 'his cruelty and brutality' and asserts that 'there is nothing new in his religion except the statement that Mohamed is the Apostle of Allah' (Andrae, 1936: 246). Thus when he died, Muhammad was 'regarded as a great man even by those who knew he was an impostor, and [was] revered as a prophet by all the rest' (cited in Daniel, 1993: 312). Voltaire's opinion of the Qur'an somewhat resembles al-Kindi's: 'every page does violence to sober reason, when he murders men and abducts women in order to force them to believe in this book' (Andrae, 1936: 245). For a more expert appraisal of French writing on Islam, see Ahmed Gunny's *Images of Islam in Eighteenth Century Writings* (1996); he also deals with English writers, including Joseph White (see below).

Humphrey Prideaux

It would be a mistake to think that all who now took up the pen to write about Muhammad had anything positive to say about him. Humphrey Prideaux's *The Nature of Imposture Fully Displayed* may, it has been surmised, have been inspired as a counterweight to Stubbe (see Bosworth, 1976: 11; I refer briefly to Prideaux in Chapter 3). This book, says Daniel, outdoes the medieval polemicists at their own game, drawing on Ricoldo and little else to portray Muhammad as having framed

such a religion as he thought might best go down, he [then] drew up a Scheme of that imposture he afterwards deluded them [his followers] with, which being a Medley made up of Judaism, the several Heresies of the Christians then in the East, and the old Pagan Rites of the Arabs, with an indulgence to all Sensual Delights, it did too well answer his Design in drawing men of all sorts to the embracing of it. (Prideaux, 1697: 13)

Like Voltaire's Muhammad, Prideaux's is consumed with 'ambition and lust. The course which he took to gain an Empire, abundantly shows the former; and the multitude of Women which he had to do with, proves the latter' (p. 35). Again, an old view of Muhammad, not lacking in the writing of the Damascene, is given new currency. Epilepsy, or something like it, is hinted at: 'And whereas he was subject to the Falling Sickness, whenever the fit was upon him, he pretended it to be a Trance, and that then the Angel Gabriel was come from God with some new revelations unto him' (p. 20). In its general outline, however, the history of Muhammad's life is accurately reflected, even in Prideaux's treatment. His primary aim was to refute Deism and what he viewed as other equally dangerous free-thinking heresies which left, in his estimate, too much room for the human, too little for the divine. In his 'note to the reader', he wrote:

Have we not Reason to fear that God may in the same Manner raise up some Mahomet against us for our utter Confusion ... And by what Socinianism, the Quaker, and the Deist begin to advance in this Land, we may have Reason to fear, that Wrath hath some Time since gone forth from the Lord for the Punishment of these our Iniquities and Gainsayings and that the Plague is already among us. (p. vii).

Like Voltaire, in writing about Muhammad Prideaux was not, primarily, writing for a Muslim audience but for a quite different constituency. Stubbe, on the other hand, appears to have set out to do justice to what he thought was the Muslim point of view, although, lacking discourse with Muslims, he was unable to ask them whether or not they agreed with his portrait. In that he had little time for any religious dimension, they probably would not have said 'amen' to his account, yet this consciousness that Muslims might read what he wrote puts him into a different category of writer from the Prideauxs and Voltaires of the time. Luther's writing on Islam, in which Muhammad is the Antichrist alongside the Pope, was also addressed to an audience other than the Muslim world. This had more to do with his eschatology, his warning that unless Europeans turned from their sinful ways the Turks would triumph, than it had to do with Islam *qua* Islam. Negatively, though, such writing did little to contribute towards a sympathetic appraisal of Muhammad since it accepted without question and thus perpetuated the traditional distorted and prejudiced image (see Fitzgerald and Caspar, 1992: 21).

The 'for' and 'against' debate

Accounts from this period usefully identify several of the issues which would occupy writers about Muhammad on both sides of the 'for' and 'against' debate: Was he sincere, or deluded? Was he just an opportunist, or in some sense a genuine religious leader? How should his 'trances' be understood (epilepsy continued to be popular)? Was his moral character reprehensible or admirable? Should he be praised for creating an empire or condemned for wielding a sword? Some writers continued to offer conventional criticisms of his sexual indulgence, imposture and general immoral conduct yet succeeded in painting a picture of Muslim history and civilization that was not altogether inaccurate or even unattractive. Indeed, as hinted earlier in this chapter, some may have found these aspects of the myth rather appealing; hence, the not insignificant success and popularity of Galland's rendering of the *Arabian Nights* (1704–17). Here,

Islam was no longer seen as the land of the antichrist but essentially that of an exotic, picturesque civilization, existing in a fabulous atmosphere peopled by good or evil, wayward genies – all this for the delight of an audience that had already shown so much taste for European fairy tales. (Rodinson, 1974: 36–7)

Simon Ockley's use of original sources (accidentally not the best!) meant that the details, if not his interpretation, of Muhammad's life might have been recognized by a Muslim as actually describing Muhammad; Muhammad, he wrote, 'was a very subtle and crafty man, who put on the appearance of those good qualities: while the principles of his soul were ambition and lust' (Ockley, 1848: 62–3). Ockley (1678–1720), a professor at Oxford, thought he was using a MS of al-Waqidi when he wrote his *History of the Saracens* (1708–18). It turned out to be a much later history by Futuh esh-Sham, which Stanley Lane-Poole describes as 'a work of little authority, which has even been characterised as "romance rather than history"'. Nonetheless, Lane-Poole comments that Ockley's work succeeded in making 'the history of the early Saracen conquests attractive for the general reader, and stimulated further research' (1968: 809).

George Sale

Within the English-speaking world especially, George Sale's English rendering, with Introduction, of the Qur'an (1734) represents a turning point in attitudes and in the provision of scholarly access to original sources. In his *Preliminary Discourse*, Sale made accurate and extensive use of Muslim traditions to critique some popular views of his subject-matter, including Muhammad's sincerity and moral character. On the latter, he thought that Muhammad had been wrongly maligned and set out to give him praise where (in his view) praise was due; 'praises due to his real virtue ought not to be denied' (Sale, 1838: vii). He was ambiguous on the issue of sincerity, but hints at this in the following passage, where he speaks of 'the wise conduct and great prudence he showed all along in pursuing his design' (p. 30). He thought there 'might be something more than what is vulgarly imagined in a religion which has made so surprising a progress' (p. v). He rejected epilepsy. Islam, though, had been violently propagated and this, perhaps more than anything else, proves it to be 'no other than a human convention' (p. 38). On the other hand, people who thought Islam spread by the sword alone were 'greatly deceived' (p. v). He also allowed allegorical interpretations of Qur'anic passages on Paradise, recognizing that Muslim scholars used allegory as a hermeneutical tool. Muhammad's multiple marriages (he had nine wives when he died) also compared favourably with the 18 which the Rabbis had allowed the ruler (p. 97). Pickthall similarly points out (1930) that 'The Prophet was himself permitted to have more wives than were allowed to others because, as head of State, he was responsible for the support of women who had no other protector' (Mentor edition, p. 406). Nor should Islam be dismissed as a merely mechanical religion: 'we must not think that Muslims, or the considerable part of them at least, content themselves with the mere *opus operatum* or imagine their whole religion to be based therein' (Sale, 1838: 77–8).

Where Sale's work represents a real break from that of most earlier writers is his willingness to listen to Muslim voices. He seems, says Daniel, 'to have no axe to grind. He wants to elucidate the facts' (1993: 322). He was probably the first non-Muslim to attempt to discuss the Qur'anic text within the context of standard Sunni exegesis and, as Daniel comments, 'the reader who wishes to know what Islam has traditionally understood can look nowhere better than Sale' (*ibid.*). Sale's Qur'an had been commissioned by the Society for Promoting Christian Knowledge (SPCK), presumably to aid the missionary effort. It is not surprising, then, that he upheld some conventional ideas about Christianity's superiority. Nevertheless, the general tone of his work was thought too positive, and he appears to have parted company with SPCK. So erudite was his Arabic scholarship that Gibbon thought him 'half a Mussalman', whilst Voltaire had it that he had spent half his life in Arabia (Lyon, 1968: 668). There is no evidence that he ever left Britain. One later writer commented that Sale's memory had been 'very undeservedly aspersed by controversial writers' (Forster, 1829, 2: 475). I find it fascinating that one response to Sale's willingness to say something positive about Islam was the charge that he must really be a closet Muslim! If an 'outsider' seems to be betraying the accepted perceptions of his or her 'group' about the 'outgroup', they may well be thought to have joined the 'outgroup'. Little wonder, perhaps, that earlier writers and translators had prefaced their work with 'Needful Caveats' as to why they were meddling with such dangerous material! For example, Alexander Ross prefaced his rendering of the Qur'an, derived from du Ryer's French version, with the words: 'Good reader, the great Arabian impostor, now at last, after a thousand years, is, by the way of France, arrived in England, and his Al-Coran, or Gallimaufry of Errors (a Brat as deformed as the Parent, and as full of Heresies as his scald head was of scurf) hath learned to speak English' (1649: i).

A new appraisal?

Now, armed with Sale's Qur'an, with various translations of Abu'l Fida, with Pocock's rendering of Bar Hebraeus and, after 1810, with copies of Captain Mathews' *Mishkat-al-Masabih*, even scholars without Arabic had access to Muslim sources. In fact, and readers might speculate why this was so, it was non-specialists rather than Arabists who began to contribute significantly towards a reappraisal of Muhammad's character and achievements. This trend began with Stubbe and Boulainvilliers, neither of whom were professional scholars of Islam or Arabic, yet unlike their professional colleagues, they had dared to suggest that Muhammad was not altogether bad. Another significant contribution of this type came from the pen of historian Edward Gibbon (1737–94) who, in his *Decline and Fall of the Roman Empire*, dealt with Muhammad and the origins of Islam.

Gibbon, a secularist, had no time for religious understandings of history but his commitment to scholarly accuracy ensured that 'he was able to avoid many of the erroneous statements about Muhammad that had been current previously' (Watt, 1955: 251). He dismissed Muhammad's supposed 'epilepsy' as a 'calumny of the Greeks' (Gibbon, 1989, 3: 160). However, he was uninterested in attempting to understand any religious dimension to Muhammad's life. Consequently, although his portrait duly acknowledges Muhammad's political achievements, it cannot be said to paint him in a particularly positive hue. Willingness to recognize Muhammad's temporal achievements often took non-Muslims some way towards a Muslim appreciation of Muhammad, but at the same time their unwillingness to consider his theological claims took them further away. Gibbon did think that before the *hijrah* Muhammad may have been sincere; afterwards he lapsed into conscious fraud and must have 'secretly smiled at the enthusiasm of his youth and the credulity of his proselytes' (3: 115). This is familiar ground – Muhammad as a self-deceived and deceiving political opportunist: 'a memorable instance ... how a wise man may deceive himself, how a good man may deceive others, how the conscious may slumber in a mixed and muddled state of self-illusion and voluntary fraud' (3: 162).

Gibbon rejected many myths about Muhammad as 'vulgar and ridiculous' and chided Prideaux and others for 'maliciously exaggerating the frailties of Muhammad' but agreed with their verdict – that 'in his private conduct, Muhammad indulged the appetite of a man and abused the claims of a prophet' (see Gibbon, 3: 114–16). Gibbon's Muhammad, with Qur'an in one hand and a sword in the other, rose triumphant over Eastern Christendom (here we have an enduring image indeed!). Nevertheless, three aspects of Gibbon's work justify Watt's statement that it represents 'the beginning of the movement for the rehabilitation of Muhammad': his careful use of Islamic sources (albeit in translation); his more positive appraisal of Muhammad's 'phase two' (pre-*hijrah* ministry); and his recognition of Islam's contribution to 'the cultural and intellectual history of mankind' which (see below) was much disputed by many who claimed expertise in all things Arabic (Rodinson,

1974: 39). Daniel says that 'if we discount Gibbon's prejudice we can measure in the story he tells the point to which scholarship had advanced' (1966: 24).

Washington Irving and others

A later, more popular *Life of Mohammed* (1850) by the novelist Washington Irving (1783–1859) shares several features in common with Gibbon's treatment (to which he refers, 1989: 228), especially the tendency to be more positive about Muhammad before the *hijrah* than after. Although written as a novel, Irving's book faithfully reproduces the outline and much of the content of Abu'l Fida, his main source. It was whilst in Spain that Irving developed an appreciation for the Moorish legacy; his books *The Conquest of Granada* and *The Alhambra* earned him an LLD from Oxford. Irving praised Muhammad's modesty, piety and generosity. He was, he said, 'undoubtedly a man of great genius and suggestive imagination'. Zeal for reform had initially motivated him, but later 'his sudden access of power' awakened in him 'human passions and mortal resentments' (pp. 84–5). He 'occasionally' availed himself 'of his supernatural machinery as a prophet' to get what he wanted (p. 204). Yet he was tolerant, kind, 'sober and abstemious' (pp. 197–9) and 'disdained all miracles excepting the Koran'. Irving, though, reproduced some of the miracle stories found in his sources as 'fables', since, surmises Patai, he 'senses that for an understanding of Mohammed's impact on the Arab world the presentation of these legends is more important than would be a painstaking tracking down of the actual events in the life of the Prophet' (1989: xxii). Irving was

far from considering Mahomet the gross and impious impostor that some have represented him but could find no other satisfactory mode of solving the enigma of his character and conduct than by supposing that the ray of mental hallucination which flashed upon his enthusiastic spirit during his religious ecstasies in the midnight cavern on Mt Hira continued more or less to bewilder him with a species of monomania to the end of his career, and that he died in the delusive belief of his mission as a prophet. (Patai, 1989: 205–6).

Muhammad, too, had drawn on Jewish and Christian doctrines in composing the Qur'an (see Irving, 1989: 36). Nevertheless, there is much accurate detail in this book, and its picture of Muhammad (which by no means lacks romance) is one which 'even today, a century and a half later, we can still find attractive, instructive and more appealing than many of the modern, more detailed, more scholarly, and more factual biographies of the Arabian Prophet' (Patai, 1989: xxvii). Irving's book is an interesting example of how a non-specialist can take, and use to good effect, the scholarly contributions of Arabists and other specialist scholars. As well as Abu'l Fida in translation, he also had access to the work of Gustav Weil (1808–89).

Weil's *Mohammed der Prophet* was published in 1843 and his rendering of Ibn Hisham appeared in 1864. Weil depicted Muhammad as an epileptic whose trances convinced him of his own sincerity. Using his own medical background (Weil was a French instructor for several years at a medical school in Cairo), he offered this as a scientific diagnosis, thus refuting Gibbon's earlier verdict (see Almond, 1989: 24). A. L. Tibawi, however, comments that Weil's rendering of Ibn Hisham's version of Ibn Ishaq is preferable to Guillaume's and did not merit the latter's criticism (see Buaben, 1996: 145 and Guillaume, 1955: xii). Similarly, Bernard Lewis (1973) praises Weil:

his Life of Muhammad was the first that was free from prejudice and polemic, based on profound yet critical knowledge of the Arab sources, and informed by a sympathetic knowledge of Muslim belief and piety. For the first time, he gave the European reader an opportunity to see Muhammad as Muslims saw him. (p. 129)

Following Weil, but supported by his own even more impressive medical knowledge (represented by a medical degree from Leiden), Aloys Sprenger (1813–97) also suggested that Muhammad's epilepsy resulted in self-delusion, deceit and imposture. Muhammad, he wrote, like all 'hysterical people' had 'a tendency to lying and deceit' (Sprenger, 1851: 210 f). Sprenger argued that Muhammad had for some time been 'a complete maniac' and that the 'fit after which he assumed his office was a paroxysm of cataleptic insanity' (p. 949). In fact, Muhammad's epilepsy, said Sprenger, probably also caused his nymphomania. Sprenger thought that Islam owed much more to Abu Bakr and other prominent Companions of the Prophet than it did to Muhammad.

Towards a new appraisal

Nonetheless, moving into the beginning of the nineteenth century, quite a few interesting, sometimes eccentric, examples of new appraisals of Muhammad can be identified. Indeed, it is perhaps to one such writer, Godfrey Higgins (1771–1833), that the credit for first asserting Muhammad's sincerity should go. His *Apology for the Life of Mohamed* appeared in 1829. He wrote:

It is unfortunate that many religious persons should imagine they are promoting their own religion by running down the character of the founders of those of their neighbours and fellow subjects. But genuine Christianity requires no such defences; and I am quite satisfied that, though Mohamed was liable to faults, like every other human being, yet that the closer his character is canvassed, the clearer it will appear that he was a very great man, both considered as a hero, a philosopher and a Christian, the latter of which he really was, as he professed to believe in the divine mission of Jesus Christ, and in the truth of the doctrines taught by him. (1830: 112)

Muhammad, he continued, was no more responsible for what has been said about him by his followers than Jesus is for what 'is said in the scores of works, called Gospels, written respecting him'. Later, Sir Sayyid Ahmed Khan remarked that Higgins had 'taken a correct view' of the Prophet (1870: xxi). Indeed, this estimate of Muhammad is very different from those surveyed above; he is no longer heretic, self-deluded, immoral but 'hero, philosopher' and even, in some sense, a Christian; in other words, a friend and not an enemy. Higgins found the type of anti-Muslim polemic which too often passed for scholarship in the work of others objectionable, but, as Almond points out, was himself somewhat partial towards 'anti-Christian polemic' (Almond, 1989: 13). Higgins thought that Jesus had been a 'Nazarite of the monastic order of Pythagorean Essenes' and 'probably a Samaritan by birth' (Gordon, 1968: 819).

From 'enemy' to friend

That Muslims might be considered 'friends', or 'brothers', not enemies, was the theme of another early nineteenth-century writer, Charles Forster (1787–1871). His *Mahometanism Unveiled* also appeared in 1829. It is therefore doubtful that Forster had read Higgins. Both, though, equally disliked Joseph White's Bampton Lecture on Muhammad. Higgins maintained that:

Since the exemplary life of the prophet could not be denied by the learned Oxonian, but as his merit could not be admitted without danger by a Christian divine, nothing remained but to attribute the conduct of the prophet to hypocrisy, and the most artful and deeply laid plot and design. (1829: 9)

Forster was a 'Christian divine' but thought it only fair to consider 'the effects which a wrong appreciation of their religious system may have had hithertofore and may continue to have on Mahometans themselves' (1829, 2: 375). The Oxford professor (Joseph White, 1746–1814), for his part, had aimed 'too manifestly to dazzle by the force of ambitious contrasts: Christianity is merciful, therefore Mahometanism must be painted cruel' (*ibid.*, 2: 469–70).

In Forster's view, to be unfair to the claims of another system was also to be guilty of gross injustice to the claims of the Gospel. 'Christian contro-versialists', he advised, ought to 'attend less to preconceptions and more to facts' (*ibid.*, 2: 464). Here, Forster recognized that a priori bias often influenced what scholars 'saw' in their sources. Previous writers, Forster says, brought 'crude and indigested theories' to bear on their subject, 'Prejudice has too often usurped the place of sound reason' (*ibid.*, 1: 4). As I have shown, many such writers addressed Muhammad in order to score points in quite different debates. They probably did not think that Muslims would read their writing, or even that they were guilty of calumny. Thus, as Edgar Taylor (1793–1839) put it so well in a valuable essay defending Sale's memory from his critics (which Forster used), these writers seem to 'lose their candour and often their love of truth when the subject is a Mussalman's religion. They stand around a cauldron, throw into it all the elements of vice and evil, and the production is a Mahomet!' (1821: 5).

Forster's own book has been much maligned, and, I believe, misunderstood. Ernest Renan (1823–92) for example, 'poured scorn on it' whilst, having read Renan's remarks, Matthew Arnold (1822–88) 'bemoaned the absence in England of any force of educated literary and scientific opinion which would make impossible the aberrations of amateurs like Charles Forster' (Almond, p. 5). Other reviewers, though, praised Forster's book as 'not merely the best work which has appeared upon the subject ... but the only one in which anything like justice has been done to the subject' (*Eclectic Review*, 1829: 384). Another praised Forster for bringing to the task a 'candid, generous and Christian spirit' (*British Critic*, 1830: 41), whilst others impugned his Christian integrity; the book represented 'a rather melancholy' example 'of the laxity and boldness of thinking' which had 'recently exhibited themselves in the Church of England', Forster could know only the 'letter' and not the 'spirit' of Christianity (*Wesleyan Methodist Magazine*, 1829: 765). Forster, however, drew on an impressive array of writers, including Sale, Boulainvilliers, Reland, as well as the *Mishkat*, in his own research.

A revolutionary thesis?

I have dealt with Forster's thesis in more detail elsewhere (see Bennett, 1992, Chapter 3) but here is a summary of its content. Forster, like earlier Christian writers, looked to the Bible for his key to unlock an understanding of Islam and its Prophet. Given Islam's survival, indeed its numerical and geographical success, he believed that it must play some part within God's plan for the world. Use of 'the sword' might explain its initial success, but not why it continues to flourish in areas 'unshackled' by Muslim powers, or indeed why it also spread in much of Africa 'among nations who never felt its swords' (1829, 1: 37). Biblically conservative, Forster therefore turned to scripture, which for him contains the blueprint of all history, to locate Islam's origin. Incidentally, he made much use of Gibbon but had few kind words for his view of history. He discovered his key in the passage Gen 17:20 (cited by Heraclius, see Chapter 2) which promised Abraham that his son Ishmael would be blessed. Abraham's prayer (Gen 17:18), Forster says, is answered in Muhammad, and in the civilization and culture which he founded. Thus Muslims stand in a covenant relationship with God, as Abraham's heirs through Ishmael, just as Jews and Christians stand in a covenant relationship with God through Isaac. The Muslim covenant is subordinate to the Christian one, because the genuine Abrahamic inheritance passed through Isaac, not Ishmael. Christianity is thus the spiritually richer of the two religions; Islam has tended towards the material yet does have its share of (lesser) spiritual fruit, which 'discover themselves in a reality of belief, a fervour of zeal and a sincerity of devotion which, it has often been remarked, might put the majority of the Christian world to shame' (1: 431).

To prove his thesis that Islam had contributed positively to human civilization, Forster undertook considerable research, especially into the period of scholarly interaction referred to above in this survey (including the Crusades, which he believed had seen much positive interaction between Christians and Muslims, see 2: 321–3). Islam, he said, had contributed much in the fields of philosophy, astronomy, chemistry, mathematics and navigation, developing and not merely passing on what it had received from the Greeks. A 'false estimate' of Islam's 'civil and intellectual influences' will only encourage Muslims to conclude that everything else Christians have to say is also untrue (see 2: 378; much evidence here of Forster's extensive use of Gibbon – although he rejected Gibbon's secular historiography). Muhammad, too, should be judged not by the standards of today but by those of his own time. Judged thus, it is remarkable that his morals were not worse, rather than better, than they were (1: 278). Forster does not clear Muhammad of all the charges made against him but he does depict him as more than an imitator of Moses, that is, a mere copyist; in some sense he was raised up by God. To 'insist on merely human causes ... is to take the world out of the hands of God' (2: 472). Thus Islam's origin is to be located within 'that one great primary cause and effect of all things, the special superintending providence of God' (1: 68).

Muslims and Christians as allies

Islam therefore 'tends towards' Christianity, of which it is a type of 'counterfeit' (a mixture of the legitimate and illegitimate), yet it is closer to the 'true faith' today than it was at its birth. It is 'fitted to prepare the way for the still more universal diffusion of Christian lights' (2: 359–60). Hence, said one reviewer, Christians might as well raise funds to print 'cheap Korans' and send 'missionary Moulahs to the heathen' (*Edinburgh Review*, 1830: 331). Sir William Muir suggested that Forster's book would, sadly, be very warmly received by the *Ulama* (Muslim scholars) of India (Muir, 1897: 43). Oddly, Forster did apply various scriptural passages to Muhammad which enabled him, as Renan (1893) pointed out, to call Muhammad by such titles as 'the Little Horn of the he-goat which figures in the 8th chapter of Daniel', whilst he also called the Pope 'the Great Horn' (Renan; 156).

Reviewers' wrath

One reviewer pointed out, though, that these references sit uneasily with the rest of Forster's book and ought to be deleted (*British Critic*, 1830: 43). 'Fraternal disposition for the Musalman' had misled Forster into assuming that 'ignorance and brutality' are not the 'universal and inevitable accompaniments of the Koran'. The reviewer found it quite absurd to claim, as Forster did, that Christianity actually stood in debt to 'this mystery of deception' (*ibid.*). It was this suggestion, that 'Isaac without Ishmael could not have been made perfect', which most infuriated his critics. Forster's conclusion was eschatological: God would eventually, as it were, re-unite Ishmael with Isaac; there would be 'one great consummation – the glorious fulfilment of the twofold covenant of God with Abraham, in its social and intellectual aspects, by the eventual re-union of his sons Isaac and Ishmael as joint civilisers of the world' (2: 36).

Many reviewers rejected any possible link between Muhammad, and Abraham (for a recent discussion of this issue, see Ibn Warraq, 1995: 131–3). Forster's book, for all its eccentricities, and (arguably) contradictions, helped to set the scene for much subsequent discussion. Widely read and consulted, it is to be found referenced in numerous nineteenth- and in early twentieth-century works. Three aspects of Forster's approach can usefully be highlighted.

First, he wanted to do 'justice to the phenomenon' of Islam (see 1: 68) and, his use of the Bible aside, turned to some of the best sources available to attempt this task. He was conscious of how Muslims might react to an unfair portrait – thus he wrote (at least potentially) *for them* as well as for his Christian readers. Given the sometimes ambiguous language of his book, it is not surprising that Muslim reaction was itself ambiguous. One recent Muslim writer refers to 'reports of the absurdity of Muslim beliefs' as 'tacitly' serving 'the purpose that [Forster] had made his express purpose' (Leila Ahmed, 1978: 70). This is not how I understand Forster's 'express purpose'. On the other hand, the Muslim modernist S. Khuda Baksh (1877–1931) wrote:'The spirit of hostility which marked the writing of early European scholars curiously continued in all its fanatical fervour till 1829, the date of the appearance of *Mahometanism Unveiled* ... But things are changing' (1926: 245).

The ambiguity here is whether Forster, for Baksh, represented the turning point in approach or the pinnacle of hostility. It is thus not easy to gauge Muslim response to Forster, but that he was concerned about their response does represent a new trend (already hinted at in the work of Stubbe and Higgins) in non-Muslim approaches to Islam – writing not only for a Western but also for a Muslim readership. Implicit in this is the hope that the account, once rendered, might command their assent. Forster saw Muslims as fellow human beings, even as allies and friends in the same enterprise. Like Stubbe and other writers who dared to question the old images, Forster's book aimed to reduce the gap between himself, and 'the other' about whom he wrote.

Second, Forster's recognition of Muslim achievements, and his idea that Islam could co-operate with Christianity in the task of 'civilizing the world' would become a hotly debated thesis. Later writers would deny that Islam had contributed anything to the enlightenment project – it had merely copied; Islam, they argued, is incompatible with social and intellectual progress, it retards rather than advances the human condition of all over whom it wields influence. Nor, they argued, could Islam 'reform' – it certainly was no *preparatio evangelium*, but instead raised up 'a thick ... veil which effectively excludes every glimmering of the true light' (Muir, 1897: 48) 'impenetrable barriers against the success of evangelical truth' (*Wesleyan Methodist Magazine*, 1829: 764). Renan's negative comment on Forster may have been prompted by Forster's rather positive view of Islam's ability to contribute to the civilizing of the species. Renan, in his work on Ibn Rushd, argued that the philosopher had substituted Aristotle for Islam; 'what is Arabic in this so-called Arab science? ... Is it at least Muhammedan? Has Muhammadanism been in any way a support for these rational studies? In no way', he concluded (Wild, 1996: 157 citing an 1883 lecture). For Renan, Ibn Rushd's death marked the end of free thought in Islam: 'When Ibn Rushd died in 1198 Arab philosophy lost in him its last representative, and the triumph of the Qur'an over free thought was assured for at least six hundred years' (1866: 1).

Thirdly, although ambiguous, Forster's 'Muhammad' was in some sense a divinely guided 'Prophet'. Certainly, he was not altogether bad. That there could be any providential and therefore benign connection between Muhammad and the Christian God was a novel idea indeed. It would not gain everyone's support, and many would continue to attribute to Muhammad self-delusion, sheer political opportunism, some sort of misguided enthusiasm, some type of epileptic malady which resulted in his fits and visions, or even, and this in works not lacking scholarship, satanic inspiration. A major difference between Forster's Muhammad and the Muhammad of many who heaped ridicule upon him was that his had genuinely set out to raise the moral standards of his people. Although Forster's unpublished *Vindication* (1830) of his theory against some of his more outspoken critics appears to have left open the possibility of a satanic influence on Islam (p. 41), he reiterated his conviction that it has 'some mysterious and inscrutable share' in God's purposes (p. 47).

Three approaches

Forster represents an early attempt by someone who did not want to 'remove God's hand from history' to understand what had motivated Muhammad *religiously*. Whilst, as has been noted, the 'development of a more secular view of history and the progressive decline' in reading all history as 'sacred history' may have enabled some to reappraise Muhammad's human achievements, at the same time it disabled them from appreciating Muhammad's religious ones (see Almond, 1989: 5). From the Muslim point of view, it is certain that any appreciation of Muhammad which *reduces* his role to that of a secular leader and does not acknowledge what he only ever claimed to be, *rasulu' Llah* (the messenger of God), will fail to command their full assent. On the other hand, many attempts at understanding what had religiously motivated Muhammad have failed to give due consideration to the political aspects of his leadership.

In the years following Forster, those who wrote about Muhammad can be divided into three broad categories:

(1) Those who wrote primarily for a Western readership, whether academic or general, either as secular historians or as writers interested in making sense of what had motivated Muhammad but from other than a Muslim perspective. Muslims might read what these writers wrote, but they were not the intended audience. Eliciting Muslim approval was not part of their agenda.

(2) Those who wrote for a Western readership and *for Muslims* but, like the above, did not care much whether Muslims approved of what they wrote. Some would claim a greater authority to write about Islam than Muslims themselves. Edward Said identifies Lord Cromer (1841–1917) as typical of this approach. Cromer, says Said, believed that 'Orientals were almost everywhere nearly the same' and thus that 'managing them, although circumstances may differ slightly here

and there', was also much the same. His 'knowledge about Orientals, their race, character, culture, history, traditions, society and possibilities' which he recorded in his *Modern Egypt* (1908) could usefully guide administrators everywhere. His 'knowledge' had been 'tested', and found 'effective': '"Orientals" for all practical purposes were a Platonic essence, which any orientalist (or ruler of Orientals) might examine, understand, and explain' – thus understanding their needs better than they did themselves (Said, 1978: 37–8). It was Lord Cromer who popularized the notion that 'Islam reformed was Islam no longer'. Such writers, too, often believe that they 'know' Islam 'for the appallingly dreadful thing it is' (Said, 1997: xviii).

(3) Those who wrote for Westerners and Muslims but who wanted to render an account which would do justice to the faith in Muslim hearts, to paraphrase Wilfred Cantwell Smith (see W.C. Smith, 1959: 44).

The first approach: Thomas Carlyle

Thomas Carlyle (1795–1881) represents an example of the first category of writer. He was interested in understanding Muhammad's 'inner experience'. Was it a sincere delusion, conscious deceit, Satanic inspiration – or were other answers possible? Indeed, although we have afforded Godfrey Higgins this honour, Carlyle's famous essay on 'The Hero as Prophet' has been described as 'The first affirmation in the whole of European literature, medieval or modern, of a belief in the sincerity of Muhammad' (Watt, 1955: 247). Carlyle declared that Muhammad was 'A silent great soul, … one of those who cannot but be in earnest; whom nature itself has appointed to be sincere' (1840: 54). Watt asks, in his *Hibbert Journal* analysis of Carlyle's essay:

How was it that in May 1840, after centuries in which Muhammad had been called an impostor, an Anti-Christ and worse, Carlyle publicly insisted that he was essentially a sincere man, sincerely following such light as he had? What were the current views against which Carlyle was protesting and how did they come to be what they were? What, on the other hand, were the existing tendencies towards a rehabilitation of Muhammad? (1955: 247).

Obviously, Carlyle was reacting to the same negative images against which Stubbe, Boulainvilliers, Sale, Higgins and Forster had all reacted. As for the existing tendencies, one was the careful historical reconstructions of Gibbon, Ockley and even Forster which did much to separate fact from fable. Watt, however, identifies two other tendencies to which I have not referred, at least explicitly, in this survey; these were, respectively, a philosophical and a romantic tendency. In fact, the latter was briefly encountered in Dante's limbo and in the translation work of Galland, whilst the former has its origin in the period of Spanish interaction, when I identified several efforts to replace polemic with reasoned discussion. Watt singles out Leibnitz (1646–1716), Immanuel Kant (1724–1804) and J. W. Goethe (1749–1832), whose works

Carlyle translated into English. Leibnitz saw Islam as a rational religion which achieved a healthy balance (unlike Catholic Christianity) between 'the needs of the body, of the senses, and of life in society' (Rodinson, 1974: 38). Kant valued 'rational religion' over its other manifestations – and may have thought that Islam qualified as a rational religion (see Hourani, 1991b: 23). Goethe (in whom the philosopher and romantic merge) wanted to discover the 'man for all times and of all places' and, thinking that it might be more profitable to search for this in the East than in the West, found himself singing Muhammad's praise in his 'poems to the glory of Muhammad' (Rodinson, 1974: 43). Rodinson suggests that Goethe's work, despite lack of 'local colour', did contribute to the 'growing understanding of the East by the West'.

Carlyle was no secularist, but nor did his world-view appeal overmuch to the religious Establishment – F. D. Maurice (1805–72), himself far from being theologically conservative, detested his 'silly rant about the great bosom of nature' (1838, 1: 282). For his part, Carlyle detested creeds, bishops and theology but believed that 'the Religious Principle lies unseen in the hearts of all good men' (Cross and Livingstone, 1974: 240). In lecturing on 'The Hero as Prophet' he appears to have taken delight in shocking his audience:

I gave them to know that ... the Arab had points about him which were good for all of them to imitate: that they were more quacks than he: that, in short, it was altogether a new kind of thing they were hearing ... The people seemed greatly astonished. (cited in L. Ahmed, 1978: 181)

Carlyle did not aim at historical but at psychological reconstruction: he wanted to understand Muhammad the man as he grappled with the problems of human life. In attempting to understand the inner experience of the Prophet, he broke new ground and, says Watt, his portrait is 'still of value in its broad outline to the historian today' (1955: 254). Carlyle's Muhammad was Nature's mouthpiece: 'The great Mystery of Existence ... glared-in upon him ... Such *sincerity*, as we named it, has in very truth something of divine. The word of such a man is a voice direct from Nature's own Heart' (1840: 54). Muhammad's inspiration came from within; it was the same type of inspiration that produces poetry, music, art, and drives great men to do great things. This, as Daniel points out, is not the sort of inspiration which comes 'unambiguously from God, and [is] not a Christian or an Islamic idea' (1993: 314). Thus Carlyle's attempt to make sense of Muhammad falls within our first category – it employs tools from outside the Muslim world-view. In fact, in a later essay, Carlyle retracted what he had written:

It was intrinsically an error, that notion of Mahomet's, of his supreme Prophet-hood; and has come down to us inextricably involved in error to this day; dragging along with it such a coil of fables, impurities, intolerances, to say, as I have done, that Mahomet was a true speaker at all, and not rather an ambitious charlatan, perversity and simulacrum; no speaker, but a Babler. Even in Arabia, as I compute, Mahomet will have exhausted himself, and become obsolete, while this Shakespeare, this Dante, may still be young; while this Shakespeare may still pretend to be a Priest of Mankind, of Arabia, as of other places, for unlimited periods of time. (1903: 392)

Buaben (1996) points out that whilst Carlyle did something to 'rescue Muhammad', he did so in a way which no Muslim could accept. Carlyle's Muhammad is, at best, a 'hero' but not a prophet (p. 108). Carlyle said:

Mahomet was ... not a sensual man [but] A poor, hard-toiling, ill-provided man ... Not a bad man, I should say ... They called him a Prophet, you say? Why, he stood face to face with them, bare, not enshrined in any mystery ... they must have seen what kind of a man he was, let him be called what you like ... I find something of a veritable Hero [in him]. (1840: 66)

Cook and Crone

I have already referred to the work of Michael Cook and Patricia Crone. This, I suggest, is an example of more recent accounts of Muhammad which, written primarily for an academic constituency, are uninterested in whether Muslims approve or disapprove of what is written. According to these writers, Muhammad's life, as recorded in the *sira*, is largely the invention of later generations; the real Muhammad was a Messianic-type figure who led a movement to repossess Jerusalem; the Qur'an was posthumously composed sometime during the Khalifate of 'Abd-al Malik. What we have in the classical account of Muhammad's life is the creation of an elaborate Arabian *heilgeschichte* to lend authenticity to the rather hybrid religion which had been put together – partly by Muhammad but more so by his successors (see Crone, 1987: 230). Cook and Crone know that their account of Muhammad does not tally with the accepted Islamic version and clearly do not care (I am not implying, incidentally, that they ought to). As Ibn Warraq observes, they 'give a new account of the rise of Islam' which 'on their own admission' is 'unacceptable to any Muslim' (1995: 81). Indeed, as Goddard (1995) points out, the book was banned in Egypt, where an '*Open Letter to the Pope*, produced in ... 1978, specifically asked his holiness to put a stop to this kind of thing' (p. 13). Buaben (1996), discussing Muslim response to the work of Cook and Crone, cites Anees and Athar: 'It is a mockery of scholarship that set[s] out to show the Muslim concepts of revelation and prophethood were born in the Judaic cradle' (p. 153).

In fact, their ideas were not altogether new – earlier writers have also depicted Islam and the Qur'an as the product of the inventive imagination of Muhammad, who changed geography and the biblical record at whim to suit his own purposes and legitimise his claims; see for example the work of Snouck Hurgronje (1855–1936), who also posited an irreducible difference between the Orient and the Occident (see Said, 1978: 256, and Hurgronje, 1957). Muhammad, according to Hurgronje, had simply invented the stories about Ishmael and Abraham at Makkah to give biblical colour to his religion. We may note, however, that Hurgronje succeeded in passing himself off as 'the skin-darkened Muslim scholar Abdul Gaffur' and 'infiltrating Dutch East

Indian Islamic circles ... wrote a major ethnographic study of Aceh' (J. R. Bowen, 1996: 13). Hurgronje saw political Islam as a threat to European values but thought that devotional Islam might be encouraged; '"Islam as worship" ... resembling European notions of religion, was to be encouraged, and "Islam as politics", contradicting European notions of what a liberal, civil society ought to be, and posing a real danger to colonial domination, was to be opposed' (*ibid.*: 12). Said says that Hurgronje 'used the confidence he had won from Muslims to plan and execute the brutal Dutch war against the Atjehnese' (1997: lvii).

There has been much written about whether the traditions of Abraham visiting Makkah are rooted in reality or not (Forster discussed this at length) and, indeed, about the genuineness of Ibn Ishaq's Isaac–Muhammad genealogy. However, the fact that the Bible provides no evidence of Abraham visiting Makkah does not necessarily rule this out, since after Ishmael's banishment from the household of Abraham it proceeds to tell Isaac's, not Ishmael's story. As Lings writes, 'After that, it scarcely mentions his name, except to inform us that the two brothers Isaac and Ishmael together buried their father in Hebron, and that some years later Esau married his cousin, the daughter of Ishmael' (1983: 2). Thus Lings accepts the Qur'anic material as supplementary, filling in the gaps of an understandable biblical silence. The relationship between the Prophet and the Qur'an (and the associated issue of authorship) is one which has long divided Muslim from non-Muslim opinion.

The second approach

I shall take as the classic example of my second approach – accounts written for both Western readers and Muslims but which claim an authority over and above that of believers themselves – the work of Sir William Muir (1819–1905), especially his four-volume *Life of Mahomet* (1857–61; third edition, abridged, 1894). I have already had cause to cite from Muir's work in this study; it aimed to make a real contribution to Oriental scholarship by using only the Muslim sources considered to be the oldest and most authentic. This evidences a genuine desire to reproduce fact, not fiction, as well as to produce a Life that Muslims would themselves recognize. However, as well as placing the facts of Muhammad's life before both Muslim and Christian readers, Muir wanted to convince Muslims that Muhammad was not worth their allegiance. He thus combined scholarly and evangelical or missionary purposes. Unlike many earlier writers, he fully understood, too, what Muslims believed about the Qur'an (as God's eternal *Kalam*), even though for him it represented 'a store-house of Mahomet's own words', that is, 'what he actually thought, or that which he desired to appear was thinking' (Muir, 1894: xxvi). He also knew the significance of Muhammad's *Sunnah* for the day-to-day practice of Islam. The result of his much more comprehensive knowledge of Islamic theory and his almost exclusive use of the early *sira* was a detailed life of Muhammad more complete than almost any other previous book, at least in English. For this reason, Muir's *Life* has been rightly praised by more recent writers such as Albert Hourani, who says that it 'is still not quite superseded' (1989: 34), and W. M. Watt, who says that it 'follows in detail the standard Muslim accounts, though not uncritically' (1961: 244).

Muir's Christian perspective

However, Muir's Christian faith was for him the only vehicle of salvation, the only message that God had given his world. By definition, then, Islam could not be a valid salvific system, nor could Muhammad have been sincere, although he may have been sincerely misguided. Muir's world-view somewhat resembled the traditional self-image of medieval Christendom – nothing outside its borders could have much value. Europe's colonial domination of much of the non-white world tended to underwrite assumptions of European superiority. Muir, himself a servant of the British Empire, was certainly influenced by these assumptions. His constant charge, for example, that Muslims were dishonest calls to mind Lord Cornwallis' words, 'every native of Hindustan is corrupt' (cited in Spear, 1965: 95). Daniel also notes (1966) how Muir could constantly criticize Muslims for neglecting to educate their women at a period when 'the long struggle for women's education was barely begun' in Britain. Muir, says Daniel, was 'acting, or thought he was acting, as an imperial ruler obliged to impose benefits upon a reluctant Islamic society' (1966: 279; see Muir's *Addresses*, 1876: 6, 8, 13, 18, 30, 35, 41, 51, 52, for references to the benefits of female education). Like Cromer, he thought Orientals much the same everywhere. Also like Cromer, he made some very magisterial statements in his writing. Let two suffice:

The Islam of today is substantially the Islam we have seen throughout history. Swathed in the bands of the coran, the Moslem faith, unlike the Christian, is powerless to adapt ... to varying time and place, keep pace the march of humanity, direct and purify the social life and elevate mankind. (Muir, 1915: 599)

And

The Christian nations may advance in civilization, freedom and morality, in philosophy, in science and the arts, but Islam stands still. And thus stationary, so far as the lessons of history avail, it will remain. (*ibid.*: 603)

Muir's, and the Englishman's, task in India, therefore, was to leave Indians the better for their having been there, as he made explicit in his *Addresses*: 'what ... are we Englishmen here in India for? ... it is that we should raise and elevate the people, make them the happier and the better for our being here' (p. 47).

Muir, who reviewed Forster's book (and roundly condemned it), read Islam quite differently: it had contributed nothing to civilization, would contribute nothing, and in everything opposed 'truth', presenting 'a thick ... veil which effectively excludes every glimmer of the true light' (1897: 48). 'They labour', he wrote, under a miserable delusion who suppose that Mahometanism paves the way for a purer faith. No system could have been designed with more consummate skills for shutting out the nations over which it has sway, from the light of truth'. (1894: 506–7)

For Muir, the Muslim and the Christian world were polarized; he lived in his world, they in theirs (see Said, 1978: 44).

On Muhammad's sincerity

Muir could endorse Muhammad at Makkah as sincerely struggling after truth, but he saw in Muhammad at Madinah a Muhammad whose ambition, lust and greed robbed him of any virtues he may have had before the *hijrah* (there is something of this in Gibbon's treatment). Muir saw every reason to criticize Muhammad on the traditional scores of violence, sexual indulgence and blasphemy, 'forging the name of God' as he put it. Muhammad, he said, had freely called down verses from heaven to justify his use of the sword, his changed attitude towards Jews and Christians, and his multiple marriages; the Zaid/Zainab affair features prominently here; 'to save his reputation, Mahomet had to fall back on the Oracle' (Muir, 1894: 282). He dealt in similar fashion with Muhammad's marriage to Mary the Copt, 'a heavenly message interposed' again (*ibid.*: 413). The 'satanic verses' affair gave Muir much opportunity to hint at something other than a divinely inspired prophet (*ibid.*: 79–84). Buaben (1996) notes that, for Muir, Muhammad's union 'to a second wife' represented 'a serious movement away from Christianity' (pp. 12, 34; see Muir, 1894: 172). Muir lists 'three radical evils' as Islam's main legacy: (1) the social – practices of polygamy, divorce and slavery; (2) the crushing and annihilation of freedom of judgement in religion; and (3) a barrier against the reception of Christianity (1894: 505). Although he claimed historical impartiality, Muir could not resist allowing personal opinion to colour his narrative. Thus in the 'final development of his creed', Muhammad 'makes the Koran to rise triumphant over both the Law and the Gospel, and casts them unheeded into the shade' (Muir, 1894: 148). He parted Christian and Jewish company with 'threats of abasement and cruel words' (1894: 440). Muir may have left his own interpretation of what had motivated Muhammad here, but instead chose to resurrect another old Christian theory – satanic inspiration:

It is incumbent upon us to consider this question from a Christian point of view, and to ask whether the supernatural influence, which ... acted upon the soul of the Arabian prophet may not have proceeded from the Evil One ... Our belief in the power of the Evil One must lead us to consider this as at least one of the possible causes of the fall of Mahomet ... into the meshes of deception ... May we conceive that a diabolical influence and inspiration was permitted to enslave the heart of him who had deliberately yielded to the compromise with evil. (1858: 90f; see also 1897: 48)

Muhammad credited as Islam's founder

Muir thought that what he called Muhammad's 'garbled' ideas about Christianity (including confusing the Holy Spirit – that is, the Spirit of inspiration – with Gabriel, and 'Mary as a person of the Trinity') to be derived not directly from Christians but via the medium of a Jewish source who had also 'furnished the more copious details of Jewish history' (1894: 152). Islam was, however, for better or for worse, the product of Muhammad and not, as Aloys Sprenger argued, of his Companions who had manipulated him. 'Islam is not the work of the impostor, it embodies the offspring of the spirit of the time ... Abu Bakr did more for the success of Islam than the prophet himself' (Sprenger, 1851: 175, 171). Muir disagreed. The process was not one of 'The material shaping its own form, much less (as some would have it) moulding the workman himself. It was Mahomet that formed Islam, it was not Islam, or any pre-existing Moslem spirit, that moulded Mahomet' (1894: lxxxvi). Muslims dislike references to Muhammad as 'Islam's founder'. However, Muir's crediting of Muhammad here may perhaps be more acceptable to Muslims than Sprenger's relegation of him to the sidelines of history.

Muir also translated, with synopsis, al-Kindi's *Risalah*, and the similarities between Muir's and the classical arguments against Muhammad's moral character are quite striking. The *Risalah* proposed a threefold distinction of dispensations: that of grace, which was divine; that of justice, which was human; whilst the third could only be diabolical (see Daniel, 1993: 210). Whilst Muir himself posed the question of satanic inspiration rhetorically, there is little doubt as to his own answer. The conclusion to his *Life* has become much quoted: 'The sword of Mahomet and the Coran are the most stubborn enemies of Civilisation, Liberty and Truth which the world has yet known' (1894: 506).

Put bluntly, Muir represents the classical Christian portrait of Muhammad writ large, more powerful, perhaps, because of his comprehensive and often faithful rendering of the *sira*. There is, however, also a hint in Muir that had Muhammad continued his original search for truth, especially had he met with orthodox Christians, he might have found himself leading a legitimate religious revival rather than a 'false one'. Thus, we might have had 'St Mahomet – more likely a MAHOMET THE MARTYR – laying the foundation of the Arabian Church' (1894: lxxxv) instead of the founder of a system which combined the worldly and the spiritual so ingenuously that

barely so much of virtue and of spiritual truth was retained to appease man's religious instincts and his inward craving after the service of his creator while the reigns of his passion and indulgence [were] relaxed to the utmost extent compatible with the appearance of Godliness. (1858, v. 2: 94)

Something here, perhaps, of the old heresy approach. Muir also rejected any legitimate link, spiritual or genealogical, between Muhammad and Ishmael (see 1897: 42). Incidentally, his view that Muhammad was more positive towards Christians and Jews in the earlier period, then 'parted company' when they failed to legitimate his prophethood with 'threats of abasement and cruel words' (*ibid.*: 440) is quite simply not justified by the evidence. Ibn Ishaq, for example, has Muhammad towards the very end of his life instructing his companions, 'He who holds fast to his religion, Jew or Christian, is not to be turned [seduced] from it. He must pay the poll tax ... He who pays that to God's apostle has the guarantee of God' (I.I., p. 643; see Lings, 1983: 324–5). Abu Bakr on the rules of war, too, commands his soldiers to leave the monks to their praise of Allah! (Nor can it be insignificant that Muhammad allowed the icon of Virgin and Child to remain at the Ka'abah (see I.I., p. 552).) The *hadith* preserve many sayings which guarantee *dhimmi*s protection, including the often-cited 'he who harms a *dhimmi*, harms me'.

Muir on the fabrication of hadith

Muir wrote his *Life* because, after reviewing 'native' biographies of the Prophet, he believed they lacked accuracy. He wanted to provide one, based on their own sources, which Muslims would recognize as authentic. In a tone remarkably near to Forster, he wrote that if Muslims perceive 'want of accuracy in our narratives and imperfections in our means of information, they will naturally doubt all our assertions and deny our conclusion' (1897: 41). 'They will thus', he continued, 'be fortified in their scornful rejection of Christian evidence and in their self-complacent reliance on the dogmas of Islam' (*ibid.*: 68). He began his *Life* with a detailed discussion of the sources available for its reconstruction in which we see the beginning of the view that they so reflect the agenda of the early Muslim community as to 'place ... details altogether beyond the reach of analytical criticism' (1894: lii). Bias, he believed, was always at work:

there exists throughout Mahometan Tradition abundant indications of actual fabrication; and there can everywhere be traced the indirect but not less powerful and dangerous influence of a latent bias, which insensibly gave colour and its shape to the stories of their Prophet. (p. xxxii)

The 'fabulous' can be easily identified, but it is less easy, Muir suggests, to 'decide what portions of these supernatural stories either originated in Mahomet himself, or received his countenance; and what portion owed its birth, after he was gone, to the excited imagination of his followers' (*ibid.*). He continues:

if it appear strange that extravagant and unreasonable tales of the kind described ... should not have been contradicted by the more upright and reasonable Moslems of the first age, and thus nipped in the bud, it must be remembered that criticisms and freedom of opinion were stifled under the crushing dogmas of Islam. (p. lvi)

Thus, Muir gave more value to any tradition 'unfavourable on the prophet' than to ones which extol him, since 'it hardly seems possible that a tradition of the kind could be fabricated. Or, having been fabricated, that it could obtain currency amongst the followers of Muhammad' (p. lxiii). He did not explain why his redactors had not expunged such traditions from their collections!

In summary, Muir was pessimistic about the historicity of much of the material but thought that a painstaking examination could identify that which was closest in origin to the time of Muhammad himself, such as transcripts of treaties purporting to have been dictated by Mahomet or verses and poetic fragments attributed to the time of Mahomet, such as the odes of Hassan Ibn Thabat on the Battle of the Ditch and on the Taking of Makkah, and the poem of Kab ibn Malik describing the second pledge of Aquaba. Given, he says, what we know about the Arab's ability to preserve poetry by memory (p. lxvi), 'it cannot certainly be deemed improbable that such poems or fragments should in reality have been composed by the parties to whom they are ascribed' (p. lxv), thus begging the question of why the bulk of traditional material should also not have been faithfully preserved. However, he considered the earliest *sira* material to be, generally, the most trustworthy: 'Whatever authentic information really existed must already have become public and available ... Every day diminished the chance that any stray traditions should still be floating downward on the swift and troubled current of time'; thus, 'later historians could not by any possibility add a single source of information to what these authors have given us' but could only draw on 'worthless and fictitious matter, gathered from the spurious traditions and romances of later times' (p. lxxv).

Material which anticipated Muhammad's victories could be rejected as a back-projection by Islam of 'some rays of its refulgence upon the bare points of its early career' (p. lxv). However, Buaben points out how other motives may have influenced Muir's selection of his material. For example, he may have deliberately omitted any reference to the 'Constitution of Madinah' so that, in his account of Muhammad's attack on the Banu Qurayzah, he could represent this as 'barbaric, inhuman and Muhammad as not worthy of the noble office of prophethood ... By omitting it, there is no basis for Muhammad accusing the Banu Qurayzah of breaking a pact' (1996: 37; see also Zakaria, 1991: 34–7 on the Banu Qurayzah's plot against the Muslims). Similarly, whilst praising Muhammad's 'magnanimity' upon entering Makkah, Muir explains this clemency in purely strategic terms, thus preserving his view that Muhammad was naturally cruel and vindictive: 'it was ... for his own interest to forgive the past, and cast into oblivion its slights and injuries' (1894: 398).

Did Muir achieve his aim?

Was Muir's aim – to construct a biography of the Prophet which Muslims would accept as an accurate and reliable account – achieved? Buaben (1996) says 'no'. What Muir did was to give a cloak of academic respectability to medieval attitudes: 'Muir was not able to divorce himself from the communal opinion dating from the medieval period. Therefore, even though in some instances, he is positively appreciative of Muhammad ... his work lacks the merit of consistent, sound academic scholarship' (p. 311). Thus, Sir Sayyid

Ahmed Khan (and other Muslims) could not recognize in Muir's Muhammad the Prophet whom they revered and whose memory they cherished, and set out to correct what they saw as Muir's distorted picture. For Sir Sayyid, 'Islam means to love Muhammad personally and to follow his *sunnah* as closely as possible' (Troll, 1978: 44); the problem with Muir's Muhammad was that no right-thinking person would dream of either loving or following him. Sayyid Ameer Ali called Muir 'Islam's avowed enemy' (1891: 211).

Sir Sayyid knew Muir personally and appointed him as a Visitor to his Mahometan Anglo-Oriental College (now Aligargh Muslim University). Speaking there in 1875, Muir refers to Sir Sayyid as 'my friend' (*Addresses*, 1876: 56) – clear evidence that Muir claimed close acquaintance with Muslims, which he probably thought added to his authority as a scholar. However, it is much more likely that Muir's opinion of Muslims and Islam was influenced primarily by his experiences in 1857–58, when he served as chief intelligence officer in the North-West Provinces during the anti-British rebellion, spending much of his time in the Red Fort, Agra. The following passages are typical of many entries from his account of the period:

The Muslims defied our Government in the most insolent manner. All the ancient feelings of warring for the faith reminding one of the days of the first caliphs were resurrected. Few of the families who were otherwise strongly loyal to us could resist the temptation. (1902, 1: 46f)

He records hearing cries of 'Deen, Deen', 'Ya Hussein', and 'Ya Mahomed' and that Mullahs were preaching 'whoever kills a European or a Christian shall get his salvation at once and will become as sinless as an innocent child, and whoever shall be killed in the righteous war against the Kafirs shall go directly to Heaven' (*ibid.*). 'It is', he wrote, 'of the very nature of the Mahometan faith to seize on such an incident as a religious principle impelling the more devoted and fanatical to an attempt for re-establishing the ascendancy of Islam' (*ibid.*: 12–13). After the cessation of hostilities, however, Muir (with others) vindicated Muslims of rape, finding no evidence to support the charges against them.

Muir narrates the killing of Ka'b in some detail as an example of 'those dastardly acts of cruelty which darken the pages of the prophet's life' (1894: 238–40). Muir probably interpreted Muhammad's response to 'O Apostle of God, we shall have to tell lies' ('say what you like, for you are free in the matter') as giving Muslims 'a general license to deceive'. Lings (1983), however, renders the incident thus:

They realized that nothing could be achieved without deception, and they knew that lying was abhorrent to the Prophet; so they went and told him what was in their minds. He said they were free to say whatever would serve their purpose, for deception was legitimate in warfare. (p. 171)

Ka'b was not merely a poet whose verses annoyed Muhammad but a prominent member of the tribe of Tayy which, after Badr, was attempting to form a tribal alliance against Muhammad; 'he urged Quraysh to redeem their honour and take their revenge by mustering an invincible quantity of troops and leading them against Yathrib' (Lings, p. 160). Muir, who was himself involved in espionage, presumably regarded it as a morally justifiable tactic yet he was unwilling to concede that the Ka'b affair was a similar, justifiable, military exercise; instead he saw it as morally reprehensible. Bukhari contains *hadith* on 'What tricks and means of security may be adopted to protect oneself against someone who is expected to be vicious' (52:160 – this includes the killing of Ka'b); and on 'Telling lies in war' (52:158). 'War', said the Prophet, 'is deceit' (52:157). Muir, who was personally involved with espionage, could not see the Ka'b affair as a covert military operation.

It was whilst taking refuge in the Red Fort that Muir 'received and corrected' some pages of his Life; 'all my MSS', he recorded, 'and books of reference have been placed in security from the ravages of our mutineer army, and are inaccessible to me at present' (Postscript to vol. 2, dated 18 July 1857). As soon as Delhi had been retaken, Muir made sure that a manuscript copy of al-Waqidi was retrieved safely (1902: 6). During this period when, I believe, Muir's image of Islam was sealed, his Christian faith was strengthened; throughout the events of 1857–58 he gave house-room to the future Bishop of Lahore, Thomas Valpy French (1825–1881). Writing to his mother, Muir assured her that 'Amid all these distresses we have, I trust, had our hearts stayed upon the consolation that the "Lord reigneth", the same God who is our father reconciled to us in His dear Son, and in Him we seek to confide' (May, 1857; 1902, 1: 32). I must admit, however, that excitement was added to my several tours of Agra's Red Fort; I recognized buildings from Muir's account, and could not but help picturing him, surrounded by the scenes of war, correcting the proofs of his *Life of Mahomet*. Muir's *Records* (1902) also describe his spy network, how loyal Indians (disloyal to others!) carried messages secreted about their persons through 'enemy lines'. Muir, it seems, who accused Muslims of 'deceit', was actually rather familiar with deceit himself!

Ibn Warraq

A more recent writer who addresses both a Western and a Muslim readership, and who wants to influence the views of the latter about their own religion, is Ibn Warraq (a pseudonym) in his *Why I Am Not a Muslim* (1995). Having ceased to regard himself as a Muslim, Ibn Warraq now describes himself as a 'secular humanist who believes all religions are sick men's dreams, false – demonstrably false – and pernicious' (p. xiii). Furthermore, the book is his 'war effort' on the side of 'freedom', against those who oppose this (see p. 360). Ibn Warraq observes:

I doubt whether many Islamic scholars would openly approve of the use I have made of their research and scholarship; thus it is no formality to emphasize that all responsibility for the harsh, final judgements on Islam in this book is mine. (p. xvi)

In his chapter, 'Final Assessment of Muhammad', he fully endorsed Muir's verdict:

Messages from heaven were freely brought down to justify political conduct, in precisely the same manner as to inculcate religious precept. Battles were fought, executions ordered, and territories annexed, under cover of the Almighty's sanction. Nay, even personal indulgences were not only excused but encouraged by the divine approval or command. (p. 347, citing Muir, 1894: 504).

Here we have a Muhammad who 'compromised his principles ... for political gain or power' (p. 349); '[when the sacred months have passed] kill, kill the unbelievers wherever you find them' (Q 9:5) is cited as evidence of 'the constant bloodshed which marked Muhammad's career at Medina' which, says Ibn Warraq, has subsequently been cited by 'Muslim governors, caliphs and viziers ... to justify their killings, lootings and destruction'. This verse has indeed been so used but this is to remove the verse both from the context of what the Qur'an says about war (defensive, or to right a wrong) and from the context of Qur'anic exegesis. Scholars point out that the words 'but if they repent ... leave their way free', contained in the same verse (but not cited by Ibn Warraq), clearly indicate that the 'unbelievers' must have initiated some type of attack against the Muslims. Indeed, the verse probably refers to the existing conflict between the Muslims and their opponents, thus giving Muslims permission to re-engage after the religious truce had ended. Arguably, the Qur'an is ambiguous on 'whether offensive war for the faith, or only defensive war' is permitted. Doner (1991) suggests that the issue is 'really left to the judgement of the exegete' (p. 47). Rahman (1980), however, states that 'Muhammad never fought against peaceful people or those who desire peace ... only against those who continued armed resistance' (p. 279). Non-Muslim images of Muhammad as warlike contrast sharply with many Muslim descriptions. For example Muhammad Ali (1948) says that Muhammad had 'no inclination for war'; the Prophet, he says, 'was peace-loving by nature' (p. 34). Forward (1997) agrees: 'The Prophet was a reluctant warrior' (p. 27).

Muir and Watt contrasted by Ibn Warraq

Muir, says Ibn Warraq, retains a 'robust sense of right and wrong' (p. 96) whilst Watt, for fear of offending Muslim friends and readers, employs 'all sorts of mental gymnastics in an effort to please everyone' (p. 26). He finds Watt's reconstruction of Muhammad's life quite unpalatable, and describes him as 'one of the few western scholars who has unqualified admiration, bordering on worship for Muhammad' (p. 344). I visit Watt below as an example of my third approach. Ibn Warraq's preference for a Crone–Cook type of reconstructed Islam is clearly expressed in his detailed summary of their view (pp. 76–85). He also cites approvingly from S. M. Zwemer (1867–1952), a missionary writer and scholar, that 'Islam is not an invention, but a concoction; there is nothing novel about it except the genius of Muhammad in mixing up old ingredients into

a new panacea for human ills and forcing it down by means of the sword'
(1900: 170).

What seems to infuriate Ibn Warraq more than anything is discussion about
whether Muhammad was sincere or not. His 'sincerity', he says, has no bearing
on 'our moral judgment of his character. One can sincerely hold beliefs that are
false. More important, one can sincerely hold beliefs which are immoral or
not worthy of respect' (p. 347). As I have indicated, much non-Muslim ink
has been spilled on the issue of sincerity. Is it relevant? Ibn Warraq is right to
say that people can be sincerely wrong. Perhaps Muhammad did sincerely
believe that Islam and the Qur'an were from God, but was wrong. However,
I think that his sincerity does matter. If Muhammad was insincere, or sincerely
wrong, Muslims are followers of a fabricated religion which enjoys no link
with the divine. What non-Muslims have to address is Muhammad's claim
that Islam was revealed to him by God. If he was sincerely misguided about
this, then Islam falls with his sincere, but wrong belief. The equation goes:
'No Prophet, No Book; No Book, No Islam'. Of course, people must look at
the evidence and draw their own conclusions. Ibn Warraq is entitled to his
opinion that Islam rests on false premisses. Readers of this book, however, are
equally entitled to decide for themselves whether Muhammad was in some
sense a divinely guided prophet or not – perhaps by judging Islam according
to its fruits, and Muhammad according to his (as Watt suggests, 1988: 1; see
also Phipps, 1996: 245).

The third approach

An example of the third approach, which made a conscious effort to see through
Muslim eyes, was Reginald Bosworth Smith's *Mohammed and Mohammedanism*
(first published in 1874). Unlike Muir, Smith (1839–1908) did not offer his
book as an original contribution to Oriental scholarship but as a serious attempt
to answer profound questions about Muhammad's status. A historian and
classicist by training, he was skilled at delving behind his texts and sources to
uncover hidden bias, fully aware that no history can be divorced from the
historians who record the history. Put bluntly, he wanted at the truth. What
had really motivated Muhammad? Thus he shares with Carlyle and Tor Andrae
(for whom see below) an interest in the psychological dimension. Could either
Muhammad or his religion be dismissed out of hand as having no connection
with God?

How could Islam's continued survival be explained? Others – Voltaire,
Joseph White, Gibbon – had explained it as a human construct. Muir thought
Satan kept it going to continue hampering the spread of Christian truth. Others
thought that Islam's appeal to sexual indulgence attracted men, if not women.
Smith asked, 'Are other explanations possible and do the facts actually support
any of these proposed solutions?' Examining not only the life of Muhammad,
but what travellers and scholars, and some Muslims, say about Islam, Smith
did not see there the immoral, degraded, profligate, worldly Islam of which
Muir wrote, but an enlightened, often egalitarian, highly moral, spiritually
devout Islam. Smith thus attempted to get close to the Islam and the

Muhammad of Muslim faith, something that Muir, despite living in proximity to Muslims and claiming Muslim friends, failed to do. What Smith also attempted, as had Forster and some of the earlier writers to whom I have referred in this survey, was to not try Islam exclusively by Christian standards. Already, notions of cultural relativity were beginning to develop – the idea of universal norms of human behaviour was giving way to the idea that context might dictate appropriate customs.

Evolutionary theory

Evolutionary theory, too, was now very much part of Smith's world-view: the noble savage's sexual code may be better suited to his environment than that of Victorian England. Islam may be better suited to certain climates or contexts than Christianity. However, where Smith really parted company with Muir was that he had expanded his world-view to liberate God from the exclusive strings of Christianity. Whilst Smith thought Christianity a superior religion to any other, he saw no reason why God might not also have revealed himself differently to other races, in a way appropriate to their evolutionary stage. Thus, instead of attempting to replace Islam, Christianity should try to reform it of any defects it might have. We may even find, he suggested, that Muhammad 'has been preparing the way for Christ' (Smith, 1876: 331). Smith did not think that Islam was perfect, although he did not think that Christianity was, either. He had much to say about African Islam; Islam, he argued, was in some respects proving itself better suited to African needs than Christianity was, at least as Africans encountered it; Christianity reached Africans as 'something foreign, alien, dogmatic'. Islam had reached the African 'when he was amidst his own surroundings ... when he was master of himself', and had 'acclimatized itself and taken root in the soil of Africa' (1887: 797).

Islam resulted, too, in some degree of 'moral elevation' (*ibid*.: 798). Aspects of 'Moslem morality', he suggested, may be 'better than our own' (1876: 331). For example, no Christian nation had 'clean hands' in Africa (1887: 805), where racism tainted the missionary effort so much that 'From the lessons he learns every day the Negro unconsciously imbibes the conviction that to be a good man he must be like the white man, not as his equal but as his parasite' (1887: 810; see also 1876: 329). In contrast, the African who converts to Islam discovers an 'energy, a dignity, a self-reliance and a self-respect which is all too rarely found in their pagan or their Christian fellow-countrymen' (1887: 800; this passage was cited by T. W. Arnold in his classic, *The Preaching of Islam*, 1896: 292). Smith constantly, as he put it, 'turned the mirror in upon himself' (1876: xii); in other words, he was willing to allow his study of Islam to interact critically with his own world-view.

The old lecher theory

In writing about Muhammad, Smith asked, 'How do Muslims view their Prophet?' He quickly noticed that Muslims simply do not see in him the traditional defects that Christians have – they do not see his military and political actions and his multiple marriages, for example, as defects. Nor do they view the Qur'an as the disjointed comedy of errors which writers from al-Kindi onwards have described. On the contrary, Muslims think that Christians have too often neglected the affairs of this world for those of the next and have probably been too ascetic in general. Censuring Sprenger for upholding what we might call the 'old lecher' theory of Muhammad, he pointed out how Muslims themselves draw attention to such considerations as the age (53) at which Muhammad had contracted his later marriages, after years of monogamy, and his need to form alliances. Muslims also (Smith noted) argue that the Prophet enjoyed certain extraordinary privileges – pointed out much earlier by Stubbe, Sale, and Forster. Ali (1948: 34) has a similar defence of Muhammad's marriages: 'living … a married life of a monogamous husband up to fifty-four … when called upon to take more women under his shelter, he answered the call of duty'. On the other hand, there are *hadith* (such as B 5:17 cited above) which attest Muhammad's virility – thus Smith's suggestion that Christian pruriency is not necessarily shared by Muslims may present a more convincing case. Parrinder (1996) tells us that Muslims consider licit sex to be God's gift (although stories of illicit sex, including homesexuality, also abound) and that 'Islamic works on sex normally [open] with the praise of God' (p. 167). Women, too, have as much right to enjoy sex as men! Smith also suggested that polygamy and even domestic slavery may be appropriate for some societies (see 1876: 326–30).

Nor could Muhammad be blamed for Islam's so-called obscurantism; Smith cites *hadith* such as 'a learned man is as superior to a worshipper as a full moon to the stars', 'the ink of the learned is as precious as the blood of the martyrs', and 'at the day of decision a special account will be given of the use made of the intellect' to evidence Islam's commitment to intellectual excellence (*ibid.*: 214–16). As for using the sword, Muhammad did so when appropriate, since his religion does not recognize the Christian divide between Church and state. He was, as it were, his own Constantine. Far from regarding Islam's refusal to separate religion from politics as its most fundamental, and ultimately damning weakness, he saw value in this: it enabled Islam to develop a social consciousness which was often denied a Church distinct from the state. Nor was Islam propagated solely by the sword; it had often spread through peaceful evangelism. Anyway, said Smith, Christians can hardly be too self-righteous on this score. In an appendix, he contrasts the 'Comparative Ferocity of Muslim and Christian Religious Wars' and concludes that Muslims have exercised the greater clemency and restraint (see 1876: 220).

A moral declension rejected

On balance, said Smith, Muhammad had improved the moral standards of his people. Smith rejected the idea that a moral declension occurred after the *hijrah* and, instead of negatively contrasting the Madinan with the Makkan years (as had Gibbon, Irving, Muir), he spoke of a 'substantial unity'. The real wonder, he suggested, is 'not how much but how little, under different circumstances, Mohammed differed from himself' (1876: 144). Thus,

In the shepherd of the desert, in the Syrian trader, in the solitary of Mount Hira, in the reformer in the minority of one, in the exile of Medina, in the acknowledged conqueror, in the equal of the Persian Chosroes and the Greek Heraclius, we can still trace a substantial unity. (1876: 144)

Instead of being a self-deluded impostor, or a satanically inspired Antichrist, Muhammad was sincere. In fact, since Islam shared so much in common with Christianity, had Satan inspired it he would have actually defeated himself. Smith accepted Muhammad as a prophet inspired by God:

he claimed for himself that title only with which he had begun, and which the highest philosophy and the truest Christianity will one day, I venture to believe, agree in yielding to him – that of a Prophet, a very Prophet of God. (1876: 344)

Exactly how he related Muhammad's prophethood to Christ as God's final self-disclosure remains unclear. However, it is likely that he saw no reason why God could not inspire men and women after Christ. Whilst Smith's Muhammad was the author of the Qur'an, which does not reflect Muslim understanding, his Muhammad *was* inspired. For Smith, inspiration was a universal phenomenon. He wrote:

in the broadest sense of the word [inspiration] is to be found in all the greatest thoughts of men and nations, for the workings of God are everywhere, and the spirits of men and nations are moulded by Him to bring about His purposes of love. (1876: xvi)

Here, he is close to Carlyle's view of inspiration and certainly to Matthew Arnold (1822–88) who, with such distinguished scholars as Charles Darwin and A. P. Stanley, was in Smith's audience at the Royal Institution when the lectures on which the book was based were originally presented.

Turning the mirror in upon himself

Points of debate between Smith's Islam and Christianity obviously remain: 'What should Muslims think of Christ?', for example. Smith probably thought this question comparatively insignificant; salvation, for him, did not depend on what you believe about Christ. It depended more on whether you lived his ethic. Smith did think that Muhammad was more Moses-like than Christ-like; thus he may have been an Old Testament-type prophet, one who, to cite Mar Timothy, 'walked in the path of the prophets' but out of chronological sequence. Whilst this might baffle men, it does not baffle a God who stands outside time. Kenneth Cragg (1984) has similarly distinguished 'cultic' and 'chronological' time: 'Prophetic meanings', he says, 'that might seem retrogressive by simple time criteria may be progressive by those of place and culture' (p. 92). Smith's view is thus reminiscent of Islam's traditional view of Christianity as imperfect but partially true, and therefore tolerable.

As I have said, neither Smith's Islam nor his Muhammad mirrors a Muslim's in all aspects, yet his effort to 'do justice to what ... has been good in Mohammed's influence on the world' (1874: xx) and his desire to 'turn the mirror in upon himself', to judge and treat others 'as we would wish to be judged and treated' represents a genuine attempt to do justice to the faith in people's hearts (p. xii). Smith's effort was rewarded with Muslim applause. Sayyid Ameer Ali wrote, 'Your book has not only confirmed me in my own faith but it has given me a far higher idea of Christianity' (cited in Grogan, 1908: 148). On Smith's death, the Muslims of Sierra Leone wrote about 'the deep feelings of sorrow with which [we have] learned of the death of [Smith] who has laboured so long and so successfully in the cause of the Holy Religion they profess' (Grogan, 1908: 156–7; see also p. 141). Smith's remarks on Muhammad are still cited in modern Muslim writing as an example of a non-Muslim who 'took a correct view'. For instance, on 6 December 1996 I down-loaded from the Internet a set of quotations on Muhammad; amongst them was Smith's

he was Pope without the pope's pretensions, and Caesar without the legions of Caesar ... If ever a man had the right to say he ruled by a divine right, it was Muhammad. ... He cared not for the trappings of power. The simplicity of his private life was in keeping with his public life. (1876: 341; cited on 'Ismaili Web Muhammad No 1', http://www.txnet.net/~graphics/ismaillim.html)

(Smith is incorrectly designated 'Revd'; he actually defended 'lay' teaching and was a member of the Anglican House of Laymen in the Representative Church Council at Westminster.)

Christian reaction was somewhat mixed; some critics said that Smith's lack of experience of Islamic society and Arabic scholarship disqualified him from addressing Islam. Readers ought instead to trust the much more expert judgement of Sir William Muir, who had 'seen the practical working of Islamism in India' (see Bennett, 1992: 95–6). Others praised his book: although written from a distance it yet penetrated to the 'true meaning of the facts' and grasped 'the complete character of the great man whose life they mark out, like the stones of a grand but intricate mosaic' (Lane-Poole, 1874: 6623). E. H. Palmer (1840–82) wrote: 'The author is not an orientalist in the technical sense of the word, but he has made such good use of the ample materials available ... that his treatment ... loses nothing in accuracy'. Palmer himself (Cambridge's Almoner Professor of Arabic) travelled in Arabia disguised as a Muslim, Abdullah Effendi; he was eventually killed there whilst on a secret mission. Buaben (1996) says that 'linguistic skill alone does not guarantee objectivity' (p. 312); lacking 'linguistic skill', Smith arguably achieved a greater degree of objectivity than did many who possessed 'linguistic skill'.

Smith gained several Muslim friends as a result of writing the book; his Harrow students were much taken by the many 'coloured guests' who visited their school master: 'we took them all for princes, and gazed on them with mingled mockery and awe' (*The Harovian* XXI, 1908, p. 82). It was also through the book that he met the remarkable African scholar, Edward Wilmot Blyden (1832–1912), who considered all Smith's writings as delivering a severe blow at the 'causes of war, aggression, cruelty and pride of race'. Smith wrote not just to fill blanks in 'religious or historical literature' but 'for high moral ends' (1967: 287).

Tor Andrae (1885–1946)

Another example of my third approach, in many respects very similar to Smith, is the outstanding scholarly contribution of the Swedish academic and bishop, Tor Andrae, an Arabist and student of religious experience. Relatively little of Andrae's work has been translated into English but, as Almond (1989) comments 'more sophisticated analysis of Muhammad's experience [dates] at least from Tor Andrae's Mohammed' (pp. 28–9). He was initially encouraged to turn to the life of the Prophet by his own professor, Nathan Söderblom (1866–1931) and was especially interested in attempting to understand 'the problem of Muhammad's response to the divine call that made him a prophet' (Schimmel, 1987: 271). His interest in religious psychology is clearly evident in his *The Psychology of Mysticism* (1926) and *Mohammed: The Man and His Faith* (ET 1936). Distinguishing between two types of mystical inspiration, the auditory and the visual, he classed Muhammad amongst the former, and, comparing reports of Muhammad's 'inspiration' with similar accounts, concluded that these were 'without a doubt psychologically possible' (1936: 66). Andrae appears to have regarded religious experience as a universal phenomenon, and quite often drew comparisons between aspects of Muhammad's life and similar phenomena elsewhere. For example, 'the conception of a spirit which literally pounces upon the inspired man, throwing him to the ground and conquering his human obstinacy, is found among various peoples' (p. 59).

Here, Rodinson seems to build on Andrae; he also draws attention to the interesting similarity between the 'cleaning of the heart' incident, and aspects of Shamanism; 'shamans of north and central Asia ... feel ... at the moment of their initiation ... that a spirit has taken away their internal organs and replaced them with fresh ones' (Rodinson, 1961: 56). Rodinson, like Andrae, discusses Muhammad within the context of mystical experience generally; see pp. 74–81, where he points out some common elements between Muhammad's experience and that of other mystics – ascetic temperament, period of bareness between Muhammad's first and later revelations. My colleague, Dr Mark Fox, has pointed out how well Muhammad's experience on Mt Hira (see Rodinson, p. 71) fits Rudolf Otto's idea of the Holy as that before which we are filled with dread, awe and a deep and profound sense of mystery. Whilst this leaves open the question of the origin or cause of such experiences, it treats Muhammad's as an example of a universal phenomenon. On the other hand, although this treatment may reduce Muhammad's religious experience to something less than unique, Andrae unambiguously accepts Muhammad's sincerity and the genuineness of his inspiration:

Was Mohammed's inspiration genuine? Did he speak in entire good faith? Formerly men thought that his character revealed a certain premeditation, a calculating cleverness, a preference for the sly methods of intrigue which could hardly be reconciled with an honourable character. Was he not dominated from the very beginning, when he first appeared as the Prophet of his People, by ambition and the greed for power? That Mohammed acted in good faith can hardly be disputed by anyone who knows the psychology of inspiration. (pp. 62–3; see also p. 253, 'he was a man of moral sincerity')

Thus Andrae saw himself and the historical Muhammad as occupants of the same world, not of different worlds – a world in which human experiences could be compared across ages and between cultures. He was personally convinced that Islam had been incorrectly maligned 'as a purely legalist religion of military uniformity'; instead, it knew 'the secret of divine grace very well' (Schimmel, 1987: 272). He did, however, think that Muhammad tended to 'take advantage of subterfuge' and, perhaps uncharacteristically, he contrasted this negatively with 'the ideals of manliness of the Nordic races' (p. 201).

Like Smith, Andrae thought it wrong to polarize Muhammad at Makkah as religious reformer, and Muhammad after the *hijrah* as empire builder, and argued for continuity, thus rejecting as false

the prevailing idea that Mohammed appeared in Mecca only as a pious messenger, with a purely religious programme, and without any associated political and social aims, and that it was entirely owing to the fact that circumstances in Medina delivered the political power into his hands that he suddenly assumed the role of a theocratic ruler and laid claim to political authority. (p. 186)

Instead, from start to finish Muhammad had conceived of a 'religious community' which was also 'a social and a political organism' (p. 186). Andrae, however, did not think that Muhammad's conduct was altogether beyond criticism and singled out some common incidents as evidence of moral lapses – such as the 'satanic verses' affair (see pp. 21–9) and the ordered execution of several enemies, especially of the Jewish poet, Ka'b ibn al-Ashraf (pp. 207f; I.I. pp. 364–9; B 59:14). Andrae's treatment of the Ka'b affair is not uncritical; he chides Muhammad for meting out death sentences to his enemies. On the other hand, he comments that the continued opposition of a man such as Ka'b represented a major obstacle to Islam; those responsible for 'political satire' posed a threat which 'for a man like Mohammed, whose success depended to a large extent upon the esteem which he could win, a malicious satirical composition could be more dangerous than a lost battle' (p. 207). Andrae did not identify Ka'b as a serious political contender, only as a bothersome poet. Yet his treatment is more balanced than Muir's.

The Zaid/Zainab affair

Andrae also discusses the Zaid/Zainab affair at some length (pp. 214–17) but on this issue shares Smith's view that Muslims themselves do not appear to see anything reprehensible about the Prophet's conduct, and comments that Zaid 'still enjoyed the full confidence of the prophet and appears to have merited it in every way' (p. 217). Citing the *hadith* (attributed to 'A'isha), 'Truly, thy Lord makes haste to do thy pleasure' (see also my discussion of Rushdie in the Conclusion), he wrote: 'A tradition which does not censor such statements must apparently possess a high degree of historical trustworthiness. The fact that they were preserved proves also that Mohammed's conduct in this affair was not regarded as a serious error' (p. 216). Andrae commends Muhammad for forgiving many of those he earlier condemned, especially after the triumphant entry into Makkah. 'It is rare', he wrote, 'that a victor has exploited his victory with greater self-restraint and forbearance' (pp. 233–4; all opponents of the Prophet were given an amnesty when Makkah fell except for about a dozen; all but four of these were eventually pardoned). Andrae also commented: 'The actions which seem to cast a shadow upon Mohammed's character are often difficult to interpret, and we are always uncertain whether we have understood and evaluated him correctly' (p. 184).

Andrae certainly tried to give credence to Muslim interpretations of some of the events he saw as moral lapses, but it seems that his own conviction that Christianity is the 'most perfect religion', and Christ the 'perfect moral ideal' (p. 269) precluded him from always conceding the Muslim viewpoint. For example, whilst aware of the Muslim view that the so-called 'satanic verses', which have Muhammad recognizing three goddesses, al-Lat, al-Uzza and Manat as genuine intercessors ('high-flying cranes whose intercession is to be hoped for'), were Satan's attempt to substitute true inspiration – what is now recorded at Q 53:19–23: 'they are but names' – with false (implied by Qur'an 22:52), he finds this unconvincing. Instead he sees the 'satanic verses affair' as an example of Muhammad attempting to 'make a place for the three goddesses in his religious system' (p. 21). Sayyid Ahmed Khan, responding to Muir's similar treatment of the affair (see Muir, 1894: 79–84), dismissed the sources here as 'unsound'; it is 'only in the category of *mursal*' and 'lacks a Companion in the *isnad*' (see Troll, 1978: 136). Muir also dismissed the Muslim explanation. The 'satanic verses' are found in Tabari and Ibn Sa'd but not in the earlier Ibn Ishaq, although Ibn Hisham may have edited them out. Buaben (1996) draws our attention to a review of Andrae by Muhammad Marmaduke Pickthall (1875–1936), the distinguished translator of the Qur'an, who identified 'two voices' in Andrae's work: 'one suave and juridical, the other harsh and fanatical ... He rules out the idea of deliberate imposture, yet on many pages he seems to write of the Qur'an as the work of the man Muhammad' (Buaben, 1996: 138). This is the very impasse to which I return in my final chapter.

Andrae may not have written primarily for Muslims but neither was he unaware that Muslims might read what he wrote; he was fascinated by the 'extent to which the difference between the believer and the non-believer exists throughout history', and touched on this in his inaugural lecture at Stockholm (Schimmel, 1987: 272). Certainly, Theophil Menzel, Andrae's English translator, thought that the 'work will appeal to students of the history of religion, lovers of biography and adherents of Islam' (Introduction to Andrae, 1936: 5). Andrae's final estimate of Muhammad, however – that we 'are not doing the Prophet of Islam an injustice when we conclude that his moral personality does not stand upon the same level with his religious achievements' (p. 269) – prompts Daniel's comment in the original version of *Islam and the West* that this conclusion to an otherwise 'very balanced judgement' suggests that 'it may well be argued that such criticism is essential to a Christian position' (1960 edn: 288). Andrae commented that Christians inevitably 'compare Mohammed with the unsurpassed and exalted figure whom we meet in the Gospels', against which measure, he asked rhetorically, 'what personality is not found wanting?' (p. 269). Andrae thought, too, that the Muhammad of Muslim faith, Muhammad as 'perfect man', was a development which went beyond what could be properly claimed of the Muhammad of history. 'It is', he wrote, 'a likeable characteristic of Mohammed that he never claimed perfection or infallibility but always admitted that he was guilty of short-comings and mistakes like other men' (p. 252). He cited as evidence Q 48:2, 'That Allah may forgive thee [Muhammad] of thy sin which is past and that which is to come'. He suggested that the 'perfect man' Muhammad (the Muhammad who is incapable of sinning) resulted from the Muslim desire to represent their Prophet as the equivalent of the Christian Christ. Thus Muslims invested the historical Muhammad with Christ-like qualities as they tried to 'exalt him' to the status of 'the perfect moral ideal' (p. 269). Nonetheless, in paying attention to the 'Muhammad of faith' in his writing, Andrae was probably the first European scholar to 'specifically ... depict Muhammad's role in Islamic piety (Schimmel, 1985: 7).

William Montgomery Watt

I have made extensive use in this book of Watt's work on the biography of the Prophet. I have drawn particular attention to his view that critical scholarship can reconstruct a largely reliable life of Muhammad, which contrasts sharply with the approach of Cook and Crone, and of Ibn Warraq, discussed above. In many respects, Watt's work resembles Reginald Bosworth Smith's. Unlike Smith, however, Watt is an accomplished Arabist. Watt's account of the Prophet, minus miracles and much of the supernatural colouring, resembles in broad outline the standard Muslim accounts. Like Smith, he tends to see Islam as valid for its own 'culture': 'Since the religions originated in different social cultures, allowance must be made for the possibility that each has a task assigned to it in God's purposes' (Watt, 1995a: 7). There is also some similarity with Smith when Watt speaks about Islam or the religion of Muhammad as 'A form of the religion of Abraham – a form, too, well suited to the outlook of men whose way of life was closer to Abraham than that of the bulk of Jews and Christians' (Watt, 1961: 118). Like Smith, Watt believes that Muhammad and Islam have often been traduced by Western writers, and in his own academic career set out to 'correct the false and negative images' of them 'current in the West' (1995b: 282).

A historical–anthropological approach

Influenced from an early period by Thomas Carlyle's psychological portrait of Muhammad (see Watt's 1955 *Hibbert Journal* article), Watt is also interested in trying to understand the inner workings of Muhammad's mind. Thus, as he writes, he attempts to take his readers into Muhammad's confidence as the prophet thinks through his options. Norman Daniel (1993) comments: 'though [Watt's work] does not revolutionize the Christian assessment of the Prophet, [it changes] the emphasis, so that the reader, through the historico-anthropological approach, is drawn into and allowed to some extent to share the Muslim awareness of the Prophet' (p. 330). It is only when Christians try to see Muhammad through Muslim eyes, asking 'How do Muslims view these events in the prophet's life?' or 'this verse in the Qur'an?' that real dialogue becomes possible. Thus Watt asks 'In what sense can we call Muhammad a Prophet?', and offers some answers. Like Smith, Watt rejects the 'moral decline theory' and the 'old lecher theory' (addressing the Zaid/Zainab affair in some detail; see 1956: 329–32) and the 'pathological theory' (1953: 336). However, his ten-page discussion of the 'satanic verses' affair (1953: 101f) interprets this as evidence that Muhammad's monotheistic stance was not then fully established, but in process. Positively, this clears Muhammad of any charge of 'compromise'. If his doctrine of God was still being formulated, then the affair tells us something about how he arrived at his strict monotheistic position. Muslims, though, believe that Muhammad was never anything but a worshipper of the one God, Allah.

Muhammad demands a theological appraisal

In his *Muhammad: Prophet and Statesman* (1961),Watt points out that 'as the founder of a world-religion Muhammad demands a theological judgement'. Similarly, Daniel (1993) states: 'it is essential for Christians to see Muhammad as a holy figure; to see him, that is, as Muslims see him … If they do not do so, they cut themselves off from Muslims'; they may not accept all that Muslims believe about Muhammad, but they ought to try to 'see things as if they did'(p. 336). 'If there is this sympathetic approach … it becomes', says Daniel, 'possible to pass into and share the state of mind of Muslims in many ages' (*ibid.*). This was the agenda which Watt set for himself in his life-long engagement with the Muslim mind. Watt's own view is that Muhammad was inspired by ideas that came from 'below the threshold of consciousness', which, he says, 'for the Christian, implies some connection with God':

> He was a man in whom creative imagination worked at deep levels and produced ideas relevant to the central questions of human existence, so that his religion has a widespread appeal. Not all the ideas he proclaimed are true and sound but by God's grace he has been enabled to provide millions of men with a better religion than they had before. (1961: 240)

Watt also argues that:

In dialogue with Muslims it is ... important that Christians should reject the distortions of the medieval image of Islam and should develop a positive appreciation of its values. This involves accepting Muhammad as a religious leader through whom God has worked, and that is tantamount to holding that he is in some sense a prophet. (1991: 148).

Elsewhere, Watt states quite unambiguously: 'I consider that Muhammad was truly a prophet, and think that we Christians should admit this' (Watt, 1988: 1); whilst in a 1993 article, he identifies Muhammad as a type of Old Testament prophet: 'Personally I hold that we must accept Muhammad as a prophet who was similar to the Old Testament prophets' (p. 245). However, whilst their task had been to call the Hebrew people back to obedience, Muhammad's was to 'bring knowledge of God to people without such knowledge'. Watt (1995b) tells us that he was at first reluctant to speak of Muhammad 'as a Prophet' lest Muslims misunderstand this as meaning that he also accepts 'that everything in the Qur'an was finally and absolutely true' (p. 283). This understanding of what motivated Muhammad does not tally with a Muslim view, but nor does it portray Muhammad as other than a sincere and successful religious leader.

Muslims: an invitation to re-think 'Muhammadology'

Watt combines the Arabic and textual scholarship of a Muir with the theological intent of a Smith to re-evaluate Christian understanding of Muhammad. Muir concluded his career as Principal of Edinburgh University; Watt was Head of Arabic and Islamic Studies at Edinburgh 1947–79. He may, though, be a better historian than theologian (in fact, he describes his theological education as a 'crash course', 1995b: 281). Accepting Muhammad as a type of Old Testament prophet, commissioned to preach to those without knowledge of God, leaves open for Christians at least the questions, 'What is Muhammad's relationship with Christ?', and 'What ought to be the nature of Christian–Muslim relations?' He believes, I think, that both Christianity and Islam are valid salvific systems of belief which ought to find ways of peacefully co-existing, perhaps as suggested by Q 5:48, 'for each we have appointed a divine law and a traced out way. Had Allah willed He could have made you one community ... so vie with each other in good works ... and He will inform you of that about which you differ.' Muslims, says Watt, would have to 'reinterpret their conception of the finality of Islam and Muhammad's being the last prophet' (1991: 149). Do Christians, then, need to rethink their view that salvation is exclusively channelled through faith in Christ? Watt says yes, and asks Christians to rethink the language they use to speak about Jesus as God and about the Trinity (to make it intelligible to more than a few!). Christians, he says, should stress Jesus' humanity (1991: 146) yet Watt still seems to demand more from Muslims than he does from Christians; for example, he writes:

doubtless a prophet or religious leader has to have many good qualities, but he does not need to be perfect in all respects; and the same holds true for transmitters of religious truth. God's use of imperfect human instruments appears to be one of the objective historical facts which many Muslims are unwilling to accept. (1991: 150)

Implying thus that Muhammad was 'not perfect', Watt asks Muslims to re-visit their 'Muhammadology' but omits to point out that the fundamental Christian dogma of Jesus' sinlessness might equally demand that Christians revisit their Christology. Yet, for most Christians, Jesus Christ's 'perfection' is non-negotiable, just as Muhammad's is for most Muslims. In my conclusion, I shall offer an alternative to Watt's call for Muslims to revise their traditional beliefs, which avoids, I believe, the need to demand that Christians also do the same.

Muslim response

Whilst it would be an exaggeration to claim that Muslims have greeted Watt's work with unanimous praise, many have studied under him at Edinburgh, whilst others express appreciation for his attempts to correct erroneous views of the Prophet. For example, Buaben (1996) cites Syed Ali Razi Naqvi's description of Watt as 'One of the most prominent modern biographers of the holy prophet' and adds: 'Considering that this statement, together with others which see Watt as rebutting the harsh criticisms of his fellow Western writers, was made in a paper read at the national Seerat conference held in Islamabad, it demonstrates the regard in which Watt is held among some Muslim scholars' (p. 157; see Buaben's much more detailed discussion of Watt in chapter 5 of his book). Buaben, however, says that Watt too often prefers a political over a theological interpretation of Muhammad's motives; 'Watt's way', he writes, 'of playing down the spiritual aspects of Muhammad's life ... comes up in his discussion on the battles that the Muslims took part in. He often assigns secular reasons for the outcome of such confrontations' (p. 323).

Buaben also points out that whilst Watt rejects the 'dominant western theory that the Qur'an is Muhammad's own composition' (p. 322) he certainly does not believe, and states this clearly, that everything Muhammad said was from God. The Qur'an contains material which can be regarded as 'revelatory' alongside much that was the product of Muhammad's environment, including 'mistaken ideas about Christian and Jewish beliefs' (p. 209). The problem is that Watt contradicts himself; if Muhammad did not compose this material and a divine source is also rejected, then how did it find its way into the Qur'an? What we see, suggests Buaben, is the historian struggling with the theologian; Guillaume has argued that the 'historian's proper position is that the Qur'an is indeed Muhammad's own composition' (see Buaben, p. 318). What we also see is a Christian who, although admitting that God might sometimes override human conscience (see Buaben, p. 209), cannot accept that the Qur'an was exclusively so revealed. Again, the question 'What is the relationship between Prophet and Book?' emerges as problematical for the outsider scholar. Watt (1988) invites Muslims to rethink the 'human element in revelation' (p. 82)

Buaben's critique

Whilst I have represented Watt as more positive than many other non-Muslims about the value of the early Islamic material, Buaben offers a less sanguine opinion. 'One of Watt's greatest faults', he writes, 'is in casting doubt on many of the classical traditions, attributing less credit to contemporary Islamic scholarship and relying often on his own conjectures' (1996: 321). Watt appears to share with many non-Muslims the view that 'Islamic thought lost its flexibility after the fourth century and became petrified' (1988: 141; see Küng, 1997: 94: 'Islam – in comparison to the European development – also seems to many Muslims to be trapped in its medieval paradigm. ... It faces a tremendous leap from the Middle Ages, through modernity to post-modernity'). This might imply that modern interpretations of Islam cannot have equal status with classical ones, although Watt does deal sympathetically with what he calls the 'liberal search for a new identity' (1988: 62–70). Buaben, however, judges this to be a rather limited treatment (p. 321). As had Forster, Watt acknowledges Europe's intellectual 'debt to the Arab and Islamic world' which it has unjustly 'belittled', exaggerating 'its dependence on its Greek and Roman heritage' (1972: 84). Watt goes on to express doubt that Muslims will prove able to extract from Muhammad 'moral principles' which can contribute positively to a global ethic, 'the one morality of the future'; 'I will not conceal my personal view that Muslims are unlikely to be successful in their attempt to influence world opinion, at least in the sphere of morals' (1956: 334). He probably did not intend this but he sounds here very much like a Muir, harping on about Islam's moral bankruptcy and inability to change for the better.

Watt may also be over-confident that the so called 'historical method' can in and of itself guarantee objectivity; 'hostility', he argues, has been 'due to personal attitudes of ... writers and not to scientific historical research.' 'On the contrary', he continues, 'these methods are essentially neutral to Islam, Christianity and other religions' (1976: 72). Thus by applying the scientific method a scholar of the biographical sources can arrive at 'the truth' about Muhammad (see Buaben, p. 191). What remains problematical, though, is 'Whose truth?' – both Buaben and I argue that careful, scientific scholarship of the sources does not of itself lead to an insider-like view of the Prophet unless the writer is predisposed towards this view. Even when the outsider is, like Watt, open to Muslim voices, he or she may still paint a different picture of Muhammad. Nevertheless, in my view Watt's work results from a genuine effort, from 'outside Islam', to understand the religious dimension of Muhammad's life and work, even if the picture painted does not fully replicate a Muslim one. Buaben says that the issue for him is not, 'Has he become a Muslim?', but has his 'expertise [led] to a fairer assessment of the Prophet?'

(p. 312). The problem I have with this statement, however, is this: what objective, neutral criterion is there with which to judge the fairness of any assessment if, as I suspect, all our assessments (insider and outsider) involve interpretations based on the theoretical stances we adopt?

Conclusion

In these two chapters surveying non-Muslim accounts of Muhammad, I have identified what could be regarded as a movement towards acceptance of Muhammad as sincere and moral, and not deluded or worse. Not all early Eastern writers, I suggested, were totally negative towards Muhammad: he was not without a measure of virtue. However, they singled out incidents in his life as points for criticism without stopping to ask how Muslims interpreted these supposed defects. This legacy passed quickly into the Christian mindset, so that even when a more holistic view of Muhammad's life emerged, a writer such as Muir could still single out the incidents which John of Damascus, the writer of the *Risalah*, Bar Hebraeus and countless others had done centuries before. He thus dismissed the *mi'raj* as 'a congenial theme to which tradition has given loose rein to pious and excited imagination' (1894: 118), without attempting to understand its importance for Muslim thought. He made no attempt to understand what Muhammad's combined roles as prophet and ruler implied, seeing his political and military involvement as evidence enough that his religious claims were invalid. Indeed, it was Muhammad's combination of the sacred and the temporal that doomed Muslim states to remain 'in a backward and in some respects barbarous state' (1891: 599).

Writers towards the end of the nineteenth century, who had access to all the best sources, and who were open to much that they thought 'good' in Muhammad, still concluded that there was an 'indelible stain' on his moral character. Thomas Patrick Hughes (1838–1911), author of the *Dictionary of Islam* (1885), an erudite, scholarly and still very useful volume (revised editions have been published by Muslim scholars), comments: 'The best defenders of the Arabian Prophet are obliged to admit that the matter of Zainab, the wife of Zaid, and again, of Mary the Coptic slave, are an "indelible stain" upon his memory' (p. 398). I also suggested that personal contact with Muslims, often within the Muslim world itself (in Muir's case in India, or in Ricoldo's case, in Iraq) did not necessarily result in Christians trying to see Muhammad through Muslim eyes. The martyrs of Cordoba, for example, preferred a Latin text to Muslim accounts, which must have been easily available had they wanted them. Willingness to give credence to Muslim voices and Muslim accounts only emerges when predisposition to find good in Islam begins to commend itself – probably because neither Islam nor Muslims seem totally bad. Early interest in trying to understand the psychological dimension of the prophet, evidenced by Carlyle, may also have assisted the process towards interest in the Muslim mindset. On the other hand, it also provided tools to explain away Muhammad's experiences as the result of some type of psychological malady – a disturbed mind, undergoing a personal crisis, results in imaginary, hallucinatory 'religious dreams'. Or, given to some form of fit, or trance, Muhammad was especially vulnerable to self-delusion. Much can be made, psychologically, of his orphaned youth and his habit of meditating alone on Mt Hira.

Recent work by neuro-psychologist Michael Persinger has isolated the 'temporal lobe' as a source of 'religious (mystical and near-death) experiences'; he suggests that seismic activity sets off atmospheric reactions which in turn stimulate unusual activity in the lobe (see Cotton, 1995). Thus an experience such as Muhammad's might be explained away biologically; if so, it was entirely internal to Muhammad, enjoying no connection with any external, God-type reality. Of course, such a chain of natural occurrences would still require a first cause or mover, to use the language of Islamic philosophy. Similarly, work on what we might call the 'charismatic phenomenon' has attempted to produce a psychological profile of the typical charismatic (see the Introduction to Storr, 1996; Storr uses the term 'guru'). These profiles can then be applied to Muhammad. Indeed, Rodinson tends to depict Muhammad as a typical charismatic: experiencing personal crises, an orphan, discontented with the ethic of his day, taunted as childless (*Abtar*, 'mutilated'; see Rodinson, 1961: 54) – 'all these things', he says, 'were capable of creating a personality thirsting to turn the tables in each particular' (p. 56). The charismatic's claim to be 'called', to receive special communication from God, gives him or her a privileged status. This may even entitle them to 'engage in sexual behaviour which would be condemned ... in an ordinary person' (Storr, 1996: xvi). This special authority invites unquestioned acceptance or total rejection. Charismatics are 'intolerant of criticism ... and anti-democratic, even if they pay lip-service to democracy' (Storr, p. xiii). Again, this places Muhammad within the context of a universal (though comparatively rare) human phenomenon. Storr (1996) does not actually say much about Muhammad in his fascinating study of 'gurus'. What he does say, however, reflects some of the criticisms encountered in this survey: 'Muhammad's injunctions concerning legal punishment and the treatment of women, as recorded in the Koran, are repugnant to modern Western ideas' (p. xii).

The details, however, of the Muhammad reality may not actually fit the profile very well. For example, whilst Muhammad was obviously not unaffected by his orphaned upbringing, the result may have been beneficial – a burning compassion towards widows, orphans and the poor, the *mustad'afun*. According to tradition, too, Arab children were reared by their nurses, often in the desert; his was Halima, who continued to visit him even after his marriage to Khadijah. Muir (1894) describes Muhammad's tenderness towards her, spreading out 'his mantle for her to sit upon – a token of especial respect' (p. 7). His childlessness, too, may have had certain advantages; Q 33:40, 'Muhammad is not the father of any of you, but the Seal of the Prophets', suggests that Muhammad, as the Prophet and divine messenger, was free from the claim of family loyalties which might have resulted in favouritism, in unfair application of *adl* (justice). What may have been a weakness was thus turned into a strength.

Muslims are unlikely to be offended by Muhammad's identification as a charismatic (Siddiqi writes of Muhammad's 'spiritual charisma', 1993: 3–4); they will, however, find an explanation of his career which reduces it to that of a charismatic theologically inadequate. Sociological, psychological and other approaches may well help us to understand more about Muhammad and are therefore useful research tools. However, if these approaches are unwilling to consider a theological dimension for Muhammad's career, alongside others, they will move away from a Muslim view. Also, if the standard account of Muhammad's life is rejected, attempts to apply psychological insight to him become somewhat fanciful (as Julian Baldick has argued in Clark, 1990).

Progress?

In some of the accounts surveyed I detected a gradual movement away from imposing Christian concepts on Muhammad (asking why he was not raised from the dead, for example) towards a willingness to at least listen to Muslim views. This willingness to listen to Muslims begins to see them as occupants of the same world, not of different worlds. The real difference, then, between those non-Muslims who make of Muhammad an impostor, an opportunist, a pseudo-prophet or worse, and those who see him as genuine, sincere and worthy of respect, is ideological premiss. A priori assumptions – for example about difference or superiority – more so than encounter, are powerful factors in determining non-Muslim assessments of Muhammad. Of course, I have also discussed some radically different assessments of the historical material – ranging from Crone's view that it is almost wholly apocryphal to the view that critical scrutiny can reconstruct a more or less reliable biography of a life that was lived, roughly, when Muslims say it was. Apart from noting that these divergent views exist, and inviting readers to draw their own conclusion, it is impossible to adjudicate between them. Clearly, assumptions (or even scholarly opinion) about the historicity and reliability of the texts themselves play no little part in how we choose to reply to the question, 'What think ye of Muhammad?'

Part Three

5 Muhammad's Significance in Muslim Life and Thought

It is not unusual for a religious tradition to continue to think about and develop ideas about the theological significance of its seminal figures after they have died (or entered another dimension of existence). These ideas, according to the tradition's self-understanding, will be rooted in its foundation documents, or teachings, even if they appear to transcend what these say about the figure concerned. For example, Christian understanding about the person and work of Christ and the relationship between Christ and God is believed to build on what the biblical record says about this, yet few Christians would claim that everything they believe to be true about Jesus is to be found explicitly in their scriptures. As previously noted, a popular view amongst non-Muslim scholars of Islam is that Muhammad developed a significance and an authority after his death which went far beyond what he had claimed about himself. I also discussed the view that Muhammad was of relatively little significance at all within the life of the early Muslim community until, for political purposes, his *sunnah* was posthumously invested with authority. I have indicated my own difficulty with this theory; it seems to me to be almost beyond belief that the majority of Muslims would have suddenly conceded authority to a legacy which, according to this view, was largely unknown (and actually fictitious) when, presumably, this would have radically altered their way of life, habits, customs and practices. The view, too, that Muhammad exercised relatively little authority is dependent on establishing that others (the early Khalifs) exercised considerable authority, yet the basis of this authority is not explained.

Personally, I incline towards the Muslim view that, from the Madinan period onwards, Muhammad's *sunnah* carried authority, was preserved in the Companions' memories, and eventually recorded by the traditionalists. My position is therefore in broad sympathy with the Muslim version, rather than with the posthumous view of Muhammad's authority advanced by Goldziher, Schacht, Coulson, Crone and others. However, there was debate within early Islam about how the community should be governed following Muhammad's death, as there is debate about this today. Not unrelated to the question of Muhammad's posthumous authority, this debate was also about the scope of any powers vested in the community's leaders. To introduce this debate, I shall first discuss the Muslim concept of 'leadership' ('*khilafat*'). I also explore Muslim understanding of 'prophethood'. Thus this chapter begins with a general introduction to 'leadership' in Islamic thought, then explores how the earliest controversy in Islam, over the question of leadership after Muhammad's death, resulted in its two tendencies or schools, the Sunni and the Shi'a. In dealing with this historical material, the questions 'What happened to Muhammad's community after his death?' and 'What significance did his legacy continue to play within the affairs of the Muslim people?' might usefully be kept in mind.

I am indebted to a number of scholars here. Amongst the texts which I found especially useful are Charles Lindholm's *The Islamic Middle East* (1996), by an 'outsider' scholar, and Rafiq Zakaria's *The Struggle Within Islam* (1988), by an 'insider' scholar. Readers interested in understanding more about some recent events in the Middle East which I have not discussed in this chapter, such as the Iran–Iraq war (1980–88) and the Gulf War (1991), will find Fred Halliday's *Islam and the Myth of Confrontation* (1996) extremely rewarding and informative. Halliday's analysis, written from an international relations perspective, is balanced and fair. He discusses events within their wider political and economic context. I commend his analysis of the Iranian revolution (pp. 42–75). Next, I explore Muhammad's significance within Sufi and popular Islam. Finally, I discuss the thinking about Muhammad within Islamic theological and philosophical discourse, including political philosophy. The question, 'Does this go beyond what can be Qur'anically justified?' will be addressed as part of this process of inquiry. I shall incline towards the view that, although the full-blown sophisticated expression of Muslim philosophical thought on Muhammad cannot be found in the Qur'an, it nevertheless represents an authentic construct. This opinion follows that of Annemarie Schimmel (1985), who judges that the 'perfect man' and 'exemplar of humanity par excellence' Muhammad of Muslim piety are a 'logical development of the Koranic *uswa hasana*' (p. 235). Schimmel's study of 'the development of the Prophet, and its reflections in literature, especially poetry' is a much more detailed study of this aspect of the Muhammad phenomenon than mine (*ibid.*: 7). Constance Padwick's *Muslim Devotions* (1996), the result of substantial field-work throughout the Islamic world, must also be recommended as a modern classic in this field. Schimmel says that it 'takes us into the very heart of Muslim piety' (*ibid.*). Padwick's Christian bias is not absent; she tends to interpret what she calls the 'sacramental tendency' in Islam as a reaction against Islam's originally austere, exoteric form (see p. xxiv). However, her work shows how an 'outsider' can develop sympathy and even love for others' spiritual practices and beliefs.

Leadership in Islam: the Qur'anic view

In the Qur'an, humans are described as God's *khilafat*, which is usually translated as viceroy (see Q 2:30). According to the Arabic lexicon, *khilafat* means 'representative' (see Maududi, 1977: 42). Adam (the first human, who thus represents the whole human race) sinned but was then forgiven by God and given a 'word' from him (Q 2:37). This is understood to refer, initially, to the *shahadah* (the affirmation that God is one, that is, sovereign and all-powerful); secondly, to the basic distinction betweeen *haram* (prohibited) and *halal* behaviour. Adam thus also became the first prophet, whose task was to order human life according to the principles found in his 'word'. 'The very first man', explains Maududi, 'received revealed knowledge from God Himself. He had knowledge of the reality and was given the code of life by following which he could have a life of bliss and success' (1977: 4). As prophet, Adam was gifted with special insight into God's will, which enabled him to lead the early human community in its affairs. I return to what Islam has had to say about 'prophethood' later in this chapter when I discuss the work of the philosophers, but briefly prophets are people of peculiar virtue who, entrusted with a word from God, are then 'assigned the task of presenting the message of truth to humanity' (Maududi, 1977: 5). The *hadith* contains a saying that there were 124,000 prophets – enough to provide humankind with adequate exposure to the divine will. All prophets are of equal status; Q 2:135–6 and 2:285: 'We make no distinction between any of his messengers'. This is also interpreted to refer to the 'oneness' of their inner nature as prophets (see also Q 4:152).

Prophets and messengers

Technically, Muslims distinguish between those who are designated as *nabi* (literally 'prophet') and *rasul* (apostle, or messenger). The former operate within the context of an existing tradition, the latter bring a 'major new revelation' (Glasse, 1991: 318). Muhammad was a *rasul*. Watt surmises that, by Muhammad's time the term *rasul* may have 'come to mean "one commissioned to do something" ... such as managing some of the affairs of Medina' (1968: 27). However, most of the discussion in Islam about Muhammad's status has focused on the nature of his 'prophethood' rather than on his 'messengership', possibly because the philosophers and theologians 'regarded prophethood as more inclusive, since all messengers were prophets but only prophets with a special call were messengers of God' (Watt, 1994: 18). Certainly, a prophet can be described as one who is uniquely fit to lead the community; they somewhat resemble Plato's 'philosopher kings' inasmuch as their leadership emerges as a result of popular recognition of their qualities (rather than by a formal electoral process). As outlined in Chapter 2, this is indeed how Muhammad's leadership evolved. He was never elected leader but emerged as such by virtue of his prophetic calling; albeit his leadership role was formally acknowledged by his followers when they affirmed that 'There is no God but God and Muhammad is the apostle of God', and when they subscribed to the Qur'anic injunction, 'And if you dispute about anything, refer it to God and the Messenger' (Q 4:59). Muhammad's prophetic office thus gave him exceptional authority, but he was neither arbitrary nor autocratic in his leadership. He both consulted and delegated: 'On every crucial occasion he consulted chiefs of different tribes and his own Companions. He took counsel when slanderous gossip was circulating against his own wife ... He chose men of impeccable character, integrity and talent to perform various governmental functions [and a] deputy to look after the affairs of state in his absence' (Zakaria, 1988: 31–32). Q 3:159 is often interpreted as ordering the Prophet to consult in conducting affairs of state: 'consult with them upon the conduct of affairs' (see also Q 42:38 and B 92:26). The Qur'an also placed limits on his leadership inasmuch as he could not act contrary to its message. There was thus some similarity between his exercise of leadership and that of the traditional Arab *sayyid* (or *shaikh*), who used to consult before taking decisions and also delegated certain functions to others, thus: 'He was not necessarily the leader in war, ... nor was he responsible for the administration of justice, except in so far as judicial matters came before the council of notables' (Watt, 1968: 20).

A shared khilafat

In the absence of a prophet, humankind corporately possesses the responsibility (as *khilafat*) to walk God's path. *Khilafat* is thus not any 'individual or dynasty or class ... but ... is bestowed on the entire group of people, the community as a whole, which is ready to fulfil the conditions of representation ... each one of its individuals shares the Divine caliphate' (Maududi, 1977: 43–4). However, in order to run its affairs efficiently the group may choose to vest *khilafat* in a suitable individual, thus 'whoever gains their confidence will undertake the duty and obligations of the caliphate on their behalf; and when he loses this confidence he will have to quit, and bow before their will' (*ibid.*). This is sometimes called Islamic democracy. Maududi, however, usefully highlights

what distinguishes Islamic democracy from Western democracy ... is [that the latter] is based on the concept of popular sovereignty ... while the former is based on popular *khilafat*. In Western democracy, the people are sovereign, in Islam sovereignty vests in God and the people are His caliphs or representatives. In the former, the people make their own laws ... in the latter, they have to follow and obey the laws (*Shari'ah*) given by God. (pp. 44–5).

Other Muslim writers think that the term *nomocracy* is better suited to the Islamic model, since 'the function of the political ruler is not to legislate laws but to execute them'. 'Islam', says Nasr (1994) is 'a society ruled by a Divine Law' (pp. 106–7). Sunni and Sh'ia both agree that the Prophetic office ceased with Muhammad. Partly, this conviction rests on Q 33:40, which calls Muhammad the 'seal of the prophets'. It also follows from several Qur'anic statements which refer to the finality or completeness of Muhammad's Book and *din* ('way of life', sometimes rendered as 'religion'; see Q 2:2; Q 3:3; Q 5:3). Earlier prophets, too, had delivered messages for particular peoples or for a particular set of circumstances, but Muhammad is the prophet for all people, as a *hadith* says: 'The prophets were formerly sent to their people alone, whereas I have been sent to all mankind' (MM, 2:XXV1, p. 1231). Thus, since the prophetic office ceased with Muhammad, whose legacy of Qur'an and *sunnah* now contains all that is necessary to live life and order society in conformity with God's will, the corporate task of the Muslim community is to apply the principles found in Qur'an and *sunnah* to the day-to-day business of attempting to live according to the divine blueprint. Indeed, it could be argued that the corporate task is to imitate Muhammad, whose own life represents the Muslim ideal (of obedience to God); thus, 'We can only know of Islam through his teachings which are so complete and so comprehensive that they can guide men for all times' (Maududi, 1960: 63).

Who should lead the Muslims?

Where Sunni and Shi'a begin to part company is on the issue of leadership after Muhammad. The Sunni view is that, in the absence of the Prophet, no single individual can exercise the unique, God-given spiritual and political authority which had been Muhammad's, nor is there any longer a need for such a person because the totality of divine revelation is now available. Instead, the community as a whole inherits this legacy and by *ijma* (consensus), itself based on the *hadith* 'my community will not agree in error', and *shura* (consultation, see Q 42:38 and 3:159) it also inherits the responsibility for correctly implementing its principles. Humans entrusted with governmental responsibility are charged with the task of interpreting and implementing God's law, not of making law. Thus, in classical Sunni thought the Khalif is not 'a religious leader but the leader of a religious community' (Peters, 1994b: 121). For the Sunnis, the Khalif possesses no extraordinary spiritual powers of his own. His office, however, symbolizes the essential unity of the *ummah* and the supremacy of the *shari'ah*; and his primary duty is to protect and uphold the Law (see Nasr, 1994: 152 and Watt, 1968: 102). Sunnis came to speak of the Khalifate as an essential institution; it is 'placed on earth', wrote Mawardi (d. 1058), 'to succeed the Prophet in the duties of defending Religion and governing the World and it is a religious obligation to give allegiance to that person' (cited in Peters, 1994b: 143). For the Shi'a, there is still scope for continued divine guidance (not, however, for revelation) after the death of Muhammad, exercised through his male descendants. What separated the two groups was therefore argument about who should lead the community after 632, and (although this may very well have emerged as a later distinction between the two schools) about the nature of the succession.

The Sunni: the Khalif as first amongst equals

The Sunni view is that Muhammad made no provision for the succession to leadership of the Muslim community before he died, and that no small degree of confusion and competition resulted because of this. In Sunni accounts, the initiative was taken by the Helpers (the Madinans, who had invited Muhammad to take refuge with them), who met immediately after the Prophet's death – possibly to pre-empt the issue before other groups could organize themselves. On hearing this, Abu Bakr and 'Umar rushed to the assembly place, anxious that whoever was appointed would be able to hold the community together. It was, they believed, unlikely that the Arabs 'as a whole would accept the authority of anyone other than a man of Quraysh' (Lings, 1983: 343; see Tabari's account in Peters, 1994b: 117–20; and B 57:6, esp. *hadith* no. 19). The accounts then have Abu Bakr asking the assembled Muslims to choose between 'Umar and Abu 'Ubaydah (both amongst the ten named by Muhammad as being 'in paradise'). 'Umar demurred, saying, 'Who would take precedence over the man whom Muhammad had chosen to lead prayers?', namely Abu Bakr – who, at Muhammad's request, had led prayers during his final illness. Seizing Abu Bakr's hand, 'Umar pledged him his allegiance, followed by all present save one. Ibn Ishaq's account, though, reflects some unease with this traditional view – that Muhammad had not appointed a successor – by making rather a meal out of Muhammad's request that Abu Bakr lead the prayers. Certainly, this *hadith* has been used to defend Abu Bakr's leadership over and against the Shi'a view that 'Ali was the legitimate heir. Ibn Ishaq felt that he had to include the words, 'So the people knew that the apostle had not appointed a successor' (I.I., p. 681) in his account, lest the opposite impression be given by the earlier part of his narrative, which says that 'When the prophet became seriously ill he ordered the people to tell Abu Bakr to superintend the prayers', and did so three times (I.I., p. 680). Another *hadith*, however, identifies Abu Bakr quite unambiguously as Muhammad's own nominee:

'A'isha told that during his illness God's messenger said to her, 'call me Abu Bakr, your father, and your brother, so that I may write a document, for I fear that someone may be desirous of succeeding me and that one may [make unjustifiable claims for himself] whereas God and the believers will have no one but Abu Bakr. (MM, 2, p. 1321 transmitted by Muslim).

We also have, 'It is not fitting for a people among whom Abu Bakr is to be led by anyone else' (MM, 2, p. 1323, transmitted by Tirmidhi as a 'rare' or *gharib hadith*). It is generally agreed, however, that 'Umar's intervention was crucial in securing Abu Bakr's appointment, and that some of those present may have been 'browbeaten ... to toe the line. "'Umar', says Zakaria (1988), 'admitted as much in a subsequent address ... He said that his intervention had saved Islam from disintegration' (pp. 45–6).

Abu Bakr: 'the best amongst us'

What is clear from the accounts is that not everyone was happy with the appointment, and that dissent began immediately. The Sunni version of events is that Abu Bakr was appointed, or chosen, by the elders of the community because he was, in 'Umar's words, 'the best amongst' the Muslims (I.I., p. 687). B 57:6 cites 'Umar thus, 'you [Abu Bakr] are the best amongst us and the most beloved of us all to Allah's Messenger' (see also MM, 2, p. 1322). In other words, having known Muhammad intimately, Abu Bakr was in an ideal position to preserve his legacy. The actual designation *Khalif* may either have been chosen by Abu Bakr himself or used of him by others. As has been noted, according to some scholars the early Khalifs saw themselves as successors in every respect to the authority of Muhammad – like his, their authority came directly from God, thus 'obedience to the caliph was deemed to be necessary for salvation'. 'The caliph', writes Rippin (1990)

acted as judge, creating the sacred law and acting as the reference point for decisions on difficult items of law. The argument was made that his rulings were based on the Qur'an, the practice (*sunna*) – not that of a fixed practice of the past embodied in the person of Muhammad but the practice as found in the territory concerned – and his own (superhuman) insight (p. 57, and see also Crone and Hinds, 1986: 1).

Crone and Hinds make much of the fact that the later Khalifs called themselves '*Khalifat Allah*, or 'God's deputy', which, they say, 'is a title which implies a strong claim to religious authority' (1986: 5); 'The caliphs are legatees of prophets in the sense that they administer something established by them, but they do not owe their authority to them (let alone to Muhammad on his own). Their authority comes directly from God' (p. 27; see my comments in Chapter 2). Abu Bakr, however, according to the traditional Sunni account, saw himself as representative of the people in safeguarding (and to some degree in interpreting) the Prophet's legacy; and is reported to have said, on the day of his election, 'obey me as long as I obey God and His apostle, and if I disobey them you owe me no allegiance' (I.I., p. 687). Abu Bakr appears to have regarded himself as merely *primus inter pares* amongst all Muslims, not as gifted with some superhuman or special authority over them. Zakaria (1988) asks:

What was Abu Bakr's contribution to Islamic polity? Foremost was his unflinching adherence to the concept of equality of all believers, irrespective of their tribe or standing. He did not allow any barriers to be created between the ruler and the ruled. The rule of law was applicable to all, he said, no one was above it, not even the caliph. (p. 47)

'Abu Bakr', says Watt (1968), 'is generally held to have taken the title of *khalifat rasul Allah*, "the caliph of the Messenger of God"' (p. 32). Thus, he did not see his authority as absolute, but as subject to the *shari'ah*. However, given his personal reputation for piety and knowledge of the Prophet's legacy, what Abu Bakr said was consistent with the spirit of Islam was likely to gain popular support. Therefore, in practice, he probably did exercise considerable power but this power could be taken away by the people. 'What distinguished the caliphs from Muhammad', says Watt (1986) 'was their lack of the office of prophet and their inability to receive further revelations' (p. 42).

The rightly guided Khalifs

Abu Bakr ruled for two years and nominated 'Umar as his successor; 'the designation, however, was preceded by an informal consultation with a few of the leading men, and was followed by the acclamation (*bay'a*), or swearing of allegiance, of the people as a whole' (Watt, 1968: 35). 'Umar's caliphate saw the rapid geographical expansion of the Islamic Empire and the putting into place of a mechanism for its government; 'he constituted the office of *amir* (governor) and chose able, energetic and competent men to administer the provinces' (Zakaria, 1988: 48). 'Umar followed Muhammad's practice of respecting local customs unless they were considered totally repugnant to Islam, and tried to ensure that old and new Muslims, Arabs and non-Arabs, were treated equally – against not inconsiderable pressure to privilege Arabs generally and the Quraish especially. From 'Umar's time, the Khalifs also became known as 'Commanders of the Faithful' (*amir-al-mu'minun*). 'Umar may have had a leaning towards authoritarianism, says Zakaria (1988), but he also had 'the sagacity to consult leading Companions on key issues' and 'occasionally also called a larger council of Tribal Chiefs to discuss broader issues and programmes' (p. 52). He appointed a Council of Six to determine the succession, which fell to 'Uthman (644–56), one of their number (all six being amongst the ten 'trusty ones'). Tradition has it that he was the 'most competent statesman' (Watt, 1968: 36) although there has been some speculation that he may have been appointed by the other five 'because he was weak and likely to leave more power' in their own hands. It is not easy to evaluate 'Uthman's caliphate. On the one hand he does not appear to have been particularly weak; on the other, he may have lacked Abu Bakr's and 'Umar's statecraft. For example, according to some accounts, he gave too many privileges to members of his own clan, the Umayyah, which obviously alienated others (not least members of the Prophet's own family and clan). His motive, though, may have been sincere; by appointing members of his own family to key posts he thought he might better control 'the growing independence of the amirs who were challenging the caliph's authority' (Zakaria, 1988: 54). Another commentator believes that they were appointed on the basis of their suitability and competency, not due to nepotism (Sayf B Umar al-Tamini, 1995: 152). Nevertheless, these appointments created resentment and helped fuel opposition to his rule. Rebellion followed. Implicated in this were 'A'isha, the Prophet's widow, and one of her brothers; 'Uthman's house was besieged, then breached and 'insurgents', says Watt, 'forced an entrance into his house and killed him' (1968: 36).

'Ali: fourth Sunni Khalif

Almost immediately after the assassination, 'Ali, Muhammad's cousin and son-in-law, appears to have been declared Khalif by 'such Muslims as were present in the city' as 'the most respected Muslim in Medina' (*ibid.*). Commenting on this lack of consultation, Watt writes, 'it could be said that in Medina in 656 'Ali was so clearly best that no consultation was needed'. In fact, it was two surviving members of the Council of Six, Talha and Zubayr, who persuaded 'Ali to become Khalif, saying that only he could 'save the caliphate from disintegration' (Zakaria, 1988: 56). Unfortunately, this proved not to be the case; 'Uthman's relatives refused to accept 'Ali's claim; furthermore, they accused him of complicity in his murder. Talha and Zubayr, too, quickly deserted his cause and, from their base in Kufa, revolted against his rule. 'Ali found himself embroiled in civil war. He won the first round (the Battle of the Camel) but the second, the Battle of Siffin (against 'Uthman's cousin Mu'awiyah, governor of Syria) continued for months, with neither side gaining any real advantage. Finally, both sides agreed to allow the conflict to go to arbitration.

What follows has been described as 'the most confused series of events in the whole of Islamic history' (Watt, 1968: 37). First, a group of 'Ali's supporters withdrew, saying that a matter of such importance could only be decided by God; their motto was 'Decision is God's alone' (they became the Kharijites, or seceders, for whom see below). 'Ali's reply to their objection is interesting: 'We did not name people the arbitrators but we named the Qur'an ... The Qur'an is a book ... and it does not speak. It should therefore necessarily have an interpreter. Men alone can be such interpreters' ('Ali, 1996: 90). Next, probably for personal gain, 'Ali's own negotiator appears to have declared 'Ali's claim to the Kalifate null and void, understanding (it is alleged) that Mu'awiyah would also withdraw his claim. In fact, Mu'awiyah's negotiator had tricked him; Mu'awiyah was proclaimed Khalif in a manner which made this seem to have been the agreed outcome of the arbitration process. 'Ali refused to relinquish his title and set up headquarters at Kufa (now loyal to him); since the negotiators had 'abandoned the course of right and come out with just the opposite of what was settled' 'Ali had 'strong ground to reject their verdict' ('Ali, 1996: 137). 'Mu'awiyah', said 'Ali, 'is not more cunning than I but he deceives and commits evil deeds' (ibid.: 174). From Kufa, 'Ali successfully won a campaign against the Kharijites (although the movement itself continued) only to lose his own life at the hand of a Kharijite in 661 – assassinated as he prepared to lead morning prayers.

Sunni Muslims (those who follow the sunnah of the Prophet) call the period from 632 to 661 the Patriarchal Khalifate, and refer to the first four Khalifs as having been 'rightly guided' (al-khulafa' ar-rashidun) – their spiritual status was such that they were truly worthy of leading the community. They were 'the most excellent of all the people after the Prophet' (Watt, 1994b: 44, from al-Ashari's creed). In other words, they were loyal to the memory and sunnah of Muhammad, whom they had all known intimately and loved. Sunni historians and theologians, retrospectively no doubt, recognize that something went wrong after 661 and refer to the period of the Patriarchs as the 'golden', or 'ideal' Khalifate when, as it were, there was almost perfect coincidence between the reality and the ideal. The creeds thus single out Abu Bakr, 'Umar, 'Uthman and 'Ali from all those who have subsequently claimed the title. In a sense, these four all perpetuated something of the Prophet's own charismatic leadership. The fact, too, that the praises of all four are sung in separate chapters of Bukhari (and in the order of their administrations) may represent a reading-back into history, suggesting that they were predestined to succeed to the Khalifate. The problem, however, with charisma is that it cannot be perpetuated permanently and, as Max Weber argued, charismatic leadership usually yields to a more routinized authority, 'which is impersonal by nature, authority resides not in the person but in the office' (Seymour-Smith, 1986: 19). We ought to note, however, that there was debate about whether 'Uthman should be included as a 'rightly guided Khalif', which is reflected in the later creeds; thus, 'some suspended judgement about 'Uthman' (Watt, 1994b: 38, 'A Longer Hanbalite Creed'). Others think that he ceased to enjoy divine favour after he lost the Prophet's ring. On the other hand, there is an alternative account of his rule which has him imitating the example of the Prophet and sees the charges against him as manufactured by the rebels in order to justify their opposition (Sayf B Umar al-Tamini, 1995: 50).

The Umayyads

Sunni historians recognize four Khalifates: the Patriarchal (described above – these Khalifs had all known Muhammad intimately and exercised authority because of this); the Umayyad (from 660 to 750); the 'Abbasids (750–1517; after 1258 only nominal), and the Ottomans (1517–1924). After 661 the mechanism for appointing the Khalif changed; no longer was the Khalif chosen for his suitability, piety and closeness to Muhammad, or for his command of Islamic dogma; rather, son followed father. In other words, the Khalifate became dynastic and therefore routinized. 'Ali's elder son, Hasan, opposed Mu'awiyah on the basis that he was personally unsuited to lead the Muslims: 'You do not possess any known merit in religion (deen), nor have you any trace (athar) of Islam in you' (cited in Zakaria, 1988: 61). Hasan urged Mu'awiyah to 'give up "his persistence in falsehood (*batil*)"' by abdicating in his own favour, 'for I am more entitled to the Caliphate than you in the eyes of God and all worthy people' (*ibid.*). Mu'awiyah disagreed. In his reply, he did not claim piety, or any particular interest in Islam as such, but he did claim much more administrative experience and ability than Hasan: 'I have better understanding of politics and also I am much older than you' (*ibid.*: 62). He assured Hasan that if he withdrew his own claim, he would succeed after his death. Hasan apparently did just this. He died before the Khalif, who may (it is surmised) have had him poisoned.

Mu'awiyah appears, all along, to have wanted the succession to go to his own son, Yazid, and 'no sooner was Hasan laid to rest ... [than he] began to plan Yazid's succession' (Zakaria, 1988: 64). He did this by persuading several leading Companions to swear loyalty to Yazid. Yazid became Khalif in 680 and immediately demanded 'allegiance from 'Ali's second and only surviving son, Husayn' (p. 65). Husayn refused. Nor was he alone in his refusal to concede the Khalifate to Yazid. There was considerable discussion about the legitimacy of his succession, as well as about his worthiness to hold that office. Abd Allah ibn az-Zubayr (the son of Zubayr – member of the Council of Six and one of the 'trusty ten') declared himself Khalif and actually controlled Makkah until about 692. Meanwhile, Husayn accepted an invitation from Kufa (where his father had enjoyed strong support) to base his opposition there, and sent one of his own cousins 'ahead to prepare the way' (Glasse,

1991: 162). He was executed before completing the journey. Husayn, with members of his household, eighteen Companions and about 600 armed supporters, still decided to proceed.

The Karbala Massacre

At Karbala in Iraq, in the year 680, during the month of Muharram, Husayn was intercepted by 'Ubayd Allah ibn Ziyad, Yazid's governor of Iraq, who commanded an army of 4,000 men and engaged the Prophet's grandson in battle. With such odds against Husayn, the outcome was no surprise. Its result, however, was indescribably tragic and casts its shadow over all subsequent Muslim history. All but two of Husayn's children were killed, including his baby son who was struck by an arrow whilst Husayn himself cradled him in his lap. Husayn's head was chopped off and sent by courier to Yazid, who 'began to poke' at it 'with a cane'. A Companion present, Tabari records, 'cried out, "Take your cane away. How often have I seen the Messenger of God kiss that mouth"' (Fishbein, 1990: 75–6). In fact, hadith tell us that Husayn 'was one of those who resembled God's messenger most closely' (MM, 2, p. 1358). Muhammad's love for his two grandsons was widely known; amongst hadith we have, 'Al-Bara told that he saw the Prophet with al-Hasan b 'Ali on his shoulder saying, 'O God, I love him, so I beseech Thee to love him' (MM, 2, p. 1351).

Husayn's supporters never acknowledged the legitimacy of Yazid's succession and permanently separated from the Sunni majority, becoming known as the Shi'a. The reality, however, was that Mu'awiyah had been a competent ruler, and the majority of Muslims found civil war distasteful; indeed for Muslims to fight Muslims was contrary to shari'ah. When Yazid succeeded, although he was weak and corrupt, the majority simply accepted that a united ummah under a bad Khalif was still better than an ummah rife with internal strife and dissension. As Max Weber has it, the office was now more important than the particular person who occupied it (see e.g. Weber, 1965). Yazid's rule, it is said, was merely tolerated. In fact, Muslims were faced with a very real dilemma – the view that God controls history is fundamental to Islam, and it could be argued that all rulers rule as a result of the divine will. Q 4:59 was widely cited to silence opposition to even the most immoral ruler: 'O you who believe, obey God and his messenger and obey those who are in power amongst you.' Others cited such hadith as 'Whosoever obeys an Amir, obeys me' (B 89:1) and 'Hear and obey, though a negro is appointed to rule over you' (B 89:4). Neutrality appears to have been the majority option, reflected in the following clause of al-Tahawi's creed:

We do not approve of the sword against any of the community of Muhammad ... We do not approve of going out in [rebellion] against ... the administrators of our affairs, even although they act wrongfully towards us ... We consider that obedience to them ... belongs to obedience to God as something prescribed by God; and we pray for soundness and pardon for them. (Watt, 1994b: 53)

The Kharijites, though, who still continued as a distinct group, found this view quite unpalatable and remained totally opposed to the hereditary principle; the Khalif, they said, must indeed be 'the best amongst us'. Nobody has the right to be Khalif just because his father had been. They argued that unworthy rulers should not be obeyed but deposed, by force if necessary, and conducted *jihad* against those whom they thought had forfeited Muslim status. The Murji'ites, who opposed the Kharijites, held that outward profession of Islam was enough; thus action should not be taken against those thought immoral as long as they continued to proclaim the *shahadah*.

Ibn Khaldun on royal authority

Ibn Khaldun (1332–1406), in his analysis of Islamic history, says that with the establishment of the Umayyad dynasty and the hereditary Khalifate, the religious influence (or feeling, *'asabiyyah*) which had originally inspired Islamic civilization waned, to be replaced by 'royal authority' (Ibn Khaldun, 1958). This followed an inevitable process of decline – away from the ideal; the original vigour, puritanism, and public mindedness of the early Muslims gave way to a more self-serving style of leadership. Royal authority vests power in itself and takes measures to protect the continuation of power down the dynastic line. This, says Ibn Khaldun, is *mulk* (the dynastic state) and not really the Khalifate at all. Yet this is a pragmatic necessity for survival. Ibn Khaldun's theory does seem to fit the facts: whilst the first four Khalifs, to a lesser or greater degree, stood for equality and fairness, Mu'awiyah and his successors furthered their personal interests and created allies by exercising favouritism in their distribution of imperial posts: 'In place of religious ties', says Zakaria (1988), 'Mu'awiyah revived tribal bonds ... The result was that religion was sidetracked and political considerations given precedence in affairs of state' (p. 64). Arabs were given special privileges over and above Muslims from other racial groups. Mu'awiyah also used the *Bait-al-Mal* (House of Property, into which taxes, war booty and treasure trove are paid) 'as if it were his personal property' instead of for the conduct of state business, for which it had been established by Muhammad. 'The dynasty', says Glasse (1991), 'became notorious for running the Empire as if it were a personal fief' (p. 408).

We shall return to Ibn Khaldun below. Umayyad history, of course, is refracted through the lens of its detractors. Some Umayyad rulers, according to Ahmed (1988), 'approximated to [the] ideal', for example, 'Umar II, who 'placated the Shi'a, stopp[ed] the condemnation of 'Ali which Mu'awiyah had instituted in the pulpits, and treated all Muslims, whether Arab or not, alike' (pp. 38–9). 'Umar II also commissioned, as noted in Chapter 2, the collection of *hadith*, and 'appointed paid teachers to teach the Qur'an to the ignorant Bedouins' (Siddiqi, 1993: 6). Another Umayyad, 'Abd al-Malik (685–705), gave us the oldest (extant) and arguably the most beautiful Muslim building – Jerusalem's Dome of the Rock. The Dome's inscriptions are replete with Islamic dogma; they proclaim Islam as the culmination of Judaism and Christianity and include texts about the status of Muhammad, whilst 'the copper inscription over the north door ... refers to Muslims as those who believe in God [and] what He revealed to Muhammad' (Rippin, 1990: 54). Incidentally, this does not, in my view, support the view that Muhammad was of relatively little importance during this period or that the Umayyads were totally indifferent to Islam.

The 'Abbasids

The Umayyads lasted just a little short of a century; their rule ended in the heartlands of Islam with the 'Abbasid coup in 750 but continued in Spain until 1236, where, under their urbane rule, Islamic civilization flowered (as noted in Chapter 3). The 'Abbasid coup, which appears to have had the support of the religious scholars, was led by 'Abu-l 'Abbas, descendant of al-'Abbas, the Prophet's uncle, and father of 'Abd Allah ibn al-'Abbas, the *hadith* collector and Qur'an interpreter. It was this familial link with Muhammad which aided the 'Abbasids in their rebellion against the Umayyads, whose father, Abu Sufyan, had been, as Hasan put it in his letter to Mu'awiyah, 'the greatest enemy of the Prophet'. The 'Abbasids went into battle with the war-cry, 'O Muhammad, helped of God'. Their first Khalif donned the Prophet's cloak 'every Friday while leading the public prayers' (Muhammad had himself worn it on ceremonial occasions; see Zakaria, 1988: 77). From the beginning, they made much of what they saw as their Islamic credentials. The Umayyads' ungodly image, which dominates the historical record, tends to suggest that the religious scholars supported their overthrow because they saw them as unworthy occupants of the Khalifate. However, what they may have found wanting was less their personal qualities than their turning the Khalifate into a hereditary office. The scholars perhaps hoped that the 'Abbasid coup would lead to a restoration of a more republican system, in which the Muslim 'best suited to rule' would become Khalif. Zakaria (1988) comments:

The theologians at the time were agreed than an Islamic state had to have a republican character. They held the Umayyads guilty of violating this principle by turning the republic into a monarchy. The Abbasids agreed and assured their subjects that this would be implemented soon. There was, however, no consensus over the means to bring this about and so the monarchical system continued. (pp. 76–7)

Thus the 'Abbasids, like the Umayyads, 'retained the caliphate within their close-knit family' (*ibid.*: 80). However, they ceased to treat the Arabs as a privileged group and increased the participation of non-Arabs in helping to run the Empire. In fact, Persians became very influential, so much so that the 'Abbasids began to model their rule on the Sassanid pattern and appear to have adopted Persian ideas about the divine nature of kingship. This may have led to their adoption of the title *Khalifat Allah* (that is, deputy of God, rather than the messenger of God), which was strongly disapproved by the *ulama*. Nonetheless, the 'Abbasids were anxious to maintain their Islamic credentials; they patronized Islamic sciences, built mosques, and generally paid much more heed to Islamic law.

Indeed, it was during the 'Abbasid period that the four schools of Sunni jurisprudence emerged and that *shari'ah* was codified into what was later considered to be a definitive form, so that future jurists 'were no longer to seek new solutions or produce new regulations and law books but instead study the established legal manuals and write their commentaries' (Esposito, 1991: 84; see also Schacht, 1964: 70–1). *Taqlid* (imitation) of the past became mandatory; *bida* (deviation, or innovation) became 'equivalent to the charge of heresy in Christianity' (Esposito, 1991: 85). There is no shortage of *hadith* (which many would dub posthumous) warning against *bida* and upholding *taqlid*, such as: 'The best discourse is God's book, the best guidance is that given by Muhammad, and the worst things are those which are novelties. Every innovation is error' (transmitted by Muslim; MM, 1, p. 39). The post of *qadi* (judge), which the Umayyads had instituted as a largely secular office, now became

inseparably linked with *Shari'a* law which it was their bounden duty to apply, they were no longer the spokesmen of a law which represented the command of the provincial or district governor but they owed allegiance exclusively to God's law. (Coulson, 1994: 121)

Islam's Golden Age

The 'Abbasid Khalifate, like the Spanish Umayyads, was a period of economic prosperity and cultural and intellectual achievement; theological and philosophical activity also reached their peak. Centres such as 'Cordova, Baghdad, Cairo, Nishapur, and Palermo emerged and eclipsed Christian Europe, mired in the Dark Ages' (Esposito, 1991: 55). Much Greek learning was translated into Arabic and profoundly influenced the development of Islamic thought. 'Towering intellectual giants', says Esposito, 'dominated this period: al-Razi (865–925), al-Farabi (d. 950), ibn Sina (known as Avicenna, 980–1037), ibn Rushd (known as Averroës, d. 1198), al-Biruni (973–1048) and al-Ghazali (d. 1111)' (*ibid.*). We shall refer to some of these intellectual giants below, when I discuss what Islamic theology and philosophy had to say about Muhammad.

Effectively, the 'Abbasids appear to have engineered their own decline. First, surrounding their office with much mystery, emphasizing its function – as they saw it – as keeper of the Islamic conscience and guardian of the Prophet's legacy, they became more and more distant from the people over whom they ruled; 'the ruler's exalted status was further reinforced by his magnificent palace, his retinue of attendants, and the introduction of a court etiquette appropriate for an emperor' (*ibid.*: 53). This included his sitting behind a veil (*hijab*), presumably to enhance the sacred nature of his office. Thus we read about visitors who thought that it was God they had come to speak with, behind the screen! Increasingly, real power passed to others, amongst them the Khalif's own chief *vizir* or minister (also hereditary – descendants of the

'Abbasids' first lieutenant), until that office was abolished as a 'Persian innovation and anti-Islamic institution' (Zakaria, 1988: 80) in 803.

Virtual independence: the age of the sultans

Many of the amirs (later known as sultans), too, were *de facto* independent kings. Watt (1968) says that they were really war-lords who 'came to rule through their military power, but ... did not claim to rule in their own right'. The Khalif, effectively, 'was powerless against them' but 'they were content to be in theory his subordinates' (Watt, 1968: 100). Khalifs, of course, had always delegated authority (sultan means 'authority'), so the theory to justify the reality was already available; 'The *de facto* rulers of the Islamic commonwealth were', says Peters (1994b), 'generally known as "Sultans" and were more often former Turkish warlords to whom the Caliphs owed the safety of their house' (p. 147). Ibn Jama (d. 1335 CE) thus wrote about the Khalif's 'right to delegate authority over any region, country, area or province to whoever is able to hold general authority there, because necessity demands it' (*ibid.*). Necessity here may well refer to the preservation of peace, which is ideally the chief characteristic of life within the world or Abode of Islam – *dar-al-Islam* is also *dar-al-salam*. From 932, although the 'Abbasids continued to hold the office of Khalif, real power was exercised by the Buyids (932–1075), followed by the Saljuks (1075–1258). The Khalif came to represent symbolic unity, continuity and legitimacy (of others' rule); 'He became', says Mernissi (1993) 'the dispenser of certificates of legitimacy' (p. 27). In 1258 the 'Abbasid capital, Baghdad, fell to the Mongols.

Although not directly the concern of this survey, it is interesting to note that the distancing of the Khalif from the exercise of effective political power appears to have contributed to the gradual marginalization of *Shari'ah* law. Its strict impartiality, together with restrictions on the amount of tax which could be levied, did not always advance the rulers' personal interests to their own liking. Thus, claiming that their responsibility was to maintain order and preserve and protect the Muslim religion (which indeed was the classical view of their function: 'the preservation of religion and the leadership of the world'), they replaced much of the *Shari'ah* with 'regulations' or 'administrative decrees' (*qanun*) which were, they said, necessary if their responsibilities were to be fulfilled. Schacht (1964) described the process thus:

The later caliphs and other secular rulers often had occasion to enact new rules. But although this was in fact legislation, the rulers used to call it administration, and they maintained the fiction that their regulations served only to apply, to supplement, and to enforce the *shari'a* ... this fiction was maintained as much as possible, even in the face of contradictions with and encroachments on the Sacred Law. (p. 54)

New courts were established to deal with these decrees, which, in practice, limited the scope of the *Shari'ah* courts; they were left to deal with personal status (marriage, divorce, inheritance) and with matters pertaining to religious endowments (*wakf*).

At first, motives may have been quite commendable – the lower magistrates might be too intimidated to judge cases concerning high officials or relatives of the Khalif, therefore 'independent' courts were established to adjudicate these. What happened, however, fits Ibn Khaldun's theory – that the religious feeling which had motivated the early Khalifs, and their servants, was gradually replaced by purely political considerations. Whilst Muslims hold up the complete unity of religion (*din*) and politics (*dunya*) (indeed, they recognize no divide) as the ideal, they have more often than not reconciled themselves to their separation (see Zakaria, 1988: 20). Lindholm (1996) argues that, having 'rejected the argument for Alide domination out of hand as both unrealistic and tyranical', Sunni increasingly found themselves 'left under the sway of an ... illegitimate secular state' (p. 181). Some Muslims criticize the religious scholars for allowing *din* to be sidetracked. However, their financial independence did allow them a degree of autonomy, which often included controlling the great centres of legal as well as religious scholarship. They were free, sometimes, to criticize the State; Al Azhar University in Cairo, for example (which is widely considered Islam's premier educational institution), was a private institution until nationalized in 1961. Following this, it lost much of the public popularity it had previously enjoyed. Rather than employ its graduates (now tainted), local mosques established their own 'informal schools'. In its turn, 'To combat the burgeoning growth of these local non-governmental religious centres, the Egyptian state' annexed the larger mosques as well (*ibid.*: 165).

Rafiq Zakaria (1988) points out, too, that Islam as *din* did not suffer from the separation of religious from political leadership. In fact, he says, it flourished (see p. 280). Sufi missionaries spread Islam through vast tracts of Africa and Asia. Islamic rule sometimes followed in their wake but often evangelized areas never came under the control of political Islam (see *ibid.*: 102). Zakaria suggests that discontent with political Islam, and inability to influence its course lent impetus to Sufi Islam; 'With the decline of central power, the people turned in greater numbers to the Sufis, men of God, who taught piety and a relaxed attitude to form and ritual' (*ibid.*: 100). We return in more detail to Sufi Islam later in this chapter. We may note, however, that scholars have tried to explain the popularity of Sufi Islam as an alternative to legal Islam by seeing it as an 'opting out' of social and political involvement. W. C. Smith (1957) writes:

Sufism differs from the classical sunni *Weltanschauung* radically; and not least in its attitude to history, the temporal mundane. It stresses the individual rather than society, the eternal rather than the historical, God's love rather than his power, and the state of men's hearts rather than behaviour. It is more concerned that one's soul be pure than that one's actions should be correct. Some Sufis thought the Law unimportant. Most regarded it as a private discipline guiding the person towards transcendent fulfilment, and paid little heed to its function in ordering society, in marshalling history into a prescribed pattern. (pp. 44–5)

Lindholm (1996), however, points out that what many Sufi orders actually established was micro social–economic systems, or

their own small sacred empires within the larger secular state, complete with a centralized administrative organisation ... a tax collection through voluntary donations and access to the military force of tribal clients. These religious enclaves offered an alternative to secular central authority, and could sometimes rise in protest against state injustice and corruption. (p. 193)

Perhaps what was difficult to sustain at the macro level was more successful at the micro; Sufism provided a micro political alternative Islamic order to that of the disintegrating Khalifate (see below). Sufis themselves have rejected the charge of indifference to social needs and social justice; Kabbani (1996) says:

It suffices to say that the lives of [the] Sufi Shaykhs are insurmountable evidence that sufism, far from encouraging escapism and quietism of the soul that causes social progress to founder, upheld the highest values of social consciousness ... In fact, they provide adequate testimony to an unremitting warfare and struggle against social injustice and social inaction that took place in Islam over the centuries. (p. 3)

The Ottomans

A surviving ʿAbbasid fled to Cairo, where his descendants continued to claim the title (and received some homage from various parts of the Muslim world) until Egypt fell to the Ottoman Turks (1517). The Ottoman Emperors later claimed that al-Mutawakkil III, the last of the ʿAbbasids to use the title of Khalif, had ceded it to them. Certainly, it was in 1517 that the staff and mantle of the Prophet (the symbols of the Khalif) found their way to Istanbul, where they remain on display in the Topkapi Palace for me and millions of visitors to gaze upon. However, there is little evidence that the Ottomans laid any claim to the title of Khalif until 1774, when they acquired some jurisdiction over Muslims living in Russia (in return for recognition of the Tsar's right to protect Orthodox Christians living in the Ottoman Empire) and appeared to think that the title matched this task. As the Ottoman Empire expanded, so did its wealth, prestige and power. Slowly, initial reluctance to accept the Ottomans as Khalif gave way to widespread recognition: 'Once the caliphate had been resurrected ... it gained some recognition ... doubtless due to the fact that the Ottoman sultan had become by far the most powerful Muslim sovereign' (Watt, 1968: 109; see Zakaria, 1988: 94–5). Following Turkey's adoption of republican government, the office of Khalif was abolished (1924). This created consternation throughout the Muslim world, which met at Cairo and Makkah in 1926 to discuss its restoration. At the time there did not seem to be any practical way of doing this, and the decision was made that 'the office must remain in abeyance for the visible future' (Watt, 1968: 109).

Muslim unity today

There have been various attempts to resurrect the Khalifate since its 'abolition'; for some time the Sharif of Makkah (a descendant of the Prophet through Fatimah), claimed the title as did his son (king of Transjordan). The kings of Morocco (also Sharifian) still use the title but none of these claimants enjoy any international recognition. A fundamental problem is who should be Khalif, and how the international Muslim community could elect or select such a person. Whilst the hereditary principle had shortcomings, and never enjoyed universal support amongst Muslims, it at least solved the problem of identifying who should wear the Prophet's mantle. Given the concern of this chapter, which is not the history of the Khalifate as such but rather its relationship with Muhammad, it is interesting to note that whilst familial links with the Prophet did not, for Sunnis, denote special status, they were often used to justify claims to the Khalifate.

As I have stated, the ʿAbbasids justified their claim on the grounds of descent from the Prophet's uncle, over against the Umayyads, whose ancestors had once been numbered amongst Muhammad's worst enemies. The ʿAbbasids may even have attracted a degree of Shiʿa support because of this link with the Prophet's household. Indeed, the Buyids (who maintained the ʿAbbasid Khalifate whilst exercising real power themselves) were actually Shiʿa. However, for the Shiʿa the line of descent must be through Fatimah, the Prophet's daughter, and her sons Hasan and Husayn. The Fatimad dynasty in Egypt, although Shiʿa, claimed the title Khalif (from 909 to 1171) on the basis of their descent from Fatimah. In response, the Abbasids appear to have developed the view that 'the claims to power of those descended from ʿAli [were] completely unfounded, because the transmission of the caliphate through women is impossible' (Mernissi, 1993: 153). We thus have traditions which restrict the Khalifate to Arabs, or exclusively to the Quraish which includes the Umayyads; 'The Khalifate will remain with the Quraish, even if only two of them were still existing' (B 89:3): the footnote reads, 'The Prophet meant that the Muslims are obliged to appoint, as their chief ruler, someone from the tribe of Quraish even if there is only one Quraish left who is fit for the caliphate' (Khan, 9: 191). In practice, Sunni rulers needed to be able to claim direct descent from the family of the Prophet, as Mernissi says: 'Every Muslim head of state who claims the title of caliph has to solve the problem of his descent from the Prophet, to certify a family tree that links him to the Prophet's descendants' (1993: 22). One reason why the Ottomans' claim was suspect was that no such link could be claimed; 'for a Turk [it] becomes a rather awkward matter' (*ibid.*). On the other hand, both the Sharif of Makkah and the kings of Morocco have claimed the title Khalif because they are descended from Muhammad through Fatimah, and some Sunni states publish official registers of those who are entitled to be called 'Sayyid' (that is, Sharifs). Such people are treated with considerable respect (see Glasse, 1991: 363) and have, at times, enjoyed special privileges (such as state allowances and exemption from certain taxes).

The Shi'a concept of leadership

The Shi'a (literally 'party', or the party of 'Ali) claim that 'Ali should have succeeded to the leadership of the community immediately after the Prophet's death. They cite, in support of this claim, the tradition that, after returning from his final pilgrimage in 632, Muhammad had taken 'Ali's hand and said, 'Everyone whose patron I am also has 'Ali as his patron' (cited in Halm, 1991: 8); or, in a different rendering, 'whomsoever I protect (*mowla*), 'Ali is likewise his protector. O God, be a friend to [or 'be close to', *vali*] whoever is his friend and an enemy to whoever is his enemy' (Richard, 1995: 16). The Sunnis (whose collections also include this *hadith*) interpret this as simply a temporary endorsement of 'Ali's authority 'in some internal conflicts' (Richard, *ibid.*) but for the Shi'a it represents his designation as successor. Other traditions have Muhammad saying to 'Ali, 'You are to me as Aaron was to Moses' (cited in Peters, 1994b: 125) and, 'I am the locality of knowledge and 'Ali is the gateway' ('Ali, 1996: i) which Shi'a also cite as proof of 'Ali's political claims. In addition, the Shi'a attach significance to a Qur'anic passage which appears to vest the family of the Prophet (*Ahl-al-Bait*) with a special spiritual status: 'Allah's wish is to remove uncleanliness far from you, O Folk of the household, and cleanse you with a thorough cleansing' (Q 33:33). 'Ali is reported to have said: 'Look at the People of the Prophet's family. Adhere to their direction. Follow their footsteps' ('Ali, p. 67). B 74:29 (and B 59:81, no. 728) has 'Ali, during Muhammad's final illness, refusing to ask him for the Khalifate, 'by Allah, if … he denied it us, the people will never give it us after that. And by Allah, I will not ask Allah's Messenger for it.' However, B 59:81, no. 736 also has 'A'isha denying that Muhammad had appointed 'Ali 'as successor by will'.

Traditional accounts of Abu Bakr's selection as Khalif tell us that 'Ali was not present at the time and that both he and his wife Fatimah (the Prophet's daughter) refused to endorse Abu Bakr's leadership, which, reluctantly, 'Ali did after his wife's death. Lings' version reads:

After the death of Fatimah some months later, 'Ali said to Abu Bakr: 'We know well thy pre-eminence and what God has bestowed upon thee, and we are not jealous of any benefit that He hath caused to come to thee. But thou didst confront us with a thing accomplished, leaving us with no choice, and we felt that we had some claim therein for our nearness of kinship unto the Messenger of God'. Then Abu Bakr's eyes filled with tears and he said, 'By Him in whose hand is my soul, I had rather that all should be well between me and the kindred of God's Messenger than between me and my own kindred'; and at noon that day in the Mosque he publicly exonerated 'Ali for not having recognised him as caliph, whereupon 'Ali affirmed the right of Abu Bakr and pledged his allegiance to him (Lings, 1993: 344).

'Ali's account is somewhat different; Abu Bakr 'knew that my position in relation to [the caliphate] was the same as the position of the axis in relation to the hand-mill'. Thus 'Ali 'put a curtain against the caliphate and kept … detached from it' (1996: 6). He 'watched the plunder of his inheritance' (p. 7) without speaking out; 'if I speak out they will call me greedy' (p. 9). He speaks, however, of possessing 'hidden knowledge' which he dare not disclose.

When 'Umar became Khalif after Abu Bakr's death, 'Ali was hurt that his claims had once more been ignored. His own supporters accused Abu Bakr of having 'stage managed' popular acceptance of 'Umar without any genuine consultation (see Zakaria, 1988: 48). 'Umar included 'Ali as a member of his Council of Six; 'Ali appears to have thought this presumptuous: 'Good Heavens! What had I to do with this "consultation"? Where was any doubt about me with regard to the first of them that I should now be considered akin to these ones?' ('Ali, 1996: 7). He regarded his own claim as incontestable: 'I am the most rightful of all others for the caliphate' (p. 4). One tradition tells us that, when asked by the other five, 'if he were made caliph' would he 'Abide by two conditions: first, whether he would rule according to the Qur'an and the sunna (the way of the Prophet), and, second, whether he would follow the precedents of the first two caliphs', he 'replied "yes" to the first question, and "no" to the second'. Instead, he said that 'he would follow his own judgement' (Zakaria, 1988: 54). 'Uthman said yes to both conditions and became the third Khalif. Following 'Uthman's assassination, 'Ali – although bitterly disappointed that his claims had now been passed over three times – hesitated before accepting office. He may have thought the task of uniting the now divided community too daunting; he finally accepted because the faithful had pleaded, 'we will accept no other but you, and we [will] not [gather] together except around you' (cited by Zakaria, 1988: 56). His own account suggests that he had no real political ambition: 'I had no liking for the caliphate nor any interest in government, but you [he was addressing Talhah and Zubayr] invited me to it' ('Ali, 1996: 177). B 57:6, no. 20 reports 'Ali saying, 'I am only an ordinary person'. Finally, however, he did become leader of the Muslims. As he had himself anticipated, his greatest challenge was trying to unite the community. His reign was in fact marked by civil war and was short-lived (as noted above). He was universally respected as a soldier (having played a vital role in the early battles against the Makkans) as well as for his piety and learning. His *Nahjul Balaaghah*, compiled by as-Sayyid ar-Raddhi (I have cited from the 1996 Ahlul-Bayt Assembly of America translation) is regarded by Shi'a as 'the greatest literary and theological composition ... after the Holy Qur'an and the Sunnah'. 'Ali remains an important figure within Sunni as well as Shi'a Islam. For the former, he was the fourth 'rightly guided' Khalif; although all four 'rightly guided' Khalifs were virtuous, the first, Abu Bakr, was the most virtuous (see Ibn Hanbal's creed which places the Companions in 'order of excellence' – Abu Bakr, 'Umar, 'Uthman and 'Ali – in Watt, 1994b: 32). For the Shi'a, however, 'Ali was the first and only legitimate successor, the first (not fourth) Khalif or Imam (which became their preferred designation for the leader of the Muslim community).

The Imamate

The word 'Imam' (literally 'he who stands before') was used during Muhammad's lifetime for the person who led prayers – thus it was either the Prophet himself or somebody designated by him. During Muhammad's last illness, Abu Bakr was appointed Imam. In later Sunni literature, the title 'Imam' is sometimes used synonymously with 'Khalif', since an important symbolic function of the Khalif is to lead communal (Friday) prayer. Any Sunni who is knowledgeable in the Qur'an can act as Imam – although the term is also applied in a more restricted sense to the most distinguished scholars and jurists (for example, 'the four Imams' – after whom the four legal schools are named: Hanifa, Malik, Shafi'i and Hanbal). Ibn Khaldun, who had much to say about the role of the Khalif, used the terms 'Imam' and 'Khalif' interchangeably:

The office may be termed the Khalifate or the Imamate indifferently. When the Khalif is called Imam, he is, as it were, compared with the leader whose movements in prayer must be imitated by the whole assembly. The great Imamate is a term used of the Caliph's office. (Guillaume, 1924: 159)

Mawardi (d. 1058) also used the term 'Imamate' in describing the function of the Khalifate.

Ibn Khaldun defined the Khalif's job as the preservation of religion and 'the political leadership of the world' (cited above). This description applies equally to the Shi'a's 'Imams', but with some significant differences – principally, that the Imam must be a male descendant of Muhammad and enjoys divine protection from error, a special type of sanctity (the Khalifs do not) and is the recipient of inspiration or *ilham* (although not of revelation). Since only the Imam enjoys this special blessing, only he can interpret the Shari'ah; thus 'the further elaboration of the law is the sole prerogative of their divinely inspired Imam' (Coulson, 1994: 106). Sunni law is 'basically immutable', but subject to 'human reason to discern the divine command'; Shi'a law is 'the direct and living expression of that command'; 'politically', says Coulson, 'it is the difference between a constitutional and an absolute form of government' (*ibid.*: 107). Sunni Islam rests on consensus (*ijma*), Shi'a on obedience. Whether the early Shi'a, who supported the Alide cause, had a very sophisticated doctrine of the Imamate or not is debatable. Some scholars think that 'Ali and his descendants simply served as convenient foci for opposition to the Umayyad and perhaps, at various stages, also to 'Abbasid rule.

Jafar (699–765)

The doctrine of the Imamate may have been developed by the sixth Imam, Jafar al-Sadiq, and the designation projected back on to 'Ali, Hasan, Husayn, 'Ali Zayn al-Abadin (the only Alide to survive Karbala) and Muhammad al-Baqir, to suggest an unbroken history of Alide support from the death of the

Prophet (see Halm, 1991: 29). Jafar was widely respected as a scholar of Islam, and at one time attracted both Imam Malik and Imam Hanifa to study under him. He is said to have mastered 'arcane sciences' such as alchemy, as well as mystical Islam (which I discuss below). The dominant legal tradition amongst Shi'a, which revolves around the role of the Imam, takes its name from Jafar – and has sometimes been considered a fifth school (alongside the four Sunni *maddhab*). It was later claimed that Jafar possessed a book of esoteric teaching (passed down the Alide line from Muhammad) and that this was the source of his doctrines. According to Jafar, the Imamate is as much part of the divine blueprint as prophethood; as a later Shi'a writer put it, 'the Imamate is a kindness from God, for, when people have a head and a true guide whom they obey ... they are in a healthy condition' (Watt, 1994b, citing i-Hilli (1250–1325)).

Thus, just as Muhammad had been preordained to be the final prophet and apostle of God, so was each Imam destined for that office from before the creation of the world. Although each must be designated (*nass*) by their predecessor, they are all predestined for designation. God, in this view, always appoints an intermediary between himself and humankind and, in the absence of the Prophet, this function devolves to the Imam, who 'cannot be chosen by fallible men and left to the vicissitudes of history' but 'must fulfil certain conditions of principle, be perfectly learned in religious matters, be absolutely just and equitable, be perfect, free from any fault (*ma'sum*), be the most perfect man (*afzal*) of his time' (Richard, 1995: 6). As descendants of the Prophet, too, the Imams can be regarded as sharing something of his nature – sometimes referred to as his essence (*al-haqiqah*), or, in later Shi'a writing, as his '*nur*' (light).

This '*nur*' was created by God before the world and incarnated in Muhammad rather as, in Christian thought, the *logos* was incarnated in Jesus of Nazareth. Sometimes Q 5:15 is cited to support this concept, 'Now hath come upon you light [Muhammad] from Allah and a plain scripture [the Qur'an]'. God, through the Prophet, said, 'I have created the light of Muhammad from the light of my own existence' (cited in al-Halveti, 1992: 54). This light is also present within the Imams – hence their peculiar ability to guide people along the straight path (indeed, to attract true seekers to themselves; perhaps this is what 'Ali meant when he spoke about possessing 'hidden knowledge'). Like prophets, Imams are infallible. Salvation depends on recognizing and following the Imam as much as on affirming the *shahadah* and fulfilling Islam's religious obligations. In later Shi'a thought, not only the Imams but their entire families, together with the Holy Family of the Prophet, pre-existed; before their birth on earth they were waiting to fulfil their destiny in heaven. Indeed, Karbala, the site of the massacre of Husayn and his companions, had also pre-existed the creation of the world and 'at the Day of Reckoning will be restored to paradise as the dwelling place of the prophets and saints' (Bennett, 1994a: 108). The Imam, in Shi'ite theory, 'is not only the head of the community but also the visible proof (*hujja*) of the truth of the divine revelation; without his presence the world would not exist for a single moment' (Halm, 1991: 45).

The Imam is spiritual and political leader, and anyone who opposes his rule is an enemy of true Islam. However, the Imams were unable to exercise any real political power; in fact, much of the Sh'ia experience has been one of suffering, martyrdom and opposition, and, in their own eyes, championing the *'adl* (justness) of God (which would not leave humanity without a Guide or Imam) against its enemies. Yazid becomes the personification of evil; Karbala is remembered as a battle between the forces of light and darkness. Akbar Ahmed writes:

A sense of sectarian uniqueness, of group loyalty, faith in the leadership, readiness for sacrifice ... marks the community .... for Shi'a's, history went awry at the source; a sense of injustice is thus rooted in the way the community perceives the world. (1988: 56–7)

This has been called the 'Karbala paradigm'. On the other hand, alongside this martyr motif, al-Jafar also taught that in the face of unfavourable 'circumstances ... one must not tempt fate, and it is preferable ... to employ that specifically Shi'ite virtue of "mental dissimulation" (*taqiyah*)' (Richard, 1995: 36). In other words, one could keep publicly silent about one's Shi'a identity whilst remaining inwardly loyal to the Imam. Muir, as previously noted, thought that *taqiyah* gave all Muslims a general license to deceive.

Shi'a's sub-traditions

The Imamate's indissoluble link with the Alide line, however, did not prevent disputes about which Alide ought to be Imam – designations could be queried, as was that of Ismail, Jafar's eldest son, who predeceased his father. The majority of Shi'a recognized Musa as Imam (believing that Ismail had been 'passed over' due to unsuitability; he was once found in a state of inebriation) but a group left the majority of Shi'a to follow Ismail's son, Muhammad, as their eighth Imam, counting Ismail himself as seventh. Numbering, however, becomes problematical as later tradition supplied 'Ali with a different title, *asas*, which makes Hasan the first Imam and Ismail the sixth! Those Shi'a who separated from the majority over the question of Ismail's Imamate became known as 'seveners' (they are also commonly referred to as Ismailis) and have themselves split into several sub-groups. Some Ismaili groups (exercising *taqiyah*) went 'underground', organizing secret opposition to the 'Abbasid dynasty. This included assassinating those whose rule they regarded as illegitimate. One group succeeded in seizing power in Egypt (the Fatimids) where they became known as Khalif-Imams, and set themselves up in opposition to the Baghdad administration. It was usually dispute over succession to the Imamate that led to these various schisms. Some Ismaili groups no longer have a 'living', but a 'hidden Imam' (see below) who is represented by a special agent on earth. The Qasim-Shahi Nizaris, perhaps the best-known Ismaili group, recognize the Aga Khan as their spiritual leader or living Imam, whilst the Bohras recognize a *da'i* as the representative of their hidden Imam, al-Tayyib (their twenty-first Imam who occulted during the final years of the Fatimids). Another Ismaili group, the so-called Assassins (or the *fidayyun*: the ones prepared to sacrifice themselves) entered the public imagination due to exotic (but not altogether accurate) tales. After the collapse of the Fatimids, a militant group of Nizari Ismailis set up headquarters in the mountain fortress of Allamut, which they controlled from 1090 to 1256. Their leader, Grand Master Hasan as-Sabbah (a *da'i*), gained considerable power in the region by winning tribes to the faith through missionary activity. Daftary describes this as a 'territorially scattered state'. It 'posed a serious challenge' to the Saljuks, and became embroiled in the Crusades, thus entering European folklore (1992: 2). Their stronghold finally fell to the Mongols, who executed Rukn ad-Din, the last Grand Master.

Ismaili doctrine

The Ismailis developed very distinctive doctrines which appear to have been heavily influenced by gnostic thought. Esoteric, inner or secret (*batini*) knowledge takes precedence over external (*zahir*) practice – thus the orthodox rites of Islam are not all that important and may or may not be practised. The esoteric teaching is believed to be embedded in the text of the Qur'an and can be decoded. The Imam possesses the key and can instruct others (who now stand in a master–disciple relationship with the Imam). As his representatives (*da'i*, literally a caller or summoner) they are then sent out to engage in *da'wa* (mission). Mission has an important place in Ismaili Islam. Ismailis stress the unknowability of God – God is equivalent to the 'Abyss', or 'Void' of the gnostics – and Allah (who can be known) is an emanation (the first emanation) or hypostasis of the Abyss (represented as light). Some Ismailis surmise that the word 'Allah' may be derived from *walaha,* which means 'to lament', because the hypostasis knows 'something' of God, who is otherwise unknowable, and mourns its own separation from God. The corporeal world, however, may be the creation of another manifestation, whose nature, in opposition to the first emanation, is evil (represented by darkness). Good, though, has hidden itself in the world and can be accessed by those who have *gnosis* (the Imams and those whom they initiate). Thus there is a cosmic battle going on between good and evil. 'Ali also assumes special status – Muhammad, as prophet, represents the *zahir* (the external, spoken) whilst 'Ali represented the ineffable, the secret or the silent. In this view, the prophet is the lesser of the two, for he is but spokesperson for 'Ali and reveals some but not all of what 'Ali knows. Sometimes Ismailis speak about a divine spark in all people ('gold fallen into mud') as a result of the Good hiding itself within creation; the job of the *da'i* is to awaken people to the realization of their true nature. Usually, the Imam is regarded as a hypostasis of the divine. Deification is the goal. Ultimately, the two rival emanations will merge and in this state of union no longer be 'good' and 'evil'.

After the Fatimid period in Egypt, Ismailis have rarely exercised political power but they have thrived as an organized community under their Imams, whose right to 'dispose of community assets freely' was upheld by the British Courts during their rule in India (Halm, 1991: 191). The Nizaris are prosperous merchants and have established their own schools, universities, social welfare, development programmes, and medical and religious institutions in many parts of the world (see Daftary, 1992: 545). As their 'living Imam', the Aga Khan 'has been able to reinterpret Islam to respond to modern life' (Esposito 1991: 48). Ismaili scholarship flourished under the Fatimids and contributed much to metaphysical speculation (influencing Jewish Kabbalah) partly through its fascination for the significance of numbers (especially the number seven). In fact, Ismaili Islam is in a sense 'apolitical'; Ismailis can live as loyal citizens of the countries in which they settle but look to their Imam for spiritual guidance. In theory, the Aga Khan's authority is absolute; in practice it covers religious and community matters; Aga Khan III is 'regarded as one of the founding fathers of Pakistan' (Halm, 1991: 191). The present Aga Khan is also a Pakistani citizen and about two million of his own followers live in Karachi (see Halm, p. 191). We may note similarities between the Ismaili model of being a 'state within the state' and our above reference to Sufi orders as micro social–economic systems.

The Zaydis

This group split from the majority of Shi'a even earlier than the Ismailis, taking their name from their fifth Imam, Zayd (d. 740), whom they followed in preference to the majority's candidate, his brother al-Baqir. Zayd was much more vigorous in opposing the Umayyads; thus radical opposition to the claims of the Khalif characterized early Zaydism. Not surprisingly, they rejected *taqiyah* as cowardly. The Zaydis represent about 40 per cent of the population of the Yemen, where their last few Imams ruled (adopting the title of king) until the revolution of 1962 established a republic. The last Imam died in London. There is, however, no reason why another should not 'emerge' (*khuruj*), although at present the Zaydis remain 'without a religious leader' (Halm, 1991: 210). Zaydi Shi'a parted company from other expressions of this tendency by allowing any descendant of the Prophet (any Zaydi) to become Imam, provided that they enjoyed the support of their peers – something in common here with the Kharijites. Rejecting 'designation' (*nass*), they opted for 'emergence'. Nor did they assign supernatural abilities to their Imams. Rather, they had to rule according to the Qur'an and *sunnah*, and were bound by these just like all other Zaydi Muslims.

Generally, later Zaydi Imams and scholars were 'hostile to undisciplined ecstasy, the veneration of saints, or millenarian longings and ... promoted instead a rather sober religious style' (Dresch, 1989: 11). It was not unusual for son to succeed father, but technically any Sayyid could be recognized as Imam, either through force of personality, military means, or his claim gaining the support of the religious scholars. The Imam, too, often delegated certain functions to the *ulama* and did not govern as an absolute ruler. There is thus little to distinguish the Zaydis from Sunnis who opposed the hereditary

Khalifate, believing that any pious Muslim could rule, except that for them the Imam must emerge from the House of Ali.

The twelvers

The majority recognized another six Imams after Jafar (through Musa's line) until their twelfth Imam, al-Mahdi, disappeared from the world, following his father's death, in 873. According to his followers, al-Mahdi had 'gone into occultation'. He continued, however, to direct the affairs of his community through a *wakil* or intermediary, of whom there were four in succession until 940, when the fourth failed to nominate a successor. After the disappearance of al-Mahdi, there has not been a 'living' Imam for the majority of Shi'a, or perhaps I ought to say an 'earth-bound' Imam, since in their view al-Mahdi is still alive and, as the spiritual centre (*axis mundi*) of the universe, remains its rightful ruler. One day he will return to usher in the age of peace, justice and righteousness. 'Ali appears to have predicted that al-Mahdi would wear 'the armour of wisdom ... if Islam is in trouble he will feel forlorn like a traveller ... He is the last of Allah's proofs' ('Ali, 1996: 141). The majority of Shi'a, known as 'twelvers' (*ithna ashariyya*), constitute the dominant tradition in Iran, where the Constitution of the Islamic Republic (declared after the overthrow of the Shah in 1979) is predicated on 'twelver' theology and principles. After the fourth *wakil* failed to nominate a successor, the twelvers were faced with the problem which had challenged the whole *ummah* immediately after the Prophet's death – in practice, how should the community be governed? Given that the Shi'a were often subject to Sunni law, this problem may have been a theoretical one. In theory, too, they are still under the guidance of the Hidden Imam, a function which nobody can usurp. Richard (1995) writes, 'The fact that the Imam is "present", though hidden, renders illegitimate any absolute claim to authority over men, as the sovereign who assumes a position of command is usurping the only existing authority' (p. 45).

Yet legal decisions must still be made and the day-to-day affairs of the community must still be supervised. What emerged in Shi'a Islam to meet this need and to help fill the vacuum left by the 'occultation' of the Imam, was a professional (often hereditary) clerical class who, whilst not infallible, could discern the correct Islamic position on a point of law or Islamic practice. This process is known as '*ijtihad*', defined thus by Kamali (1991): 'lit. "exertion", and technically the effort a jurist makes in order to deduce the law, which is not self-evident, from its sources' (p. 405). In other words, if a particular situation is not explicitly covered by legal codes in either the Qur'an or *hadith*, a competent scholar, by applying Qur'anic principles, can deduce an authentic Islamic position or ruling. In Sunni Islam, the legal deductions of the four Imams or jurists after whom the recognized schools of law were named, exercised *ijtihad*, and were known as *mujtahid* (plural, *mujtahidun*). This extension of Islam's legal code's scope to cover new situations was an essential part of its development as a comprehensive social and economic legal system. However, after the tenth century, and with the work of the four Imams generally recognized as more or less definitive, Sunni Muslims became reluctant to allow further *ijtihad*. Even though the decisions of the *mujtahidun* had to be accepted by the *ijma* (consensus) of the community, there were dangers inherent in this process: first, that individuals exercised undue influence, over and above others, in interpreting Islam; second, that personal interests might result in corruption or in self-serving legal rulings. Thus, Sunni *ijma* decided that the 'gates of *ijtihad*' were closed. *Bida* (innovation) became a mortal sin, *taqlid* (imitation) of the past the duty of all Muslims, as Esposito (1991) comments:

Belief that the work of the law schools had definitively resulted in the transformation of the Shari'a into a legal blueprint for society reinforced the sacrosanct nature of tradition; change or innovation came to be viewed as an unwarranted deviation (*bida*) from established sacred norms. (p. 84)

As I have already suggested, what actually happened was that, since rulers could not change *Shari'ah*, they increasingly sidelined it instead.

Akhbaris versus the Usulis

Used to the idea that the Imam possesses special, indeed unique, authority to interpret Islam, the Shi'a have had less difficulty with *ijtihad* – although its *mujtahidun* have had to be careful not to claim for themselves all the prerogatives of the Imam. Whilst his decisions were inspired and infallible, they have to be content with fallibility. In fact, within twelver Shi'ism, there was opposition to the continued exercise of *ijtihad* for the very reason that it could be seen as usurping the authority of the Hidden Imam. One school, the Akhbaris (traditionalists), held that the Qur'an and the 'sayings of the Imams' were the 'guiding principles for believers' (Halm, 1991: 101), and that the *ulama* could not add to this corpus but must imitate the past. The scholar may know more about the tradition but has no greater authority to interpret it than does any other believer. Thus the Akhbaris' position resembles the Sunnis' (as does the Sayyid view, described above). They were eventually ousted, however, by their rivals the Usulis (rationalists), who asserted the right of the *mujtahidun* to deduce original legal rulings; indeed, according to the Usulis, all Muslims should imitate a living, not a dead, man. All Usulis follow a living *mujtahid* who becomes their 'reference of emulation' or *marja'-al-taqlid,* whose opinions and judgements they consider binding. These rulings 'die' with the *mujtahid.* The *ulama,* amongst the Usulis, became a highly organized body of scholars of varying rank and competency. Only the highest rank function as *mujtahidun,* as Halm (1991) explains:

The majority of simple mullahs only had jurisdiction over the application of already unambiguously laid-down rules and regulations in Islamic law, the *furu* (literally: branches), while a group of highly qualified scholars selected on the basis of their knowledge of the principles of legal ruling, the *usul* (literally: roots), was qualified to reach independent and binding decisions (*ijtihad*). (p. 104)

In earlier times, there were very few scholars of *mujtahid* status. Later, their numbers increased, which resulted in the creation of additional ranks within the hierarchy. The most senior *mujtahidun* (in practice, those who attracted a large following) became known as *hujjat-al-Islam*, or proof of Islam, whilst the higher title of 'Ayatollah' (sign of God) went to the most senior of all. Eventually, the most senior of these became known as the *Ayatollah-al-Uzma* (the greatest sign of God) or the *marja'-al-taqlid al-mutlaq* (absolute point of reference). Although such a person is still not, as such, a substitute for the Hidden Imam, nor does he share the Imam's infallibility, he may well be regarded as speaking on behalf of the Imam. Indeed, the group appears to have come very close to claiming infallibility. Collectively, the *ulama* certainly came to be recognized as substituting for the Imam, and gradually took upon themselves some of his prerogatives, such as collecting the *khum* (tax), imposing corporal and capital punishment (*hudud*), leading the Friday prayers and, finally, the right to declare a *jihad* (see Halm, 1991: 107).

Shah Ismail and Mahdism

The authority of the *ulama* waxed and waned somewhat, but was usually strengthened when they were seen as defenders of true Islam against rulers whose rule few saw as guided by Islamic principles. It was under the Safavid dynasty in Persia (1501–1732) that Twelver Shi'ism as it is known today really developed and became the majority religion of that state. The first Safavid, from a long line of Sufi revivalists who 'called for a restoration of a purified Islam' (Esposito, 1991: 64) came to power by rallying Shi'a opposition to the Khalif to support his own claims – descended from the family of the Imams, he came to see himself as 'personifying the Hidden Imam in the flesh' (Ahmed, 1993: 84). Shah Ismail saw himself as a religious as well as a political leader and took the title 'Shadow of God on earth'. Indeed, his charismatic personality resulted in many believing him to be the Mahdi. Islamic history is littered with what has been called 'Mahdism' – the phenomenon of religious and political leaders who either claimed to be the Mahdi or who were regarded as such by others. Sayyid 'Ali Muhammad (1819–50), for example, predicted that the Mahdi would soon return, and called himself the *bab* (gate, a John the Baptist type forerunner). His followers continued to expect the Mahdi; then in 1863, one of their number, Mirza Husayn 'Ali Nuri, or Baha'u'llah (1817–92), announced that he was the Mahdi and the 'inaugurator of a new religious dispensation' (Momen, 1996: 121). This, of course, would place him 'on a par with Muhammad' (p. 116) as a new prophet, which immediately attracted opposition. However, the Bahai faith, which developed from his leadership, now numbers some six million and is committed to the unity of the human family. Amongst Sunni, there is also popular belief in the coming of the Mahdi, who is often thought to be a descendant of the Prophet. Claimants have included Ibn Tumart (d. 1130), founder of the puritan Almohads, who ruled north Africa until 1269; and the famous Mahdi of Sudan (d. 1885), who besieged General Gordon at Khartoum, then took the town and killed the General in the process.

Esposito describes Shah Ismail as 'both temporal and spiritual ruler, emperor and messianic messenger' (*ibid.*). In some popular accounts, he is depicted not only as the Mahdi but also as the reincarnation of ʿAli and of all twelve Imams (see Halm, 1991: 82). Under him, such practices as pilgrimage to the shrines of the Imams and to Karbala for the annual 'passion play' (*ta'ziya*), were established. In Shiʿa piety, the Imams are not regarded merely as good men who are now dead, but as 'friends of God' through whom prayers can be offered. Shiʿa 'believe that the intercession of the Imams is a necessary part of history, from the redemptive death of Husayn to the return of the Hidden Imam at the end of time' (Esposito, 1991: 110). The Safavids continued to claim to 'represent' the Hidden Imam, which somewhat by-passed the *ulama*. However, the Shahs were not experts in religious law, and required advice; thus they appointed a 'deputy' or *Sadr* (although early holders do not seem to have been especially well versed in this either!). Gradually, the *Sadr* were able to curb the excesses of the Safavid's charismatic claims, and even succeeded in transferring some of these to themselves. Al-Karaki, who became *Sadr* in 1531, was given powers to appoint and dismiss all religious functionaries. He, not the Shah, became *na'ib al-Imam,* deputy of the Imam. By the sixteenth century, the *mujtahidun* were all but claiming that they were infallible guides of a fallible Shah. Halm (1991) comments that it is 'by no means the case that – as it is occasionally claimed – the Twelvers recognize no legitimate government and administration whatsoever in the absence of the Iman'. Rather, there can be legitimate government but this requires the Imam's 'explicit authorization' (p. 57). What we see happening here, then, was a contest between the charismatic Imam-family related rulers, and the not necessarily charismatic scholars, to claim true representation of the hidden Imam.

The 1979 Revolution

Under the Safavid's successors, the Qajars (who made no charismatic claims for themselves) the doctrine of dual functions developed: 'the Shah dealt with law and order and thus produced the external conditions for the application of the *shari'a* over which the *ulama* for their part had jurisdiction' (Halm, 1991: 111). Later, however, rulers found themselves wanting to reform, that is, to secularize the legal and administrative systems or to get their hands on the wealth of the endowed shrines which the clergy controlled, which brought them into increasing conflict with the *ulama*. The last Shah certainly saw 'the independent and wealthy clergy as a major threat to his power. He expelled them from their old jobs as teachers and judges, replacing them with government appointees' (Lindholm, 1996: 178). The *ulama* regarded Iran's increasing involvement with Europe and Russia as responsible for the introduction of un-Islamic practices and values. This century, the contest between secularizing rulers of the Pahlavi dynasty (1925–1979) and the *ulama* reached its climax in 1979 when, under the leadership of Ayatollah Khomeini, the Shah was replaced with a revolutionary Islamic government. Khomeini appears to have been regarded by many as the *marja'-al-taqlid al-mutlaq* or absolute point of reference, although he was 'neither the senior nor the most learned' clergyman (Halliday, 1996: 221). His speeches clearly indicate his view of the Shah's government as a 'puppet' of the Godless West:

They do not want us to be true human beings [real Muslims], for they are afraid of true human beings. Even if only one true human being appears, they fear him, because others will follow him and he will have an impact that can destroy the whole foundation of tyranny, imperialism, and government by puppets. (cited in Markham, 1996: 309)

The Shah was the modern Yazid, rebellion against him was of the just against the unjust and represented a religious duty. The time had come for 'the learned *ulama*, as heirs of the Prophet, interpreters of the law, and proxies of the Imam, finally to take the authority that had been denied to them by secular usurpers and reunite the state and faith' (Lindholm, 1996: 179).

According to Lindholm, Khomeini claimed what earlier *ulama* appear to have almost – but not quite – claimed: infallibility:

Under the new sacred polity the findings of a juriconsult are no longer conditional or contingent, and ordinary persons can no longer shop around to discover the spiritual leader most in tune with their own predilections. Instead, the old informal contestation between religious leaders for followers in an open spiritual marketplace was to be superseded by a new centralized organization of seventy faqih elected by the people; this assembly would in turn elect an Absolute Guide from amongst the ulama most qualified. (pp. 179–80)

The government established by Khomeini has thus been described as a 'mullacratic' system, since it allows for the election of a Consultative Assembly whilst also ensuring that the authority of the *mujtahidun* remains paramount; Khomeini himself often cited the following *hadith*: 'The direction of public affairs is in the hands of those who are learned concerning God and are trustworthy in matters pertaining to what He has made lawful and unlawful' (cited in 'The Constitution of the Islamic Republic of Iran', *Al-Tawhid*, 13, 2, Summer 1996). Article 2 upholds the right of the *mujtahid* to engage in 'continuous *ijtihad* ... exercised on the basis of the Qur'an and the Sunnah of the infallible ones (*Ma'sumin*)'. During the occultation of the Imam, Article 4 states, 'leadership of the *Ummah* devolves upon the just and pious jurist, fully aware of the times, courageous, possessing administrative and problem-solving abilities'. A mechanism for the removal of the Leader, or Absolute Guide, however, does exist – should he fail to fulfil his function properly.

After 1979 Khomeini used the title Imam (which is not used by his successor), which seems to suggest that he regarded himself in some sense as a substitute for the Hidden Imam. Halm (1991) describes Khomeini's authority as a 'an anticipated plebiscitary de facto Imamate'. In other words, even before his return, 'the rule of the Mahdi is already being enforced by the will of the people' (Halm, p. 128; see Richard, 1995: 108). There is little doubt that many Shi'a saw Khomeini's rule as the restoration of legitimate government; as Lindholm (1996) says, 'Khomeini's central claim was that he was refinding a divine order that had been lost' (p. 179). Khomeini may well have believed that his leadership anticipated the Mahdi's return, which might lie behind these words which conclude the Constitution's preamble:

It consists of twelve chapters comprising one hundred and seventy-five articles and was completed ... on the eve of the fifteenth century of the hijrah of the Noble Messenger, may Peace and blessings be upon him and his family, the founder of the redeeming school of Islam, hoping that this century will witness the establishment of a world government of the *mustad'afun* and the defeat of all *mustakbirin*. (see *Al-Tawhid*, 13, 2, p. 39)

Certainly, there was much that was 'Imam-like' about Khomeini, himself a *sayyid*. Richard (1995) compares his 15 years in self-imposed isolation at Najaf, when he 'continued to communicate with the Iranians with the aid of a few messengers', with the occultation of al-Mahdi (p. 106). Iranians have claimed to see Khomeini's face in the night-moon (p. 197). They often performed ritual ablution before meeting him (p. 108). To non-Muslims, for whom Khomeini has become something of a bogey, it is difficult to appreciate the love and respect he commanded; a deeply mystical personality, there is no doubt that his followers regarded him as Muhammad's heir in directing the affairs of Iran. He combined within himself routinized (legal) and charismatic (Sufi) leadership and thus, in his own person at least, resolved the struggle between these two which has often troubled Iranian Islam (see Richard, 1995: 58–60).

Summary

What, then, can we say about the significance of Muhammad within Shi'a Islam? First, that Shi'a Muslims share with Sunni the belief that Muhammad is the Final Prophet, that they share with Sunni the view that his life represents a source of emulation for all Muslims and that his *sunnah* is binding. However, unlike Sunni, they add to this the continued ability of his descendants to interpret Islam for each new generation, indeed, to add newly inspired (though not revealed) content to Islamic law. Believing that God does not leave the *ummah* without living leaders, the Imams (and their *de facto* successors, the *mujtahidun)* enjoy unique authority within the Shi'a world. It can be said that this authority substitutes for that of Muhammad, who is dead; indeed, according to the Usalis, 'one should not imitate a dead man (*taqlid-al-mayyet)*', which includes Muhammad (Richard, 1995: 69). In some Shi'a sub-traditions, too, we saw how 'Ali's role becomes elevated at the expense of Muhammad's. On the other hand, the concept of the 'light of Muhammad', which we shall also encounter in Sufi Islam, makes much more of Muhammad than an ordinary flesh and blood mortal.

Sunni Islam, having called a halt to its ability to 'extend' Islamic law (with the emulation of the past as its highest ideal), often seems to experience difficulty in responding to new challenges. On the other hand, because it refuses to give too much authority to individuals, it has (in the Prophet's absence) acted cautiously in its juridical endeavours; thus 'its legal theory regards its own judgements as only probable regardless of their practical necessity and compulsion' (al-Azmeh, 1993: 97). For its part, with infallible (or nearly so) leaders, Shi'a Islam has had less difficulty with change. One Muslim friend once told me that he became a Shi'a because he sees Shi'a Islam as more dynamic than Sunni, better able to adjust to new circumstances. Of course, one can say that the 'truth' does not have to adjust to the world, rather the world has to adjust to the truth. This, however, can seem to relegate Muhammad's role to the past, and to concede more importance to those who exercise leadership today.

Sufi and popular Islam

This section explores the Prophet's role within Sufism (*tasawwuf*), which is usually identified as Islam's mystical tendency. Some writers object to the designation 'mystical Islam' since, in their view, Sufism is quite simply 'Islam', or 'spiritual Islam' and not a particular development, or branch of Islam. Paul Yachnes (1995) writes, 'Sufism is a continuous historical and even institutional phenomenon in the Muslim world' (p. 1). Hixon (1989) thinks that 'the Sufis shouldn't be identified with any sort of narrow-minded Islam, with any cultural chauvinistic Islam, but definitely with Islam itself. Sufism and Islam are one' (p. 2). Similarly, when asked, 'What is a Sufi?', a former Shaikh-al-Azhar replied, 'A Sufi is a good Muslim' (Eyre, 1979: 148). Sufism shares certain features in common with Shi'ism, and has always provided something of a bridge between the Sunni and Shi'a strands of Islam, as Akbar Ahmed (1996) notes: 'Its message of *sulh-i-kul*, peace with all, has endeared it to Muslims and non-Muslims alike. It appeals to all Muslim sects and social classes' (p. 55). Below, illustrating the degree to which Sufi Islam crosses boundaries, I have cited from such contemporary authors as Seyyed Hossein Nasr, a Shi'a scholar influenced by Sufi thought, and Frithjof Schuon (Isa Nusruddin) and Martin Lings (Abu Bakr Siraj Ad-Din) who are both Sunni Sufis, as well as from classical Sufi writers.

Islam's mystical tendency emerged early in its historical development; Hasan of Basra (642–728) helped to formulate mystical thought and provides an important link with the Prophet himself. Hasan is often cited as an authority in the *isnad* of *hadith* transmission. He also contributed to the theological debates of his day; the Mu'tazalites are said to have broken away from his school. According to Louis Massignon (1883–1962), the influential French Islamicist, it was the early traditionalists who 'evolved into the pioneers of Sufism' (Lindholm, 1996: 181). Studying the *hadith*, they came to love the figure of Muhammad found therein; they were especially inspired by the example of his simple lifestyle and selfless habits. At what was probably quite an early stage in the development of Sufi thought and practice, its devotees became known as Sufis, from *suf* (wool), because they apparently wore distinctive woollen clothes. However, a device of the mystics (note here similarity with Ismaili theology) is to see different layers of meaning in Qur'anic verses, ritual acts and technical and theological terms, usually an inner and an outer meaning. Later Sufis spoke of a secret identity between the word 'sufi', and the word '*safi*' (pure). Bishr al-Hafi, an early Sufi of Baghdad, said, 'The Sufi is he who keeps his heart pure' (Lings, 1975: 77). The origin of the term Sufi has been subject to much speculation. Another possible derivation is from *suffe* or bench; thus, the earliest Sufis (*ahle suffe*) would sit on a bench in the Prophet's mosque discussing the spiritual meaning of the Qur'an, and how to walk in the footsteps of the Prophet.

Asceticism, devotion to God and to his prophet characterized Sufism from the very beginning; Rabi'a (d. 801) was amongst the first to introduce the language of love (*mahabba*), love between the 'beloved' (God) and the 'lover' (the Sufi) which she spoke of as transcending any duality between the two: 'she taught', says Lindholm, 'that self-immolation in divine love was the only worthwhile end for Muslims' (1996: 182). Nor should Muslims worship or serve God because they hope thereby to gain Paradise or to avoid Hell; they should do so 'for God's own sake' alone:

> O my Lord if I worship thee from fear of Hell,
> burn me in Hell, and if I worship thee from hope
> of paradise, exclude me thence, but if I worship Thee
> for Thine own sake then withhold not from me Thine
> Eternal Beauty. (M. Smith, 1994: 50)

Incidentally, non-Muslim writers have often regarded the 'love-talk' of the Sufis as a reaction to lack of love within classical Islam's doctrine of God – it was thus supplied 'from without'. However, *hubb* is one of God's Beautiful Names, and not a few Qur'anic verses speak of God as 'lover': for example, Q 5:54, 'Allah will bring a people whom He loveth and who love Him'; other verses, for example Q 2:165, speaks of the believers' love for God. B 72:41 says, 'Love is from Allah'.

The doctrine of the Oneness of Being

Our concern is with Muhammad's role within Sufism, but in order to understand this it is first necessary to explore some of the most important features of Sufi Islam. Given the popularity of Sufi Islam, to which I shall refer later in this section, I make no apology for this quite detailed description. Sufi thought begins with an interpretation of the doctrine of *tawhid*, as contained in the first statement of the *shahadah*: 'I testify that there is no God but God'. Martin Lings explains:

Every Muslim is obliged to believe in theory that there is no Reality but the Reality, namely God; but it is only the Sufis ... who are prepared to carry this formulation to its ultimate conclusion. The doctrine which is based on that conclusion is termed 'Oneness of Being', for Reality is that which is, as opposed to that which is not; and if God alone is Real, God alone *is*, and there is no being but His Being. (Lings, 1975: 65)

Muslim philosophers, too, developed a cosmology which saw all 'being' as essentially singular (*wahdat al-wujud*). Like the Ismailis, Sufis tend to regard 'creation' as an 'emanation' from the divine presence. The world was not created *ex nihilo*, nor at a point in time, but eternally proceeds from the 'essence' of God: 'There is One Real Being, the Ultimate ground of all existence. This Reality may be viewed either as God (the divine Essence) or as the world (phenomena) by which the hidden essence is made manifest' (Nicholson, 1995: 23). God manifests forth, as creation, in order to 'be known'; God cannot be 'known' if there is nothing to 'know him', as Rumi (1207–73), founder of the Mevlevi (the whirling dervishes) wrote: 'Divine Wisdom created the world in order that all things in His knowledge should be revealed' (cited in Nicholson, *ibid.*). According to various traditions, the first emanation was either 'knowledge' itself, or 'the intellect', or 'The Perfect Man' within whom 'knowledge' resides, as Nicholson explains:

According to the Holy Tradition, 'I created the creation in order that I might be known' [this tradition begins thus, 'I was a hidden treasure, I willed to be known. I created the ....'; see al-Halveti, 1992: 53], the entire content of God's knowledge is objectified in the universe and pre-eminently in Man. The divine mind, which rules and animates the cosmos as an indwelling rational Principle (Logos), displays itself completely in the Perfect Man. The supreme type of the perfect Man is the pre-existing reality or Spirit of Muhammad, whose 'Light' irradiates the long series of prophets beginning with Adam and, after them, the hierarchy of Muslim saints, who are Muhammad's spiritual heirs. Whether prophet or saint, the perfect Man has realized his Oneness with God: he is the authentic image and manifestation of God. (1995: 24)

Two of Muhammad's titles are thus *al-ʿaql al-Kull* (the total intellect) and *al-qalam* (the Pen) because 'he poured knowledge into the realm of letters' (al-Halveti, 1992: 6). The Sufis tend to say that God's ultimate essence (*dhat* or *zat*) is unknowable; what can be known of God is knowledge of him which has been 'objectified' within the Universe; Muhammad is thus 'the essence of all beings, the beginning and reality of the universe' (*ibid.*). Sometimes, however, Sufi cosmology begins with an ineffable, unknowable God, who first manifests that which can be known about God's-self as Allah, the Personal God, who then manifests forth 'knowledge of himself' as creation, beginning with Paradise where human souls reside with the angels in full knowledge of their relationship with God, and finally culminating with humankind. Humanity, however, has 'forgotten' its true nature; people think that they exist independently of God. In reality, we are 'non-existent'; Rumi wrote, 'We and our existences are non-existent: Thou art the Absolute appearing in the guise of mortality' (Nicholson, 1995: 107). In this cosmology, God's 'terrible' and 'benign' attributes both manifest or irradiate into the universe (again resembling Ismaili dogma). Thus we have the apparently real but really unreal universal struggle between 'good' and 'evil'. Nicholson, in his introduction to *Rumi: Poet and Mystic* (1995) writes;

Though essentially identical, from our point of view, the divine attributes are diverse and opposed to each other, and this differentiation constitutes the phenomenal world, without which we could not distinguish good from evil, and come to know the absolute good. In the sphere of reality there is no such thing as evil. (p. 23).

The Tariqah

The mystic's concern is to journey from asserting self-existence, false-self, or ego (*nafs*) to a conscious merging of self with the ultimate and only reality (again, note the similarity with Ismaili thought; we all contain a divine spark). This goal is called both *fana* (the passing away of self, a type of death) and also *baqa* (union with the one reality, a type of rebirth), or *tawhid*, a 'making one' of the human and divine. Al-Ghazali's description of this state is worth citing in some detail since, as we shall see below, he is widely regarded as having reconciled Sufism with the more legalistic expression of Sunni Islam:

It is the condition called 'annihilation' or 'not-being' by the Sufis. That is to say, all that is becomes non-existent as a result of his meditation, and that too becomes non-existent because [the mystic] has forgotten himself as well. And just as God possesses universes of which we have no knowledge and which, as far as we are concerned, do not exist, so our existence is [simply] that of which we have consciousness and about which we have information. When someone forgets these worlds which constitute created beings, they cease to exist: and when he forgets his own selfhood, he too ceases to exist so far as a self is concerned: and since he is left with nothing but God, his existence is God, neither more nor less. And just as you survey heaven and earth and all that in them is and only see part of it, you will say that the universe extends just so far as this and that this is all. So too does this man also see nothing but God, and he says, 'All is He and apart from him there is nothing at all. (Zaehner, 1994: 167)

Whilst travelling, the mystic is a *salik* (traveller) and the journey takes him or her along the *tariqah* or path. Along the way, the *salik* is usually guided by a teacher, who is known as a *murshid*, *shaikh*, or *pir* (or marabout in North Africa). Here a direct link with Muhammad can be identified; every Shaikh is believed to stand in a direct initiatic succession (*silsilah*) with Muhammad, often through Hasan of Basra and 'Ali (providing a bridge with Shi'ism). In Sunni Islam, Abu Bakr is also an important link in various *silsilah* or chains. These Shaikhs, like Muhammad, are 'perfect men'. Hence, the mystics do not neglect the significance of the second statement of the *shahadah*. Indeed, like the Shi'a, they believe that their doctrines originate from Muhammad's esoteric teaching. Al-Jilani (1077–1166), founder of the Qadiriya order, wrote: 'A living teacher must have connection with our Master the Prophet of Allah – that is, if he is truly the inheritor of the state of the Prophet. In his teaching he receives guidance from the Prophet' (al-Halveti, 1992: 113). Schuon, says Qadir (1988), sees Muhammad as 'the manifestation and the mouthpiece of the Almighty' – thus, when Muslims recite the second statement of the *shahadah* ('and Muhammad is the apostle of Allah') they are affirming that apart from God 'nothing else is real ... everything else [symbolized by Muhammad] because it is a manifestation, is real to the extent that it has divinity in itself' (1988: 148).

Before the goal of union with reality can be realized, various stages (*maqamat*) and states of perception (*ahwal*) mark the Sufis' journey along the path. Their *niyya* (intent or desire) must be pure; this marks the beginning of the journey towards what is often called 'perfection' but the goal itself is not earned: 'The thing we tell of', said the Persian mystic al-Bistami, (d. 874) 'can never be found by seeking, yet only seekers find it' (Glasse, 1991: 377). Bistami founded the popular Naqshbandi order or *tariqah* (path); Naqshbandi means 'to engrave the name of God in the heart'. Selflessness, renunciation of extreme wealth (*faqr* – hence fakir), love of others, all help to purify the Sufi. The goal, however, can only be realized through God's love (*hubb*) and grace (*karamat*). These are frequently used terms in Sufi writing, much of which has been poetic in form. Just as we did not ask to be created, but receive existence (*wujud*) as a divine gift, so *ma'rifah* (gnosis) or knowledge of our true nature can only be realized when this is gifted us by God. Ibn Sina, one of Islam's most distinguished philosophers, who was also a renowned physician and an acclaimed Sufi writer, wrote:

Every created thing, by its nature, longs for the perfection which means its well being, and the perfection of the created being is brought about by the grace of that One who is essentially perfect. The most perfect object of love is the First Cause of all things. (Quoted in M. Smith, 1950: 47)

This reference to Aristotle's 'First Cause' clearly illustrates the connection between Ibn Sina's metaphysical and mystical thought. It is, however, his use of the term 'perfection' here which connects with Muhammad's role and significance within Sufi thought.

The Perfect Man

As noted above, Sufis often refer to the goal of their path as 'perfection'; thus one who realizes union with God may also be called a 'Perfect Man' (*ihsan-i-kamil*). This is a generic term and includes women:

He to whom this supreme happiness has been granted has become a perfect man and the most exalted of creatures, for his own existence has become merged in that of the Absolute Being ... Whether woman or man, such a one is the most perfect of human beings. This is the grace of God which He gives to whom He will. (The Mughal princess Jahanara, d. 1681, quoted in M. Smith, 1950: 133)

Since human intellect is but the cosmic intellect within, and since the object of both normative and Sufi Islam is to achieve a complete identification between the individual and the divine will, it follows that human perfection is an inherent possibility. In a real sense, the Sufis are saying that if you want to picture God, picture the perfect man, picture the individual whose life is so tuned into the will of God, whose life so reflects the qualities of God, that duality between creature and creator is annihilated. 'Every man', says al-Karim Jili (d. 1428), 'is a copy of God in His perfection; none is without the power to become a perfect man' (quoted in M. Smith, 1950: 119). In Sufi thought, as I have already stated, the model of the 'Perfect Man' is Muhammad; in him, the human will and the divine existed in complete (perfect) harmony. In a sense, the 'divine' and the 'human' met in his person, as they were from eternity intended to meet; 'he is human equilibrium', the 'Universal Man' in whom 'God contemplates Himself'. The Prophet is thus the mirror in which God and all the divine qualities 'are fully reflected and through which the purpose of creation itself is fulfilled' (Nasr, 1994: 137–8). Muhammad, then, represents for Sufis the 'return to the origin which we bear within us', he becomes the 'archetype', the 'primordial and normative form' (Whole Man, al-Insan-el-Kamil, and also Ancient Man, el-Insan el-Qadim).

The way of imitation

The Sufi path is pre-eminently the way of imitation, of imitating the Prophet's inner devotion to, and outer conformity with, God's will. Sufis also believe that as the prophetic cycle culminated with Muhammad (which means that God no longer sends messengers to remind people of their true nature), a spiritual energy continues to emanate from him; many believe that this energy was manifest in his person, and identify it as the 'light of Muhammad'. *Hadith* such as 'I was a Prophet when Adam was still between water and clay' and 'I have been charged to fulfil my mission since the best of the ages of Adam, from age to age down to the age in which I now am' (Schuon, 1976: 90, MM, 2, p. 1230) are cited as proof of Muhammad's 'avataric nature'. Sufis are not saying that Muhammad is inherently 'different' from any other human being but rather that he was the first to reach the goal of human fulfilment – of extinction to self, and total at-one-ness with God. Nasr (1994) describes Muhammad as 'inwardly the beginning and outwardly the end of the prophetic cycle'. Thus, his 'being' becomes indistinguishable from the Being of God. Those who attain the goal after Muhammad do so because he has opened up the way – and continues to guide travellers along the *tariqah*. Having reached the spiritual centre, he remains there and

has the power to throw out a 'life-line', that is, a chain (*silsilah*) that traces a spiritual lineage back to himself. Every Sufi order is descended from the Prophet in this way, and initiation into a *tariqah* means attachment to its particular chain. This confers a virtual centrality, that is, a virtual reintegration into the primordial state which has then to be made actual. (Lings, 1975: 39; see Nasr, 1994: 87)

For Nasr it is through the Shaikhs that Muhammad's spiritual legacy is perpetuated via the initiatic cycle, the *da'irat al-wilayah*. Whilst not all Sufis attach themselves to a Shaikh, most do; love of the *shaikh* is a metaphor for love of God, thus:

the *murid* [disciple] even more than the student of law, had to enslave himself to his teacher in a relationship of absolute trusting submission (*tawakkul*) ... above all, the *murid* was taught that 'nothing is achieved without love for the shaikh, and obedience is the mark of love'. (Lindholm, 1996: 184, citing Nusayb)

Rumi is famous for his love poetry, expressing the *murid–murshid* relationship as one of 'two bodies with one soul'. Rumi says that their souls were once playmates in Paradise; until re-united, co-attracted as spiritual lovers by their respective 'auras', or *barakah*, they are destined to wander the earth in search of each other (see Lindholm, 1996: 198). Al-Khayr (967 – 1049) wrote:

God created the souls four thousand years before He created their bodies and placed them near to Himself and there He shed His light upon them ... those who in this world live in fellowship and agreement ... must have been on terms of intimacy there. (Cited in M. Smith, 1994: 206–7)

Pious excess?

Murid and *murshid* can both be saints; 'In the beloved', sainthood manifests itself 'under the aspect of lordship and self-sufficiency, in the lover it takes the form of servitude, abasement and tribulation' (Nicholson, 1995: 123). Some thought that the Sufis went too far in their claim to mirror God perfectly; this meant that they mirrored God's 'terrible' as well as 'benign' attributes, 'evil' as well as 'good', and sometimes led to claims that, as Perfect Men, they could transcend normative morality. The mask of sanctity could easily be misused. By asserting 'spiritual authority', the Shaikh could avoid 'personal responsibility for his acts by claiming to be an extension of the Almighty' (Lindholm, 1996: 204).

The tasliya

The main concern of this survey is Muhammad's continued significance in Islamic faith and practice. The rituals which surround invocation of his blessing and the celebration of his birthday give popular expression to this significance. Many of these practices are commonplace within the Muslim world and form part of the devotional life of many Muslims who do not, in any formal way, associate with an organized Sufi order. Foremost is the *tasliya* or salutation of the Prophet. This has a Qur'anic mandate at Q 33:56, 'Lo! Allah and his angels shower blessings on the Prophet for saluting the Prophet (*salatu 'ala al-Nabi*). O ye who believe, ask blessings on him and salute him with a worthy salutation' (Muslims, in fact, never pronounce Muhammad's name without asking God to bless him, saying 'peace be upon him'). Padwick (1961) tells us that one third of the popular prayer manuals she collected on her journeys throughout the Muslim world (for her *Muslim Devotions*) 'consists of variations on a single sentence, 'May God call down blessings on our Lord Muhammad and on the family of our Lord Muhammad and greet them with peace' (p. 152; see pp. 152–66, 'The calling down of the blessing of the prophet').

Cragg (1984) has a detailed discussion and description of *tasliya* in Chapter 4, 'Muhammad in the Soul'. This aspect of Sufi (and popular) devotion to God and God's Prophet also takes its mandate from Q 3: 31; 'If you love God, then follow me, and God will love you and forgive you your sins.' 'No one', says Padwick, 'can estimate the power of Islam as a religion who does not take into account the love at its heart for this figure [Muhammad]' (1961: 145). Cragg tells us that *tasliya* 'has been likened to the *mihrab*'; just as the *mihrab* orients Muslims' prayers towards Makkah, which serves as their physical *qiblah*, so the *tasliya* orients them towards Muhammad, who is

the *qiblah* of the heart. He thus becomes in turn the imam through whom one faces the face of God. This *tawajjah*, or seeking the light of the divine countenance, comes to pass by virtue of setting one's sight on the merit of the Prophet. Thereby, as in a *mihrab*, the desire to appear before God is made good. (Cragg, 1984: 56)

In popular piety, the Prophet is 'saluted' by reciting his many honorific names or titles, of which there are two hundred, or by reciting (*dhikr*, remembering) the Names and Qualities of God, or by dwelling 'in particular on one of these names'. As Lings explains, the aim here is to 'become like him [like Muhammad] a personification of all that this name implies' (1975: 44; and see Padwick, 1961: 138f, 'The Names of the Prophet in Worship'). Al-Jilani wrote:

When the mirror of the heart is completely cleansed by being polished with continuous invocation of the divine Names, one has access to and knowledge of the divine attributes. The witnessing of this vision is only possible in the mirror of the heart. (al-Halveti, 1992: 76)

Since Muhammad's life and person reflect or mirror the totality of divine qualities (compassion, justice, mercy, selflessness, generosity, and so on), what believers must do is to cultivate these virtues in their own lives. One way is by practical action (being generous, upholding justice) but another is by tuning yourself into Muhammad's spiritual essence or nature (which you hope to mirror) by the constant use of *dhikr*, *tasliya* and other expressions of love for the Prophet. Eventually, we become our own 'prayer'. 'Prayer in this sense makes and transforms man until he himself becomes "prayer", identified with the *dhikr* which becomes his real nature and in which he discovers who he really is' (Nasr, 1994: 142). Islam, writes Schuon, 'is the Prophet' (1976: 91). Padwick (1961) stated: 'Muhammad is the pattern of life for his people, ever occupied with his *sunna*' (p. 140). Love for the Prophet becomes total identification with his 'reality'; 'In this union of loving souls all distinctions vanish: nothing remains but the essential Unity of love, in which 'lover' and 'beloved' have merged their separate identities' (Nicholson, 1995: 21). Love (*hubb*) has been described as the beginning, and the end, of the Sufi way. 'God', says Nicholson 'reveals Himself in every union of loving souls' . (*ibid.*: 33). By 'mirroring' the life of the Prophet, the Sufis 'purify' the 'mirror'.

Muhammad as intercessor

Many *hadith* have the Prophet claiming intercessory power, for example, 'I shall be the first intercessor in paradise, no prophet having been believed to the extent I have' (transmitted by Muslim) and, 'I shall be pre-eminent among the descendants of Adam on the day of resurrection, the first from whom the grave will be cleft open, the first intercessor and the first whose intercession will be accepted' (also transmitted by Muslim). In Bukhari and Muslim, 'I have been granted five things which no one else before me has been given', of which the fifth is 'the right of intercession' (MM, 2, p. 1231). These *hadith* reflect the belief that on the Day of Judgement each prophet will be called upon to intercede on behalf of his people; Q 4:159 and 5:117, for example, refer to Jesus as witness (*shahid*) for his people, whilst Q 43:86 ('And those unto whom they cry instead of him possess no power of intercession, saving him who beareth witness unto the Truth knowingly') is widely believed to refer to Muhammad.

Others, however, argue that not only is there no explicit Qur'anic reference to Muhammad fulfilling this role but that God has reserved the prerogative for himself (see Q 6:51, 70; 10:19). Thus Rippin (1990) believes that there is no 'explicit support' within the Qur'an (which emphasizes individual responsibility) to justify the 'commonly held belief that Muhammad will act as an Advocate before God' (p. 43). Nevertheless, Muhammad is the object of intercessory prayer (*shafa'at*), and many Muslims believe that practical benefit can be obtained by receiving *barakah* (blessing) from the Prophet; see Padwick, 1961: 42–5, 143–9 and 281–6 on various forms of prayers to the Prophet. Muhammad's universal significance for all people, Muslims and non-Muslims, is clearly evident in traditions regarding death and resurrection. On the day of reckoning all will be asked, 'Who is thy lord and who is thy Prophet?', to which the correct answer will be, 'God is my lord and Muhammad is my Prophet, the Qur'an is my *iman* and the Ka'bah my *qiblah*' (Padwick, p. 279). The question, 'what think ye of Muhammad?' is one which cannot be avoided. Indeed, a *hadith* has God saying to Muhammad, 'But for you I would not have created creation' (cited in al-Halveti, 1992: 54).

Dreams and visions

In popular Islam, Muhammad is regarded as still able, beyond death, to intervene in the affairs of his community, either directly or through his spiritual heirs. Two highly regarded scholars, al-Ashari (see below) and al-Bukhari, attached significance to dreams in which Muhammad appears to have communicated his wishes to them. There are *hadith* which attribute bad dreams to the devil and good ones to God (see B 87:3, *hadith* nos 113, 114, 115). Al-Ghazali also wrote about dreams, and their interpretation: 'We hold that many a vision seen during sleep is genuine, and we acknowledge that it has an interpretation' (Watt, 1994b: 45). Esack (1997) comments on the role which dreams have played within Qur'anic exegesis, 'Muhammad, it is claimed, appears to the interpreter in a vision, to clarify a difficult point or to indicate the correct interpretation' (p. 74). Al-Halveti's rendering of al-Jilani's *The Secret of Secrets* has a chapter on visions. Dreams feature in the story of Rabi'a (d. 801), Islam's pre-eminent woman saint, whose father, himself a devout Sufi, fell asleep in some distress after her birth because of his inability to provide adequately for her, his fourth child. Then he saw Muhammad, who 'appeared to him in his sleep and said, "Do not be sorrowful, for this daughter who is born is a great saint, whose intercession will be desired by seventy thousand of my community"' (M. Smith, 1994: 23).

Rabi'a herself relates how she saw 'the prophet in a dream, and he said ... "O Rabi'a, dost thou love me?". I said, "O Prophet of God, who is there who does not love thee? But my love to God has so possessed me that no place remains for loving or hating any save Him"' (M. Smith, 1994: 123–4). E. W. Lane (1801–76) in his classic work of enthnographical observation, *Manners and Customs of the Modern Egyptians* (1836), describes how disputes were often settled 'by a dream; and when the dreamer is a person of reputation, no one ventures to contend against him' (1978: 218). At B 87:10 (*hadith* no. 123) Muhammad says, 'Whoso seeth me in his sleep seeth me truly, for Satan cannot assume the similitude of my form' (see also no. 124). Padwick translates for us prayers for visions of the Prophet (*ru'yatu n'nabi*); 'The prayer-books are eloquent of the longing of his people to see the face of the Prophet they love ... not only in the hereafter, but here and now' (1961: 149; see pp. 149–51). On the other hand, al-Kaysi (1986) in his 'compendium of rules regulating Islamic conduct' (described on the back cover as a 'brief and comprehensive handbook for Muslims') felt he had to issue a warning: 'If a Muslim feels he has seen the Prophet ... and/or received from him some kind of instruction or advice, he must keep it to himself and not divulge it to others. Islam is complete and has never acknowledged dreams as a source of Islamic teaching' (p. 59).

Barakah

It is debatable whether the conviction that blessing the Prophet may result in receiving blessing, referred to above, is or is not justified by Q 33:56. However, *barakah* is also believed to be available from Muhammad's spiritual successors, the Shaikhs of the Sufi orders. When pilgrims visit their shrines, not only do they expect spiritual blessing but healing miracles and other 'interventions' as well (*Karamat*, such as a much-wanted pregnancy). Discussing *barakah*, anthropologist Michael Gilsenan (1990) wrote: 'through the mediation of a holy man or the free gift of blessing by God (*baraka*), flow forces and powers that are witness to the interrelations of God and man and nature' (p. 79). Having, as it were, 'broken through' into the really real, Muhammad and his spiritual heirs become conduits through which movement from either side can occur – disciples can pass through from this realm into the really real, whilst blessings can flow from there into this realm. The tombs of the Shaikhs, suggests Hixon, act like crystal sets. Their physical remains many times remain uncorrupted, that is, not decaying in an ordinary sense ... Of course, their souls have melted into the divine attributes. So they're not there in their tombs, so to speak, but these crystal sets are there, and they're very important places for making spiritual progress. (1989: 2; see Lindholm, 1996: 188–90 on the 'superhuman powers' of the saints)

Much is made of Muhammad's Ascent from Jerusalem into Paradise as a metaphor or paradigm for the spiritual journey. Consider the architecture of Jerusalem's Dome of the Rock, for example, which has replicated itself in Sufi shrines throughout the Muslim world: the square foundation represents fixity (the *nafs*, unconscious of its true nature, is trapped in the not-really-real phenomenal world); the octagonal base represents the start of the *salik*'s journey away from self-exertion towards enlightenment; whilst the perfect circle, the Dome, represents *ma'rifah* (its colour, gold, is the symbol for knowledge). Just as Muhammad travelled through the heavens into Paradise, so have the Sufi Shaikhs and so can their disciples. The saints (Arabic *wali*, friend), having completed the *tariqah* or journey, themselves become indispensible parts of the cosmic order, assisting in the task of maintaining the Balance, 'God has lifted up the heavens, and has set up the Balance' (Q 55:7). R. A. Nicholson explains:

The saints form an invisible hierarchy on which the order of the world is thought to depend. Its supreme head is entitled the *Qutb* (Axis). He is the most eminent Sufi of his age, and presides over meetings regularly held by this august parliament ... below the *Qutb* stand various classes and grades of sanctity. (1963: 123–4; see Bennett, 1994a: 108)

The *qutb*, or 'world pivot of the day', had 'the legal authority equal to that of Muhammad since the power of both came from the same source: God Himself' (Lindholm, 1996: 189). As such, they could pose a threat to routinized Sunni authority, which made no such claim. The Sufi lodges or *khaniqas* also provided alternative venues for prayer and devotion to officially recognized mosques. On the other hand, many Muslims took comfort from the fact that whilst the Khalif no longer exercised any real power, 'there remained a true spiritual Caliph, the immediate representative of God, who bore a more basic sway than any outward Caliph' (Hodgson, cited in Lindholm, 1996: 190). Geertz (1983) has usefully explored the relationship between the *barakah*-authority of the marabouts of Morocco and the more routinized authority of the king: 'To ... prevail over others' the King had to demonstrate that he 'had *baraka*, that God had gifted [him] with the capacity to dominate' (p. 136).

Kabbani (1996) tells us that the axis of each age could 'project their spiritual power through time and space' so that 'millions of people' have reached 'the Divine Presence, many without ever encountering the master in physical form' (p. 5). In practice, disputes sometimes occurred between rival *murshids* for recognition as the *qutb*, each claiming 'metaphysical superiority' (Lindholm, 1996: 201). For many, however, any claim to spiritual merit disqualifies you as a true saint; indeed, some Sufis prefer to practise a type of *taqiyah*-like concealment, rather than identify openly with Sufism, lest they be thought spiritually arrogant; cf. Ronald Eyre looking for Sufis in Cairo during the still unsurpassed series, *The Long Search* (1977). Others proudly wear the distinctive dress of their orders (see Lindholm, p. 183). Also, whilst the ecstatic cries of some Sufis, uttered whilst experiencing God-intoxication (their sense of oneness with God), have led to the charge of blasphemy, for which, for example, al-Hallaj was executed in 922, others warn against speaking about the unspeakable; al-Ghazali rebuked al-Hallaj for doing just this. This important passage is also worth citing in full; al-Hallaj and those in the state of God-intoxication, said al-Ghazali, had felt themselves

drowned in the absolute of Oneness, and their intelligences lost in Its abyss ... they become persons struck dumb, and they [have] no power within them except to recall God, not even the power to recall themselves. So there [remains] with them nothing but God. They become drunk with a drunkenness wherein the sense of their own intelligence disappeared, so that one cried out 'I am the Truth' [Al-Hallaj], and another 'Glory be to me' ... But the words of lovers passionate in their intoxication and ectasy must be hidden away and not spoken of. (Peters, 1994b: 342–3)

He continues: 'when their drunkenness abates ... they know that this was not identity, but that it resembled identity'. There is a difference between saying, 'the wine is the wine-glass' and saying, 'It is as if it were a wine-glass' (Zaehner, 1994: 165, citing the same passage as above). Here, al-Ghazali uses a phrase familiar to orthodox Sunnis; this is how al-Ashari explained how Muslims could speak of God seeing, hearing, and sitting on a throne whilst avoiding the impression that God does so exactly as we do.

Whilst writers have often highlighted tension between Sufi Islam and the political–religious establishment, al-Ghazali is to be credited with helping to reconcile this tension. After a highly successful academic career in Baghdad, he became disillusioned with what philosophy and the legal tradition could offer (he thought that the former made God redundant, whilst the latter could be too formally mechanical). Success had brought him wealth but not spiritual satisfaction. Following a mental breakdown, he went off in search of inner peace and found it amongst the Sufis: 'I learnt with certainty that it is above all the mystics who walk on the road to God; their life is the best life, their method the soundest method, their character the purest character' (Watt, 1994a: 63). Al-Ghazali was now convinced that knowledge of God results only from the gift of divine illumination. However, anxious to 'keep his mysticism in harmony with orthodox dogma' (*ibid.*: 12), al-Ghazali told the Sufis that they must not neglect the external aspects of Islam, which must go hand in hand with the inner:

There [thus] emerged the image of a new organism, a complete body with mysticism or Sufism as the heart, theology as the head, philosophy as its rationality binding the different parts together, and law as the working limbs. (Glasse, 1991: 138)

The Birthday of the Prophet

The annual celebration of *Milad-al-Nabi* provides millions of Muslims with the opportunity to express their love for Muhammad; many Muslims will perform *dhikr* and *tasliya* in their homes (see Gilsenan, 1990: 182), special prayers will be recited in the mosque, and street parades and marches make public demonstration of Muhammad's significance. I have often observed these in predominantly Muslim areas of Birmingham when I was also resident there. Lane (1978) spends some 16 pages describing popular Birthday celebrations:

before the doors of most private houses of the middle and higher classes of Muslims throughout the city, lamps were hung to be lighted in the ensuing night, the night of the Moolid ... Almost all the inhabitants of the metropolis seemed to be in the streets. (p. 459)

It is interesting to compare this with a more recent description of the festival in the same city, Cairo, by Ahmed (1996) and to note many similarities:

Here Sufism and popularism, private joy and public festivity, belief and custom met as thousands and thousands of people danced, sang, cheered and chanted ... 'The full moon has arrived and grace is upon us, the messenger is with us. He came in accordance with God's order, welcome the best of messengers to Madinah'. (p. 48)

This was, says Ahmed, sung on the Prophet's Birthday in Cairo, just as it had been first sung when Muhammad entered Madinah on the occasion of the *hijrah*.

The Prophet's Tomb

It is at the Prophet's Tomb, in the mosque at Madinah, that popular devotion to Muhammad might be said to reach its climax. Although officially frowned upon by the Wahhabis who dominate Saudi Islam (see below), most Muslims who perform the *hajj* also pay a visit (known as the *Ziyarah*) to the Prophet's tomb. Traditional prayers are recited at various 'stations' within the mosque, where Abu Bakr and 'Umar are also buried. Standing before the tomb, the pilgrim recites:

I bear witness that thou art the Apostle of God. Thou hast conveyed the message. Thou hast fulfilled the trust. Thou hast counselled the community, and enlightened the gloom, and shed glory on the darkness, and uttered the words of wisdom. (Padwick, 1961: 137)

Between the Prophet's Tomb

[and a] 'free standing *mihrab* a short distance away [which is] especially sought after as a place of prayer of exceptional potency ... is a space called the *rawdah* ('garden') ... so named because the Prophet said, 'Between my house and my pulpit is a garden of the gardens of paradise.' (Glasse, 1991: 277; see B 30:13 and Peters, 1994b: 304–6).

Lane tells us how dust or soil from the Prophet's Tomb was sold in Cairo as amulets to warn bad luck away (1978: 258). See Peters (1994b: 302–3) for al-Ghazali's meditation on the value of the *Ziyarah*.

We could include much more in this chapter about the Prophet's role within both popular piety and Sufi thought but the above will suffice to illustrate his unparalleled importance as the 'door' through which one has to pass in order to realize one's true nature. Arguably, this elevates the messenger above the message, the Prophet above the Qur'an. However, as Nasr (1994: 83) points out, without the Messenger the Book 'would be a closed book'. What some Muslims find problematic, too, is the role of the 'saints', for whom special *ilm* (knowledge) is claimed. This challenges the fundamental Islamic concept of equality, elevating some above others, and smacks of gnostic influence – some, an élite, know what others do not know. Here, overlap between Sufi and Shi'a Islam may again be noted; Nasr cites al-Jafar:

The Book of God contains four things: the announced expression (*ibarah*), the allusion (*isharah*), the hidden meaning related to the suprasensible worlds (*lata'if*), and the spiritual truths (*haqa'iq*). The literary expression is for the common people (*'awamm*); the allusion is for the elite (*khawass*); the hidden meaning is for the friends of God (or saints (*awliya'*); and the spiritual truths are for the prophets (*anbiya'*). (*Ibid*.: 59).

Hostility towards Sufi Islam

Sayyid Ahmed Khan rejected 'any kind of mediation, such as the intercessionary power of a *pir* – in life, in the hour of death, or after death – as pure error' and was uneasy about the role played by *pirs* in Sufi Islam. Even so, he did not 'want to abolish the *pir-muridi* and the devotional practices that go with it' but to 'place them in the right perspective'. Thus,

If you become a *pir* become one in accordance with the *sunnah* alone, if a *murid*, then in accordance with the *sunnah* alone. Be ready in the service of the elders and opt for the affection of the one who is obedient to the *sunnah*, so that you may be blessed with good company ... the perfect *murid*, in the final analysis, is the one who keeps to the way of God – all the rest is idle talk. (Cited in Troll, 1978: 47–8)

There is much evidence that even where official hostility is expressed towards Sufi Islam, it remains the Islam of the masses. The Wahhabi movement, founded by Ibn Abd al-Wahhab (1703–87) of Saudi, and the Deobandi and Jamaat-i-Islam movements from the sub-continent, amongst other contemporary schools, are anti-Sufi. They also regard the *Milad-al-Nabi* as an uncanonical festival. They criticize Sufis for overstepping the mark in their devotion to Muhammad. Often the charge is of *bida*, theological heterodoxy (having introduced un-Islamic practices into Islam), but political motives can also be identified. The authority of regionally based *pirs*, together with their micro-systems, can rival centralized power; the religious 'centralization and homogenization under the title of *shari'a* was a cultural precondition for political centralization' (al-Azmeh, 1993: 99). Pilgrimage to the tombs of the saints could substitute for the *hajj*.

Thus, whilst Sufis have no difficulty with such practices, Wahhabis and others condemn them as *haram*, and cite *hadith* forbidding the veneration of tombs. The *Mishkat* cites *hadith* which forbid ostentatious tombs, especially those built above the ground: 'Do not leave an image without obliterating it, or a high grave without levelling it' (MM, 1, p. 355). It also has *hadith* which permit visiting graves (although some appear to cancel an earlier prohibition): 'I forbade you to visit graves, but now you may visit them'; 'visit graves, for they make you mindful of death' (MM, 1, p. 369). In Pakistan (and amongst the Pakistani community in Britain), the Islam of Ahmed Riza Khan (1856–1921), or Barelvi Islam, which emphasizes Muhammad's 'uniqueness, his esoteric gifts and roles' remains the dominant tradition (D. Bowen, 1992: 23). In Bangladesh, despite the efforts of the 'militant Islamic revivalist and purificatory movements', Sufi practices and *pir* veneration persist today 'at every level of Bengali Muslim society' according to anthropological research (see Roy, 1983: 252). Bowen observes that 'There is a marked tension between [the] iconoclastic zeal' of the Wahhabis and 'the devotion to the Prophet that prevails in [many] areas of South Asia [where] "Wahhabi" has become a derogatory term, even sometimes a form of abuse' (D. Bowen, 1992: 26). Barelvis and their Wahhabi-influenced rivals, the Deobandis, have both declared each other 'non-Muslim, Kafir', and have 'sought endorsement of their respective anathemas from religious scholars' in Saudi Arabia (P. Lewis, 1994: 40). Akbar Ahmed (1996: 116) describes the Sufi Barelvis as a group of 'mainstream Sunni Muslims who ... see the Prophet as semi-divine, present everywhere and not made of flesh'. Ahmed Khan stressed the Sufi concept of 'the "light" of the Prophet ... which came from God's own light and existed before the foundation of the world'.

In Birmingham, a Barelvi mosque, related to the contemporary Sufi *pir*, Sufi Abdullah, has recently opened; claiming to be the largest in Europe, it also supports a job club, schools, an advice centre, youth work and a myriad of other activities. As Zakaria (1988: 113) put it, Sufism is 'still a force to be reckoned with'. I recently conducted an Internet search and identified 1,000 Sufi sites, some very useful, such as International Association of Sufis home page (http://www.ias.org); Kabbani's *Sufism Today* (http://www.naqshbandi. net/haqqani/sufi/tariqat.html), cited above; 'Sufism: A Way of Life' (http:// www.qadiri-rifai.org/sufismdefined.html); and *Sufi: A Journal of Sufism* (http:// www.nimatullahi.org/MAG.HTM). There is also Yachnes' 'Sufism: An Annotated Resource Guide' (http://www.ziplink.net/~salik/sufres.html) and, on 'Dreams and Sufism', an interview with Muhammad Nur (Les Hixon; http://www.naqshbandi.net/haqqani/Sufi/M_Nur_interview.htm).

Theology, philosophy and political discourse

Time now to turn to Islamic theology and philosophy (which cannot altogether be separated from Sufism). One of the earliest debates within Sunni Islam surrounded the question: Was the Qur'an created in time by God, or had it eternally existed? It was this, amongst other issues, which divided the Mu'tazalites from the Asharites: the former take their name from a word meaning 'to distance yourself from', that is, to disagree with; the latter from al-Ashari (873–935). Elsewhere I have explored in more detail aspects of the Mu'tazalites debate with the Asharites (see Bennett, 1994b) but here I shall focus on the createdness versus the uncreatedness of the Qur'an controversy. The Mu'tazalites were influenced by Greek thought. They flourished during the early 'Abbasid Khalifate and stressed the role of 'reason' – and of human ability to deduce the 'good life' without the aid of the divine. Sunni orthodoxy wanted to assert the Qur'an's 'uncreatedness'; thus the Qur'an was not composed or created by God at the moment of *tanzil* (sending down) but had always existed within the Being of God. In fact, several verses in the Qur'an seem to refer to some type of pre-existence. For example, Q 85:21–2 refers to a 'Glorious Qur'an on a heavenly table' (*lawh*), or 'guarded tablet' in some English renderings. This and other verses were interpreted to mean that the Qur'an was uncreated. It may, though, have existed – and may still exist – as a heavenly reality created outside of God's divine being before it was 'sent down' (*tanzil*) to Muhammad, but this heavenly book is an exact replica of that which had eternally existed within God. The Mu'tazalites rejected this, arguing that a verse such as 'we have made it an Arabic Qur'an' (Q 43:3) clearly indicates that God made or created it. Political considerations influenced their stance here; wanting to give more scope to reason, they needed to reduce the authority of the Qur'an which, if it was created, might have been created other than it is,

whereas, if it is uncreated it presumably expresses something of [God's] own being which is unchangeable. If the Qur'an could have been created other than it is, the work of the *ulama* in interpreting it loses much of its authority; and a divinely-inspired imam (caliph) would be entitled to say how the law was to be changed. In practice this would almost certainly mean more power for the caliph's ministers and secretaries. (Watt, 1985: 35; see also Watt and Bell, 1970: 170–2)

Thus the Mu'tazalites enjoyed the support of at least three 'Abbasid Khalifs. However, their argument here was also predicated on *tawhid*. The idea of an uncreated Qur'an, perhaps transcribed on to a heavenly tablet, suggested that both God and God's book existed separately. This not only compromised *tawhid* but verged on associating a partner with God, albeit an inanimate partner. The Mu'tazalites challenged their opponents to explain what happens when someone recites the Qur'an: are the words, as uttered, created or uncreated? Orthodoxy, represented by the Asharites, which eventually won popular acceptance of the Qur'an's uncreatedness, replied like this:

The Qur'an is the speech of Allah ... uncreated, that is his revelation and what he has sent down. It is not he, but neither is it other than he, but in a real sense it is one of his attributes ... The ink, the paper, the writings are created things, for they are the work of men, but the speech of Allah ... is uncreated. The writing, the letters, the words, the verses, are an adaptation of the Qur'an to human needs, but the speech of Allah ... exists in itself, though its meaning comes to be understood through these things. (Imam Hanifa, cited in Zakaria, 1991: 89)

Part of the background to the created/uncreated debate was undoubtedly a power struggle between those who asserted more scope for human government and those who wanted to limit human ability to legislate. It may be possible to identify the Asharites' desire to assert the absoluteness of the Qur'an, over against those who gave more scope to human reason, with the theory that the religious scholars 'created' the authority of the *Sunnah*, thus effectively wresting power from the hands of the Khalifs. Clearly, if the Qur'an might have been other than it is, so might the example, indeed the life, of its messenger. If the Qur'an becomes less than absolute, so does the role of the messenger as its best and only safe interpreter. Diminish the importance of the Qur'an and you automatically diminish the importance of its messenger. On the other hand, if the Qur'an existed as 'sent down' to Muhammad eternally within the Godness of God, then Muhammad's life was also 'pre-ordained'. Since the Qur'an was 'revealed' to the Prophet over a period of 22 years, and sometimes addressed specific events, circumstances and relationships, these too must have been, if not planned then foreseen by God. In a sense, then, Muhammad was also 'waiting' to 'be' from eternity, at least as an 'ideal', alongside the book he was to receive. This tends to support the Sufi viewpoint, outlined above, that Muhammad as the perfect synthesis of the divine with the human will, as an archetype, was always waiting to be born. This does not make Muhammad anything other than human; it does make him unique, not as a result of accident or historical or personal circumstance, but by divine gift. As Muslims put it, Muhammad is 'a mortal, but not as other mortals; he is like a jewel amongst pebbles'. Or, as al-Ghazali said, Muhammad 'is the prince of the human race' (Watt, 1994a: 19, 77). Al-Ashari certainly saw himself as defending the legacy of the Prophet and recounts how Muhammad appeared to him in a series of dreams:

In the first of these the Prophet told him to defend what had been related from himself, that is, the Hadith, and in the second he asked how he had been fulfilling this task ... in the third dream ... the prophet, when told that [al-Ashari had given up rational methods] angrily said that he had commanded him to defend the doctrines related from himself, but had not commanded him to give up rational methods. (Watt, 1985: 65)

What the theologians taught about Muhammad is summed up for us in the more detailed confessional or doctrinal statements which were developed by them from the eighth century onwards. His sinlessness, inability to err and the finality of his message are emphasized. There are also references to his intercession ('Belief in the intercession of the Prophet', Watt, 1994b: 31), and to the importance of his role on the Day of Judgement, as identified above.

Philosophy

The Muslim philosophers were concerned with epistemology. They were dissatisfied with the reluctance of the theologians to concede human ability to 'know' very much without revelation, but they did not want to exclude the Prophet from their system; they saw the 'intellect' as a 'divine emanation' within creation. There is Cosmic Intellect (God), then there is 'intellect' which extends into our beings. This is of three types: the Active Intellect (the world of immutable ideas or forms – clear evidence here of Platonic influence); the Potential Intellect (human potential to acquire eternal truths about God, that is, to tune into Active Intellect); and Acquired Intellect (learned knowledge, with which most of us operate much of the time). In the Prophet, Active and Potential Intellect were identical – thus he knew his true nature and, in tune with God's will, he could teach this to the masses. Ibn Sina held that

not all people are capable of moral insight; only Prophets, because of their contact with active intellect, can arrive at results without the employment of moral syllogism ... Active Intellect is ... insight which in the case of the Prophet creates knowledge and values. (Qadir, 1988: 84)

Ibn Sina was also insistent that such insight had to result in action; a prophet 'moves to the higher stages of prophecy only by turning towards society and converting [moral truths] or at least some of them, into an idiom comprehensible to the masses ... who need guidance on their path to happiness and salvation' (Peters, 1994b: 189). However, whilst prophets are born with this insight, it is possible for some, by philosophical training, to attain the same relationship with Active Intellect. We see this in the work of Ibn Rushd, for whom the perfect society would be governed by such enlightened rulers. In al-Farabi, this would be the 'virtuous city', which he clearly identified with Madinah under the Prophet,

through the political life and the relationship between the best regime as Plato understood it and the divine law of Islam ... the good city resembles a sound body in which all the members co-operate and of which the ruling member is the heart. (Lambton, 1974: 420–1)

For Ibn Rushd, too, once the philosopher has acquired scientific truth he must use it on behalf of the masses. If the only difference between philosophers and prophets is that the former need to arrive at enlightenment whilst the latter are born enlightened, this leaves open the question whether the philosopher is equal to the Prophet. Of course, since the truths which a philosopher-king must rule by are identical with those revealed through the Prophet, there ought to be no need for the philosopher-kings to change these rules. However, maybe these eternal rules might be applied differently.

Political philosophy

Who should rule the Muslims? How should such a ruler be selected? These are amongst the questions about which there is much contemporary debate throughout the Muslim world. For the philosophers, as for the Kharijites, such a person would emerge; their gifts, their piety, their 'knowledge', their ability to substitute for, whilst not exceeding, the authority of the Prophet, would be recognized by the Muslim people. This could be routinized by allowing pious Muslims to elect a Consultative Assembly, which would discuss how best to implement and administer the *Shari'ah*. However, how much of what Muhammad said must be regarded as legally binding? For some, everything he said or is believed to have said has authority. Others allow that there was a degree of particularity involved in the Prophet's mission; in other words, his mission was grounded in a specific historical and cultural context. Thus, what is eternal and immutable are the principles or values (*usul*) which resulted in particular laws or, as Sardar (1979) calls them, 'norms', not these norms themselves. Sardar distinguishes between 'norms' which, as ideals for particular social contexts, can change and 'values' which are absolute and do not change. There are, though, *hadith* which discourage believers from seeking power: 'Do not seek to be a ruler, for if you are given authority you will be held responsible for it' (B 89:6). This raises a question about the integrity or motive of anyone standing for public office.

Some think there no need to 'elect' anybody, since the *ulama*, who know the law best, are the obvious candidates for leadership; the *hadith* cited above continues, 'but if you are given it without asking for it, then you will be helped by Allah'. Yet this would make the *ulama*'s interpretation of Islam somehow better than anybody else's, which Sunni Islam especially has been unwilling to concede; the scholars' 'claim to moral authority has never been completely accepted by the egalitarian Muslim masses' (Lindholm, 1996: 163). Thus, as Schacht (1964) pointed out, even when *ulama* have been appointed by governments to 'provide the general public, and government officials, with authoritative opinions on problems of religious law', their opinions, or *fatwas*, have been essentially 'private'. 'Appointment by government', says Schacht, 'does not add to the instrinsic value of their opinions, they have no monopoly on giving fatwas, and the practice of consulting private scholars of high reputation has never ceased' (p. 74; see also Lindholm, 1996: 159). As I wrote this chapter, the Taliban (from *talib*, one who seeks, that is, knowledge) in Afghanistan were decreeing that all Muslim men must wear beards, because we know from the *sunnah* that Muhammad had a beard. For other Muslims, this simply misses the point; one's faithfulness to the *sunnah* of the Prophet is not to be measured by the length of one's beard, but by the quality of one's life; 'love God', said Muhammad, 'with all your hearts ... Love one another in the spirit of God' (I.I., p. 231).

Muhammad Iqbal

It was Sir Muhammad Iqbal, amongst others, who did much to open up the possibility of reconstructing *Shari'ah*; for example, so that a *hadd* (extreme, that is, corporal or capital) penalty prescribed in the Qur'an or *Sunnah* might be revisited today. In his view, the absoluteness of Qur'an and prophetic *sunnah* is to be understood dynamically. Islamically, how did he justify this understanding of *Shari'ah*? First, he argued that Muslims had wrongly called a halt to the dynamic process of *ijtihad* which had once creatively extended *Shari'ah*. 'During the last five hundred years religious thought in Islam', he wrote, 'has been practically stationary' (1930: 6). Next, he said, Muslims have confused the real *Shari'ah*, its eternal, immutable principles, with particular applications of these principles to tenth-century contexts. This had brought about a legal and dogmatic slumber, a preoccupation with the past which needs to yield to confidence in human ability to create an even better future. 'A false reverence for past history', he wrote, 'and its artificial resurrection constitute no remedy for a people's decay' (*ibid.*: 151). 'The teaching of the Qur'an that life is a process of progressive creation necessitates that each generation,' he wrote, 'guided but unhampered by the work of its predecessors, should be permitted to solve its own problems' (*ibid.*: 160). He argued that the 'completeness' of the Qur'anic revelation, and the Prophet's mission, was 'potential' rather than 'realized'. The Prophet 'accentuates the principles underlying the social life of all mankind' but 'applies them to concrete cases in the light of the specific habits of the people immediately before him'. Laws resulting from this 'application are in a sense specific to that people' and 'cannot be strictly enforced in the case of future generations' (p. 163). Muhammad's message was 'final' only in the sense that 'it was', and remains, 'eternally valid'. Its function is to 'awaken' in us consciousness of our real relationship with the universe. By assuming our God-given responsibility as *Khalif* we can actualize the ideal society which lies 'dormant in our minds'. 'Man', insists Iqbal, can progress 'onward to receive ever-fresh illuminations from an Infinite Reality which "every moment appears in a new glory"' (p. 123).

Man has the power to shape and direct the forces around [him;] in his innermost being man, as conceived by the Qur'an, is a creative energy, an ascending spirit who, in his outward march, rises from one state of being to another. It is the lot of man to share in the deeper aspirations of the universe around him, and to shape his own destiny as well as that of the universe. (Iqbal, 1930: 11)

God God's-self, said Iqbal, is dynamic, not static. God's essence contains within itself unrealized potentiality; creation had lain dormant until actualized. As creation, aided by its *khilafat*, unfolds towards the perfection it can achieve, God's own potentialities will also unfold. Thus 'The Ultimate Ego [God] exists in pure duration wherein change ceases to be a succession of varying attitudes, and reveals its true character as continuous creation' (1930: 56). All life and all creation is in process – the process of becoming what it is intended to be and capable of being; 'Professor Whitehead', comments Iqbal, 'describes the universe not as something static, but as a structure of events possessing the character of a continuous creative flow' (*ibid.*: 47). Whilst drawing on Sufi thought (and himself a Sufi-like poet of distinction) Iqbal also criticized the Sufis for, as he saw it, neglecting the 'circumference' (this world) for the radius, for wanting *baqa* (oneness) rather than *firaq* (separation – to shoulder our full responsibilities). Sufism, he believed, stifled development of the human personality. The *khudi* (ego, self, personality) was central to Iqbal's thought. This drew on Nietzsche's concept of the 'superman', but also on the 'Perfect Man' (*insan-al-kamil*) of the Sufis. Muhammad was the prototypal 'Perfect Man' but all can realize this at-one-ness with the divine will by right effort and constant struggle. 'In this process of progressive change', says Iqbal, 'God becomes a co-worker' with us, 'provided man takes the initiative' (1930: 13).

Annemarie Schimmel (1985) devotes her last chapter, Chapter 12, to a study of 'The Prophet Muhammad in Muhammad Iqbal's Work' (pp. 239–56). She points out how love of the Prophet was a dominant theme in Iqbal's writing; Muhammad was his 'Arabian friend', a 'faithful, loving and consoling friend'. 'Love of the Prophet', said Iqbal, 'runs like blood through the veins of his community' (1930: 256). The Prophet, for Iqbal, represents God's activity; 'God cannot be seen with human eyes ... but the Prophet is visible' (*ibid.*: 241). After ascending the heights of heaven, however, the Prophet returns to the valley, 'to transform the human world', to translate 'his spiritual experience into a living-force' (*ibid.*: 242).

Muhammad Taha

Muhammad Taha, leader of the Republican Brothers in the Sudan (executed in 1985), spoke about 'The Second Message of Islam'. The Qur'an, he says, 'contains two messages: one, corresponding generally to the early chapters, is a spiritual message of peace, tolerance and human brotherhood, while the other, corresponding to the later chapters, is the more legalistic' (Shepard, 1991: 60). The first message is the primary, or essential message of Islam. However, the world was not quite ready for this, so it was 'suspended and replaced by the Madinan Message'. The time has now come for the Makkan message to replace the Madinan, which 'opens the way to a number of radical reforms, such as the equality of men and women, and, it would appear, to a future of unlimited progress' (*ibid.*).

Muslim writers are often highly critical of Western secularism, which they reject (for examples of recent comment on secularism, in the context of a Christian–Muslim dialogue, see Atabani, 1995 and Ben-Yunusa, 1995). However, there are Muslim secularists; with Muhammad Taha, they regard Islam as essentially *din*. For example, Taha Husayn argues that human history progresses through three evolutionary stages: in the first, religion dominates; in the second, human reason asserts itself against religion; in the third 'human reason directs human actions', whilst 'religion inspires human feeling'

(Shepard, 1991: 55). Muhammad's rule at Madinah was an appropriate experiement for the first phase of human progress but Islam's enduring contribution to the world is as an essentially 'rational religion which allows for further cultural progress on the basis of reason without the need for any more change in basic religious doctrines' (*ibid.*).

For Sayyid Ahmed Khan, Muhammad's message was fundamentally *din*; '*din* – the one basic revealed message of all prophets – does not change, but Shari'ah laws, by their very nature and purpose [are] closely bound to the circumstances and nature of different societies, do change with human society' (Troll, 1978: 92). 'In religious matters we are', he said, 'bound to obey the *sunnah* of the prophet and Islam, in worldly (*dunyawi*) matters we are allowed to do so but it is not binding upon us' (*ibid.*: 277). For Muhammad Ali Jinnah (1876–1948), Pakistan's founder, Islam was to provide the moral and cultural ethos, whilst law (informed by this ethos) would be democratically determined. 'Whose *shari'ah*?' he once replied when asked why he was unwilling to substitute *Shari'ah* for the colonial legal legacy (see Zakaria, 1988: 8–9). Zakaria – a former Deputy Leader of the Congress (I) Party of India – also favours Islamic secularism (*ibid.*: 20). Similarly, Ali Abd al-Raziq (d. 1966) 'challenged the link between Islam as a faith and any particular form of government'. This link, he said, represented, 'the road to despotism and authoritarianism' (Halliday, 1996: 234). Al-Azmeh (1993: 14) describes 'the frequently heard calls for the 'application'' of *shari'ah* as 'meaningless'; the idea that Islamic Law can be 'applied' as a ready-made code 'has no connection with the Muslim legal tradition built upon multivocality ... it is a political slogan, not a return to a past reality'.

Conclusion

What clearly emerges from this chapter is that Muhammad is vitally important for every tradition within Islam, which he himself predicted would accommodate many (73) tendencies (see MM, 1, p. 45). Each 'tendency' finds in the prophet's legacy what it needs to legitimize its particular version of Islam. Annemarie Schimmel (1985: 238) put it like this:

Every modern writer sees in the beloved Prophet the ideal realization of those qualities that he himself considers highest and most needed in the world – and the multicoloured image of the Prophet which thus emerges draws on the most divergent strands of the centuries-old tradition and translates the praises of the 'best of mankind' into modern times.

All forms of government which have been encountered, or which currently exist, which some Muslims advocate ought to replace current regimes, are believed to be in full conformity with the Prophet's legacy. Democracy, rule by the *ulama*, rule by descendants of the Prophet, are all advanced as genuinely Islamic. *Shari'ah* as contained in the tenth-century manuals, *shari'ah* as re-interpreted, are both advanced as Islamically bona fide. Muslims who oppose veneration of the Prophet's and the saints' tombs, and those who approve of such veneration, all regard themselves as loyal to Muhammad's memory. The Taliban who decree that men must wear beards, and that women must stay at home, believe that they are implementing *Shari'ah*. Some Muslims believe that the ideal society lies in the past and think it their duty to replicate that past, to resurrect the Madinah that was. Others, such as Sardar (1979), believe that 'it is possible, now or in the future, to create a society that achieves a realization of Islamic values greater than that achieved by the society of the Companions of the Prophet' (Sardar, 1979: 52); see also his much-reproduced graph (*ibid.*: 117–20), which shows the Madinan ideal as a straight line, whilst the possible norms are represented as progressing upwards. Incidentally, Ziauddin Sardar once told me that he was quite surprised by the excitement his graph has generated, amongst some Muslims at least. Islam is not a 'platonic essence', a monolithic, static tradition in the singular, but people's existential and pluralist responses to the revelation of God's-self through Qur'an and Prophet. Essentially, as W. C. Smith (1957: 17–18) says, 'The reality of Islam is a personal, living faith. New every morning in the heart of individual Muslims.'

Yet are Muslims justified in their claim that Muhammad's legacy, however they interpret this, is the 'supreme guide'? Christians and others have seen faults in Muhammad which, in their view, disqualify him from fulfilling this role. Tor Andrae could not but conclude that Muslims have tried to exalt Muhammad too highly (1936: 269). Argument about whether Muhammad is or is not the 'examplar of humanity par excellence' (Schimmel, 1985: 238) may well be with us until the end of time. When Muslims look at Muhammad they do so through the eyes of faith; seen thus, however differently they understand, apply and interpret his *sunnah*, it *is* supreme. This belief is *theological*; it may or may not be historically sustainable. Hence my claim that no attempt to understand what Muhammad means, and has meant, to Muslims can neglect the theological dimension. Yet, given that we do possess certain historical documents about Muhammad, it seems to me that the claims which Muslims make about the *sunnah* – including theological claims – are subjects for critical inquiry. Personal inclination and bias will influence the judgements we make – some claims to interpret the *sunnah* for today may appeal to me more than others! However, scholarly scrutiny may be able to identify whose claims harmonize more, whose less, with the classical texts. Anticipating what I shall have to say in my concluding chapter, and making explicit my own bias, I passionately agree with Sardar's powerful critique of the so-called 'fundamentalists':

By emphasizing the precision in the mechanics of prayer and ablution, length of beard and mode of dress, they have lost sight of individual freedom, the dynamic nature of many Islamic injunctions, and the creativity and innovation that Islam fosters within its framework. They have founded intolerant, compulsive and tyrannical orders and have provided political legitimacy to despotic and nepotistic systems of government. They have closed and constricted many enquiring minds by their insistence on unobjective parallels, unending quibbles over semantics.

They have divorced themselves from human needs and conditions. No wonder then that the majority of Muslims today pay little attention to them and even foster open hostility towards them. (1979: 78)

6 Conversations Islamic

This chapter presents some data gathered from what I might call the interpersonal as opposed to the textual phase of my research. What follows is deliberately reflective and impressionistic. My presence in the research is made explicit. This account does not claim scientific objectivity; rather, it is an exercise in qualitative analysis. What I offer here is an imaginative reconstruction, or perhaps a recreation, of conversations and encounters. Throughout, I oscillate between two different perspectives: the perspective – or my understanding of the perspective – of my Muslim partners, and my own Christian world-view. The latter, because I am who I am, is prone towards theology! Clifford Geertz (1988: 5) suggests that the task of the anthropologist as author has

less to do with either a factual look or an air of conceptual elegance than it has with their capacity to convince us that what they say is a result of their having penetrated (or, if you prefer, been penetrated by) another form of life, of having, one way or another, truly 'been there'. And that, persuading us that this off stage miracle has occurred, is where the writing comes in.

Elsewhere (cited in my Introduction) Geertz describes this as a type of 'fashioning'. My task, then, is vicariously to transport my readers with me into the world I have visited, albeit virtually. This chapter is thus a 'fashioning': a 'fashioning' of real conversations which took place with real people, into which, to maximize the information available to me, I integrate some data collected via the questionnaire (which is reproduced at Appendix 3). Much of this text does replicate exactly what I heard or gleaned. However, I have tried to construct a narrative account which, whilst true to the facts, is not slave to the verbatim. My theologically discursive reflections, too, represent what I thought at the time, although references and quotations have been added *post hoc*. When circumstances allowed, my consultants have verified my rendering. However, I take sole responsibility for my 'fashioning' and leave those who so generously assisted me to judge whether I have fulfilled the 'go-between function'; does what I have written 'command their assent'?

When I began this project I was determined to bring the results of some first-hand data-collecting research into dialogue with my textual and historical analysis. I decided to combine use of a questionnaire as a data-collecting instrument with some opportunistic interviews. The questionnaire focuses on issues generated by my work on the texts, which seem to have divided Muslim from non-Muslim opinion. It usefully sums up the conclusions drawn from that phase of my research. The responses were thin in quantity but thick (or rich) in quality (at least, so it seems to me!). Several of my own Muslim students, to whom I distributed copies, indicated that they did not think themselves 'competent' to answer my questions. One expressed reluctance to do so because she did not 'know where I was coming from'. Both sets of comments dented my self-confidence. They were second-year students and I had thought that my interests and intentions were transparent through my teaching and writing! Apparently, I am more opaque than I would like to be. Another, however, returned a very full response; yet another volunteered several hours of his time to converse with me about my research. Much of my field-work took place during two visits to Bangladesh (in August–September 1996 and August–September 1997). The conversations were in Bengali; they were organized with generous help from my brother-in-law and a Muslim friend. My wife was also present for some of the sessions.

In the courtyard of a Dhaka mosque

My brother-in-law, who directs a non-governmental organization in Dhaka and enjoys wide contacts in the community, arranged for me to meet some Muslims at a local mosque to talk with them about my research. He was responsible for choosing my consultants, so I cannot be accused of selecting those who would tell me what I wanted to hear!

It was just after sunset when we arrived at the gate of the mosque compound. *Maghrib* prayer was about to begin. We decided to go to a nearby sweet-shop to pass some time. The sweets were very enjoyable. The shop, however, especially when the electricity failed and the fan stopped, was extremely hot! On our return to the mosque, the congregants were finishing their prayers. Many were still inside the prayer hall, offering personal, informal supplication. Others were busy conversing in the courtyard. On one side of this was the mosque itself, on another a Qur'an school, on another a tin-roofed office-type building to which my brother-in-law and I were led. Whilst some of the men who had agreed to meet us were completing their prayers, another handed round cups of tea and a plate of biscuits. Then the others arrived. They were an Imam, a bank manager, a businessman, a hafiz (a Muslim who can recite the Qur'an by heart) and a schoolteacher. One of the group was a member of my brother-in-law's NGO committee. There followed intro-ductions and the usual polite, indeed laudatory, comments about my Bengali. Appreciation was also expressed about my interest in Islam. As the conversation proceeded, and I quoted from such texts as Ibn Ishaq and Bukhari, as well as from the Qur'an, and used some of my limited Arabic, these comments became almost embarrassing.

'I am writing', I said, 'a book about the Holy Prophet' – should I add, I wondered, 'Peace be upon Him' or would the *'Hazrat'* prefix suffice? As we continued to talk, no one gave me the impression that they were offended by my referring to the Prophet in this way, so I kept saying 'the Holy Prophet'. 'I am especially interested', I told them, 'in why non-Muslims do not view the

Prophet in the way Muslims do, even when they have access to the texts which Muslims use.' I thought an example might be needed: 'For instance,' I said, 'many supply a human dimension to the Qur'an. They think that Muhammad must have composed it himself.' The response was fascinating. A non-Muslim, they said, must recognize that Muhammad (peace be upon him) is God's messenger, and that the Qur'an is God's definitive word to humankind. If they do not recognize this, they will fail to appreciate who Muhammad really was even if they do read the earliest sources and texts. In other words, lack of faith in Muhammad will result in a deficient understanding of him. Naturally, since it confirmed my own conclusion that a non-Muslim reading the same texts as a Muslim is still likely to arrive at a different view of the Prophet, I was delighted by this response. Another consultant commented:

I think non-Muslims have formulated this negative picture because you can never fully understand a religion unless you are a part of it, and have the same respect for their beliefs ... people such as Salman Rushdie don't really help the situation ... what I mean to say is that it doesn't matter what evidence you have – if you hold certain prejudices deep down, then that evidence will mean nothing to you.

Others, however, have put to me that all someone who wishes to learn about Islam has to do is to read the Qur'an; 'Tell your students to read the Qur' an, then they'll accept Islam.' During my next field-work visit to Bangladesh, in reply to my question, 'Why do you think non-Muslims have formed an unfavourable picture of Muhammad?', a consultant replied, 'If they read the Qur'an and *hadith* they'll get the right information.' Yet in my experience many non-Muslims, who bring negative stereotypes of what Islam is to their reading of the Qur'an, simply find that it confirms many of their worst preconceptions. What is to all Muslims a book of great beauty and eloquence becomes, especially in translation, confusing, 'prosaic and even incomprehensible' to non-Muslims. 'It seems', says Kabbani (1989: 33), 'that our texts are destined to remain only semi-comprehensible to those who read them in translation.' Thus William Gladstone could hold up a Qur'an in the House of Commons, and proclaim, 'So long as there is this book, there will be no peace in the world' (cited in Zakaria, 1991: 59).

Shortly before I left Oxford, the newspaper headlines were reporting on the Taliban siege of Kabul and about their decrees concerning women, and men's beards:

Witnesses said that Taliban fighters with long chains beat at least four women in public in three separate incidents for violating Islamic dress codes. The Taliban also closed schools for girls and instituted the death penalty for adulterers or drinkers of alcohol. (*Feminist News*, 30 September 1996)

Looking around at my hosts and noticing that some of them were clean-shaven, I was slightly nervous when I asked my next question, 'Must all good Muslim men wear beards and all good Muslim women the *hijab*?' Bangladesh has a woman Prime Minister, who in fact succeeded another woman; she wears a head-scarf but many Bangladeshi Muslim women wear exactly what Hindu women wear. It was now very hot in the tin-roofed room; the electricity had failed again. 'No,' they said, 'these dress-codes are cultural.' 'You don't have to wear a beard?' 'This is a personal matter. Some men do because they want to imitate the Prophet, upon whom be peace.' My hosts indicated that, in their view, only the *qudsi hadith* had to be accepted by all Muslims; other *hadith* were open to critical scrutiny.

A Muslim woman should not be thought a bad Muslim because she wears a *sari*. Many of the *hadith*, they said, are advisory, not mandatory. (Some jurists do think it *haram* to trim the beard; others say it is *makruh*.) During my next field-work, a heated debate developed amongst a group of consultants about the requirements of Islamic dress. My hosts implied (or seemed to) that only the *qudsi hadith* could be trusted as a source for Muhammad's biography; if so, we would know very little about him.

It seemed to me, however, that the Taliban version of Islam, and my hosts' version were somewhat divergent. They both deduce their versions from the same prophetic 'tradition' but their rendering of that tradition varies.

My conversation in the Dhaka mosque continued for a little while longer. I managed to drink my by now cold tea. A coffee addict, I only drink tea when politeness demands it! Unfortunately, we meandered away from the concerns of my research, down other interesting but research-irrelevant avenues. Perhaps what most impressed itself upon my thinking during my mosque conversation was the difficulty of talking about Muhammad and Islam separately. Increasingly, I have realized that the Prophet and Islam are so intricately inter-linked that any real distinction between them blurs. Writing this book, I have worried about saying too much about Islam, about drifting away from my primary focus on Muhammad. However, whatever Muslims take to be Islamic is so taken because they derive it from the Book which Muhammad recited, or from the life which he lived. When non-Muslims make any statement about Islam, negative or positive, they are at the same time commenting on Muhammad. If Islam is criticized as intolerant, violent or sexist – so is Muhammad. If Islam's social conscience and spirituality are praised, so are Muhammad's. I decided to test this identification of Prophet and Islam during subsequent conversations

Then it was time to leave – my brother-in-law wanted me to meet another friend, so we made our farewells. On the way out of the now dark mosque courtyard, I was introduced to some other members of the congregation. Again, appreciation was expressed for my interest in the Prophet: 'He's writing about the Prophet, peace be upon him'; 'He's written several books already', 'His wife is Bengali'; 'He's not a Muslim but he reads the Qur'an', 'He's trying to do a good job', they said. That remains to be seen ...

Inside a village mosque

My host's family had originally donated the land on which the mosque was built and still contributed generously to its upkeep. My wife's uncles' and cousins' homes spread out into the thick, green woods around the mosque.

News of my visit had been sent on ahead and the Imam appeared on the doorstep to greet us. He did so with genuine warmth. My host (a woman) declared, 'Women have the right to enter the mosque.' It was not a question but a claim, a statement of her rights as a Muslim. She was not contradicted. We entered and sat down in the centre with about 18 members of the congregation who had just finished their prayers. Later, we were joined by my wife. This was, for me, a moment of some significance; previous conversations with Muslims in Bangladesh had taken place in educational institutions or various mosque outhouses and not in the prayer hall itself. My wife, too, had not (as an adult) entered a mosque before. Our overnight stay in our friend's brother's house was also the first time that either of us had slept in a Muslim home.

As in Dhaka, I began by explaining that I was writing a book about the Prophet, about what different people have said about him. My first question was about the *hadith*: 'Were they all of equal authority?' The replies affirmed the authority of the classical collections: 'There is no doubt about them', said the Imam, quoting the Qur'an. When it was pointed out that this verse of the Qur'an (2:2) refers to the text of the Qur'an itself, the hafiz present said, 'The *qudsi hadith* are in the Qur' an'. The *qudsi hadith* are not found in the Qur'an. However, they share the same, or very nearly the same, status as the Qur'an; he was thus extending the 'no doubt' of Q 2:2 to the *hadith*.

'What role do *hadith* play in daily life?' My consultants said that the uneducated do not have much knowledge of the *hadith* but do what the *ulama* tell them. 'The *hadith* prohibit begging', I said, 'but I see lots of beggars!' 'Yes', they responded, 'the Prophet had rebuked people for begging and had advised them to collect firewood and sell it in the market so that they could buy a tool to work for their livelihood [see B 34:16]. Healthy people should work, not beg. Those that cannot work ought to be looked after voluntarily by the Muslim community. They should not have to beg but sadly people do not always help them.' An admission here, perhaps, that the ideal is difficult to attain, especially in a country as poor as Bangladesh.

'I'm interested in hearing what you think about miracles.' 'Yes', they said, 'there was the splitting of the moon, and the feeding of the crowd, and stones that spoke. Allah supported the Prophet with miracles.' 'What about prayer? Do you pray to and through Muhammad?' 'We pray to God', they said. 'Muhammad is the "method", the guide.' I would like to have pursued this interesting metaphor further but my host whispered 'What about marriage?' to me, so I posed a question instead about Muhammad's marriage to Zainab, singled out for censure by so many non-Muslim writers. Confirming my impression that this incident does not present any moral difficulty for Muslims, they replied that since Zaid was not Muhammad's natural son, nothing illicit was involved. My wife intervened here with a question about polygamy: 'did they agree that men could have more than one wife?' The replies all agreed that in certain circumstances, and with the first wife's permission, men could marry a second, third or fourth wife. However, they must be able to treat all of them equally.

Next, the conversation moved on to the issue of Islamic dress. Is the *hijab*, or a head-to-foot covering for women, compulsory in Islam? One man replied that dress varied from place to place because of climate. This provoked an angry response from another man: 'It has nothing to do with climate. The *Shari'ah* demands that women cover themselves.' On this issue, opinion clearly differed, suggesting that Muslims can and do argue about what is and is not Islamically acceptable. Incidentally, I did not see any woman in the village wearing anything other than a sari.

'What do you think about *pir*s?' I asked. 'Some are rogues', they said, 'but some of them are sincere ... Their role is to point people to "The *Pir*", who is Muhammad.' More than an echo here, I thought, of Sayyid Ahmed Khan's view of the *pir*'s proper function. The conversation ended with the Imam enquiring of my host if I was about to convert to Islam! 'Could I take a photograph?' I asked. 'Yes, but not inside,' so we crowded in front of the mosque and posed (somewhat tourist-like) for the camera.

Conversation with a *hafiz* and a liberal Muslim

Next day, my wife and I visited a very impressive local non-governmental organization, the Dulai Polli Unnaon Sangstha, which runs a children's clinic, a micro credit support programme, a legal aid centre, and other development projects. My wife interviewed the director and staff to gather data for her Master's research; I was joined by a local *hafiz*. My host had sent a messenger to a nearby mosque to see if anyone was interested to meet me. On the *hadith*, miracles and prayer, the young scholar's answers were all but identical to those I had heard the previous night. However, he had less time for *pir*s; the Qur'an and the *hadith* need no supplement. It was *shirk* to put anyone between oneself and Allah. Towards the end of our conversation, I asked him whether he thought Bangladeshi law (in the main inherited from the colonial period) and Islamic law sufficiently compatible; what did he think about countries which had *Shari'ah* law, such as Pakistan or Saudi Arabia? 'Not Pakistan', he replied, 'Afghanistan, they have *Shari'ah* law and I think that the people there are very glad.' The Taliban's version of Islam held more appeal for him than it had for my Dhakka consultants!

My host took us to the home of her sister's father-in-law, a retired medical doctor who laughingly described himself as 'not a true believer'. He expressed scepticism about some aspects of Islam. However, he had great regard for its cultural achievements. 'We don't know which *hadith* are genuine and which are not,' he said, 'they were recorded too long after Muhammad's death.' 'Miracles! I don't believe in them.' 'Why is Muhammad special?' asked my wife. 'Ah! He gave Arabia and the Muslims a sense of unity. Before Muhammad, Arabia was divided by tribal feuds. Other countries were united. This is what Muhammad achieved.' 'What do you think about Sufism?' I asked. 'The Sufis came from Persia,' he replied, 'when they got here they encountered Buddhists and Hindus and their holy teachers. They took advantage of the ordinary people's respect for the holy teacher and for sacred shrines, to preach Islam and to make it attractive to the masses. So we get a bit of a mixture.'

What the doctor was describing was Islam's evolution in Bangladesh into the type of absorbent, tolerant, mystical Islam which I personally find very attractive: a pragmatic blend of classical Islam with the 'givenness' of the pre-existing Bengali Hindu–Buddhist cultural milieu into which Islam was propagated. This very special blend, says Asim Roy (1983: 251), was created 'by the conscious efforts of the Bengali cultural mediators, with a view to disseminating Islam in a more locally familiar and meaningful form'. I shall argue in my Conclusion that outsiders can express their views about what, in their view, promotes human well-being and about what hinders it, although they must take care not to 'misconstrue' what they are seeing.

We talk, in academic circles, about objectivity, or sometimes about neutrality – if I am lecturing about aspects of the Roman Catholic tradition within Christianity, for example, I try to refrain from expressing a Baptist critique. However, it is quite likely that something of my personal beliefs will colour what I say. Similarly, when lecturing about different Islamic movements, it is not part of my brief to say which ones I happen to prefer! Yet my enthusiasms inevitably emerge. During a recent lecture, several Muslim students present became visibly excited when I spoke about Muhammad Iqbal – and afterwards expressed their appreciation for that part of the lecture. Sensing their enthusiasm, I suspect that I gave way to my own (see my chapter on Iqbal in Brown *et al.*, 1997). In contrast, they had been somewhat agitated whilst I outlined the Wahhabi version of Islam. This experience reinforces my view that a progressive interpretation of Islam is an authentic rendering of the tradition; certainly, *those* Muslims believe it to be so.

I meet a Sufi

One of my Muslim students, a married man with his own business who put several relatives through university before starting to study himself, kindly agreed to discuss my research with me. Hasan (let's call him that) is British born; his wife and parents originate from Kashmir. He regards himself as British. When pushed, he'll speak about Kashmir rather than about Pakistan as his family homeland. Hasan has not taken the *bay'at* (which marks formal membership of a Sufi order) but he regularly attends public *dhikr*. He hopes to become an Imam. Hasan spent about three hours at my home, on campus here at Westminster College. As we conversed, the following thesis was forming in my mind and therefore influenced our conversation: what is non-negotiable in Islam is the authority of the Prophet's *sunnah*, whilst how this impacts on Muslim life is open to different interpretations. Positively, this has enabled Islam to adapt itself to very diverse contexts by stressing those aspects of Islam which are especially suited to local needs. This is how, according to Roy (1983), Islam inculturated itself into Bengal; Clifford Geertz (1968), has also usefully contrasted Moroccan and Indonesian Islam. As Islam in these two different contexts responded to the particular conditions in which it found itself, it developed differently. Morocco needed a unifying force to prevent the disruption of tribal, and rural–urban clashes. This produced an Islam with a strong 'centre' – the Sharifian king. Indonesia's ethos of 'each to their own' produced an Islam which developed differently amongst different social strata (see Bennett, 1996a: 144). Negatively, however, different interpretations may result in conflict between different interpreters. We have already in Chapter 5 referred to hostility between Barelvis and Deobandis.

I started our dialogue by putting my thesis to Hasan. 'Yes,' he agreed with me, 'all Muslims regard the way of the Prophet as the way of Islam. The two are quite inseparable.' This response was almost identical, I thought, to Schuon's statement, 'the Prophet is Islam'. Indeed, all of my Muslim friends were very clear about this; another replied, 'If there was no Muhammad, peace be upon him, there would be no Islam.' My conviction that Prophet and Islam overlap inextricably was strengthened by these responses. However, I wanted to probe further into what we might call the authority of the *hadith*, so I asked, 'Is everything that the Prophet said or did binding, or are there some areas where Muslims are free to exercise personal choice?' Hasan did not think that all Muslim men had to grow beards or wear what the Prophet had worn. On the level of personal piety, though, he could fully understand why some Muslim men do choose to wear what the Prophet wore (in fact, he was in the process of buying this dress for himself) but he certainly did not want to call those who do not bad Muslims. However, nor did he mince his words; he expressed distaste for the Taliban interpretation of the Prophet's legacy. 'Piety', he said, 'is within.' Another student gave me a similar response, but from a woman's perspective: 'I don't wear the *hijab* because the *hijab* is supposed to be worn for modesty but to me it's the modesty of the heart that counts – not how you dress.'

Hasan's comment led us to talk about the traditional distinction between Islam's '*zahir*' (external) and '*batin*' (inner) dimensions, which have such an important place in Sufi thought and practice. As we chatted, Hasan commented that, in his view, the Sufi version of Islam *was* Islam – thus expressing a view which we also encountered in Chapter 5. We were to return to things Sufi later in the conversation but I was anxious to raise with Hasan the issue of how non-Muslims and Muslims have differed in their evaluation of the historical sources for Muhammad's life, so I asked, 'Must Muslims and non-Muslims inevitably view the sources differently? Non-Muslims often supply a human element into the Qur'an, for example, because they do not believe what Muslims believe about its divine origin.' Hasan agreed; belief or lack of belief in the Qur'an and Prophet distinguish between a Muslim's and a non-Muslim's reading of both 'texts', so to speak. 'Miracles', I said, 'have caused non-Muslims to reject much of the material as unreliable. They think that Muhammad as miracle-worker contradicts the Qur'an.' 'In fact,' I commented, 'rather a lot of ink has been devoted to this issue; I've devoted quite a lot to it in my book but I'm beginning to think that few Muslims find the miracles at all problematic.' Hasan's reply confirmed this conviction; he had no problem whatsoever with a Muhammad who, by Allah's leave, worked miracles. Another student expressed the view that Muhammad is 'slightly below Allah' and can more or less do what Allah, who said to him 'You are my equal', can do. I cannot locate this *hadith* but the following *hadith*, cited by al-Jilani, carries much the same import:

Allah said, 'When I love My servant [Muhammad] I become his eyes, his ears, his tongue, his hands and his feet, he sees through Me, he hears through Me, he speaks in My name, his hands become mine and he walks with me.' (al-Halveti, 1992: 42)

Incidentally, it was Hasan who lent me a copy of al-Jilani's *The Secret of Secrets*, as rendered by al-Halveti. Hasan then shared with me a moving personal testimony about answered prayer which involved the *karamat* of the Prophet. An outsider might scoff but Hasan does not doubt that Muhammad intercedes on behalf of his supplicants.

For Hasan, Muhammad is not 'dead' but very much alive. I could not help but compare the language he used to describe his relationship with Muhammad with the language I use to speak about my relationship with Christ, as my 'saviour and friend'. There may very well be a world of difference between Jesus and Muhammad, Islam's view of Jesus may very well be irremediably different from the Christian view, yet at the level of devotion Muslims and Christians seem to me to be very close to each other in how they regard their examplars. Hasan began to describe what he feels when he attends *sama* and performs *dhikr* in salutation of the Prophet. As he spoke, I felt exactly as I sometimes feel at a prayer meeting. I experience what I can only describe as an intense feeling of God's reality, God's proximity, God's presence with me, in me, near me, around me. My hair seems to stand on end. Despite all my doubts, my questions, my theological liberality, I find myself believing what I preach. As Hasan spoke about his sense of intimacy with his God, I felt intimate with mine. No. With ours. Kenneth Cragg (1992: 73), writing about Constance Padwick's exploration of *tasliya*, has said that '*tasliya* and eucharist can at least converse'. In what for me was an unscheduled and unexpected moment, I experienced not *tasliya* conversing with eucharist but *tasliya* conversing with my own sense of at-one-ness with God through Christ.

Missionary musings

One of my passionate interests is missionary biography (to which I've tried, over the years, to make a contribution). Sitting in my lounge reflecting on the above experience, I found that my mind had wondered back in history (virtually, that is) to the famous Missionary Conference of 1938 at Tambaram, India. There, A. G. Hogg (1875–1954), who had just retired as Principal of Madras Christian College (where, amongst many other Hindus, he once taught the eminent Radhakrishnan (1888–1975), former President of India and sometime Oxford's Spalding Professor of Eastern Religions and Ethics), declared 'the reality of non-Christian faith':

Why ... am I so convinced of its actual existence? Most of all because I am sure I have already met with it. I have known and had fellowship with some for whom Christ was not the absolute Lord and only Saviour, who hold beliefs of the typically Hindu colour, and yet who manifestly were no strangers to the life 'hid in God' (1939: 101).

Hogg was reacting against the assertion by Hendrik Kraemer (1888–1965) that there is a radical discontinuity between God's revelation in Christ and all other religions. The former represents the exclusive movement of the divine towards the human and is uniquely saving; the latter represent human striving or seeking after God. Other religions may glimpse something of God but they do not save; faith in them is faith misplaced. Over against this, Hogg maintained that Hinduism and other faiths evidence a 'finding' as well as a 'seeking' of God (see Bennett, 1989: 22).

Hogg's opinion may well have been subjective; my opinion about the validity of Hasan's experience of God was also subjective. Nonetheless, it must impact on my actions and my intentions towards him as well as on my attitude towards his faith. Just as Hogg could feel no 'religious concern', as he put it, for Gandhi, whom he already held to be 'so clearly ... a "man of God"' (*ibid.*: 106), so I cannot but think that God is happy with Hasan just as he is. Would he be a better person were he to convert? Would he be closer to God than he is already? Yet I want to talk with him about what Christ means to me. I do not want to remain silent about my faith. This begs the question, must either I abandon my faith, and adopt his, or he abandon his faith and adopt mine, before true religion is served? Were the village Muslims being truer to their faith than I am to mine because they hoped for my conversion whilst I cannot feel this 'religious concern' for Hasan? Or can I claim that Christ has a universal message to which the world ought to listen, and can Hasan claim that Muhammad has a word for all people, without our claims resulting in conflict, or in one of us out-claiming the other?

I am posing questions here, not offering answers. Some Christians will not hesitate to say that Hasan must become a Christian if he is to enjoy any genuine relationship with God. When people do convert, I rejoice that they have experienced what I experience but I find it difficult to deny that those who do not convert may enjoy a genuine relationship with God. What I do know is that, for me, my own spiritual experience of Christ as real, for me, in my life, is primary. I shall talk about this experience with passion and conviction, but no amount of 'talking' ever does justice to the inner experience of faith. I think that Newbigin (1989) was right when he suggested that we 'should not imagine it is [our] responsibility to insure that the other is persuaded. That is in God's hands.' I cannot control what the Spirit does in the hearts and lives of others: 'it is not [the Christian's] duty to convert the others. ... This will always be the mysterious work of the Spirit, often in ways which no third party will ever understand. ... We do not', Bishop Newbigin continued, 'presume to limit the might and the mercy of God for the ultimate salvation of all people, but the same costly act [the Cross] ... which gives us that assurance and promise also requires that we share with our fellow pilgrims the vision that God has given us' (1989: 182–3). It is less a matter of us finding Christ than of Christ 'finding us', as Charles Wesley's hymn puts it: ''Tis Mercy all, immense and free, For O My God it found out me' (from the hymn 'And can it be').

'So', asked Hasan, 'what conclusions are you beginning to draw?' This question jolted me back from Tambaram into the present. 'Well,' I said, 'I'm still thinking about that. But I will be making use of a brilliant book I've just received for review – by Farid Esack. He …' and I started to tell Hasan something about Farid's thesis.

Finally, because I wanted very much to hear his opinion about this, I asked Hasan whether the role played by *pir*s troubled him at all; 'Do they not relegate Muhammad to a less significant role?' Hasan did not think so – they represent Muhammad, their authority is derived from Muhammad, they are 'nothing' apart from him. Another student said, replying to the same question:

No, the role of *pir*s and devotion to their shrines does not relegate Muhammad to a less significant role because the *pir*s are supposed to be mediators between Muhammad and Muslims. Even though Muslims can pray directly to Muhammad, they often feel that their prayers will be heard sooner if they visit these *pir*s or their shrines – Muhammad still comes at the top.

As the villagers had put it, 'The *Pir*' is 'Muhammad'.

Conversations analysed

What conclusions do I draw from this attempt to create discourse between my textual and historical research and my dialogue with Muslims? I conclude that: (1) there are some issues that non-Muslims have traditionally found problematical, such as Muhammad's miracles, the role of Sufi *pir*s and the reliability of the textual sources, which, generally, Muslims have found non-problematical; (2) Muslims are broadly agreed about Muhammad's status as the sinless recipient of God's revelation and its best interpreter; (3) any view of Muhammad as less than this is inadequate from the Muslim perspective.

Conclusion: Towards a Postmodern Theology of Religions

In this chapter I shall discuss whether, in the light of the material that has been examined in this book, what Muhammad means and has meant to Muslims can be justified on the basis of what can be known about him historically. As I argued in my survey of non-Muslim accounts of Muhammad, many non-Muslims have made moral judgements about Muhammad which have been unacceptable to Muslims. This difference, between insider and outsider accounts, raises the questions, 'Is Muhammad inevitably viewed differently from without Islam?', and 'How much of the Islamic view of Muhammad can outsiders share without becoming Muslims and ceasing to be outsiders?' 'Can outsiders be expected to regard Muhammad with the reverence Muslims do?' If they do not believe in any possibility of a link between Muhammad, or any other religious leader, and the supernatural, are they inevitably going to find themselves at odds with the Muslim viewpoint? If they do believe that such a supernatural link is possible but restrict this to their own religion's seminal figure, must they either explain Muhammad's career in human terms, or see his inspiration as demonic? What happens if they can accept that Muhammad was divinely guided but cannot accept everything which Muslims believe about this – for example, that there is absolutely nothing in the Qur'an which did not come from God but originated with Muhammad.

The Salman Rushdie affair

However, I begin this chapter with the Salman Rushdie affair. There are at least two reasons for exploring the Salman Rushdie affair in some detail in this chapter: first, the controversy about his book, *The Satanic Verses*, serves as a useful peg on which to hang many of the points I want to cover in this conclusion. Second, the affair underscores the importance of trying to understand Muhammad's significance as part of any attempt to study Islam itself. Whilst the following quite lengthy treatment could be seen as a diversion from the main business of this 'conclusion', I think that a book primarily concerned with 'accounts of the Prophet' can hardly ignore Rushdie's version. Finally, this chapter will try to integrate what I have discovered in the process of researching this book within my own world-view.

Rushdie the man

The Rushdie affair was cited by Akbar Ahmed (1992) as an example of how a recent event has been manipulated by the Western media to reinforce old stereotypes of Muslims and Islam. The media image created, he says, was of intolerant, obscurantist, anti-intellectual, illiberal Muslims versus the liberal literary establishment. *The Satanic Verses*, by prize-winning novelist Salman Rushdie, was published in September 1988. Before publication, an Indian critic warned Penguin Books, India, that publication there was likely to cause 'a lot of trouble'. In India, the book was placed on the proscribed list on 5 October. Article 295A of the Indian penal code makes it illegal to 'insult or outrage the religious feelings of any class of people' (see Ruthven, 1990: 86–7). In the United Kingdom, the book met with immediate critical acclaim. Although it failed to win its author a second Booker prize – the first was won by his earlier *Midnight's Children* (1980; judged the 'Booker of Bookers' in 1993) – it did gain the almost equally prestigious Whitbread Prize for Novels. Its inventive use of language, its rich kaleidoscope of characters and metaphor, its eloquent plea for meaning and purpose, not to mention its open criticism of racist immigration policy, makes it a powerful novel in which real issues are confronted and explored. 'If', says Rushdie (1991:394),

The Satanic Verses is about anything, it is a migrant's-eye view of the world. It is written from the very experience of up-rooting, disjuncture and metamorphosis ... that is the migrant condition, and from which, I believe, can be derived a metaphor for all humanity.

Sadly, as Cundy (1996: 65) comments, 'the text has all but lost its ability to be judged as an artistic enterprise rather than as a cultural and political crisis'.

Clearly, there is much of Rushdie's own background, interests and experience in his writing. Born in Mumbai (Bombay) in 1947 (the year India gained independence), his parents were wealthy Muslims who chose, initially, to stay in India (like the Sinais in *Midnight's Children*) instead of migrating to Pakistan (as did other characters in the same book). Bombay, says Rushdie, is where 'all Indias met and merged', and where 'all-India met what-was-not India' (1996: 350). Rushdie, who had 'a Christian *ayah* [nanny]', tells us that his 'friends were Hindus, Sikhs, Parsis'; and adds, 'none of this struck me as being particularly important' (1991: 377). His parents were Muslims but neither of them 'was insistent or doctrinaire'. 'My writing and thought', he continues, 'have ... been as deeply influenced by Hindu myths and attitudes as Muslim ones' (*ibid.*: 404). Rushdie was sent to the famous Rugby School in England when he was 13 (1961) and a year later (with his parents) became a naturalized British citizen. In 1965 he followed his father and uncle to King's College, Cambridge, where he read history. His relationship with his father, however, became strained when the senior Rushdie moved to Karachi, established a factory there and asked graduate Salman to manage it. Life in Pakistan had little appeal for Rushdie; venturing into film and publishing in Karachi ('I never forgave Karachi for not being Bombay', *Midnight's Children*,

p. 307), he encountered censorship and 'newspapers of whose stories the only thing that can be confidently said is that they are lies' (*Shame*, p. 70; see also 1991: 37–40 on 'Censorship'). Instead, he moved to London where for several years he was an occasional actor, claimed social security benefit and worked as a freelance writer of 'ads'. Writing novels, however, not 'ads', was to become his principal occupation.

Rushdie has a long-standing interest in anti-racism. For him, 'multiculturalism' is just another catchword'. The real issue, he says, is 'facing up to and eradicating prejudice' (Rushdie, 1982; 1991: 138). Rushdie became convinced, whilst working for a local project among Bangladeshis in 1977, that 'racism permeated British society' (Brians, 1996: 6). Having exploited and lorded it over non-whites in the days of Empire, the British have now imported an 'Empire' which they can continue to treat as inferior. Rushdie was especially annoyed by being considered 'more English than the English', with the assumption that in the process he had lost his own culture:

I point out to these people that if there was an English person living in India who adopted Indian dress, who has learnt to speak Urdu or Hindi or Bengali fluently without an accent, nobody would accuse him of having lost his culture. They would be flattered and pleased that the language had been acquired so efficiently. And they would see it as a compliment to themselves. But they wouldn't accuse him of having betrayed his origins. (Cited in Brians, 1996: 6)

Rushdie detests the way Westerners think that 'India – like radium – had been "discovered"' by them, making Indians 'somehow the invention of their ancestors' (*Midnight's Children*, p. 11). He writes about the need for a 'freedom movement' against the British until the prejudice 'within almost all of you' has been eradicated (1991: 138). His 1982 article, 'The New Empire Within Britain' (reprinted in the 1991 collection), concludes thus:

And so it's interesting to remember that when Mahatma Gandhi, the father of an earlier freedom movement, came to England and was asked what he thought of English civilization, he replied, 'I think it would be a good idea'. (1991: 138)

According to Parekh (1989), 'Rushdie is both drawn towards and repelled by his fellow-immigrants. He both fights them and fights for them.' Rushdie, says Parekh, sometimes seems annoyed that 'everyone around him is not an immigrant', yet he also tramples on their 'dearest memories and sentiments'. Parekh suggests that they have become, for Rushdie, an 'abstraction'; he loves them as 'real human beings', yet uses them to people an abstract, make-believe world of cartoon characters and caricatures (p. 31). Perhaps the ease with which Rushdie himself is able to move within different cultures is not shared by all those who have settled in Britain. His characters are often torn between cultures. In *The Satanic Verses*, some enjoy a ghetto-type existence; more interested in Pakistani or Indian politics than in the affairs of their adopted home, they actually occupy a world that is not quite East or West but somewhere in-between, a world of 'hybridization and ghettoization, of reconciling the old and the new' (Brians, 1996: 4). It is this 'inbetweenness' of many members of minority groups which Rushdie, I think, finds both fascinating and irritating. Rushdie's literary style and themes are 'postmodern': Cundy (1996: 5) thinks that 'the extent to which Rushdie would embrace the label 'postmodern' [is] debatable', but Rushdie himself proposes 'the novel as the crucial art form of what I can no longer avoid calling the post-modern age' (1990a: 12). Together with such postmodern authors as Kazuo Ishiguro (Japanese–British) and Timothy Mo (English–Chinese), Rushdie (Indian–British) enjoys a double 'ethnicity'. Postmodernity, says Ahmed (1992: 25) 'allows, indeed encourages, the juxtaposition of discourses, an exuberant eclecticism, the mixing of diverse images'. Professor Ahmed might well have written this as a description of *The Satanic Verses*. I shall return, below, to the postmodern agenda as part of my attempt to sum up the research offered in this book.

East meets West

Most of Rushdie's writing has explored different aspects of the meeting and mingling of cultures. His first book, a science fiction fantasy called *Grimus* (1975), drew on Sufi imagery. Brians (1996: 4) writes:

The mixing of cultural influences, or what Rushdie calls the 'chutneyfication' of culture, is one of the most enlivening aspects of his work. He throws off phrases in Hindi, Arabic, and Urdu ... and delights in playing with those aspects of Indian and Arabic culture which have been trivialized in the West in what Edward Said calls 'orientalism', satirizing the failure of Europeans to grasp what they persistently exoticize.

(Rushdie (1991:166) writes, 'For those of us who see the struggle between Eastern and Western descriptions of the world as both an internal and external struggle, Edward Said has been for many years an especially important voice.')

Midnight's Children (1981) and *Shame* (1983) mirror the politics of India, Pakistan and the emergence of Bangladesh. Both resulted in controversy. Indira Gandhi, 'who was not only Prime Minister ... but also aspired to be Devi, the mother-goddess in her most terrible aspect ... a multi-limbed divinity with a centre-parting and schizophrenic hair' (*Midnight's Children*, p. 438) won an injunction against *Midnight's Children* (as a consequence, it was re-issued with various passages deleted or revised). *Shame* was banned in Pakistan (anticipated, it seems, by Rushdie, p. 70; 'the book would have been banned ... burned ... however, I am only telling a sort of modern fairy tale'). Relatives also recognized 'unflattering portraits of themselves' in the text (Brians, 1996: 6). *The Moor's Last Sigh* (1996) wrestles throughout with the tension between pluralism and particularity (communalism) that plagues India; its love–hate story of a family's rise and fall (in explosive self-destruction) refers, in passing, to many historical events (such as the end of Portuguese rule in Goa; p. 155) and to some more recent events (such as the destruction of the Babri Masjid; pp. 351, 363). The collapse of the 'Khazana Bank International' reads very much like that of the Bank of Credit and Commerce International (p. 360)! We also have a fascinating reference to Thomas

Babington Macaulay's infamous 'Minute' of 1835, resolving 'To form a class of persons, Indian in blood and colour, but English in opinions, morals, and in intellect', which goes on to deride all things Indian: 'Thus, a class of "Macaulay's minutemen" would hate the best of India' (Rushdie, 1996). But, says Rushdie's character, 'we were not, had never been, that class. The best, and worst, were in us, and fought in us, as they fought in the land at large' (p. 376; see also pp. 165–6). Here, I think, we hear Rushdie's own voice, speaking about the East–West, West–East struggle within himself (see also Rushdie, 1983: 29; the East is 'a part of the world to which, whether I like it or not, I am still joined, if only by elastic bands').

Rushdie's writing often verges on the magical (or veers towards surrealism; see Cundy, 1996: 96–9 on Rushdie and magical realism): in *Midnight's Children*, for example, baby Saleem (who later develops telepathy – initially he thought the 'voice' in his head might be Gabriel but no, 'the Recitation was completed in Arabic long ago', 1981: 168) seems to work 'changes on the people around him' (p. 130). All 581 of the Midnight Children are 'endowed with features ... which can only be described as miraculous' (p. 195), whilst Ahmed's private parts freeze up as his assets are frozen (p. 136)! Or Rushdie introduces a magic lamp: in Saladin's childhood this had summoned up images from *The Thousand and One Nights*, where 'the true djinns of old had the power to open up the gates of the Infinite, to make all things possible, to render all wonders capable of being attained' (*The Satanic Verses*, p. 546).

Rushdie views the novel as the ideal forum for exploring ideas, challenging accepted axioms and furthering the processes of human thought. His aim, as a novelist, is not only to write entertaining stories, but to re-imagine, question and doubt. As one of his own characters says,

A poet's work is to name the unnameable, to point at frauds, to take sides, start arguments, shape the world, and stop it from going to sleep. And if rivers of blood flow from the cuts his verses inflict, then they will nourish him. (*The Satanic Verses* p. 97)

In demonstrations against the book, and as a result of the *fatwa* (see below), a number of people have indeed lost their lives. In *Is Nothing Sacred?* (1990b) Rushdie speaks of the novel as a privileged arena of discourse. For him, it is the one arena in which everything can be discussed 'in every possible way' (p. 16; thus his dislike of the 'barren certitudes of the land of the pure [Pakistan]', *Midnight's Children*, p. 316). Indeed, apart from this privileged arena of discourse, nothing is sacred, although Rushdie is reluctant actually to call even the novel 'sacred': 'we do not need to call it sacred, but we do need to remember that it is necessary' (1990b: 16).

Thus far, this introduction to Rushdie the novelist has identified several themes which are not irrelevant to the concerns of this book: Rushdie's fascination with the meeting and mingling of cultures, his belief that one can belong to more than one culture, for example, go right to the centre of our own quest for an outsider understanding of Islam which resembles, but which does not become, an insider view. *The Satanic Verses*, says Rushdie, rejoices in mongrelization and fears the absolutism of the Pure. Melange, hotchpotch, a bit of this and a bit of that is how newness enters the world. It is the great possibility that mass migration gives the world, and I have tried to embrace it. *The Satanic Verses* is for change by fusion, change by conjoining. It is a love song to our mongrel selves. (1991: 394; *The Satanic Verses* (p. 8) asks, 'How does newness come into the world?').

Rushdie comes even closer to the concerns of this book when he writes about wanting to explore in the novel what might 'fill our God-shaped holes' in the absence of any belief in God or in the possibility of divine revelation (1990b: 11). He writes, he says, 'in part, to fill up that emptied god-chamber with other dreams' (1991: 377). Here we have another Rushdie theme; in *Midnight's Children*, the world is remade for Aadam Aziz when he 'resolved ... never again to kiss earth for any god or man' (p. 10); this resolve, however, resulted in 'Permanent alteration: a hole', which subsequently needed to be 'filled up' with something else. Later, Aziz's daughter thinks she sees 'a dark shadow, like a hole' at 'the centre of her father's body' (p. 138). Similarly, in *The Moor's Last Sigh*, the Jewish mother-character, Flory, discovers that 'There is no world but the world ... There is no god ... *There is no spiritual life*' (p. 84). Having stopped believing in 'God, Satan, Paradise and Hell' when he was 15 (1991: 377), Rushdie speaks about wanting to fill the 'God-shaped hole' with some meaning, or sense of purpose (1990b: 11). This quest permeates much of his writing; above all, his characters want 'to end up meaning something – yes, meaning something', and 'fear absurdity' (*Midnight's Children*, p. 9).

Rushdie's own location within the insider–outsider framework is difficult to identify; he tells us that he has lived his whole adult life as a 'secular, pluralist, eclectic man', (1991: 405). His personal 'world-view' is far removed from an Islamic world-view: 'To accept that the world, here, is all there is; to go through it alone, towards and into death, without the consolations of religion seems, well, at least as courageous and rigorous ... as the espousal of faith' (1991: 413). However, it would be incorrect to say that he is in no sense 'an insider'. Brought up within a Muslim family, he obviously has some 'insider' knowledge. 'Muslim culture', he says, 'has been very important for me' (1991: 404). In more than one novel he uses material drawn from Muslim (including Sufi) sources. References, however, to 'the last prophet' coming 'only to announce the End' (*Midnight's Children*, p. 168) and to Muhammad as 'the Penultimate', 'the Last-But-One' (*Ibid.*: 163) seem distinctly odd. In 1981, Rushdie chided V. S. Naipaul for not trying hard enough to find Muslims who would denounce the 'terrible things being done in the name of Islam': 'Naipaul never mentions the Mujahideen-e-Khalq, whose leader Rajavi is committed to a "multi-party democratic system of government"; but the Mujahideen are certainly "believers"' (1991: 374). He describes the Islam of the sub-continent in positive terms; it 'developed historically along moderate lines, with a strong strain of pluralistic Sufi philosophy' (1991: 54). Writing in 1991, however, he describes his failed attempt to join 'the fight for the modernization of Muslim thought, for freedom from the shackles of the Thought Police' (*ibid.*: 436).

He wanted the West 'to understand a little more of the complexity of Muslim culture' (which Naipaul had failed to do), but in the face of 'the utter intransigence, the philistine scorn of so much of Actually Existing Islam [he] reluctantly concluded that there was no way [he could] help bring into being the Muslim culture [he had] dreamed of'. Philosophically open Islam, he seems to suggest, ended with Ibn Rushd whose 'ideas were silenced in their time' (*ibid.*: 437; an echo here of Renan). 'Actually Existing Islam', he continued, has 'almost deified its Prophet, a man who always fought passionately against such deification' and, making 'literalism a weapon and redescriptions a crime', this Islam 'will never let the likes of me in'.

The Satanic Verses

Characters in the novel are torn between East and West, India and Britain, Bombay and London, good and evil, between their lost faith and the need to find something to substitute for that faith. In scenes in the novel which depict the beginning of a new world religion (which, as I shall show, more than resembles Islam) Rushdie set out to explore how a religion might have begun if God is subtracted from the equation. For example, its scripture must be explained as in some sense the product of the Prophet's own imagination; Rushdie asks, 'if we accept that the mystic, the prophet is sincerely undergoing some sort of transcendant experience, but we cannot believe in a supernatural world, then *what is going on?*' (1991: 408). He set out to explore 'the extent to which the mystic's conscious personality informs and interacts with the mystical event ... to try to understand the human event of revelation' (*ibid.*). Here we are close to one of the explanations which non-Muslims have often applied to the Qur'an; as Muir put it, it is a 'storehouse of Mahomet's own words' (1894: xxvi). In several respects, Rushdie is very close to Muir – it was whilst at Cambridge that Rushdie first discovered the account of the 'satanic verses', which gives the book its title and provides the data for pages 118–25. Rushdie was also aware of the incident when 'Adballah ibn-Abi Sarh tampered with the verses of revelation without Muhammad noticing (which Tor Andrae had discussed at some length) and he has a similar scene in his novel (see *The Satanic Verses*, p. 367). Rushdie's Mahound, like Muir's Muhammad, 'manufactured revelation'.

Like Muir, Rushdie also appears to hint at a satanic explanation for the Prophet's behaviour; 'It is a wonderful thing I did. Deeper truth. Bringing you the Devil. Yes, that sounds like me' (p. 125). This might identify an inconsistency in Rushdie's treatment; if he does not believe, as he has stated, 'in the supernatural', does this not preclude belief in Satan and the demonic as well as belief in God and the angelic? For Rushdie, however (unlike Muir, for whom God and Satan were realities), such terms are metaphors for 'good' and 'bad'; also, Rushdie more than hints that what we think is 'bad' may actually be good, and vice versa. Here we see something of Blake's 'Marriage of Heaven and Hell' (cited on p. 304 of *The Satanic Verses*). Blake was not at all convinced that the two realms were all that different; indeed, hell might be the more liberating of the two. 'By 1790', says King (1991: 82), Blake 'had come to believe that the world of hell was the only alternative open to him. In fact, it was superior to the world of heaven, and, paradoxically, it was the source of revolutionary fervour'. Similarly, Rushdie tells us that, 'Appearances deceive; the cover is not the best guide to the book' (*The Satanic Verses*, p. 257; Rushdie's fascination with the concepts of 'heaven' and 'hell' also features in *The Moor's Last Sigh*). He often explores 'opposites' and juxtapositions – especially the East–West juxtaposition. He is fascinated by the idea that they can meet and mingle, that they are not, as Kipling would have it, irreconcilably different, 'East is East, and West is West, and never the twain shall meet' ('The Ballad of East and West', 1889). Although, to do Kipling justice, he did believe that differences disappear when 'two strong men stand face to face'; then there is 'neither East nor West, Border, nor Breed, nor Birth' (for Rushdie on Kipling, see 1991: 74–80).

Why have Muslims objected to *The Satanic Verses*? Before referring to some of the scenes in the book which have offended Muslims, it is important to note that there is much material in the book which has not caused offence. Indeed, the main plot (there are numerous sub-plots running through the text, especially within dream sequences) is not explicitly about religion at all. In this, two characters are torn within themselves between cultures, loyalties, dreams, fears, hopes and aspirations. They are (to use their truncated names) Saladin Chamcha and Gibreel Farishta. The first is an Anglophile Indian and naturalized British citizen living in England, whose 'mutation … began long before he got close enough to hear the lions of Trafalgar Square. When the England cricket team played India at the Brabourne Stadium, he prayed for an England victory' (*The Satanic Verses*, p. 370). Then he was given 'an English education' (as was Rushdie; as noted, Rushdie is also a naturalized Briton). Rushdie's description, too, of Saladin's parents as 'Muslims in the lackadaisical, light manner of Bombayites' (*ibid.*: 48) matches his own background. In India, the Chamchawalases run 'a fertilizer business' (*ibid.*: 64). Rushdie's portrait of Saladin Chamcha, whilst reflecting something of his own story, is far from flattering; he describes him as a 'collaborator'; 'colloquially', he explains, 'a *chamcha* is a person who sucks up to a powerful people, a yes-man, a sycophant. The British Empire would not have lasted a week without such collaborators among its colonized peoples' (cited by Brians, 1996: 9). Elsewhere, Rushdie renders a 'chamcha' as a 'toady' (*The Moor's Last Sigh*, p. 133). Saladin's 'mutation', however, was not painless:

One day soon after he started at school he came down to breakfast to find a kipper on his plate. He sat there staring at it, not knowing how to begin … his fellow-pupils watched him suffer … It took him ninety minutes to eat the fish. (*The Satanic Verses*, p. 44)

This experience only made Saladin more determined 'to conquer England'. This scene is based on an incident during Rushdie's own early days at Rugby.

Married to an estranged wife, Pamela Lovelace (possibly an allusion to Rushdie's own first wife, Clarissa Luard, as well as to a 1960s porn star, Linda

Lovelace; see Ruthven, 1990: 21f), Saladin later becomes a successful actor, often doing commercial voice-overs:

A Man of a Thousand Voices and a voice. If you wanted to know how your ketchup bottle should talk in its television commercial, if you were unsure as to the ideal voice for your packet of garlic-flavoured crisps, he was your very man. (*The Satanic Verses*, p. 60)

Would he have succeeded, we wonder, in front of the camera where his skin colour would have attracted more notice? Then Saladin visits India 'to interpret the role of the Indian doctor in *The Millionairess* by George Bernard Shaw'. On stage 'he tailored his voice to the requirements of the part, but those long-suppressed locutions, those discarded vowels and consonants, began to leak out of his mouth' (*ibid.*: 49). An Indian mistress (Zeeny Vakil; she reappears, to be blown up, in *The Moor's Last Sigh*) follows – and a battle begins between Saladin's sublimated Indianness and his acquired Englishness. Like Rushdie, Saladin has a very strained relationship with his father.

Gibreel Farishta is a superstar of the Indian movie business. Although a Muslim, he is renowned for playing the role of Hindu gods. He has lost any religious faith he may have had and seeks to find meaning in success and fame, and by drowning himself in a life of sexual debauchery: 'He had so many sexual partners that it was not uncommon for him to forget their names even before they had left the room' (*The Satanic Verses*: 25). After a filming accident, he actually began to feel better when he realized that there was no God 'out there' looking after him; 'one day he found that he no longer needed there to be anything to feel. On that day of metamorphosis the illness changed and his recovery began' (*ibid.*: 30). Gibreel falls in love with Alleluia Cone, the 'climber of mountains, vanquisher of Everest', who is described as an 'ice queen' (*ibid.*: 31) Cundy (1996) points out that whilst Rushdie's women are often 'centre stage' (p. 116) he also tends to 'demonize female sexuality' (p. 12). Gibreel meets up with Saladin when he follows Cone to London.

Thus, in Rushdie's narrative, Saladin and Gibreel find themselves aboard the same flight, A1-420, from Bombay. The plane is hijacked by Sikh separatists, and our two protagonists spend 111 days 'marooned on a shimmering runway' (*The Satanic Verses*, p. 77). Alone amongst the 50 hostages who were not released, both miraculously survive the plane's destruction when Tavleen releases the pin on her grenade during a final fight with her co-conspirators, 'at that moment Buta and Dara rushed at her and she pulled the wire anyway, and the walls came tumbling down' (*ibid.*: 87). Watched by one Rosa Diamond, who rescues them, the two land in the sea and wake up on the beach amidst 'not sand. Snow' (*ibid.*: 130; the book actually begins with this miraculous tumble, pp. 3–10). Meanwhile, however, Gibreel has grown angel-wings and acquired a halo, whilst Saladin has grown devil-horns and cloven hooves. He is arrested as an illegal immigrant (despite his British passport) and experiences some 'Packy bashing' at the hands of the police, who find his claim to be British highly amusing: 'look at yourself. You're a fucking Packy billy. Sally – who? – what kind of name is that for an Englishman' (*ibid*.: 163). The Police National Computer, though, reveals him to be 'a British citizen first class' so he is unceremoniously dumped into the detention centre's medical facility. Rushdie is asserting that, whilst 'migrants' are often 'demonized by the host culture's attitude to them', this 'does not really make them demonic' (1991: 402). Escaping from hospital, Saladin takes refuge in the attic of a bed and breakfast guest house (*The Satanic Verses* pp. 251–2). His bank accounts are frozen, however, and, as the story continues, Gibreel becomes for him the object of hate and resentment.

Not only had the Bombay superstar failed to help him when the police arrived to arrest him but he was now enjoying considerable success in London. Claiming that he had never boarded the plane (to explain why he is still alive), Gibreel becomes a London celebrity and is to star in a series of films as none other than the Angel Gabriel, 'a trilogy at least. "Don't tell me", Allie said "*Gibreel in Jahilia, Gibreel Meets the Imam, Gibreel with the Butterfly Girl*"' (*ibid*.: 345). However, Gibreel has also started to dream his dreams; interspersed between page 86, which has the two protagonists surviving the fall out of the sky, and page 129, which describes their rescue by Rosa Diamond, we have the first of the really controversial dream sequences. This dream continues as Chapter 6 (p. 359–94). The real mixes with the unreal (evidence here of Gabriel Garcia Marquez's acknowledged influence) as Gibreel dreams that he is an angel and plays the same angel in front of the cameras; thus we read that the dream-world begins 'to seem as tangible as the shifting realities he inhabits when he's awake' (*ibid*.: 205). 'I am bound to [the angel]', says Gibreel, 'by a shimmering cord of light' and it is 'not possible to say which of us is dreaming the other' (*ibid*.: 110). In one scene, thinking himself really Angelic, he steps into moving traffic and gets hit (*ibid*.: 337). Of dreams, Rushdie writes, 'The dream is part of our very essence. Given the gift of self-consciousness, we can dream versions of ourselves, new selves for old' (1991: 377).

In these dream (to be made film) sequences, Gibreel witnesses the birth and development of a 'new religion'. Its prophet, Mahound, is a womanizing, profiteering scoundrel, who has 'no time for scruples, no qualms for ends and means' (*The Satanic Verses*, p. 363). Cundy (1996: 102) points out how, 'In both *Midnight's Children* and *The Satanic Verses*, the communication networks of advertising and cinema compete with the written word for man's attention and allegiance.' Rushdie knew that he had chosen for his prophet's name a medieval Christian corruption of 'Muhammad' and addresses this in the text, 'Here he is neither Mahomet nor MoeHammered; has adopted, instead, the demon-tag the faringis hung around his neck. To turn insults into strengths, whigs, tories, Blacks, all chose to wear with pride the names they were given in scorn' (*The Satanic Verses*, p. 93; see also *Midnight's Children* p. 163: 'Muhammad ... also known as Mohammed, Mahomet, the Last-But-One, and Mahound'). Rushdie's choice of the name 'Mahound' was part of a 'process of reclaiming language from one's opponents' (1991: 402). According to Cundy (1996: 108) this is the very 'project in which *The Satanic Verses* itself is engaged – to refute the insult of difference by embracing it', thus empowering the 'post-colonial subject' to define 'his or her own identity' instead of passively being defined by others.

Before I proceed to cite further passages, I want to add a note about my reason for doing so, fully aware that Muslim friends (who I hope will read this book) find *The Satanic Verses* deeply offensive. In August 1994 I delivered some lectures at the Henry Martyn Institute of Islamic Studies, Hyderabad, India, to a mixed Muslim and Christian audience, about non-Muslim images of Muhammad. Indeed, some of the material I used then is reproduced in earlier chapters of this book. I chose, instead of simply saying 'non-Muslims have had some negative images', to give examples, prefixing them with such words as 'myth', 'legend', and 'calumny'. Nevertheless, despite these comments – and the scholarly context in which I was speaking – some Muslims present were offended by what I said. I did not intend this. Nor do I intend to offend here by citing passages from *The Satanic Verses*. It seems to me impossible to explore why Muslims dislike the book without giving examples. These seem to be necessary, just as they seemed to be necessary in my Hyderabad lectures. However, citing passages on the basis that they have given offence almost certainly gives a distorted picture of the book. For example, these passages contain what is actually a disproportionate number of swear words, as Rushdie has commented:

I remember someone who didn't like *The Satanic Verses* went through it and ... counted the number of times I said 'fuck' and 'shit' and so on, and ... it was incredibly low ... There was something like 16 fucks and, you know, 25 'shits' and this – and in a novel of 550 pages long it struck me as being incredibly clean. But this point is not generally accepted. (*Gleaner*, 1996: 1)

But to return to Gibreel's 'dream' religion: its scripture, with its 'rules about every damned thing' (*The Satanic Verses*, p. 364) is portrayed as either satanically inspired ('Being God's postman is no fun, yaar. Butbutbut: God isn't in this picture. God knows whose postman I've been' *ibid.*: 112), or as conveniently tailor-made to suit the prophet's own inclinations – as his wife, Ayesha, is made to say, 'Your God certainly jumps to it when you need him to fix things up for you' after the angel gave Mahound, 'God's own permission to fuck as many women' as he liked (*ibid.*: 386). According to Bukhari, Ayesha (or 'A'isha), often described as Muhammad's favourite wife, once said 'Messenger of God, I see that your Lord makes haste to satisfy your desire' (cited by Robinson, 1992: 36). Rushdie may well have had this tradition in mind when he wrote the above line for his fictitious Ayesha. Here, Mahound resembles Gibreel – like the actor, he is very fond of women. However, he 'didn't like his women to answer back' (*The Satanic Verses*, p. 366). We read:

so ... out comes the rule book, the angel starts pouring out rules about what women mustn't do, he starts forcing them back into the docile attitude the Prophet prefers .... but the man is a magician, nobody could resist his charm; the faithful women did as he ordered them. They submitted: he was offering them Paradise after all. (*ibid*, p. 367)

We saw in Chapter 3 how non-Muslims have often represented Muhammad as sexually indulgent – and therefore as morally suspect. Rushdie writes about 'stories of Muhammad's doubts, uncertainties, errors, fondness for women' abounding 'in and around Muslim traditions' (1991: 409). What distinguishes Muslim from non-Muslim here (as I have already argued) is not the texts used but how they are handled and interpreted.

Mahound is described as a 'fit man, no soft-bellied usurer he' (*The Satanic Verses*, p. 93). He has three powerful opponents: Baal, a 'blood-praising versifier' (p. 98), Abu Simbel, who is able to 'make his quarry think he has hunted the hunter' (p. 98), and Abu Simbel's wife, Hind, 'that famous Grecian profile with the hair that is as long as her body' (p. 113). These three can all be identified with actual opponents of Muhammad; for example, Abu Simbel is based on Abu Sufyan, chief of Makkah, whose real wife was indeed called Hind (Hind bint 'Utba; briefly referred to in *The Moor's Last Sigh*, p. 368), a renowned beauty who had a love affair with ''Umar before his conversion' (see Mernissi, 1991: 117). 'Historians', says Mernissi, 'have been so fascinated by Hind's personality that they have devoted pages and pages to her' (*ibid.*: 118). The Makkan chief converted to Islam just before the Battle of Hunayn. Hind did so only after the fall of Makkah. In *The Satanic Verses*, Abu Simbel finally delivers Jahilia into Mahound's hands; Hind for her part appears to be arcanely responsible for causing Mahound's fatal illness (see *The Satanic Verses*, p. 393). The passages which Muslims find objectionable are too numerous to list – they include the satanic verses affair (see *ibid.*: 107), the brothel scene in which the whores in 'the most popular brothel in Jahilia' have each taken the name of one of Muhammad's (Mahound's) wives (see pp. 376f), and allusions to such historical figures as Bilal (the first Muezzin) as 'the one Mahound freed, an enormous black bastard ... with a voice to match' (p. 101). *Jahilia* is the Muslim term for pre-Islamic Arabia, the 'age of ignorance'; Bilal is especially popular with Black and African Muslims, who regard him as a type of 'patron saint' (see Craig, 1977; also *Midnight's Children*, p. 294 for another Rushdie reference to Bilal). B 57:23 reports Muhammad saying to Bilal, 'I heard the sound of your shoes in Paradise just in front of me.' After taking control of the city, Mahound is persuaded not to close the brothel, 'take things slowly', he is advised, 'Jahilians are new converts', and, 'most pragmatic of prophets', he agrees (*The Satanic Verses*, p. 381).

Throughout, Gibreel's own identity is problematic – he dreams that maybe he is not the Angel, but Satan (see *ibid.*: 91, 367). Sometimes he dreams that he is 'actually inside the Prophet' (*ibid.* 110). Sometimes the Prophet seeks his advice; thus, 'Mahound comes to me for revelation, asking me to choose between monotheist and henotheist alternatives, and I'm just some idiot actor having a bhaenchud nightmare, what the fuck do I know'(*ibid.*: 109). The angel seems to speak just what the Prophet wants him to: 'then he did his old trick, forcing my mouth open and making the voice, the Voice, pour out of me again, made it pour all over him like sick' (p. 123; note a similarity here with how Rodinson uses the word 'Voice', for example: 'The Voice itself insisted, 'We have not taught him poetry, nor does it beseem it', 1961: 95). After the satanic verses affair, we read: 'but Gibreel, hovering-watching from his highest camera angle, knows one small detail, just one tiny thing that's a bit of a problem here, namely that it was me both times ... From my mouth, both the statement and the repudiation' (*The Satanic Verses*, p. 123). Mahound is depicted as somewhat scathing about literature; Baal, sentenced to death, shouts, '"Whores and writers, Mahound. We are the people you can't forgive." Mahound replied, "Writers and whores. I see no difference here"' (p. 392). Rushdie may have been expressing criticism of the way in which literary freedom has, in his view, been restricted in Islam by the 'shackles of the Thought Police'; '"Free speech is a non-starter"', says one of my Islamic extremist opponents' (1991: 436, 439).

We also have a revolution-plotting, anti-Western Imam in exile (from Desh), who is 'wont to thunder. Apostate, blasphemer, fraud' (*The Satanic Verses*, p. 209). The similarity with Khomeini is striking; like Khomeini, 'in exile' Rushdie's Imam refuses to 'put down roots': 'The curtains ... are kept shut all day, because otherwise the evil thing might creep in ... foreignness' (p. 206). In *The Satanic Verses*, the Imam flies to Desh on Gibreel's back (p. 211f). What is clear, however, is that Muslims identify the religion portrayed in the book as a deliberate and offensive parody of Islam. Rushdie himself has said that the religion takes its starting point from Islam but, as portrayed, the dream religion is a device for exploring how human weakness can corrupt the search for divine meaning. The religion is, he says, the product of Gibreel Farishta's fevered imagination.

To complete the narrative, Saladin (alone in his attic) actually appears to recover, 'it seemed a cure was in progress' (*ibid.*: 406). He begins to go out and about again. There is a hilarious reunion between Saladin and Gibreel at a London party; then Gibreel saves Saladin from the fire which destroys his bed and breakfast retreat (p. 468). Recalled at the end of the novel to Bombay to attend his dying father (the reconciliation that follows, p. 523, may well be based on Rushdie's death-bed reconciliation with his own father), Saladin finds peace (and Zeeny) when, 'His old English life, its bizarreries, its evils', suddenly begins to seem 'very remote, even irrelevant, like his truncated stage name'. Gibreel, meanwhile, has become more and more consumed with religious megalomania – insisting that 'people get down and kneel' (p. 539) – the result of his dreams. His debauchery also reaches new limits. He, too, returns to Bombay where, in a final scene at the house of Saladin (who has now inherited his father's fortune) he commits suicide (p. 545).

The controversy

Muslims view Rushdie's *The Satanic Verses* as a gratuitous and scurrilous attack on Islam; 'in most parts of the Muslim world – the novel was seen as a deliberate attempt to humiliate and ridicule the most revered figures in Islam' (Ahmed, 1996: 114). For them, it constitutes libel, since Islamic law makes provision for safeguarding the honour of the dead as well as the living. In the United Kingdom, they called for legal redress and tried to invoke the English blasphemy laws. These laws (of blasphemous libel and blasphemous slander), however, only protect the Christian religion and the Church of England in particular. On 14 February 1989 Ayatollah Khomeini, then spiritual leader of Shi'a Iran, issued a *fatwa* (legal opinion) pronouncing that Rushdie, and those publishers aware of the book's contents, were *'madhur el dam'* (those whose blood must be shed): 'I call on zealous Muslims to execute them quickly, wherever they find them, so that no one will dare to insult Islam again' (cited in Markham, 1996: 310). Only three offences carry the death sentence in Islamic law: premeditated murder, adultery (for married partners) and attacking Islam – usually closely associated with apostasy. Attacking Islam and apostasy both represent treason; as I have stated throughout this book, Islam draws no distinction between 'religion' and 'state', the 'secular' and 'the sacred'; see also Forward (1997: 62) on apostasy as an 'example of the tension in Islam between individual responsibility and choice, and community identity'.

Legal texts, however, devote much space to discussing whether apostates must first be given the chance to repent; indeed, both repentance and forgiveness play significant parts in Islamic law. Ibn Ally (1989: 26) explains:

Apostasy is mentioned in the Qur'an in thirteen verses ... but in none of these ... can one find any mention of the punishment ... The only occasions when specific penalties have been mentioned in the Qur'an has been when apostasy is accompanied by fighting ... a quiet desertion of personal Islamic duties is not a sufficient reason for inflicting death on a person. Only when an individual's desertion of Islam is used as a political tool for instigating state disorder, or revolting against the law of Islam, can the individual apostate be put to death.

Rushdie has rejected the charge of apostasy:

To put it as simply as possible, I am not a Muslim. It feels bizarre, and wholly inappropriate to be described as some sort of heretic after having lived my life as a secular, pluralist, eclectic man ... When I am described as an apostate Muslim, I feel as if I have been concealed behind a false self. (1991: 405).

In *The Moor's Last Sigh*, when secular Aurora is described by critics as 'a Christian artist', Rushdie comments: 'How easily a self, a lifetime of work and action and affinity and opposition, could be washed away under such an attack' (p. 234).

Islamic law, however, only passes sentence following a trial in which the accused have the opportunity to defend themselves. Almost by definition, this can only happen when the offence has occurred in a Muslim state. Mehdi Mozaffari, a professor at Aarhuus University in Denmark, argues that the so-called *fatwa* is in fact nothing but Khomeini's personal opinion:

Nothing in the decree's form, procedure, or substance indicates that it is a *fatwa* ... Neither can Khomeini's decree be considered a judicial act following a judgement. The Iranian Constitution does not allow the leader to give orders to kill someone in the absence of trial and judgement. (1996: 13)

However, as 'the ears and eyes' of the Hidden Imam on earth, Khomeini may well have felt able to move beyond traditional legal conventions, especially if, as suggested in Chapter 5, he regarded himself as 'infallible'. Perhaps he even recognized himself as the book's revolution-plotting Imam in exile.

Although the *fatwa*'s authority, even amongst Muslims, is debatable (and it is difficult to see how Britain's predominantly Sunni Muslims could recognize its validity), the possibility of a murder attempt remains – perhaps by an Iranian, or by someone else who decides that God's law may sometimes ignore national borders. Consequently, Rushdie is still in hiding – in 'spiritual isolation', as he has himself described the experience ('In the shadow of the *fatwa*', Channel Four programme broadcast 7 February 1993). Something of the impact that the *fatwa* has had on Rushdie, I think, informs the plot of *The Moor's Last Sigh*, in which Moor is born with an incurable premature ageing disease, and says to himself, '*So you made it today. Will you still be here tomorrow?*' Moor lives 'with the minute-by-minute fear of death … a toothache for which no soothing oil … could be prescribed' (p. 340). The *fatwa* has been renewed by the Iranian authorities on several occasions since Khomeini's death. For Shi'a, who do not follow dead men, *fatwa*s die with their authors. The Italian and Japanese translators of the book have been killed, as were two Imams in Belgium whose views on the affair were thought to be too moderate. The Norwegian publisher was injured by gunfire. As I was writing this chapter, headlines in *The Times* (14 February 1997 – eight years after the *fatwa*) announced that a 'shadowy Iranian foundation' had increased the bounty on Rushdie's head to $2.5 million, and that non-Muslims were also eligible to claim the sum.

What the affair represents is a clash of values; Lord Justice Watkins, who rejected the plea to prosecute Rushdie, stated that there was little doubt that the book had 'deeply offended many law-abiding Muslims who are United Kingdom citizens' but that the 'law covered only Christianity'. Indeed, he advised that it ought to be abolished: 'I join with many persons of good will in urging Parliament to end this discrimination [between religions as well as against humanists and non-believers] by abolishing an anachronistic crime which still, notwithstanding today's decision, carries dangers for freedom of expression' (Queen's Bench Divisional Court, 9 April 1990). The Court also ruled that no offence had been committed under the Public Order Act. Whether the law should be extended to protect all faiths or be abolished altogether as unworkable in a secular and pluralist society, or whether alternative laws – making 'incitement to religious hatred' an offence, for example – might be introduced, remains a subject for debate. (See *Second Review of the Race Relations Act, 1976* (1991), published by the Commission for Racial Equality, pp. 58–61, for an important discussion of this issue.) On the one hand, Rushdie has been defended by the literary establishment as the champion of free speech. Indeed, the question about whether the religion pictured in the book is or is not identical with Islam remains, in my view, unanswered; yes, there are obvious references to historical Islam, but in the book fact mingles with fiction to create a mélange. It is by no means uncommon for novelists to use history as the base-line from which their imaginations take off into a world of make-believe. Perhaps the following description of Aurora's art in *The Moor's Last Sigh* might equally describe Rushdie's literary style: 'the mythic-romantic mode, in which history, family, politics and fantasy [jostle] each other like ... great crowds' (pp. 203–4). Just as the country in *Shame* 'is not Pakistan, or not quite', so the dream religion could be called 'not Islam, or not quite Islam'. In *Shame*, Rushdie's narrator says, 'There are two countries, real and fictitious, occupying the same space ... My story [exists] like myself, at a slight angle to reality' (p. 29).

On the other hand, Muslim response in the form of book-burnings and mass marchers waving placards reading 'Rushdie Must Die' have confirmed many non-Muslims' images of Islam. Said (1997: xiii) comments that Khomeini's *fatwa*, 'and the multimillion dollar reward' associated with it, seem 'to epitomize Islam's viciousness, its resolute war against modernity and liberal values [and] its capacity of reaching across the oceans into the heart of the West in order to challenge, provoke, and threaten'. Rana Kabbani (1989: ix) writes about her own feeling of being trapped between 'two tyrannies – that of Ayotollah Khomeini's unacceptable death sentence ... and, in reaction, the harsh condemnation of the West of what it saw as an alien culture'. As a Muslim, Kabbani admires and wishes to adopt aspects of Western life, but equally wishes to uphold 'many things about Islam' (p. 11). Like Rushdie, Kabbani wants to bridge cultures. However, in her view, *The Satanic Verses* failed to achieve what it set out to accomplish. Instead, it 'added dramatically to the clash of cultures [and] has set back the cause of anti-racism, to which Rushdie himself has over the years been so eloquent a contributor' (p. 68). In trying to bridge the East–West divide, it seems, Rushdie has fallen into the gulf between them. Or, having (like his character, Aurora) made 'the ideas of impurity, cultural admixture and mélange' closest to 'a notion of the Good' he has discovered that these are 'in fact capable of distortion, and [contain] a potential for darkness as well as for light' (*The Moor's Last Sigh*, p. 303).

The insider–outsider polarity

According to Kabbani, Rushdie misused his 'insidership':

Writers who lose sight of accountability risk becoming self-indulgent and politically irresponsible. Their position as 'privileged insiders', with unique insight into their own communities, gives them an authority and credibility that no outsider has. The danger is that their texts may be read as truths. (1989: 67)

As Ahmed points out, libraries are full of books which treat the Prophet of Islam similarly, but what has angered Muslims is a sense of cultural betrayal. 'What really agitated them', writes Ahmed (1993: 115),

was the breach of *adab*. By violating the rules of *adab* [Rushdie] appeared to be saying to Muslims: I understand your rules of behaviour and culture and I am violating them; let us see what you can do about it.

My own view is that the book is witty, inventive, peopled with real characters experiencing real dilemmas. In places, too, I find the book very funny – even though I laugh at what ought to make me cry. Rushdie's aim, to hold up 'chutneyfication' as something to be affirmed – denying that intermingling inevitably weakens – is close to my own passion for a cultural and religious pluralism that enriches our understanding of what it means to be equally human but culturally and religiously different. The global village is, for better or for worse, a reality; we live in a world of many cultures in which there is movement, migration, trade, marriage and, too often perhaps, conflict between different human groups. Either we prepare for continual confrontation between ourselves and others, or we develop strategies to enable peaceful co-existence with, if not creative exchange between different civilizations. I shall return to this below.

However, what conclusions can I draw about Rushdie's treatment of Mahound? It makes little difference, in what follows, whether Mahound and Muhammad are identical, since what I focus on are similarities between Rushdie on the 'prophet' and what others have made of Muhammad. I am not especially interested in analysing his motive. He has clearly stated his own difficulty with belief in revelation from without and his view that the human personality of the prophet must have interacted with any sense, however genuine, of divine inspiration. What results from this, in the book, is a Prophet who was inspired from within, whose motives appear to have been, at the very least, mixed, who willingly compromised his principles in order to achieve success. Whether Rushdie is to be considered an 'insider' is, I think, doubtful. Muslims do not regard the Prophet's inspiration as internal, or think that he was anything less than sincere, honest and single-minded in pursuing his commission. In fact, Rushdie's Prophet resembles traditional non-Muslim accounts which, convinced from the outset that Muhammad's career represented something negative, that he enjoyed no link with the divine, set out to offer an alternative explanation for his success. In these accounts, Muhammad succeeded through compromise, resort to violence, silencing his enemies, appealing to human licentiousness and the force of his charismatic personality. Some suggest satanic inspiration; for others, an origin within Muhammad's gifted but deluded personality has sufficed. Incidentally, Rushdie's Hindu boy-guru character, Lord Khusro, lacks genuine religious bona fides; he is 'the wholly spurious creation of his mother' (*The Moor's Last Sigh*, p. 163; see *Midnight's Children*, p. 269).

Of course, it is possible to reject belief in Muhammad's divine inspiration and uphold a human explanation for his success without also portraying Muhammad in a negative light – here we may recall the accounts of Voltaire, Stubbe and Carlyle, which interpret Islam as a successful secular movement and credit Muhammad accordingly. Rushdie's decision to portray the Prophet negatively may suggest an a priori animosity towards Islam. Also, Rushdie does have knowledge of Islam's sources; his account was not dependent on myth, legend, or pure invention – unlike the early Byzantine and Latin accounts. What is different, then, between Rushdie on his Prophet, and Muslims on theirs, is how the sources and primary texts are interpreted.

It seems that such people as Muir, Rushdie, and others look at the sources available for reconstructing Muhammad's biography and see there someone who, as one writer put it, 'is in every way unfit to be the ideal of a single human being' (Tisdall, 1916: 221), whilst the vast majority (if not all) Muslims look at the same sources, and see Muhammad as 'the model of righteousness, the perfect individual' (Akhtar, 1992: 3). One can hardly imagine two more different appraisals. When, as with Byzantine, Latin, and medieval European writing about Muhammad, the sources used were of very dubious historical value, the result was far from surprising. What accounts for radically different images of Muhammad when these are derived from identical sources? In my view, and based on the research out of which this book has evolved, the explanation lies in what different writers bring to their sources. Muslims bring to the sources what can be called a hermenuetic of faith. For them, Muhammad's example is *uswatan hasanah* (noble) and they see nothing but beauty in his Life. Others, convinced from the outset that Muhammad was insincere, or that he was sincere but misguided, or that he enjoyed no link with any divine reality, find in the sources what they need to confirm their particular view of Muhammad. They bring a different hermeneutic to the same material – one of suspicion or doubt, or perhaps a hermeneutic which must explain the phenomenon humanly, sociologically or psychologically, or which can credit Muhammad's political achievements but cannot accept that God played any part in his career.

Just as, according to Adam Kuper, anthropologists have found data within the cultural texts they have studied to support their a priori beliefs – that societies are all based on kinship, or on territoriality, for example – so scholars of Islam's foundational documents have found data to support their a priori convictions about Muhammad (see Kuper, 1988: 169). Those who approach the sources with a hermenuetic of faith interpret an incident such as the killing of Kaʿb Ibn al-Ashraf as a wholly justifiable act which does not in any way reflect negatively upon Muhammad's character. Someone such as Muir, approaching the sources with a hermeneutic of doubt, reads the same incident as an example of Muhammad's moral culpability: 'I have been thus minute', Sir William wrote, 'in the details of the murder of Kaʿb, as it faithfully illustrates the ruthless fanaticism into which the teaching of the Prophet was fast drifting' (1894: 240).

I argue, then, that it is the a priori hermeneutic which we bring to the material that, to a great degree, determines what we make of the Prophet. A predisposition to see goodness or greatness in the Prophet will construe the evidence to confirm this, whilst a predisposition to see Muhammad as morally culpable, suffering from some form of psychological malady, or as a clever political leader, will find what it needs to justify these views. To pose our questions again, 'Is Muhammad inevitably viewed differently from without Islam?', and 'How much of the Islamic view of Muhammad can outsiders share, without becoming Muslims and ceasing to be outsiders?', it seems to me inevitable that our a priori agendas and hermeneutics influence how we interpret Muhammad's career, and that a believer is therefore likely to construe a different picture from a non-believer. Non-believers, who reject any link between Muhammad and the divine, may very well treat him in a way which Muslims find offensive. The specific question raised by the Rushdie affair is: Should such treatment, if it causes offence, be liable to legal challenge?

Personally, I think that extending the blasphemy laws in England would be very problematical and, since this survey has shown that people can interpret the same material in radically different ways, who would be qualified or competent to say whose interpretation should stand? An insider interpretation is an authentic interpretation, but so are outsider interpretations, however different these are from each other. They may even be mutually contradictory yet, based on the same data, they carry their own authenticity. Postmodernity upholds the view that texts do not speak – rather, they are read, and their reading is always mediated by the mind of the reader: 'There is no innocent interpretation, no innocent interpreter, no innocent text' (Tracy, 1987: 79); 'Every interpreter', says Said, 'is a reader, and there is no such thing as a neutral or value-free reader' (1997: 164). Or, as W. C. Smith (1980: 492) put it:

If you yourself are a Muslim writing a commentary; or a *sufi pir* instructing your *murid*; or are a conscientious juriconsult deciding a tricky point of law, or are a modern Oxford-educated Muslim reflecting on contemporary life, or a twelfth-century Shirazi housewife ... or are a left-wing leader of the slave revolt of the Zanji protesting against what to you are the exploitation and hypocrisy of the establishment – in all such cases the correct interpretation of a particular Qur'an verse is the best possible interpretation that comes to you or that you can think up.

Here we encounter plurality of interpretation amongst insiders; when we extend interpretation of the same text to outsiders we can expect even more variety. For example, a Muslim man interpreting Q 4:3 may claim that it allows polygamy – that polygamy is wholly moral, and rightly a feature of Muslim life. The Qur'an, he may say, is the definitive revelation of God's will, of that which is permitted, and contains universally valid rules of conduct. A Muslim man may cite some of the misogynist *hadith* which I discussed in Chapter 2 and find nothing objectionable in attributing these to valid sayings of the Prophet. Another Muslim, perhaps a woman, may read the same texts and reject their authenticity. Similarly, she may read Q 4:3 and claim that it does not permit polygamy (strictly speaking, polygyny) for all Muslims; rather, it permits polygamy only in situations when war has left women and children bereft of financial support, which only marriage can provide. Another may say, yes, Q 4:3 does permit, but does not encourage, polygamy; and, given that other Qur'anic verses speak of husband and wife as having been created from a single soul (see Q 4:1, for example, only a few verses removed from Q 4:3), the ideal relationship envisaged by the Qur'an is monogamous; see, for example, 'Ali (1948: 127), 'The Prophet recognised, as a rule, only the union of one man and one woman as a valid form of marriage' except in 'exceptional circumstances'.

Here, Muhammad's own multiple marriages will not be held up as the example for Muslims to follow, but will be understood as peculiarly appropriate for him, given his unique role and mission. A non-Muslim, convinced that Muhammad achieved success through pandering to men's sexual desires, may interpret Q 4:3 as an example of Islam's moral bankruptcy. To this, they will add Muhammad's multiple marriages (which exceeded the four allowed at Q 4:3) as additional evidence to support their theory. As Forward asks, 'Which Muhammad are we to affirm? The polygamist patriarch or the devoted and consultative companion?' (1997: 97). What kept occurring again and again in my research was the fact that insiders have had no difficulty with Muhammad's multiple marriages, with participation in war, the miracle *hadith*, or some of his dealings with opponents, whilst outsiders have very often seen all these as reasons for censuring the Prophet. My conversations with Muslims, too, during my attempt to gather some first-hand data for this book, confirmed that none of the above are regarded as problematic.

Of course, any interpreter may claim that their interpretation is the only valid one; in this view, there is present in the text a single true meaning which can be retrieved; Esack (1997: 74) comments that 'Traditional Islamic scholarship ... effectively worked along the lines of a pious form of historical positivism. Meaning ... is located within the text and can be retrieved by "pure minds".' Similarly, Muir would have claimed that, by applying the so-called scientific method, he had read in the texts what was there to be read. Any interpreter can claim that their piety, academic skills, or privileged hermeneutic has enabled them, and only them, to understand correctly (see *ibid.*: 75). Does this postmodern view of the relationship between text and reader mean, then, that Muslims cannot claim, on the basis of the biographical data we possess, that what they believe about Muhammad is justifiable? It may mean that their interpretation of what can be said about Muhammad will not be universally accepted, since scripture – like any other text – has no objective meaning. However, communities have the right to develop a shared interpretation of their sacred texts - thus 'the Qur'an as scripture has meant whatever it has meant to those Muslims for whom it has been scripture' (W. C. Smith, 1993: 88), just as Muhammad's life has meant what it has meant to those Muslims for whom it has carried authority.

What a scholar may ask is whether a Muslim interpretation of Muhammad is plausible, given what the historical records say. Quite possibly, this is where a theologian may differ from an historian; a theologian may supply a supernatural element about which the historian must remain agnostic. However, my reply to the question, posed at the start of this chapter, 'Can outsiders be expected to treat Muhammad with the same reverence as Muslims do?' must, I think, be 'no'. I do believe, however, that if we are to find strategies for peaceful co-existence within our pluralist world, it is incumbent upon us all to develop sensitivities towards others' most cherished beliefs. We may not be *legally* obliged to take off our shoes when we tread on other people's sacred territory – I do not believe that legislation could enforce this – but we may well feel that common courtesy, and a desire for social harmony, represent a moral obligation to do so.

Towards a Muslim view of the Prophet?

Outsiders, then, do not bring to the texts, or to Muhammad's life, a hermeneutic of faith – that is, the conviction that Muhammad's life is exemplary and divinely guided. The Muslim views the Qur'an as wholly inerrant. A non-Muslim may totally reject the view that the Qur'an was revealed and presuppose an origin within Muhammad's mind (Rushdie's verdict), or view it as the creation of a particular cultural, social and religious context. Watt, who, in my view, of all the non-Muslim scholars examined in this survey moves closer than any other to a Muslim view, does not accept that 'everything in the Qur'an was finally and absolutely true' (1995b: 283). He does believe that Muhammad was 'genuinely inspired by God' (*ibid.*: 284) but not that 'all [his] revelations ... were infallible' (1991: 148).

Another Christian writer who, I believe, can be said to have moved towards a Muslim view of Muhammad is Hans Küng. Like Watt, he recognizes Muhammad as a 'prophet'. He writes: 'Muhammad ... can be accepted as an authentic prophet, though at the same time (like all prophets) he had his human limitations and weaknesses' (1997: 93). For Küng, too, 'Christians will always ask whether [the Qur'an as] Word of God is not at the same time a human word, the word of a prophet, like the Bible' (*ibid.*). Küng's parenthetical 'like all prophets' is a giveaway – here he is superimposing his Christian understanding of prophets as fallible humans responding in faith to God's calling on to Muhammad; Muslims believe in the sinlessness of all the prophets. For them, the Qur'an is not human attestation to divine self-disclosure, but God's speech mediated through the Prophet. I shall, however, suggest below that in our responses to the 'word of God' revealed through Qur'an/Prophet, there is inevitably a degree of human interpretation.

For many Muslims, the idea that context may have 'called forth' revelation, as implied by Watt's and Kung's approaches, devalues the Qur'an. Esack (1997: 53) explains:

The reluctance to explore the question of temporal causality that might be present in the background is a direct consequence of the passionate commitment to the preservation of the Otherness of the Qur'an as God's speech. The reasoning seems to be that if this-worldly events caused revelation then somehow revelation is not entirely 'other-worldly'.

If the Qur'an is to be regarded as a 'guide for humankind' (Q 2:185) it must, in this view, contain universally applicable rules of conduct. However (as Chapter 5 indicated), not all Muslims think that recognition of the Qur'an as a book revealed in and for a context (which is not the same as saying that the context created the text) implies that the values it teaches cannot be universally applied, even if its norms are adjusted. Outsiders, suspicious of any divine origin for the Qur'an and Muhammad's mission, must find other explanations.

As I have demonstrated, even when these explanations do not result in an inherently negative view of Muhammad, they nevertheless result in a view which differs from the Muslim view. If Muhammad is seen as anything other than a divinely guided, inspired recipient of God's word, its best interpreter, a model of conduct for all humanity, Muslims will find the account wanting. Some outsiders will already acknowledge another 'divine self-disclosure' as the definitive revelation of God's will and another messenger as the perfect example; thus, to accept Muhammad's claims would appear to demand abandoning existing loyalties. This seems to be true for Christians.

Goddard (1995: 173) concludes his excellent comparative study, *Christians and Muslims*, with this statement:

At the end of our review of the two faiths, therefore, these are the two fundamental options which need to be considered – the person of Jesus and the Christian scriptures on the one hand, and the message of the Qur'an and the person of Muhammad on the other – and we are therefore ultimately confronted with the need to make a choice. The question which remains before us at the end of our review of the two faiths is thus very simple yet also very complex; which of these two should be seen and accepted as supreme examplar and source of guidance.

Expressed thus, I have several problems with this choice. There are some who would question the theological correctness of a Christ–Muhammad comparison at all; we are not, it can be argued, comparing like with like: (see, for example, Jones, 1938: 53; for what the Qur'an says about Jesus, see Parrinder, 1995). Forward (1997: 72), too, argues that 'core Christian and Muslim beliefs about Jesus are so different that it is difficult to believe that he could ever be other than a divisive figure'. Forward also draws our attention to the fundamental difference between how Muslims and many Christians understand 'issues of revelation, prophetic authority and the origins of religion' (p. 119), which probably makes any comparison of Christian and Muslim 'revelations' theologically suspect – including that which follows in this book!

Reviewing William E. Phipps' *Muhammad and Jesus* (1996), Oliver Leaman (1996) takes Phipps to task for ignoring the 'extensive discussion of Muhammad within Islam ... which radically distinguishes him from Jesus' and 'the variety of interpretations of the Prophet and Islam itself which is commonplace even in elementary discussions of the religion'. He implies that Phipps is simply not comparing like with like. He concludes that this is not how to do comparative religion (p. 62). Leaman, I think, does an injustice to Phipps, although I agree that he fails to explore the diversity of Islamic 'Muhammadology'. Phipps' book, however, is not 'Comparative Religion' but 'Comparative Theology' and, as I argue below, a comparison between Christ and Muhammad may very well be justified.

Here, however, is the problematic: in Christian thought, God's self-disclosure is a person, God made flesh, whilst in Islam God's self-disclosure is a Book, the Qur'an. Christ was himself the messenger. Christian scripture represents human attestation to that Message – hence, as I have indicated,

Watt and Küng find it difficult to regard the Qur'an as totally ahuman. Küng asks:

Must an unconditional divinity and therefore perfection, infallibility and immutability of the 78,000 words of the Qur'an (but indirectly also those of the Prophet's Sunna and the shariah generally) be maintained? Or, as in the case of the Bible, may the historical character of divine revelation (God's word in the word of the prophet, God's word attested by the human word) be taken seriously? (1997: 96).

In Islam, however, the message was the Book; its recipient was merely the virgin human channel or instrument through which it was communicated. Muhammad was not the message. Thus it seems to be the case that the correct comparison would be Christ with Qur'an, not Christ with Muhammad. However, during this research I have personally become more and more convinced that this view fails to take account of the intimate relationship between Book and Prophet; the Qur'an was not only communicated through Muhammad but 'lived' by him. He is its best interpreter; without his *sunnah*, it remains a closed book. Also, Muhammad's status within Islam is so closely linked with that of the Book he brought, that he stands or falls with the Book. As Schuon (1976: 91) – and one of my own Muslim students – put it, 'Islam is the Prophet'. We have noted, too, how Muslim devotion to Muhammad can be said to resemble Christian devotion to Christ, as Cragg (1984: 65) writes:

Islam, even in despite of itself, finds place for categories of relationship between divine ends and human means, between the eternal and the historical, unlike and yet akin to those that are at the heart of Christian experience in Jesus as the Christ.

Thus, whilst Christ and Muhammad may not be commensurate in every respect *theologically*, they can be regarded as *functionally* commensurate; in believers' hearts, they occupy a commensurable place.

The Christ–Muhammad option

However, whilst I uphold the Christ–Muhammad comparison, one problem I have with the 'choice' so starkly put by Goddard is: which Muhammad, indeed which Christ, should I choose? We have argued above that different Muslims, and indeed different non-Muslims, depending on their presuppositions, view Muhammad differently. Which Muhammad should I follow? Similarly, Christians are far from unanimous in their understanding of Christ. Leaving aside differences of opinion about his exact relationship with God, which is actually to leave rather a lot to one side, Christians also differ in their views about Christ's ability to perform miracles, the extent of his special knowledge, whether the Sermon of the Mount is an ethic for today or the blueprint of the Kingdom that is yet to come, whether the resurrection (indeed the incarnation) is metaphor or scientific fact. Christians differ, too, in whether they interpret Christian obedience as primarily a matter of spiritual devotion, a bringing of lost souls into membership of the Church, or a matter of living Christ-like lives and working for peace, justice and improved quality of human living. And so on. Thus, which Christ must I follow, and what will my life be like as a result of following that Christ?

The second difficulty I have with the choice between Christ and Muhammad, put so starkly, is existential. For the vast majority of Christians whom I know, and for the vast majority of Muslims whom I know, there is simply no question of making such a choice. Ahmed (1988: 21) lists the following qualities which, for him, make Muhammad's *sunnah* worth following: 'respect for learning, tolerance of others, generosity of spirit, concern for the weak, gentle piety and desire for a better, cleaner world' ... 'constitute', says Ahmed, 'the main elements of the Muslim ideal'. We may note how Muir and Rushdie would substitute opposite qualities for almost all those listed above! We may also note how many of the above – such as generosity of spirit, concern for the weak, gentle piety – would be affirmed by Christians of Christ and stated as reason enough to accept Christ's claims. However, for Muslims who share Ahmed's view of Muhammad, his example is altogether adequate.

I know many Muslims who are not (as many of my Christian friends think) hankering for something else, something better, something more spiritually fulfilling, but who are happy, content, full of kindness and humaneness, because they try to imitate the Prophet. For most Muslims, the option of abandoning the *sunnah* is a non-starter. Similarly, for most Christians who love and cherish Christ and feel that they enjoy spiritual communion with him and through him with God, the idea of transferring loyalty to Muhammad is an existential impossibility. Quite simply, it isn't an option. Indeed, neither Christian mission to Islam, nor Muslim to Christian, has met with much success. Christian missions in Muslim countries boast few converts. In the very heartland of Islam – the Middle East, Egypt – significant Christian minorities survive to this day, despite centuries of Muslim rule. See Julian Pettifer and Richard Bradley's chapter, 'The Greatest Challenge' (1990) for some salutary reading here: 'In Morocco, for example, one missionary who worked for the Frontline mission reported that there were only about 300 Christians in a population of 26 million; more missionary graves than converts' (p. 190).

Goddard's choice, too, is between Christ and Muhammad as supreme example and guide. In posing this choice, he is assuming that there can be only one supreme guide. There is logic in this assumption; indeed, for both Christians and Muslims it is absolute commitment that Christ and Muhammad respectively claim. The faith of Christians and Muslims, who have faced persecution and even death, stems from an absolute, not a partial, commitment. A pluralist, who believes that all religions represent different and partial human apprehensions of that which is ultimately ineffable and beyond comprehension, might be happy to say that Christ can be *the example* for Christians, whilst Muhammad is *the example* for Muslims, Buddha for Buddhists, and so on. However, this type of pluralism runs counter to the claims that Christians and Muslims have made for their exemplars; it also runs counter to traditional belief that Christ and Muhammad did not just 'apprehend' what they taught but mediated (in different ways) divine self-disclosure. Thus, throughout the history of Christian–Muslim encounter, the choice between Christ and Muhammad has often been proposed. Another presupposition, as well as the view that there can only be one supreme guide, has often been behind this choice; namely, the conviction that, of the two, one is indeed better than the other. In other words, it is not really a choice at all, because any self-respecting person would choose your ideal candidate. Karl Gottlieb Pfander (writing in 1835) put it thus:

You have to choose between the Lord Jesus Christ, the Word of God, and Muhammad ibn 'Abdu'llah, between Him who went about doing good, and him who is called the Prophet of the sword: between Him who said, 'love your enemies', and him who said, 'slay your enemies and the enemies of God'; between him who prayed for his murderers, and him who caused those who lampooned him to be murdered ... you have seen what Muslim writers tell us about the life and character of Muhammad. You must now judge for yourself whether these were so superior to Christ's that you are justified in rejecting Christ, and entrusting your eternal salvation to Muhammad instead. (1986: 368; for Pfander, see Bennett, 1996b)

For Pfander, there is no choice; Christ is in every respect the better of the two and therefore the only option is to follow him. Muslims, however, may well express the opposite opinion. For them, both Christ and Christianity may seem distinctly lacking. As Nasr pointed out, 'Islam criticises Christianity for not having a Divine Law, a Shariah, in the strict sense of the term, and does not understand why Christianity did not follow Mosaic Law or bring a law of its own' (cited in Griffiths, 1990: 130). In other respects, too, Jesus' example may be thought Islamically wanting; as Ronald Eyre commented during his *Long Search* (1979), Jesus 'never married'. Reflecting popular Muslim belief, Eyre continued, 'His Second Coming may be to take a bride and rise to His full prophetic height' (p. 148).

But must we choose only one?

Yet is the only option to follow Christ or Muhammad and therefore to choose between the two? Is there any possibility that we are faced not with a choice between rivals but with complementary exemplars, both rooted in divine self-disclosure? If we abandon the idea that either one is inherently better than the other, then I think that we might be able to see Christ and Muhammad as complementary, not as rivals. A difficulty here, as we have already noted, is that Christians and Muslims have both claimed universal recognition for their exemplars. Thus, when I concluded my review of Goddard's book by stating, 'My own view is that such a stark choice may not be necessary. Rather, we may choose to see Muhammad as "supreme exemplar and source of guidance" in some areas of human life, Christ as supreme in others' (Bennett, 1996c: 66–7), I was rebuked by some Christian friends: either I recognize Christ as my absolute Master or I am guilty of compromise. I have thought long and hard about this and disagree. However, I think that my position needs clarification. What I want to argue is that, for me, Christ is indeed supreme exemplar; his love and compassion, his concern for the poor and outcast, his stress on the spirit rather than on the letter of the law, are all absolute values. I do not want to negotiate these. Also, I believe that God was present in the life of Christ in a unique way, conferring a new dignity on human life; I also believe that the qualities and values we see in Christ are those which God wants to govern our conduct. I believe that there is, in Christ, all that is necessary to live according to God's will; nothing more is needed. For me, too, the events of Easter say something about the nature of God which takes us to the very core of the divine character: love in the face of hate; restraint in the face of violence; suffering with all who are oppressed and abused – and through all of this there shines the hope of new life. Believing that God was present in the life of Jesus, for me there is something universally significant about the cross and resurrection. Otherwise, the cross would have been senseless: a tragic end to a failed life which achieved little if anything of value. Indeed, this may be why Muslims find the cross a scandal, and think that the crucifixion did not take place; no prophet's life could end so ignobly. If loving your enemies, putting away your sword, and being kind to the poor leads to crucifixion, then the real politic of life would lead us to regard such behaviour as absurd. It is the seal of the resurrection that has motivated Christian faith and enabled Christians to 'turn the world upside down'. Lesslie Newbigin (1988: 328) is right, I think, to claim that

If, in fact, it is true that almighty God, creator and sustainer of all that exists in heaven and on earth, has – at a known time and place in human history – so humbled himself as to become part of our sinful humanity and to suffer and die a shameful death to take away our sin and to rise from the dead as the first-fruit of a new creation; if this is a fact, then to affirm it is no arrogance. To remain quiet about it is treason to our fellow human beings ... One can, of course, deny the story. One can say it is not fact but legend. But if it is fact it cannot be slotted into some way of understanding the world based on other presuppositions, it can only be the starting-point, the presupposition of all our struggle to understand the world, including our struggle to understand the world of history.

However, Hick also rightly states the problematic:

We say as Christians that God is the God of universal love ... that he wills the ultimate good and salvation of all men. But we also say, traditionally, that the only way to salvation is the Christian way. And yet we also know ... that the large majority of the human race ... have lived either before Christ or outside the borders of Christendom. Can we accept the conclusion that the God of love who seeks to save all mankind has nevertheless ordained that men must be saved in such a way that only a small minority can in fact receive this salvation? It is the weight of this moral contradiction that has driven Christian thinkers in modern times to explore other ways of understanding the human religious situation. (1988: 122–3)

In other words, the scandal of the cross suggests that, on the one hand, it must have universal meaning, whilst on the other hand, its parochialism and particularity appear to contradict this claim.

What is at issue here is whether only Christians possess genuine knowledge of God, or other religious traditions are also valid paths from which Christians can learn something about their God. Hick sees all religious claims as relative; all represent apprehensions of the ultimately ineffable Real; all are particular because they are mediated by particular historical and cultural contexts. Thus,

all human thoughts, beliefs, theories, conceptions, are generated by particular men and women, or groups of men and women, living at a particular time and within a particular culture, with its particular presuppositions and modes of thought and its particular social and economic basis; and to say that thought is relative to those circumstances is simply to acknowledge that it takes different forms within different contexts. (1994: 21)

Religions, for Hick, are different human responses to the one ultimate Real. This 'relativising of Christian doctrine', he says,

by accepting that it is a human creation, always in principle subject to development and revision in the light of new information and new experience – seems to me to be incumbent upon us as Christians living in the humanly one but religiously plural world of today. (*Ibid.*: 22)

Hick prefers to talk about the Real or the Ultimate, rather than about 'god', in an effort to include those who do not believe in a personal divine entity. He writes:

We shall therefore postulate the ultimately Real, whose nature is beyond the network of human concepts – personal/nonpersonal, one/many, substance/process, purposive/nonpurposive, good/evil – but is humanly thought and experienced through the personal concept of deity or the non-personal concept of the absolute, in each case made concrete in the particular forms of Jahweh, the Holy Trinity, Vishnu, etc., or of Brahman, the Dharmakaya, the Tao, etc. (1994: 21)

Hick tends to say that there is no special self-disclosure or revelation; thus we are always dealing with partial, limited human apprehensions. Presumably, however, there is something about the nature of the Real that allows us to glimpse aspects of its nature. Although unknowable in its totality, there is an element of 'knowableness' about the Real. Indeed, Christians, Muslims, Jews and others traditionally go further; they believe that through their prophets and scriptures, God God's-self has taken the initiative. God has revealed to us something about God's nature, qualities, attributes and will.

Unlike Hick, for whom there is no special movement from the divine towards the human, I believe in revelation. Partly, this is based on the fact that human beings have long believed that God makes God's-self known – to Moses at the burning bush, to Job in the whirlwind, through the Christ event, through the scripture revealed to Muhammad. Thus one can either say that this belief is wrong, and that we are always dealing with people who think that God has spoken, or we can say that the Real is by nature a Reality which communicates with humanity. If we claim that our religion enables us to enjoy some sort of relationship with the Ultimate and that this relationship is life-enhancing, we are by definition claiming that the relationship is two-sided. Again, we might simply be wrong. However, those of us who opt for religion, who want to argue that it has some value, do so because we believe that it rests on something other than the human. Yet Hick, I think, is right to call our attention to the human element in religion; without human response, we would also be talking about the overriding of human free will.

Some regard the traditional Islamic view of *wahy*, in which God's word is communicated through an unconscious Muhammad who 'added nothing to this revelation himself' (Nasr, 1994: 44), as indeed 'overriding human freewill'. Nasr (as noted in Chapter 3) has compared Muhammad's unletteredness with Mary's virginity:

the human vehicle of a Divine Message must be pure and untainted. ... If this word is in the form of flesh the purity is symbolized by the virginity of the mother ... if it is in the form of a book this purity is symbolized by the unlettered nature of the person who is chosen to announce this word (*Ibid.*: 44).

However, what I think significant about Muhammad, and Mary, was their willingness to be used by God as God's mediators – in other words, they were receptive to God's revelation. There was, as it were, a meeting between the divine Will and their individual human wills. God wanted to make something of God's-self known; Mary and the Prophet were willing to be used, to place themselves completely in God's hands. Thus, whilst my world-view has a place within it for 'revelation', I also believe that what God reveals must be humanly encountered. Therefore, whilst Christ and Qur'an/Prophet may be regarded as mirroring the divine (although only as much of the divine as the divine wills to reveal), what we perceive about them will always be tainted by our own agendas and contexts. Unlike Küng, then, I would not insist that Qur'an/Prophet must be regarded as 'God's word attested by the human word', but I do maintain that our 'reading' of this 'book–prophet text' is a human activity, although one which may be divinely inspired.

If it is possible to claim that our knowledge of God is not merely human apprehension (us talking about God) but God talking about God's-self, or 'God-talk' (albeit this 'God-talk' must be heard through human ears), certain consequences follow; there will be a truthfulness, even an authority, about our apprehending. This is why Christians and Muslims have said: God has spoken, we have heard; his will for us is set forth in Christ or in Qur'an/Muhammad – so, if you want to 'get with the Real' (so to speak) follow us. Newbigin is right to say that if the Christian (and I would add, the Muslim) message is real, 'then to affirm it is no arrogance. To remain quiet about it is treason to our fellow human beings.' The challenge of religious pluralism is this: since we have more than one claim to be 'revelation', how are we to choose between them? Accept one, reject others? Or, as Hick suggests, regard all as partial? Or, as I am suggesting, regard them as of equal but complementary, rather than rival validity?

My proposal is rooted in the postmodern view of reality. I accept that we are all captive to our contexts; we all view, indeed construe, reality through the lenses we bring to bear on the data available to us. I am who and what I am – and I need not be anyone else. There is no 'meta-narrative', there is my narrative and there is yours. Postmodernism has unmasked the element of control behind the meta-narratives we previously took for granted; they are not all to be trusted. They represent the inventions of whatever authority happens to dominate at the time at the centres of power; therefore they can be challenged (for this unmasking, see Foucault, 1977, and the Introduction to this book). This, however, does not mean that we cannot claim that our discourse is worth listening to – but we must relinquish, perhaps, some of the imperialist ways in which we have proclaimed this conviction.

Samuel P. Huntington has been much criticized for singling out Islam as the next 'enemy' of the West (and, therefore, of democracy, free-speech, liberal values, and so on) in his controversial article, 'The Clash of Civilizations' (1993). He cited M. J. Akbar, '[the] next confrontation ... is definitely going to come from the Muslim world' (p. 32). In fact, his thesis was that 'a central area of conflict for the immediate future will be between the West and several Islamic–Confucian states' (p. 48). Huntington sees the Muslim world's lack of what he calls a 'core state' as 'a source of weakness to Islam' and 'a source of threat to other civilizations' (1996b: 177). He also regards Islam as inherently violent (see *ibid.*: 258). Its claim to cultural universality, he says, fuels 'conflict between Islam and the West' (*ibid.*: 118). However, in his recent writing he similarly castigates the West for its arrogance in assuming that the 'rest of the world' wants, or needs, its 'values, institutions, and culture' (1996a: 41). Describing this as 'immoral', he calls on the West to 'abandon the illusion of universality and to promote the strength, coherence, and vitality of its civilization in a world of civilizations' (*ibid.*). Huntington is no postmodernist – indeed, he is somewhat scathing about multiculturalism and values cultural homogeneity. Chutneyfication, for Huntington, is dangerous. The USA, he says, must resolve the question, 'Are we a Western people, or are we something else?', since 'history shows that no country' without a cultural core 'can long endure as a coherent society' (1996b: 306–7). Said describes Huntington's 'clash of civilizations' thesis as 'diatribe' (Said, 1997: xxxiv). However, there is some similarity between Huntington's concept of 'civilizations in a world of civilizations', in which the West, having stopped trying to 'reshape other civilizations' in its own image, lives 'side by side in peaceful interchange' with them and even *learns* from them(!) (Huntington, 1996: 321), and what has been described as postmodernity's political agenda:

The unanswered question at the heart of the postmodern political agenda is how to make common cause to preserve difference, how to create a sense of solidarity that will be both 'more expansive ... than we presently have' (Rorty, 1989: 196) and conducive to the preservation and enhancement of difference. (Smart, 1993: 105)

Similarly, Akbar Ahmed (1992: 27) writes about the 'positive and exhilarating offering, what Barthes calls "jouissance"', which 'postmodernism brings to us: the importance of diversity, the need for tolerance, the necessity for understanding the other' (see Barthes, 1989; for a reference to Barthes, see Rushdie, 1991: 391). Thus, in the postmodern world, we can claim to have a message of universal significance but must renounce the type of 'universalism' that seeks to 'impose' this on others. Christian and Muslim evangelism have both, at times, enjoyed an alliance with political and economic structures which has left people with little real 'religious freedom'; they have found conversion the most pragmatic option. Postmodernity invites us to win the intellectual debate – and to re-examine how we may have converted people in bygone days.

A Trinitarian world-view

However, there is a difference (or so it seems to me) between saying 'Jesus is universally significant' and 'only Christians are saved'. There is, I think, a difference between saying 'Christ mirrors all that we need to know about God', and saying, 'there is no other mirror which reflects anything of God'. Nor do I want to say that Christ mirrors 'everything' there is to know about God. Whilst the Christian doctrine of the Trinity is not unproblematic for Muslims (see Q 4:171 but also my comments below), as D'Costa (1990) has argued, it can help Christians to 'dialectically relate the universal and the particular' which I have identified as problematical in this chapter. Christians, he points out, have never claimed that Christ is *totum Dei* (the whole of God) but that he is *totus Deus* (wholly God). Thus we may view Christ as 'normative' in 'revealing God' but not as God's exclusive revealer (Küng calls Christ the 'crucial standard', 1984: 129). D'Costa writes: 'It is ... possible to argue that Christ is normative, not exclusive or absolute in revealing God. Without Jesus we cannot speak of God', because God has peculiarly and particularly revealed God's-self in Christ, 'but that speaking is never completely exhausted in history, for the Spirit constantly and in surprising ways calls us into a deeper understanding of God in Christ' (1990: 18–19). A. G. Hogg (1939: 100) put it like this;

Whether to Christian faith or to non-Christian, God reveals Himself; he does not reveal ready-made truths about himself. And the thought and language in which a man expresses to himself or others his apprehension of that supernatural self-disclosure has to be human thought, human language – always defective, sometimes gravely distorting.

Incidentally, I have, at times, found Unitarianism very attractive – due in no small part to the challenge of Islam's unitarian understanding of God (see Bennett, 1981). Muslims have relatively little doctrinal quarrel with Unitarianism, apart from the fact that Muhammad plays no significant part in its world-view. However, over the years my Christianity has become firmly Trinitarian. For me, there was a merging of the human with the divine, and vice versa, in Christ, which means that it makes sense for me to call him 'God'; whether Jesus was always God, or was 'adopted', or became God through his own God-consciousness, or exactly how his identification with God happened,

I do not know. Christian scripture, for me, attests to what Jesus Christ said about himself and about God; thus its witness to the Spirit as the dynamic agent of God (see John 3:8) enables me to recognize God's action and presence outside the historical person of Christ, whilst the Spirit's implicit link with Christ (see John 16:15) suggests that Christ's role is somehow definitive, yet not exhaustive.

Paul Knitter (1996), drawing on the theology of the Orthodox bishop George Khodr, points out that if Christians accept that the Spirit moves beyond the Church, indeed beyond Christ (as the free-ranging aspect of the Triune God; see p. 112) then we ought also to 'accept that the kingdom of God beyond the Church is independent; that is, not to be submerged or engulfed or incorporated into the economy of the Word represented in the Christian churches' (pp. 113–14). 'The Spirit can never be understood and experienced without reference to [Christ] but nor can it be reduced to the Word, subordinated to the Word. ... There is "hypostatic independence"' (p. 113). Thus, whilst I want to affirm Christ as my critical standard, I must also be open to surprises; the Spirit beyond Christ may also 'make known to me what is to come' (John 16:13). The Spirit beyond Christ may blow from, and towards, the most unexpected places (John 3:8). That which complements but does not contradict, which supplements but does not supplant, may be affirmed. That which reflects nothing of the Kingdom, however, must be exposed; the world must be transformed

in order to foster the well-beings of persons *in this world*, we will have *to change* this world ... for it is painfully evident [that] so many practices and structures of nations and of the international community [and of religions, including the Christian] are death-dealing rather than life-giving for millions of people. (Knitter, 1996: 116).

What I want to argue, then, is this: Christ, for me, will be the mirror which I shall hold up before any claim to reflect the will of God. In applying this measure, I am not claiming superiority; my only claim is that I have something that works for me, which enables me to make sense of the world. It is my hermeneutical framework. However, not everything which claims to be of God, inside the Christian religion as well as outside it, will match the image in my mirror. Sometimes, beliefs or practices will strike discord. Christ condemned that which enslaves or manipulates people; he spoke out against oppression. He affirmed the dignity and worth of all. He rejected the accumulation of wealth – he encourages us to store up treasure which endures eternally. Thus systems which privilege some over others, which elevate profit above people, will find no reflection in my mirror. I will need to reflect, 'Have I seen aright?' before I speak, lest I be guilty of misconstruing what I see. However, I believe that the Gospel does compel me to oppose the forces of darkness. There are moral principles which inform my world-view and I will not yield ground when these principles are threatened. I will always remain open to dialogue. I will listen to my enemies. However, if their arguments do not convince me, I will do all I can to persuade others that my view, not

In Search of Muhammad

theirs, is right. 'Enemies', of course, is a strong term; yet those who value
success, wealth, possessions, over against fairness, compassion, justice, may
well qualify as such. So might those who think that some ethnicities are
inherently better than others! In other words, whilst I do not want to privilege
my way of seeing the world over-and-above other peoples', I also uphold my
right to argue for what I believe is just and right. I agree with Küng (see
below) and Halliday that the goal may be to achieve a consensus on core
values. I am not yet willing to concede that no moral principles can be
regarded as absolute. Halliday (1996: 154) writes:

we are to some degree in a common ethical universe in which an absolute 'cultural
relativist' position is untenable ... If, as is often argued, attempts to produce moral
codes on the basis of an irreducible, internationally recognized minimum have not
yet succeeded, this does not gainsay the principle that some such elements are to
be acknowledged.

Jesus and Muhammad

What can I say of Muhammad, when thus addressed? Here, I follow Küng's
view that, for me as a Christian, Muhammad can serve as a 'prophetic
corrective' – summoning me to re-examine what stands at the centre of my
life, reminding me that there must be symmetry between what I say and what
I do: 'That faith and life, orthodoxy and orthopraxy, belong together
everywhere, including politics' (1984: 129). Jomier (1989) suggests that
Christians might regard Muhammad as a 'charismatic reformer'; Jomier's book
How to Understand Islam, with a chapter on 'The Problem of Muhammad',
enjoys the *nihil obstat* and *imprimatur* of a Catholic bishop. Jomier is a
Dominican priest and missionary. Muslims, though, may think that this view
of Muhammad falls short of what the *shahadah* demands – belief in his
messengership, 'And Muhammad is the messenger of God'. Incidentally, I do
not know *how* the Qur'an was communicated by God through Muhammad,
but I can accept that it was; as I view the incarnation as a mystery, so I view
the *bookification* of the Qur'an.

As I look at the life of Muhammad, I see a life which, although Christians
have contrasted it negatively with Christ's, can be interpreted as
complementary; Christ said 'Render to Caesar' but did not give us instructions
on how Caesar ought to spend the tax to which he is entitled. Muhammad's
sunnah can help to supply some detail here; see Zakaria (1988: 36–7) on 'the
rate of taxation and the mode of collection ... determined by the Prophet'.
Christ appears to have been a pacifist. This may indeed be the Christian ideal.
However, in practice, Christians have had to develop theories to justify war
in certain mitigating circumstances; Phipps (1996: 156) comments that
'Christian rulers from Constantine onwards have been as interested in
legitimizing war as in making peace'. Muhammad's use of war, thus
interpreted, does not contradict Christian practice. Indeed, as Esack (1996)
says, Muhammad was given 'permission for the armed struggle' in order to

help preserve the sanctity of Christian and Jewish, as well as Muslim, institutions; 'But for the fact that God continues to repel some people by means of others, churches, synagogues and mosques, [all places] wherein God's name is mentioned, would be razed to the ground' (p. 161; Q 22:40).

F. D. Maurice (1805–72) addressed the relationship between Christianity and other faiths in his classic *The Religions of the World* (1846) and, anticipating Küng by almost 140 years, spoke about 'The Mahometan side of Christianity', and about Muhammad as 'one of God's witnesses before the Cross' (p. 238). Muhammad's insistence that 'God is' and is 'the ground of action, history and knowledge' challenges a Christianity which has too often tried to substitute 'notions and theories about [God's] nature' for the simple, uncompromising message that it is God who 'is himself the ground of man's being' (p. 33; note this pioneer use of the expression 'ground of being' usually associated with Paul Tillich). Maurice, who believed that God 'had not given swords to men in vain' (1838: 353) could hardly censure Muhammad for believing that 'men must be taught [God's mind and will] by the sword, if they would be taught no other way' (1846: 135). On the other hand, and I am personally inclined towards a pacifist stance, it can be argued that the rules governing war which have been handed down from the Prophet, through Abu Bakr especially, are such that no modern war could meet them. These protect non-combatants, crops, houses, places of worship; prisoners of war must be properly fed and clothed, although they may be ransomed. I recently heard a Muslim colleague endorse this view.

My own perception (drawing on Maurice) is that Islam has veered towards over-emphasis on the letter of the law, whilst (as Nasr has pointed out) Christianity has been too 'esoteric'. What is needed is a meeting of the ways; Christ may challenge Muslims to re-examine the ethical intent of the Qur'an, to pursue the Qur'anic spirit rather than the Qur'anic 'letter'. Christ, as 'a Spirit from God' (Q 4:171) may be a *sunnah* here for Muslims. Christianity may have neglected justice in the here and now in favour of reward tomorrow, and has rightly attracted Marxist critique. As Harvey Cox (1988) points out, religious institutions have often 'played an almost exclusively reactionary role. Marx and his followers took deadly [but accurate] aim ... controlled by the dominant groups, religion can be a tool of manipulation' (p. 214). Here, Muhammad's *sunnah*, with its many safeguards against the misuse of power (even if these have not always been practised by his successors) may serve as a 'prophetic corrective' for Christians.

For Muhammad's 'preferential option for the *mustad'afun*' (oppressed of the earth, marginalized) see Esack, 1997: 100–1:

to facilitate the empowerment of the poor and dispossessed, the qur'an announces that in the wealth of the rich there is an intrinsic share for them (70:25; 51:19). The principle of distributive justice was unambiguously affirmed ... elaborating on this principle, the Prophet mentioned various forms of wealth and power that had to be shared with those who did not have them. (p. 101)

We know that Muhammad had to be persuaded to take enough from the *Bait-al-Mal* to provide for himself and his family, and that at the height of his success he chose to live quite frugally (see Muir, 1894: 515–16). Phipps (1996) has a useful discussion of 'Getting and Giving' in Islam and Christianity (pp. 127–34), 'Giving to the needy should be viewed as a dividing of wealth that does not ultimately belong to the human giver' (p. 128). The preacher in me says, 'Surely here is a *sunnah* for me, as a Christian, which complements Christ's concern for the poor and marginalized who, he said, "would inherit the Kingdom".' A more systematic comparison of Christ–Muhammad may or may not support my thesis. Phipps (1996) goes some way towards such a comparative study, although I have reservations about aspects of his treatment of Muhammad; see his comments about Muhammad displaying 'no magnanimity in an expedition he led against the Jewish settlement at Khaibar' (p. 65; compare Buaben, 1996: 86–7), and on Muhammad's 'sexual drive' (p. 143), which do not suggest much effort at 'insidership'. Muhammad's alleged sexuality has proved to be a persistent stumbling-block for non-Muslim biographers.

I am not persuaded that attributing validity to aspects of Muhammad's *sunnah* (example) reduces Christ to anything less than Christians have traditionally believed him to be – God made human, in whom the fullness of God's will for human life was revealed. To say that aspects of Muhammad's *sunnah* have a validity for me which equals Christ's teaching is to say no more than that these aspects are wholly consistent with what I know of God in Christ; they do not *contradict*, but are *consonant with*, that revelation. This does not mean that God cannot use other channels to flesh out the details of the life he wants us to live. Saying that God speaks to us through other religions is not the same as saying that he 'saves' through them. God will, I am convinced, save whom he wills to save. Personally, I believe that all salvation is mediated through Christ; however, I agree with Newbigin (1989) that to affirm the 'unique truth of the revelation in Jesus Christ' does not 'limit the saving grace of God to members of the Christian church', nor does it deny 'the possibility of the salvation for the non-Christian' (p. 182). Thus, the Christian must 'tell the story' of what God had done in Christ: 'The story is itself, as Paul says, the power of God for salvation. The Christian must tell it, not because she lacks respect for the many excellencies of her companions – many of whom may be better, more godly, more worthy of respect than she is [but] as one who has been chosen and called by God to be part of the company which is entrusted with the story' (*ibid.*).

What remains problematical for me is Muslim denial of Christ's crucifixion. This event is central to my faith. I have not addressed this issue in detail in this book, although its place within early Christian–Muslim disputation was discussed. An option is obviously to say that the Qur'an is simply wrong at Q 4:157: 'They slew him not nor crucified, but it appeared so unto them.' Another option might be to invite Muslims to look again at how they understand the text. Does it actually deny that Jesus was crucified, or rather suggest that attributing blame or credit for his death is complex and contentious? 'They slew him not' may seem difficult to gloss, but what is at issue here may not be the fact of Christ's death, but its cause. Who, in Christian theology, is responsible for Christ's death? The Jews have traditionally been blamed, yet under Roman rule they did not have authority. Pilate, despite his hand-washing, had the legal power; yet was he not just the agent, the instrument through which all human brokenness and rebellion crucified Christ? If Christ's death was an integral part of God's redemption plan, so that there was 'no other way', no human agent or agents can properly be blamed. The blame rests with us all

Farid Esack and a Qur'anic liberational ethic

Esack, from a Muslim perspective, argues a view which brings him remarkably close to Küng and even closer to Knitter, with whom he shared a platform here in Oxford a year or so ago. Knitter, in fact, hails Esack's book as 'extraordinarily good': 'Esack offers a challenge for all religions: that human liberation and interreligious dialogue cannot be realized without each other' (back cover). Indeed, there seems to be a real meeting of minds between this Muslim and these Christian scholars. Examining Qur'anic passages which address 'Others', especially those who have had prophets and who possess scriptures, Esack points out that there is an ambiguity in the text – these Others are criticized for corrupting their scriptures, and for making exaggerated, indeed exclusivist, statements; Q 2:111: 'And they say, "None entereth paradise unless he be a Jew or a Christian." These are their own desires.' However, the Qur'an also indicates that there are some amongst the Others who remain faithful to God; for example, 'And lo! Of the People of the Scripture there are some who believe in Allah' (Q 3:199; see also 4:113).

The traditional view that these 'some' are those who have converted to Islam, Esack says, fails to explain why they should be identified as 'People of the Scripture'; 'there is no convincing need to single them out as Jews, Christians and Sabeans' (p. 164). Esack prefers to accept a text such as Q 2:62, 'Surely those who have faith who are Jews, Christians and Sabeans ... have their reward', as meaning exactly what it seems to mean, instead of trying to 'circumvent [its] apparent meaning' (p. 162). He criticizes the 'widespread acceptance, among the more conservative Muslims, of respect for the laws of the religious Other, even if only in theory, and the equally widespread rejection of their salvation' (p. 159). Esack rejects (p. 162) the argument that Q 2:62 (and similar verses) were abrogated by 3:85, 'Whosoever desires a *din* other than *islam* shall not have it accepted from him', pioneered by Ibn Abbas, for whom see Chapter 1 above. Whilst upholding that Muhammad's call was to present 'to all of humankind ... the Qur'an's own guidance for consideration and acceptance' (p. 173), Esack argues that the Prophet's role *vis-à-vis* the Other was sometimes to invite them to become Muslim, sometimes to 'challenge them regarding their commitment to their own scripture (Q 5:68), their deviation from these, and their distortion thereof' (p. 173). The Qur'an, says Esack, affirms in such passages as Q 2:148 and Q 5:48, that 'religious diversity is the will of God'. When Muslims deny this and claim exclusive status for Islam, they become guilty of doing what the Qur'an condemns in Others: 'the Qur'an is explicit in its acceptance of religious pluralism. Having derided the petty attempts to appropriate God, it is inconceivable that the Qur'an should itself engage in this' (p. 159). Esack, whose book arises out of the anti-apartheid struggle for justice and liberation in South Africa (which he extends, however, to other contemporary issues, including gender), argues in favour of mutual interreligious solidarity against oppression, as Muslims and Others 'vie with one another in good works'.

Küng, similarly, calls on Islam, Christianity and Others to 'do more for peace than they have in the past' (1984: xiii); commenting that, 'Peace (*shalom, salam, eirene, pax*) is a central feature in the programme of most religions.' 'Their first task', he suggests, 'in our age must be to make peace with each other' (1997: 100). Küng's call for a 'global ethic', without which he fears that the globe itself may not survive, directly addresses the postmodern world in which we live:

A global ethic has become particularly urgent in a world which has become secular, which is characterized by pluralization of truth and individualization of life: a minimal fundamental consensus concerning binding values, irrevocable standards, and fundamental moral attitudes, which can and should be affirmed by all religions despite their dogmatic differences. (1997: 101)

Theological issues or 'dogmatic differences' will no doubt continue to divide Christian and Muslim. Fazlur Rahman (1921–88), whose influence Esack acknowledges, comments that 'the unacceptability of Jesus' divinity and the Trinity to the Qur'an is incontrovertible, as is the fact that Jesus and his followers are regarded as exceptionally charitable and self-giving'. However, he continues,

I believe something can still be worked out by way of positive cooperation, provided the Muslims hearken more to the Qur'an than to the historic formulations of Islam and provided that recent pioneering efforts continue to yield Christian doctrine more compatible with universal monotheism and egalitarianism. (Cited by Griffiths, 1990: 109–10)

Esack writes movingly, on the last page of his book, about his personal commitment to a liberational ethic which can unite people across faith-divides:

Let us hope that, because of, and not despite, our different creeds and worldviews, we are going to walk this road side by side. Let us hope that we will be able to sort out some of the theological issues whilst we walk the road. If not, then at least we will get another opportunity after we have ensured our survival and that of our home, the earth. ... The struggle for justice, gender equality and the re-interpretation of Islam is one to which I am deeply committed. My own humanity is intrinsically wedded to this struggle. (p. 261)

Again, Esack is very close to Küng. Esack is openly critical of interpretations of his own tradition which, in his view, violate the Qur'an's liberational ethic.

My world-view, if it is truly pro-liberation, will need to examine critically whatever seems to restrict human freedom, wherever I perceive this – within and without my own tradition. We must tread carefully, however, when we point the finger of accusation at others, lest we ignore the log in our own eye! Nevertheless, I see no reason why I should not lend my support to those interpretations of Islam which seem to me to uphold the 'no compulsion in religion' (Q 2:256) dictum just as vigorously as I support those interpretations of Christianity which I believe allow and encourage open and critical enquiry. Sharing W. C. Smith's view that a 'flourishing Islam is important not only for the Muslims but for all the world' (1957: 304), and that this depends on 'whether Islam's contemporary renascence or reform succeeds in bringing a renewed vitality and power to Muslim society' (*ibid.*: 305), but not Watt's pessimism about the success of this enterprise, I see no reason why I should not express my personal enthusiasm for the versions of Islam which I prefer. Like Said (1997), I find the idea that 'recourse to a hazy fantasy of seventh century Mecca' can be 'a panacea' for all the ills of 'today's Muslim world' too fanciful, and 'it would be rank hypocrisy to deny' this (p. xv). I fully realize, however, the dangers inherent in making my preferences explicit – potentially, it may become a covert form of Christianization (see Bennett, 1993).

Finally, is there any scope for a theological meeting of minds between Christians and Muslims? Two options can be identified. One option is for Christians and Muslims to abandon some of their traditional convictions. Watt and Küng, sympathetic as they are towards Islam, have both called upon Muslims to revisit their understanding of the Qur'an as God's infallible word, and to accept that Muhammad contributed something to the Qur'an, as 'word of God and word of the prophet'. Muslims may call upon Christians to abandon the doctrine of the Trinity. Indeed, some Muslims have argued that Christianity was originally unitarian and deviated into Trinitarianism at an early point in its historical and theological development. The popular *Islam: the First and Final Religion* suggests that 'Christianity started with belief in one God [but] Due to Paul Jesus acquired a dual personality and became both man and God' (p. 187); thus 'Unitarianism can play a very significant part in the World today. It can ... act as a bridge between the Islamic and the Christian world' (p. 192). Hence what I have called my own 'flirtation with Unitarianism', to which I made reference above. Although Hick and other Christian theologians argue for a radical rethinking of traditional Christian dogmas, including the Trinity, few Christians show any inclination to follow this option. Similarly, whilst Muslims such as Esack, Zakaria and others are willing to revisit Qur'anic texts, to understand them 'in their historical context' (Zakaria, 1988: 32), I have never met a Muslim for whom the Qur'an is not wholly divine speech.

However, just as Christians distinguish between Christ as 'wholly God' and 'the whole of God', so Muslims may view the Qur'an as 'wholly divine word' but not as 'the whole of God's word'. Esack usefully summarizes the thought of Muhammad Arkoun, who (influenced by Paul Ricoeur; see Ricoeur, 1989) 'distinguishes between three levels of the word of God'. First, there is the 'transcendent, infinite and unknown' word. Second, 'fragments' of this 'word' are 'revealed through the prophets' (see also Q 2:255). Third, there is the 'textual objectification of the word' when 'Qur'an becomes a *mushaf*, i.e., written text' (p. 70; see also Arkoun, 1994: 37, in an accessible English translation of his thought). Thus we know as much of God as God has revealed of God's-self, but we do not know the whole of God. The language of the Qur'an, too, is language adapted to the needs of human minds; 'scripture is itself communicated through natural languages [which are] used as systems of signs' (Esack, p. 69). Similarly, addressing Muslims, a Christian writes as follows about the early Church's attempt to express, within 'the poverty of human language', what it had experienced about the nature of God; 'for want of better language', it spoke, he says, of 'the threefoldness of God'. Yet, 'No Christian claims that even the most widely-accepted definition of the Trinity is adequate to the ultimate truth about God' (Jones, 1938: 95). At what we might call the 'highest level' (the 'whole of God' level) it is inadequate, I suggest, for us to speak of God as One or as Three. This reduces God to a mathematical concept. It fails to do justice to the *mysterium* of God. The 'ineffable God' whom Muslims and Christians worship is ultimately beyond 'number'. On the other hand, there may not be as great a gap between Christian and Muslim doctrines of God as we have usually assumed: Muslims do not understand the 'Oneness' of God simplistically – *tawhid* is an active, dynamic concept; God is continually holding all God's qualities and attributes in balance. Muslims, too, whilst affirming the 'unity' of God, believe that God has many Names, qualities and attributes – indeed, 99 of them. Is this as radically different from Christian belief in a threefold experience of God as has often been supposed? I may be mistaken. However, I have argued that whilst Muslims find traditional Christian Trinity-language problematical, they have no difficulty accepting God's reality as complex. If this is true (dialogue may help me determine whether it is) it will not resolve all our theological debates, but it might invite us to listen more carefully to what each of us really believes, and to examine whether our beliefs are actually as contradictory as we have sometimes thought they are.

Standing between a rock and a hard place, Muslims and Christians might ask: Would the God whose will we discern through Christ (see Matthew 25) and Qur'an/Prophet (see Q 5:48) rather hear us debating endlessly about Unity and Trinity, or see us liberating the oppressed, seeking the welfare of the poor, and meeting our neighbours' needs? I also agree with Knitter that 'A missionary who has filled the church with converts without seeking to change a society that condones dowry deaths or bonded labor is a failure' (1996: 121). My second, and preferred option, is therefore for Christians and Muslims to accept that whilst on the one hand our theological formulations do not lack 'truthfulness', on the other hand they do not exhaust the mystery of God. Indeed, it might be the Spirit who inspires our dialogue who will 'guide us into all truth' (John 16:13). Have we found Muhammad during this search? My search suggests that what we bring to the historical record determines, to a large extent, what we take away, how we see Muhammad. There may be as many images of Muhammad as there are readers of this book. None the less, I hope that something of Muhammad's undeniable genius, perhaps even of his 'excellence', might be found reflected in this account of my search (see (Phil, 1: 9–11). For me, Muhammad's *sunnah* contains much that is worth putting into practice.

Appendix 1

Time-Line of Main Events*

570	Birth of Muhammad; death of father, Abdullah; Makkah invaded by Abraha the Abyssinian.
576	Death of Muhammad's mother, Aminah.
578	Death of grandfather/guardian, Abdul Mattalib.
572–82	Muhammad as a shepherd-boy.
582–95	Accompanies uncle, Abu Talib, on trade missions; gains reputation as '*al-amin*'; employed by Khadijah as factotum.
595	Marries Khadijah.
605	Muhammad appointed to adjudicate dispute between tribes over restoration of the black stone to the rebuilt Ka'aba.
c. 607/8	Begins to meditate on Mt Hira.
610	Revelation of Q 96 during 'night of Power' in the month of Ramadan; Khadijah, Zaid, 'Ali, Abu Bakr, become *mu'minun* (believers).
613	Summoned to preach publicly; attracts more followers but also Quraishi opposition.
614	Despatches refugees to Abyssinia.
615	Despatches second contingent to Abyssinia, where the Christian emperor refuses Quraishi request to deport them.
619	Deaths of Khadijah and Abu Talib.
620	Muhammad's Night Journey and Ascension; first pledge of Aquaba – allegiance of men from Yathrib.
621	Second pledge of Aquaba – 70 more pledge allegiance.
622	*Hijrah* – migration – to Yathrib, renamed Madinah-al-Nabi; residents agree to form a commonwealth under Muhammad; the Constitution is ratified. Followers become known as Muslims; mosque built, etc.
623 or 624	Battle of Badr – Quraish army suffers a defeat.
624	Bani Qaynuqa, Jewish tribe, is implicated in an anti-Muslim plot and punished.
625	Defeat at Uhud: blamed on sedition.
626	Plot by Bani Nadir is thwarted. Defensive ditch is dug around Madinah.
627	Punitive action against Jewish tribe, Bani Qurayzah.

628	Muhammad performs the *hajj*; treaty of Hudaybiyyah – truce during pilgrimage season. Battle of Khaibar – punishment for breach of treaty.
630	Battle of Hunayn – Abu Sufiyan converts. Makkah is taken peacefully; idols destroyed, 'truth has come and falsehood is banished'.
632	Last pilgrimage and sermon. Death of Muhammad.
632–34	Abu Bakr as Khalif.
634–44	'Umar as Khalif; Jerusalem taken in 638.
644–56	'Uthman as Khalif – Qur'an codified.
651	'Ali's army fights Mu'awiyah's.
656	'Ali becomes Khalif.
661	'Ali's assassination; Mu'awiyah becomes first Umayyad Khalif.
670	Death of Hasan, Muhammad's grandson.
680	Yazid becomes Khalif. The battle of Karbala and death of Husayn. Beginning of real division between Sunni and Shi'a.
684	Ibn Zubayr takes Madinah and Makkah and claims Khalifate; this ends in 692.
691	Dome of the Rock built. *Hajj* performed there until Makkah is recovered.
711	Spain invaded.
732	Battle of Tours: northern advance halted by Charles Martel.
750	End of Umayyad Khalifate at Baghdad – continued in Spain until 1236; beginning of 'Abbasid Khalifate.
765	Death of Shi'a's 6th Imam, al-Jafar, and dispute over succession. Majority follow Musa, d. 818; minority follow Ismail's son, Muhammad (the Aga Khan belongs to this lineage).
767	Death of Ibn Ishaq, Muhammad's first biographer.
800	Charlemagne becomes first Holy Roman Emperor.
819	Death of legalist, al-Shafi'i.
870	Death of traditionalist, al-Bukhari.
895	Death of philosopher, al-Farabi.
909	Rival Ismail Khalifate established in Egypt, the Fatimids.
940	12th Shi'a Imam, al-Mahdi, becomes the 'Hidden Imam'.
1009	Church of the Holy Sepulchre, Jerusalem destroyed by Fatimids.
1037	Death of philosopher, Ibn Sina (Avicenna).
1055	'Abbasid Khalif appoints the Saljuk general, Tughril Beg, 'Sultan'; effective power exercised by the Saljuks until 1260.
1095	Pope Urban I announces 1st Crusade.
1099	Jerusalem captured by Crusaders.
1111	Death of theologian and Sufi, al-Ghazali.
1143	First rendering of Qur'an into Latin.
1171	Fall of the Fatimids; remnant at Allamut until 1256 (the Assassins).
1187	Saladin re-takes Jerusalem.

1198	Death of Ibn Rushd (Averroes).
1219	St Francis of Assisi visits Sultan of Egypt.
1229	Jerusalem restored to Crusades by treaty between Frederick II and the Ayyubids.
1244	End of Crusaders' Kingdom of Jerusalem.
1258	Sack of Baghdad by the Mongols. 'Abbasid Khalif flees to Egypt.
1291	Fall of Acre, last Crusaders' fort.
1316	Lull, Christian evangelist, dies in Morocco.
1321	Death of Dante, who alone amongst the moderns exempted Ibn Rushd, Ibn Sina and Saladin from hell.
1378	Death of Ibn Batutah, who left an account of travels in Africa, the Middle East, India (where he served as a judge), China and Indonesia.
1389	Serbia conquered by the Ottomans.
1406	Death of Ibn Khaldun, father of the social sciences.
1453	Constantinople falls to Sultan Mehmet the Conqueror.
1492	Fall of Grenada; Christian re-conquest of Spain complete.
1501	Sha Ismail establishes Safavid dynasty in Iran. Iran becomes Shi'a.
1517	Ottoman Khalifate begins (last 'Abbasid is said to have ceded the title).
1526	First Mughal emperor in India.
1529	Vienna almost taken by Sulayman. Luther's *Against the Turks*.
1539	College of France appoints Professor of Arabic.
1638	Edward Pocock becomes Oxford's first Professor of Arabic.
1683	Vienna again under siege.
1732	End of the Safavid dynasty in Iran.
1734	Sales' English rendering of Qur'an: Gibbon thought the author 'half Muslim'.
1787	Death of al-Wahhab, founder of the *Muwahhidun* (Unitarians) who control Saudi Arabia.
1806	End of the Holy Roman Empire.
1829	Charles Forster's *Mahometanism Unveiled* – Islam fitted to prepare the way for Christianity.
1858	Victoria proclaimed Empress of India; end of the Mughal period.
1860	Muir's *Life of Mahomet* complete: Islam as enemy of civil society.
1870	Sir Sayyed Ahmed Khan's response to Muir.
1874	R. B. Smith's *Mohammed and Mohammedanism*; Smith criticizes Gladstone's animosity towards the Ottomans.
1884	The Mahdi of Sudan storms Khartoum; General Gordon is killed.
1898	Kitchener's victory over the Mahdi's successors.
1892	Death of J. E. Renan: Ibn Rushd's death had marked the end of free thought in Islam.
1924	Khalifate abolished.
1928	Muslim Brotherhood founded by Hasan al-Banna (1906–49).
1938	Death of Muhammad Iqbal, poet and philosopher of Islamic reconstruction.

1948	Creation of the State of Israel; death of Jinnah, founder of Pakistan.
1965	Death of Sayyid Qutb, ideologue of Muslim Brotherhood.
1967	Jerusalem captured by the State of Israel.
1971	Bangladesh achieves independence from Pakistan; 1977, Islam declared a 'principle of state'; 1988, Islam declared the state religion.
1977	Patricia Crone and Michael Cook's *Hagarism*: Islam a seventh- to eighth-century invention.
1979	Islamic revolution in Iran. Death of Abul Ala Maududi, founder of Jamaati-i-Islam; *Shari'ah* Act passed in Pakistan.
1981	Egyptian President Sadat assassinated by Jihad Organization.
1988	Salman Rushdie's *The Satanic Verses*.
1989	Khomeini's *'fatwa'*.
1996	Taliban coup in Afghanistan.

*(following traditional chronology; some dates are disputed)

Appendix 2

Muhammad's Marriages

Accounts vary. The chronology of Muhammad's marriages differs in some versions, some accounts also list additional wives. What follows has been reconstructed from a range of sources (see Hughes, 1988; Muir, 1876; Glasse, 1991; Zakaria, 1991; and Siddiqi, 1983).

1st marriage, 595 CE Muhammad married his employer, the wealthy widow Khadijah, who may have been widowed twice, or even three times. He was 25/26, she was 40 – according to the traditional chronology. They had 6 or 7 children: 2 or 3 sons and 4 daughters, but only Fatimah (a daughter) survived. She married Muhammad's cousin, 'Ali. Khadijah died in 619.

2nd marriage, 620 About two months after Khadijah's death, Muhammad married another widow, Sawda (aged between 35 and 40, possibly older), probably to provide his children with a stepmother. Sawda had returned from Abyssinia.

3rd marriage, 620 Shortly after, Muhammad became betrothed to 'A'isha (d. 678) who was then 6 or 7 years old. The marriage was consummated after the migration to Madinah (probably in 623). 'A'isha, who adored the Prophet, became 'Muhammad's undisputed favourite' (L. Ahmed, 1992: 51). Following the raid on the Bani Mastalik, 'A'isha was accused of adultery but vindicated; verses at Q 24:11–20 which denounce slander probably relate to this incident (see Pickthall, Mentor edition, p. 253; Lings, 1983: 243–6). This was also Muhammad's first political alliance; Aisha's father was Abu Bakr.

4th marriage, February 625 Muhammad contracted marriage with the 18-year-old Hafsa, also a widow and 'Umar's daughter. Muhammad thus forged another important political alliance with one of his most respected supporters (Hughes places Juwairiya 4th – see 8th marriage).

5th marriage, March 625 (one year after Badr) Muhammad married Zainab, widow of his cousin Ubaidah, killed at the battle of Badr. He thus took a vulnerable relative under his care. She died before Muhammad – perhaps within eight months of their marriage (Zakaria says 'three', p. 48, although I have seen 630 cited as the year of her death). Hughes places Hafsah 5th.

6th marriage, 626 The prophet married Salama, whose husband had died at the battle of Uhud. Salama has been described as 'no longer young' but Lings (1983) writes: 'despite what has been said of her age' she was 'no more than twenty-nine' (p. 206). This marriage fits the context of Q 4:3, thought to date from after Uhud when 'many Muslims were killed ... hence the concern for orphans and widows' (Pickthall, p. 79). Salama was at first a reluctant bride, saying: 'I have a nature of exceeding jealousy and thou, O Messenger of God, hast already more than one wife.' 'A'isha admitted to being jealous of Salama! (Lings, p. 207; Hughes places Zainab 6th).

7th marriage, June 626 About six months later, Muhammad married another Zainab and cousin, 40-year-old Zainab bint Jahsh (Forward, 1997: 87, says 35 or 38; Lings, 1983: 213, says 'almost 40') who was already married to his adopted son, Zaid. Qur'anic verses which abolish adoption (Q 33:4–5), and allow Muhammad to marry her following divorce from Zaid (Q 33:37) are associated with this marriage. Non-Muslims have often singled this marriage out for moral censure, arguing that Muhammad was sexually attracted by Zaid and manufactured revelation to endorse this irregular marriage. If the first Zainab was dead (and if my list's chronology is correct), then it was after this marriage that the number of Muhammad's wives exceeded the four allowed at Q 4:3. Thus, Lings (1983) comments, 'the Prophet ... already had four wives, the most that Islamic law allows' (p. 213). Q 33:50 is cited as granting Muhammad permission to marry beyond the four (whilst imposing certain restrictions). In Hughes's order, Salama is 7th.

8th marriage, circa December 626–January 627 After the Battle of the Trench, Muhammad married Juwairiya, captured during the raid on the Bani Mastalik. She was the widow of the tribal chief. This represents a political alliance: 'When it became known that the Bani Mustaliq were now the Prophet's kinsmen by marriage, the Emigrants and helpers set free their captives' (Lings, p. 242). 'A'isha is reported as saying, 'When I saw her ... I was filled with misgiving, for I knew that the Prophet would see in her what I saw' – her 'great loveliness and beauty' (*ibid.*).

9th marriage, circa 627/8 Muhammad married Umm Habiba, who had accompanied her husband to Abyssinia where he had become a Christian. She was given in marriage to Muhammad by the Negus (see Lings, p. 259). Her father was Abu Sufyan, then Muhammad's arch-enemy. Her brother, Mu'awiyah, became Khalif and 'Ali's arch-rival (see Chapter 5). She was herself an early Muslim convert. By marrying Habiba, Muhammad was exercising a duty of care and registering a political point. Indeed, it may have encouraged Abu Sufyan to convert, which he did before the conquest of Makkah. Lings says that Habiba dreamt of marrying Muhammad.

10th marriage, circa 628 After the battle of Khaibar, Muhammad married Safiyah, the 17-year-old widow of the defeated Jewish chief. She was renowned for her beauty. This was a political, peace-making marriage. She also appears to have dreamt of marrying Muhammad; see Lings, p. 269.

11th marriage, circa 629/630 Muhammad married Maimunah, a widowed relative. She was 51 when her first husband died. This marriage also created important alliances (see Lings, p. 282).

Was there a 12th marriage? Most accounts say that Muhammad contracted 11 marriages and that Khadijah and Zainab predeceased him, which left 9 wives living when Muhammad died. Accounts list two concubines, Mary the Copt (a Christian) and Rihana (a Jew; see Muir, 1876: 499). Rihana was acquired after the battle with Banu Qurayzah, Mary was given him by the Archbishop of Alexandria in about 630. She bore him a son, Ibrahim, who died before he reached the age of two. However, Zakaria (1991: 53) states that Muhammad married Mary, which would make her Muhammad's 12th wife. Muhammad's wives may have expressed jealousy of Mary. Muhammad may have responded by resolving to cease relations with Mary (for a period he refrained from all marital relations, and rumour spread that he had divorced his wives; see Lings, pp. 277–8) but Q 66:1 told him not to refrain from what 'Allah had made lawful for him'. His wives are chided: 'if he divorce you, he may get instead wives better than you, submissive to Allah'. Lings points out that all Arabs are descended from Abrahams's bondwoman, Hagar; 'the Koran itself expressly allowed a master to take his handmaid as concubine on condition of her free assent'.

Other marriages? Hughes (1988) says that some Shi'a accounts list as many as 21 wives (see p. 400). Shi'a (twelvers) recognize a form of temporary marriage (*mu'ta*), and cite Q 4:24 to support this practice: 'lawful to you are all beyond those mentioned, so that ye seek them with your wealth in honest wedlock'. Some sources say that Muhammad himself had temporary wives. If so, this might explain the '21'. All the wives of the Prophet qualify for the title, 'Mothers of the believers'. Some Qur'anic verses address them specifically, especially Q 33:53 which forbids their remarriage after Muhammad's death and instigates the *hijab*, 'when you ask his wives anything, ask them from behind a veil'. Q 33:30–40 says that Muhammad's wives are 'not like other women' – they will be doubly rewarded for piety and doubly punished for wrongdoing. Muslims texts, collected by Siddiqi (1993) attest to the 'mothers' high moral characters, and faithfulness to the way of Islam. Lings says, 'whatever jealousies there may have been between one and another, the wives of the Prophet were all women of piety' (p. 243).

The idea that Muhammad was allowed special licence, as head of state, to exceed the four wives allowed at Q 4:3 is often advanced to explain why he had 'more wives than was allowed others' (Pickthall, p. 406). However, Zakaria (1991) appears to date Q 4:3 as a very late verse, since he argues that:

> After the promulgation of the restriction to four wives, Muhammad never took another wife. So the charge that he had eleven or twelve wives while his followers were allowed only four is baseless; surely his critics did not expect him to divorce some of his wives to bring their number to four! (p. 45)

As I have illustrated in this book, non-Muslims have criticized Muhammad for his multiple marriages. They argue that Muhammad was monogamous whilst Khadijah was alive because she was the dominant partner and would not allow him other women. As soon as she died, he gave vent to his subdued sexual passion: 'Once the natural limits of restraint were overpassed, Mahomet fell prey to his strong passion for sex' (Muir, p. 499). Muslims, however, regard Muhammad's multiple marriages either as politically necessary or as examples of him exercising compassion towards the vulnerable. Certainly, Muslims do not view them as immoral (see Pickthall, pp. 300–1, for a typical 'defence'). The idea that Muhammad was inclined towards sexual indulgence does not seem to fit the facts. He was about 50 when he married Sawda, 53 or 54 when he consummated his marriage with 'A'isha (whose age, it must be said, raises some people's eyebrows!). He was probably closer to 60 when he married Hamsa, although dating is problematic. On the other hand, Muslims do not appear repelled by the fact that Muhammad enjoyed sexual relations. Muir had it that the Qur'an's descriptions of paradise's black-eyed houries emanated from Muhammad's young mind – perhaps composed even before he had lost his virginity! (ibid.). Muhammad's sexuality continues to divide Muslims from non-Muslim opinion.

Appendix 3

Dr Clinton Bennett
Senior Lecturer in Islamic Studies,
Westminster College,
Oxford OX2 9AT

October 1996

Dear respondent

I am currently writing a book for Cassell Academic [provisionally] entitled *Muhammad: An Interpretive Study.* What I am exploring are different understandings/accounts of Muhammad, that is, who he was, his significance and role within Islam, and accounts of him by non-Muslims. I am interested in listening to a range of Muslim and non-Muslim voices in order to draw out similarities and differences. What I call the 'insider-outsider polarity' is a central concern; do non-Muslims inevitably produce different accounts of Muhammad? Is it possible for a non-Muslim to properly comprehend what Muhammad means to a Muslim? I am especially interested in whether what I have written does justice to Muslims' own understanding of who the Prophet is, in whether they are offended by anything I have written, and in whether they think that, as an outsider, I have began to approach their insider view. To help me address these issues I am asking some Muslim friends to read what I have written. However, to enable me to engage with a larger number of respondents I am also asking Muslim colleagues, friends and students to complete this questionnaire.

I thank you for taking time to respond. Below, I summarize aspects of my research and invite you to respond. Most of the questions are 'open' in that they invite you to record your own response, in your own words, to what I have written.

Issue No: 1: examining the *Sira* (early biographies of the Prophet) and the collections of *hadith*, I discuss their usefulness and reliability for reconstructing Muhammad's biography. Some Western scholars consider these so influenced by the agenda of the ninth/tenth century Muslim world that they tell us very little about the Prophet – and say that the standard account of the Prophet is more or less fictitious. Other Western scholars say that the broad outline of the standard account is reliable but that traditional accounts also contain much material that is historically suspect – miracle stories, material which depicts the Prophet's behaviour as exemplary, and so on. They tend to say that the Prophet's *sunnah* gained posthumous authority – displacing that exercised by the Khalifs and thus enhancing the role of the religious scholars.

Arising out of this research, I am interested in your comments on:

(1) Do you find the miracle material in the *Sira/Hadith* problematical or not?

(2) Do you find material in the *Hadith* in which Muhammad predicts people's death, future events, problematical or not?

(3) If miracle stories, and claims to know about future events, were redacted from the biography, would what is left be more credible?

Issue No: 2: Non-Muslim Responses
Early non–Muslim responses singled out certain events/issues for criticism – especially Muhammad's marriage to Zainab (arguing that the Qur'an was 'made' to condone this), and the so-called 'satanic verses' affair, when Muhammad is said to have compromised his stern monotheism (in order to gain support). Accounts depict him as an opportunist who changed his mind, and manufacturd 'revelation' in order to gain power, and wealth. His supposed 'cruelty' towards enemies is also highlighted. Of course, this picture does not resonate at all with a Muslim account. Dismissing the notion that Muhammad was unlettered, they see the Qur'an as the invention of his own mind. Even when non-Muslims have had full access to traditional Muslim lives of Muhammad they have still found Muhammad 'guilty' of the above charges.

(1) Why do you think non-Muslims have formulated this picture of Muhammad?

(2) How would you try to correct it?

(3) Do you think that lack of belief in Muhammad's uniqueness (e.g. prophethood, divine inspiration, etc) makes it impossible for a non-Muslim to fully understand Muslim belief about Muhammad/what Muhammad means to Muslims?

(4) How would you describe your belief in Muhammad's uniqueness?

Issue No: 3: discussing Muhammad's continued significance in Islamic thought, faith and practice, I discuss arguments about who should succeed him, popular devotion to him, and some of the writings of the philosophers and mystics. The following questions arise:

(1) Do such terms as 'light of Muhammad', 'spiritual energy' and belief in Muhammad's ongoing power to intercede/bless, used by the Sufis and other Muslim writers, claim of him more than he claimed for himself?

(2) Does the role of *Pirs*/devotion to their shrines relegate Muhammad to a less significant role?

(3) Does popular belief that Muhammad can intercede on behalf of Muslims go beyond what the Qur'an says about Muhammad?

Please summarize below your understanding of the Prophet's significance within your practice of Islam.

Finally, would you describe how you locate yourself within the Muslim perspective, e.g. Sunni, Shi'a, Hanafite, Shafite, Sufi etc., indicating nationality, gender and age.

References

Ahmad, Aziz (1990) 'Islah' in *Encyclopaedia of Islam* (new edition), vol. 4, Leiden, E.J. Brill, pp. 141–71.

Ahmed, Akbar (1988) *Discovering Islam: Making Sense of Muslim History and Society*, London, Routledge.

Ahmed, Akbar (1992) *Postmodernism and Islam: Predicament and Promise*, London, Routledge.

Ahmed, Akbar (1993) *Living Islam: From Samarkand to Stornoway*, London, BBC Books.

Ahmed, Akbar (1996) *Living Islam*, second edition, Harmonsdworth, Penguin.

Ahmed, Leila (1978) *Edward W. Lane*, London, Longman.

Ahmed, Leila (1992) *Women and Gender in Islam: Historical Roots of a Modern Debate*, New Haven, Yale University Press.

Ahsan, Muhammad Manazir (1996), Preface to Jabal Muhammad Buaben *Image of the Prophet Muhammad in the West*, Leicester, Islamic Foundation, pp. xiii–xvi.

Akhtar, Shabbir (1992) *Be Careful With Muhammad*, London, Bellew.

al-Azmeh, Azz (1993) *Islams and Modernities*, London, Verso.

al-Halveti, Shaikh Tusun Bayrak al-Jerrahi (1992) *The Secret of Secrets*, Cambridge, Islamic Texts Society.

'Ali ['Ali Ibn Abi Talib] (1996) *Nahjul Balaaghah*, Potomac, MD, Ahlul-Bayt Assembly of America.

Ali, Muhammad (1948) *The Living Thoughts of the Prophet Muhammad*, London, Cassell.

Ali, Muhammad (1977) *A Manual of Hadith*, London, Curzon Press. Originally published in 1944.

Ali, Sayyid Ameer (1922) *The Spirit of Islam*, London, Chatto & Windus. Originally published in 1891.

al-Kaysi, Marwan Ibrahim (1986) *Morals and Manners in Islam: A Guide to Islamic Adab*, Leicester, The Islamic Foundation.

Ally, Mashuq Ibn (1989) 'Second introductory paper' in *Law, Blasphemy and the Multi-Faith Society*, London, Commission for Racial Equality and the Inter Faith Network for the United Kingdom, pp. 21–9.

Almond, Philip C. (1989) *Heretic and Hero: Muhammad and the Victorians*, Wiesbaden, Otto Harrassowitz.

Al-Tawhid: A Quarterly Journal of Islamic Thought and Culture 13:2 (1996), pp. 31–89, 'The Constitution of the Islamic Republic of Iran'.

Anawati, George C. (1994) 'Philosophy, Theology and Mysticism' in Joseph Schacht with C.E. Bosworth *The Legacy of Islam*, Oxford, Oxford University Press, pp. 350–92.

Andrae, Tor (1936) *Mohammed: The Man and His Faith*, London, George, Allen and Unwin.

257

Arkoun, Mohammed (ET 1994) *Rethinking Islam*, translated and edited by Robert D. Lee, Boulder, CO, Westview Press. Originally published in French in 1969.

Arnold, Thomas Walker (1896) *The Preaching of Islam*, London, Constable.

Arthur, C.J. (1986) *In The Hall of Mirrors: Problems of Commitment in a Religiously Plural World*, London, Mowbray.

Asad, Muhammad (1981) *Sahih-al-Bukhari: The Early Years of Islam*, Gibraltar, Dar-al-Andalus. Originally published in 1938.

Atabani, Ghazi Salahuddin (1995) 'Islamic Shariah and the Status of Non-Muslims' in Tariq Mitri (ed.) *Religion, Law and Society: A Christian–Muslim Discussion*, Geneva, WCC and Kamen, Kok Pharos Publications, pp. 63–9.

Azami, Mohammad Mustafa (1978) *Studies in Early Hadith Literature*, Indianapolis, American Trust Publications.

Baker, Dwight (1980) *The People of the Mosque*, Delhi, ISPCK.

Baksh, S. Khuda (1926) 'A Muhammedan View of Christianity' in A.S. Peake and R.G. Parsons, *An Outline of Christianity: The Story of Our Civilization*, vol. 5, London, Waverley, pp. 245–55.

Baldwin, Marshall W. (1984) 'Crusades' in *Encyclopaedia Britannica* (15th edn), vol. 5, pp. 297–310.

Barthes, Roland (1989) *Barthes: Selected Writings*, edited by Susan Sontag, London, Fontana Press.

Bell, Richard (1945) 'Muhammad's Knowledge of the Old Testament' in C.J. Munro Weir (ed.) *Studica Semitica Orientalia*, vol. 2, Glasgow, Glasgow University Oriental Society, pp. 1–20.

Ben-Yunusa, Mohammed (1995) 'Secularism and Religion' in Tariq Mitri (ed.) *Religion, Law and Society: A Christian–Muslim Discussion*, Geneva, WCC and Kamen, Kok Pharos Publications, pp. 78–86.

Bennett, Clinton (1981) 'Flirtation with Unitarianism', *The Inquirer*, March 7, p. 3.

Bennett, Clinton (1989) 'Tambaram Re-visited: An Interpretive Essay based on the Published Proceedings (IRM, July, 1988) of the Consultation on Mission and Dialogue', *Faith and Freedom* 42:124, pp. 21–6.

Bennett, Clinton (1992) *Victorian Images of Islam*, London, Grey Seal.

Bennett, Clinton (1993) 'The Din-Dunya Paradox: Contemporary Debate about the Nature and Scope of Islamic Law', *Bulletin of the Henry Martyn Institute of Islamic Studies* 12:1–2, pp. 58–73.

Bennett, Clinton (1994a) 'Islam' in Jean Holm with John Bowker, *Sacred Place*, London, Pinter, pp. 88–114.

Bennett, Clinton (1994b) 'Islam' in Jean Holm with John Bowker, *Picturing God*, London, Pinter, pp. 113–41.

Bennett, Clinton (1996a) *In Search of the Sacred: Anthropology and the Study of Religions*, London, Cassell.

Bennett, Clinton (1996b) 'The Legacy of Karl Gottlieb Pfander', *International Bulletin of Missionary Research* 20:2, pp. 76–81.

Bennett, Clinton (1996c) 'Review of Hugh Goddard's *Christians and Muslims*', *Discernment: An Ecumenical Journal of Inter-religious Encounter* NS 2:3 and 3:1, pp. 64–7.

Bennett, Clinton (1997) 'Islam and Muhammad Iqbal' in Laurence Brown, Bernard C. Farr, and Joseph R. Hoffmann *Modern Spiritualities: An Inquiry*, Amherst, NY, Prometheus, pp. 127–43.

Benthall, Jonathan (1995) 'Missionaries and Human Rights', *Anthropology Today* 11:1, pp. 1–3.

Berthrong, John (1995) 'A Confucian-Christian?' in Martin Forward (ed.) *Ultimate Visions: Reflections on the Religions We Choose*, Oxford, Oneworld, pp. 22–37.

Blyden, Edward Wilmot (1967) *Christianity, Islam and the Negro Race*, Edinburgh, Edinburgh University Press. Originally published in 1887 by W.B. Whittingham.

Bosworth, C. Edmund (1976) 'The Prophet Vindicated: A Restoration Treatise on Islam and Muhammad', *Religion: A Journal of Religion and Religions* 6, pp. 1–12.

Bosworth, C. Edmund (1977) Preface to Muhammad Ali, *A Manual of Hadith*, London, Curzon, pp. v–viii.

Boulainvilliers, Henri (1731) *The Life of Mahomet*, London, W. Hinchcliffe.

Bowen, David G. (ed.) (1992) *The Satanic Verses: Bradford Responds*, Ilkley, Bradford and Ilkley Community College.

Bowen, John R. (1996) 'Religion in the Proper Sense of the Word', *Anthropology Today* 12:4, pp. 12–14.

Brians, Paul (1996) *Notes for Salman Rushdie: The Satanic Verses*, Pullman, WA, Washington State University; http://www.wsu.edu:8080/~brians/anglophone/satanic_verses/intro.html (downloaded 18 December 1996).

The British Critic 7 (1830), pp. 1–44, 'Review of Charles Forster's *Mahometanism Unveiled*'.

Brown, Laurence, Bernard C. Farr and Joseph R. Hoffmann (1997) *Modern Spiritualities: An Inquiry*, Amherst, NY, Prometheus.

Buaben, Jabal Muhammad (1996) *Image of the Prophet Muhammad in the West: A Study of Muir, Margoliouth and Watt*, Leicester, The Islamic Foundation.

Burton, John (1994) *An Introduction to the Hadith*, Edinburgh, Edinburgh University Press.

Burton, Sir Richard (1997) *Arabian Nights*, adapted by Jack Zipes, Harmondsworth, Penguin. Orignally published in 1885–8.

Carlyle, Thomas (1840) *On Heroes, Hero Worship and the Heroic in History*, London, Chapman and Hall.

Carlyle, Thomas (1903) 'The Hero as Poet: Dante, Shakespeare. A Lecture' in W. Peacocke (ed.) *Selected English Essays*, Oxford, Oxford University Press, pp. 357–95.

Caspar, Robert (1987) *Traité de Théologie Musulmans*, Rome, PISAI.

Chadwick, Henry (1967) *The Early Church*, Harmondsworth, Penguin.

Clark, Peter (ed.) (1990) *The World's Religions: Islam*, London, Routledge.

Commission for Racial Equality (1992) *Second Review of the Race Relations Act, 1976*.

Cook, Michael (1981) *Early Muslim Dogma: A Source Critical Study*, Cambridge, Cambridge University Press.

Cook, Michael (1983) *Muhammad* (Past Masters Series), Oxford, Oxford University Press.

Cotton, Ian (1995) *The Hallelujah Revolution*, London, Little, Brown.

Coulson, Noel J. (1994) *A History of Islamic Law*, Edinburgh, Edinburgh University Press. Originally published in 1964.

Cox, Harvey (1988) *Many Mansions: A Christian's Encounter with Other Faiths*, London, Collins.

Cox, James L. (1992) *Expressing the Sacred: An Introduction to the Phenomenology of Religion*, Harare, University of Zimbabwe.

Cragg, Kenneth (1984) *Muhammad and the Christian: A Question of Response*, London, Darton, Longman and Todd; Maryknoll, NY, Orbis Books.

Cragg, Kenneth (1992) *Troubled by Truth*, Durham, Pentland Press.

Craig, H.A.L. (1977) *Bilal*, London, Quartet Books.

Cromer, Lord (Evelyn Baring) (1908) *Modern Egypt*, London, Macmillan & Co.

Crone, Patricia (1987) *Meccan Trade and the Rise of Islam*, Princeton, Princeton University Press.

Crone, Patricia (1995) 'Review of F.E. Peter's *Muhammad and the Origins of Islam*', *Journal of the Royal Asiatic Society*, 3rd Series, 5:2, pp. 269–72.

Crone, Patricia and Cook, Michael (1977) *Hagarism: The Making of the Islamic World*, Cambridge, Cambridge University Press.

Crone, Patricia and Hinds, Martin (1986) *God's Caliph. Religious Authority in the First Centuries of Islam*, Cambridge, Cambridge University Press.

Cross, F.L. and Livingstone, E.A. (eds) (1974) *The Oxford Dictionary of the Christian Church*, Oxford, Oxford University Press.

Cundy, Catherine (1996) *Salman Rushdie*, Manchester, Manchester University Press.

Daftary, Farhad (1992) *Ismailis: Their History and Doctrines*, Cambridge, Cambridge University Press.

Daniel, Norman (1966) *Islam, Europe and Empire*, Edinburgh, Edinburgh University Press.

Daniel, Norman (1993) *Islam and the West: The Making of an Image*, revised edition, Oxford, Oneworld. Originally published in 1960 by Edinburgh University Press.

D'Costa, Gavin (1990) 'Christ, the Trinity and Religious Plurality' in Gavin D'Costa (ed.) *Christian Uniqueness Reconsidered: The Myth of a Pluralistic Theology of Religion*, Maryknoll, NY, Orbis, pp. 16–29.

Dietrich, Stefan (1992) 'Mission, Local Culture and the "Catholic Ethnology" of Pater Schmidt', *Journal of the Anthropological Society of Oxford*, 23:2, pp. 111–25.

Doner, Fred (1991) 'The Sources of Islamic Conceptions of War' in John Kelsay and James Turner Johnson (eds) *Just War and Jihad: Historical and Theoretical Perspectives on Peace and War in Western and Islamic Traditions*, New York, Greenwood Press, pp. 31–69.

Dresch, Paul (1989) *Tribal Government and History in Yemen*, Oxford, Clarendon Press.

Dyson, A. (1983) 'Christian Anthropology' in A. Richardson and J. Bowden (eds) *A New Dictionary of Christian Theology*, London, SCM, pp. 23–6.

Eclectic Review, 3rd series, VIII (1829), pp. 681–90, 'Review of Forster's *Mahometanism Unveiled*'.

Edinburgh Review, Oct 1829–Jan 1830, L (1830), pp. 287–344, 'Review of George Miller's *Lectures on the Philosophy of Modern History* and Charles Forster's *Mahometanism Unveiled*'.

Esack, Farid (1997) *Qur'an, Liberation and Pluralism*, Oxford, Oneworld.

Esposito, John L. (1991) *Islam: The Straight Path*, Oxford, Oxford University Press.

Esposito, John L. (1992) *The Islamic Threat: Myth or Reality?*, Oxford, Oxford University Press.

Eyre, Ronald (1979) *Ronald Eyre on the Long Search*, London, Fount (and BBC Television series, broadcast 1977, presented by Ronald Eyre).

Fishbein, Michael (1990) *The History of al-Tabari*, vol. 21, Albany, NY, SUNY Press.

Fitzgerald, Michael and Caspar, Robert (1992) *Signs of Dialogue: Christian Encounter With Muslims*, Zamboanga City, Philippines, Sisilah Publications.

Forster, Charles (1829) *Mahometanism Unveiled*, 2 vols, London, James Duncan and John Cochran.

Forster, Charles (1830) *Vindication of the Theory of Mahometanism Unveiled ... In a Letter to the Revd Hugh James Ross, BD, Christian Advocate in the University of Cambridge*, unpublished (British Library Ref 4504 d 14 29).

Forward, Martin (1994) 'Islam' in Jean Holm with John Bowker, *Myth and History*, London, Pinter, pp. 97–118.

Forward, Martin (1997) *Muhammad: A Short Biography*, Oxford, Oneworld.

Foucault, Michel (1972) *The Archaeology of Knowledge*, London, Tavistock Books.

Foucault, Michel (1977) *Discipline and Punish: The Birth of the Prison*, London, Allen Lane.

Gagnier, John (1723) *Abu'l Fida de Vita et Rebus Gestis Mohammedis*, Oxford, Oxonia.

Galland, Antoine (1704–17) *Les Mille et Une Nuits*, Paris.

Geertz, Clifford (1968) *Islam Observed: Religious Development in Morocco and Indonesia*, Chicago, University of Chicago Press.

Geertz, Clifford (1973) *The Interpretation of Cultures*, New York, Basic Books.

Geertz, Clifford (1983) *Local Knowledge*, New York, Basic Books.

Geertz, Clifford (1988) *Works and Lives: The Anthropologist as Author*, Stanford, Stanford University Press.

Geertz, Clifford (1996) *After the Fact: Two Countries, Four Decades, One Anthropologist*, Cambridge, MA, Harvard University Press.

Gibb, Hamilton (1969) *Islam*, Oxford, Oxford University Press.

Gibbon, Edward (1869) *The Rise and Fall of the Roman Empire*, vol 3, New York, Scribner. Originally published in 1776–83.

Gilsenan, Michael (1990) *Recognising Islam*, London, I.B. Tauris.

Glasse, Cyril (1991) *The Concise Encylopaedia of Islam*, London, Stacey International.

Gleaner (1996) *Exclusive: The Rushdie Tapes*, http://www.merlin.com.au/gleebooks/gleaner/march96/rushdie.html (downloaded 25 November 1996).

Goddard, Hugh (1995) *Christians and Muslims: From Double Standards to Mutual Understanding*, London, Curzon Press.

Goldziher, Ignaz (1967–71) *Muslim Studies*, London, Allen and Unwin. Originally published in 1889–90.

Goldziher, Ignaz (ET 1981) *Introduction to Islamic Theology and Law*, Princeton, Princeton University Press. Originally published in 1910.

Gordon, Alexander (1968) 'Godfrey Higgins' in *Dictionary of National Biography*, vol. 9, pp. 819–20, Oxford, Oxford University Press.

Griffiths, Paul J. (1990) *Christianity Through Non-Christian Eyes*, Maryknoll, NY, Orbis.

Grogan, Ellinor F. (1908) *Reginald Bosworth Smith: A Memoire*, London, James Nisbet.

Grotius, Hugo de (1627) *Grotius de veritate religionis Christianae*, Paris. Editio nova, Paris, 1640; editio novissima, Paris, 1650.

Guillaume, Alfred (1924) *The Traditions of Islam*, Oxford, Oxford University Press.

Guillaume, Alfred (1955) *The Life of Muhammad: A Translation of Ibn Ishaq's Sirat Rasul Allah*, Oxford, Oxford University Press.

Guillaume, Alfred (1973) *Islam*, Harmondsworth, Penguin. Originally published 1954.

Gunny, Ahmed (1996) *Images of Islam in Eighteenth Century Writings*, London, Grey Seal.

Halliday, Fred (1996) *Islam and the Myth of Confrontation. Religion and Politics in the Middle East*, London, I.B. Tauris.

Halm, Heinz (1991) *Shi'ism*, Edinburgh, Edinburgh University Press.

Hammersley, Hugh and Atkinson, Paul (1995) *Ethnography: Principles in Practice*, London, Routledge.

Hick, John (1988) *God and the Universe of Faiths*, London, Macmillan. Originally published in 1973; 1996 edition published by Oneworld.

Hick, John (1994) 'Christianity Among The Religions of the World', *Discernment*, NS 1:3, pp. 11–24.

Higgins, Godfrey (1829) *Apology for the Life of Mohamed*, London, Rowland, Harper.

Higgins, Godfrey (1830) 'Mr Higgins' Reply to Mr Upham', *The Gentleman's Magazine and Historical Chronicle*, C, pp. 112f.

Hitti, Philip K. (1961) *A History of the Arabs: From the Earliest Times to the Present*, 7th edn, London, Macmillan & Co.

Hixon, Les (1989) *Dreams and Sufism*, KGNO Boulder, CO, hhtp://www.best.com/~Nur_interview.html (downloaded 20 December 1996).

Hodgson, Marshall G.S. (1974) *The Venture of Islam: Conscience and History in a World Civilization*, 3 vols, Chicago, University of Chicago Press.

Hogg, Alfred George (1939) 'The Christian Attitude to Non-Christian Faith' in *The Authority of the Faith* (Tambaram Series 1), New York, International Missionary Council, pp. 102–25.

Holt, P.M. (1972) *A Seventeenth Century Defence of Islam: Henry Stubbe (1632–76) and His Book*, London, Dr William's Library.

Hourani, Albert (1979) 'The Road to Morocco', *New York Review of Books*, March, pp. 27–30.

Hourani, Albert (1989) *Europe and the Middle East*, London, Macmillan.

Hourani, Albert (1991a) *A History of the Arab People*, London, Faber and Faber.

Hourani, Albert (1991b) *Islam in European Thought*, Cambridge, Cambridge University Press.

Hughes, Thomas Patrick (1988) *A Dictionary of Islam*, Calcutta, Rupa & Co. Orignially published in 1885 by W.H. Allen.

Humphreys, R. Stephen (1991) *Islamic History: A Framework for Inquiry*, Princeton, Princeton University Press.

Huntington, Samuel P. (1993) 'The Clash of Civilizations', *Foreign Affairs* 72:3, pp. 22–49.

Huntington, Samuel P. (1996a) 'The West Unique, Not Universal', *Foreign Affairs* 75:6, pp. 28–46.

Huntington, Samuel P (1996b) *The Clash of Civilizations and the Remaking of World Order*, New York, Simon and Schuster.

Hurgronje, Snouck (1957) *Selected Works*, Leiden, E.J. Brill.

Ibn 'Abbas, 'Abd Allah (n.d.) *Majmu'ah min al-Tafasir*, Beirut, dar al-ahya al-Turath al-'Arabi.

Ibn Sa'd, Abu 'Abd Allah Muhammad (1967) *Kitab al-Tabaqat al-Kabir*, 2 vols, translated by S. Moinul Haq, Karachi, Pakistan Historical Society Publications.

Ibn Warraq (1995) *Why I Am Not a Muslim*, Amherst, NY, Prometheus.

Iqbal, Muhammad (1930) *The Reconstruction of Religious Thought in Islam*, Oxford, Oxford University Press.

Irving, Washington (1989) *Life of Mohammed*, Ipswich, MA, The Ipswich Press. Originally published in 1850 by Henry G Bonh.

Islam: The First and Last Religion, Karachi, Ashraf Publications.

Johnson, Paul (1987) *A History of the Jews*, London, Weidenfeld.

Jomier, Jaques (1989) *How to Understand Islam*, London, SCM.

Jones, Lewis Bevan (1938) *Christianity Explained to Muslims*, Calcutta, YMCA Press.

Kabbani, Rana (1989) *Letter to Christendom*, London, Virago.

Kabbani, Shaikh Muhammad Nazim al-Haqqani (1996) *Sufism Today*, http://www.nayshbandi.net/haqqani/sufi/tariqa.t.html (downloaded 18 December 1996).

Kamali, Mohammed Hashim (1991) *Principles of Islamic Jurisprudence*, revised edition, Cambridge, Islamic Texts Society. Originally published in 1989.

Khaldun, Ibn (1958) *The Muqaddimah: An Introduction to History*, translated by Frank Rosenthal (3 vols), New York, Pantheon Books.

Khan, Muhammad Muhsin (1987) *Sahih al-Bukhari*, 9 vols, revised edition, New Delhi, Kitab Bhavan. Originally published in 1984.

Khan, Sayyid Ahmed (1862, 1865) *The Muhammedan Commentary on the Bible*, Ghazipur, Private Press of the Author. Published in two parts.

Khan, Sayyid Ahmed (1870) *Essays on the Life of Muhammad and Subjects Subsidiary Thereto*, London, Trubner.

King, James (1991) *William Blake: His Life*, London, Weidenfeld and Nicolson.

Knitter, Paul (1996) *Jesus and Other Names: Christian Mission and Global Responsibility*, Oxford, Oneworld.

Küng, Hans (1984) *Christianity and the World Religions*, London, SCM.

Küng, Hans (1997) 'Farewell Lecture' in W. Jens, K.-J. Kuschel and H. Küng, *Dialogue With Hans Küng*, London, SCM, pp. 71–111.

Kuper, Adam (1988) *The Invention of Primitive Society: Transformations of an Illusion*, London, Routledge.

Kuper, Adam (1994) 'Culture, identity and the project of a cosmopolitan anthropology', *MAN*, NS 29:3, pp 537–54.

Kurtz, Paul (1996) 'Intellectual Freedom, Rationality and Enlightenment: The Contribution of Averroes' in Mourad Wahba and Mona Abousenna (eds) *Averroes and the Enlightenment*, Amherst, NY, Prometheus, pp. 29–40.

Lambton, A.K.S. (1974) 'Islamic Political Thought' in Joseph Schacht and C.E. Bosworth (eds), *The Legacy of Islam*, Oxford, Oxford University Press, pp. 404–25.

Lammens, Henri (1968) *Islam, Its Beliefs and Institutions*, London, Frank Cass & Co. Originally published in 1929.

Lane, Edward William (1978) *Manners and Customs of the Modern Egyptians*, London, East-West Publications. Originally published in 1836 by John Murray.

Lane-Poole, Stanley (1874) 'Mohammed and Mohammedanism', *The Academy*, 5, Jan–June, pp. 6623–4, 6684–5.

Lane-Poole, Stanley (1968) 'Simon Ockley' in *Dictionary of National Biography*, vol. 14, Oxford, Oxford University Press, pp. 807–10.

Latourette, Kenneth Scott (1975) *A History of Christianity* (2 vols), revised edition, New York, Harper and Row.

Leaman, Oliver (1996) 'Casual Views on Muhammad and Jesus', *The Expository Times* 108:2, p. 62.

Lewis, Bernard (1973) *Islam in History*, London, Alcove Press.

Lewis, Bernard (1982) 'The Question of Orientalism', *New York Review of Books*, June, pp. 49–56.

Lewis, Philip (1994) *Islamic Britain: Religion, Politics and Identity Among British Muslims*, London, I.B. Tauris.

Lindholm, Charles (1996) *The Islamic Middle East: An Historical Anthropology*, Oxford, Blackwell.

Lings, Martin (1975) *What is Sufism?*, London, George, Allen & Unwin; reprinted 1993 by Islamic Texts Society.

Lings, Martin (1983) *Muhammad: His Life Based on the Earliest Sources*, Lahore, Suhail Academy.

Lott, Eric (1995) 'When Methodist and Hindu Meet: Confessions of a Compulsive Re-Visionary' in Martin Forward (ed.) *Ultimate Visions: Reflections on the Religions we Choose*, Oxford, Oneworld, pp. 176–86.

Lyon, Harold Thomson (1968) 'George Sale' in *Dictionary of National Biography*, vol. 17, Oxford, Oxford University Press, pp. 668–70.

Malinowski, Branislaw (1967) *A Diary in the Strict Sense of the Word*, London, Routledge.

Margoliouth, David Samuel (1905) *Muhammad and the Rise of Islam*, London, G.P. Putnam.

Markham, Ian S. (ed.) (1996) *A World Religions Reader*, Oxford, Blackwell.

Masri, B.A. (1987) *Islamic Concern for Animals*, Petersfield, The Athene Trust.

Maududi, Abul Ala (1960) *Towards Understanding Islam*, London, UK Islamic Mission.

Maududi, Abul Ala (1977) *Islamic Way of Life*, Dhaka, Adhanik Prakasani.

Maurice, Frederick Denision (1838) *The Kingdom of Christ*, London, Darton and Clark.

Maurice, Frederick Denison (1846) *The Religions of the World*, London, Macmillan

Maurice, John Frederick (1884) *The Life of Frederick Denison Maurice: Chiefly Told in His Own Letters*, London, Macmillan.

Meadows, Philip (1996) 'Virtual Insidership: Interreligious Dialogue and the Limits of Understanding', *Discernment*, NS 3:2, pp. 29–41.

Mernissi, Fatima (1991) *Women and Islam: An Historical and Theological Inquiry*, Oxford, Blackwell. Originally published in French in 1987.

Mernissi, Fatima (1993) *The Forgotten Queens of Islam*, Cambridge, Polity Press.

Miller, James (1744) *Mahomet the Imposter: A Tragedy*, London, J. Watts.

Mingana, Alphonse (1928) *Timothy's Apology for Christianity*, Manchester, John Rylands Library.

Momen, Moojan (1996) *A Short Introduction to the Bahai'i Faith*, Oxford, Oneworld.

Mozaffari, Mehdi (1996) 'The Fatwa That Wasn't', *Guardian*, 13 November, p. 16.

Muir, William (1858) *Life of Mahomet*, vol. 2. Original edition of Muir (1894)

Muir, William (1876) *Addresses Made in the North-West Provinces*, Simla, Government Press.

Muir, William (1882) *The Apology of Al-Kindy*, London, SPCK.

Muir, William (1891) *The Caliphate. Its Rise, Decline and Fall*, London, Religious Tract Society.

Muir, William (1894) *Life of Mahomet*, third (abridged) edition, London, Smith, Elder and Co. Originally published in 4 vols in 1857–61.

Muir, William (1897) *The Muhammedan Controversy*, Edinburgh, T. & T. Clark.

Muir, William (1902) *Records of the NWP Intelligence Department*, vol. 1, Edinburgh, T. & T. Clark.

Muir, William (1915) *The Caliphate, Its Rise, Decline and Fall*, ed by T.H. Weir, Edinburgh, John Grant.

Muslim Abu'l Hussain (1975) *Sahih Muslims*, (4 vols) translated by Abdul Hamid Siddiqi, Lahore, Muhammad Ashraf.

Muslim, Hajjaj ibn (1960) *Al-Jami al-Sahih*, Cairo, Sharika Maktabah wa Mustafa al-Babi al-Halabi.

Nasr, Seyyed Hossein (1993) *A Young Muslim's Guide to the Modern World*, Cambridge, Islamic Texts Society.

Nasr, Seyyed Hossein (1994) *Ideas and Realities of Islam*, revised edition, London, The Aquarian Press. Originally published in 1966.

Neuman, Lawrence W (1994) *Social Research Methods: Qualitative and Quantitative Approaches*, Boston, Allyn and Bacon.

Newbigin, Lesslie (1988) 'A Sermon Preached at the Tambaram Service for the Fiftieth Anniversary of The International Missionary Council', *International Review of Mission*, 78: 307, pp. 325–31.

Newbigin, Lesslie (1989) *The Gospel in a Pluralist Society*, London, SPCK.

Nicholson, Reynold A. (1963) *The Mystic of Islam*, London, Routledge. Originally published in 1914 by George Bell.

Nicholson, Reynold A. (1995) *Rumi: Poet and Mystic*, Oxford, Oneworld.

Ockley, Simon (1848) *The History of the Saracens*, 5th edn, London, Henry G. Bohn. Originally published in 1708–18.

Padwick, Constance (1961) *Muslim Devotions: A Study of Prayer Manuals in Common Use*, London, SPCK.

Palmer, Edward Henry (1877) 'Mohammed and Mohammedanism', *Quarterly Review* 143, Jan & April, pp. 205–37.

Parekh, Bhikhu (1989) 'Between Holy Text and Moral Void', *New Statesman and Society*, 24 March, pp. 29–33.

Parrinder, Geoffrey (1995) *Jesus in the Qur'an*, Oxford, Oneword. Originally published in 1965.

Parrinder, Geoffrey (1996) *Sexual Morality in the World's Religions*, Oxford, Oneworld. Originally published in 1960.

Patai, Raphael (1989) Introduction to Charles Getchell (ed.) *Washington Irving's Life of Mohammad*, Ipswich, MA, The Ipswich Press, pp. xvii–xxvii.

Peters, F.E. (1991) 'The Quest of the Historical Muhammad', *The International Journal of Middle East Studies* 23, pp. 202–325.

Peters, F.E. (1994a) *Muhammad and the Origins of Islam*, Albany, NY, SUNY Press.

Peters, F.E. (1994b) *A Reader on Classical Islam*, Princeton, Princeton University Press.

Pettifer, Julian and Bradley, Richard (1990) *The Missionaries*, London, BBC Books (and television series, broadcast 1990).

Pfander, Karl Gotlieb (1986) *Mizan-ul-Haqq,* translated by William St-Clair Tisdall, Villach, Light of Life Press. Originally published in 1835 by the Religious Tract Society.

Phipps, William E. (1996) *Muhammad and Jesus: A Comparison of the Prophets and Their Teaching*, London, SCM.

Pickthall, M. Marmaduke (1930) *The Meaning of the Glorious Koran*, New York, Mentor; London, Ta Ha.

Pocock, Edward (1650) *Specimen historiae Arabum sive Gregorii Abu'l Fargii … de origine et moribus Arabum … narratio*, Oxford.

Polo, Marco (1946) *The Travels of Marco Polo* (translated by William Marsden), London, Everyman Library.

Poonawala, Ismail (1990) *The History of al-Tabari: The Last Years of the Prophet*, Albany, NY, SUNY Press.

Prideaux, Humphrey (1697) *The True Nature of Imposture Fully Displayed in the Life of Mahomet*, London, William Rogers.

Qadir, C.A. (1988) *Philosophy and Science in the Islamic World*, London, Routledge.

Qutb, Muhammad (1954) *Islam: The Misunderstood Religion*, Dhaka, Associated Printers.

Rahman, Afzalur (1980) *Muhammad as a Military Leader*, London, The Muslim Schools Trust.

Reat, Ross (1983) 'Insiders and Outsiders in the Study of Religious Traditions', *Journal of the American Academy of Religions* 51:3, pp. 459–76.

Reland, Adrian (1705) *Adriani Relandi de religione Mohammedica*, Utrecht.

Renan, Ernest (1866) *Averroes et l'averroisme – essai historique*, Paris, A. Durand.

Renan, Ernest (1893) *Studies of Religious History*, London, William Heinemann.

Richard, Yann (1995) *Shi'ite Islam*, Oxford, Blackwell.

Ricoeur, Paul (1989) *Hermeneutics and the Human Sciences*, translated and edited by John Thompson, Cambridge, Cambridge University Press.

Rippin, Andrew (1990) *Muslims: Their Religious Beliefs and Practices: The Formative Period*, vol. 1, London, Routledge.

Robinson, Neal (1991) *The Sayings of Muhammad*, London, Duckworth.

Robinson, Neal (1992) 'Reflections on the Rushdie Affair' in David G. Bowen (ed.) *The Satanic Verses: Bradford Responds*, Ilkley, Bradford and Ilkley Community College, pp. 33–44.

Robinson, Neal (1996) *Discovering the Qur'an: A Contemporary Approach to a Veiled Text*, London, SCM.

Robson, James (1986a) 'kudsi hadith' in *Encyclopaedia of Islam*, vol. 3, Leiden, E.J. Brill, pp. 28–9.

Robson, James (1986b) 'Bukhari' in *Encyclopaedia of Islam*, vol. 1, Leiden, E.J. Brill, pp. 1296–7.

Robson, James (1986c) 'Hadith' in *Encyclopaedia of Islam*, vol. 1, Leiden, E.J. Brill, pp. 23–8.

Robson, James (1990) *Mishkat-al-Masabih: English Translation with Explanatory Notes*, 2 vols, Lahore, Muhammad Ashraf.

Rodinson, Maxime (1961) *Muhammad*, Harmondsworth, Penguin.

Rodinson, Maxime (1974) 'The Western Image and Western Studies of Islam' in Joseph Schacht and C. Edmund Bosworth (eds) *The Legacy of Islam*, Oxford, Oxford University Press, pp. 9–62.

Rodinson, Maxime (1981) 'A Critical Survey of Modern Studies on Muhammad' in Merlin L. Swartz (ed.) *Studies on Islam*, Oxford, Oxford University Press, pp. 23–85.

Rodinson, Maxime (1988) *Europe and the Mystique of Islam*, London, I.B. Tauris.

Rorty, Roland (1979) *Contingency, Irony and Solidarity*, Cambridge, Cambridge University Press.

Ross, Alexander (1649) *The Alcoran translated out of Arabique into French ... and newly Englished, with The Life of Mahomet, and a Needful Caveat*, London.

Roy, Asim (1983) *The Islamic Syncretistic Tradition in Bengal*, Princeton, Princeton University Press.

Rushdie, Salman (1981) *Midnight's Children*, London, Jonathan Cape.

Rushdie, Salman (1982) 'The New Empire Within Britain', reprinted in *Imaginary Homelands: Essays and Criticism 1981–1991* (1991), London, Granta Books. Also published on the Internet, http://www.cwrl.utexaseduc/mbenjamin/316kfall/

316unit4/studentsprojectsspring/group2/rushdie.html (downloaded 25 November 1996).

Rushdie, Salman (1983) *Shame*, London, Jonathan Cape.

Rushdie, Salman (1988) *The Satanic Verses*, London, Viking Books.

Rushdie, Salman (1990a) 'In Good Faith', *Independent on Sunday*, 4 February.

Rushdie, Salman (1990b) *Is Nothing Sacred?*, Cambridge, Granta.

Rushdie, Salman (1991) *Imaginary Homelands: Essays and Criticism 1981–1991*, London, Granta Books.

Rushdie, Salman (1996) *The Moor's Last Sigh*, London, Vintage.

Ruthven, Malise (1990) *A Satanic Affair: Salman Rushdie and the Rage of Islam*, London, Chatto and Windus.

Sahas, Daniel J (1991) 'The Seventh Century in Byzantine–Muslim Relations', *Islam and Christian–Muslim Relations* 2:1, pp. 3–23.

Said, Edward (1978) *Orientalism*, London, Routledge. Reprinted by Penguin in 1985.

Said, Edward (1997) *Covering Islam*, London, Vintage. Originally published in 1981.

Sale, George (1838) *The Koran and Preliminary Discourse*, London, Thomas Tegg. Originally published in 1734.

Sarder, Ziauddin (1979) *The Future of Muslim Civilization*, London, Croom Helm.

Sayf B Umar al-Tamini (1995) *Kitab Al-Rida and Kitab Al-Jamal Wa Masir Aisha Wa Ali*, edited by Qasim Al-Samara, Leiden, Smitekamp Oriental Antiquarian.

Schacht, Joseph (1950) *The Origins of Muhammadan Jurisprudence*, Oxford, Oxford University Press.

Schacht, Joseph (1964) *An Introduction to Islamic Law*, Oxford, Oxford University Press.

Schimmel, Annemarie (1985) *And Muhammad Is His Messenger – The Veneration of the Prophet in Islamic Piety*, Chapel Hill, North Carolina University Press.

Schimmel, Annemarie (1987) 'Tor Andrae' in Mercea Eliade (ed.) *The Encyclopaedia of Religion*, vol. 1, New York, Macmillan, pp. 271–2.

Schuon, Frithjof (1976) *Understanding Islam*, London, Unwin Paperbacks.

Seymour-Smith, Charlotte (1986) *Macmillan Dictionary of Anthropology*, London, Macmillan.

Shepard, William (1991) 'The Doctrine of Progress in Some Modern Muslim Writings', *The Bulletin of the Henry Martyn Institute of Islamic Studies* 10:4, pp. 51–64.

Shore, Chris (1996) 'Anthropology's identity crisis. The politics of public image', *Anthropology Today* 12:2, pp. 2–5.

Siddiqi, Muhammad Saeed (1983) *The Blessed Women of Islam*, Delhi, Taj Co.

Siddiqi, Muhammad Zubayr (1993) *Hadith Criticism: Its Origins, Development and Special Features*, Cambridge, Islamic Texts Society.

Smart, Barry (1993) *Postmodernity*, London, Routledge.

Smith, Jane (1996) 'French Christian Narratives Concerning Muhammad and the Religion of Islam from the Fifteenth to the Eighteenth Centuries', *Islam and Christian–Muslim Relations* 7:1, pp. 47–61.

Smith, Margaret (1950) *Readings from the Mystics of Islam*, London, Luzac & Co.

Smith, Margaret (1994) *Rabi'a: The Life and Work of Rabi'a and Other Women Mystics of Islam*, Oxford, Oneworld.

Smith, Reginald Bosworth (1876) *Mohammed and Mohammedanism*, revised edition, London, Smith, Elder & Co. Originally published in 1874.

Smith, Reginald Bosworth (1887) 'Mohammedanism in Africa', *Nineteenth Century* 22, pp. 791–816.

Smith, Wilfred Cantwell Smith (1950) *The Comparative Study of Religion: An Inaugural Lecture*, Montreal, McGill University.

Smith, Wilfred Cantwell (1957) *Islam in Modern History*, New York, Mentor.

Smith, Wilfred Cantwell (1959) 'Comparative Religion - Whither and Why?' in Mercea Eliade and Joseph Kitagawa (eds) *The History of Religions: Essays on Methodology*, Chicago, University of Chicago Press, pp. 31–58.

Smith, Wilfred Cantwell (1980) 'The True Meaning of Scripture: An Empirical Historian's non-Reductionist Interpretation of the Qur'an', *International Journal of Near East Studies*, 11, pp. 487–505.

Smith, Wilfred Cantwell (1993) *What is Scripture?*, London, SCM.

Southern, R.W. (1962) *Western Views of Islam in the Middle Ages*, Cambridge, MA, Harvard University Press.

Spear, Percival (1965) *A History of India*, vol. 2, Harmondsworth, Penguin.

Sprenger, Aloys (1851) *The Life of Mohammed from Original Sources*, Allahabad, Presbyterian Mission Press.

Storr, Anthony (1996) *Feet of Clay: A Study of Gurus*, London, HarperCollins.

Stubbe, Henry (1911) *An Account of the Rise and Progress of Mahometanism with the Life of Mahomet*, London, Luzac & Co.

Sweetman, James Windrow (1945) *Islam and Christian Theology*, part 1, vol. 1, London, Lutterworth.

Sweetman, James Windrow (1955) *Islam and Christian Theology*, part 2, vol. 1, London, Lutterworth.

Taylor, Edgar (1821) 'Sale's Koran', *Retrospective Review* 3:1, pp. 1–22.

Tisdall, William St-Claire (1901) *The Sources of Islam*, translated by William Muir, Edinburgh, T. & T. Clark.

Tisdall, William St-Clair (1916) *The Religion of the Crescent*, London, SPCK.

Tracy, David (1981) *The Analogical Imagination*, London, SCM.

Tracy, David (1987) *Plurality and Ambiguity: Hermeneutics, Religion and Hope*, London, SCM.

Troll, Christian (1978) *Sayyid Ahmed Khan: A Reinterpretation of Muslim Theology*, New Delhi, Vikas Publishing House.

ur-Rahman, Muhammad 'Ata (1977) *Jesus the Prophet of Islam*, Wood Darling Hall, Norfolk, Diwan Press.

Vahiduddin, Syed (1986) *Islamic Experience in Contemporary Thought* (Islam in India series, vol. 3, edited by Christian Troll), Delhi, Chakya Publications.

Voltaire, François Marie Arouet (1826) *Oeuvres Completes*, Paris, E.A. Lequien.

Wansbrough, John (1977) *Qur'anic Studies: Sources and Methods of Scriptural Interpretation*, Oxford, Oxford University Press.

Watt, William Montgomery (1953) *Muhammad at Mecca*, Oxford, Clarendon Press.

Watt, William Montgomery (1955) 'Carlyle on Muhammad', *Hibbert Journal*, 52, pp. 247–54.

Watt, William Montgomery (1956) *Muhammad at Medina*, Oxford, Oxford University Press.

Watt, William Montgomery (1957) 'Early development of the Muslim attitude to the Bible', *Transactions of the Glasgow University Oriental Society, 1955-6*, pp. 50–63.

Watt, William Montgomery (1961) *Muhammad – Prophet and Statesman*, Oxford, Oxford University Press.

Watt, William Montgomery (1968) *Islamic Political Thought*, Edinburgh, Edinburgh University Press.

Watt, William Montgomery (1972) *The Influence of Islam on Medieval Europe*, Edinburgh, Edinburgh University Press.

Watt, William Montgomery (1976) 'Western Historical Criticism and the Prophet of Islam' in *Message of the Prophet*, Islamabad, First National Conference on Seerat, pp. 68–75.

Watt, William Montgomery (1985) *Islamic Philosophy and Theology*, Edinburgh, Edinburgh University Press. Originally published in 1962.

Watt, William Montgomery (1988) *Muhammad's Mecca – History in the Qur'an*, Edinburgh, Edinburgh University Press.

Watt, William Montgomery (1991) *Muslim–Christian Encounters: Perceptions and Misconceptions*, London, Routledge.

Watt, Willaim Montgomery (1993) 'Islamic attitudes to other religions', *Studia Missionalia* 42, 245–55.

Watt, William Montgomery (1994a) *The Faith and Practice of Al-Ghazali*, Oxford, Oneworld. Originally published in 1953.

Watt, William Montgomery (1994b) *Islamic Creeds: A Selection*, Edinburgh, Edinburgh University Press.

Watt, William Montgomery (1995a) *Religious Truth For Our Time*, Oxford, Oneworld.

Watt, William Montgomery (1995b) 'Ultimate Vision and Ultimate Truth' in Martin Forward (ed.) *Ultimate Visions: Reflections on the Religions We Choose*, Oxford, Oneworld, pp. 280–8.

Watt, William Montgomery and Bell, Richard (1970) *Bell's Introduction to the Qur'an*, Edinburgh, Edinburgh University Press.

Weber, Max (1965) *The Sociology of Religion*, trans. E. Fischoff, ed. T. Parsons, London, Methuen.

Weil, Gustav (1843) *Mohammed der Prophet, seine Leben und seine Lehre*, Stuttgart, J.B. Metzler.

Weil, Gustav (1864) *Das leben Mohammed: nach Ibn Ishak bearbeit van Ibn Hisham*, 2 vols, Stuttgart, J.B. Metzler.

Wesleyan Methodist Magazine, 3rd series, VIII (1829), pp. 681–90, 753–65, 'Review of Forster's *Mahometanism Unveiled*'.

Whaling, Frank (1984) *Contemporary Approaches to the Study of Religions: The Humanities*, vol. 1, Berlin, Mouton.

Wild, Stefan (1996) 'Between Ernest Renan and Enst Block: Averroes Remembered, Discovered, and Invented. The European Reception Since the Nineteenth Century' in Mourad Wahba and Mona Abousenna (eds) *Averroes and the Enlightenment*, Amherst, NY, Prometheus, pp. 155–71.

Yachnes, Paul (1995) *Sufism: An Annotated Resource Guide*, http://www.ziplink.net/~salik/sufres.html (downloaded 16 December 1996).

Zaehner, R.C. (1994) *Hindu and Muslim Mysticism*, Oxford, Oneworld. Originally published in 1960.

Zakaria, Rafiq (1988) *The Struggle Within Islam: The Conflict Between Religion and Politics*, Harmondsworth, Penguin.

Zakaria, Rafiq (1991) *Muhammad and the Qur'an*, Harmondsworth, Penguin.

Zwemer, Samuel Marinus (1900) *Arabia: The Cradle of Islam*, New York, Fleming H. Revell Co.

Index

Abbas, ibn 33, 46,
151, 239
'Abbasids 55, 62, 71,
74, 85, 148, 151–3,
155, 156, 185, 246,
247
Abd-al-Malik, Khalif
150
Abdallah ibn Abi
Sarh 23, 211
Abraha 29, 245
Abraham 29, 51, 104,
105, 110
Abu Bakr 30, 57, 59,
114, 115, 144, 145,
146, 147, 158, 159,
173, 182, 245, 246,
249
Abu'l Fida 30, 93,
100, 101
Abu Jahl 51
Abu Sufyan 151, 216,
246, 250
Abu Talib 245
adab (manners) 23,
220
Adam 140, 141
adultery 43, 91, 218,
249
Afghanistan 188, 199
Africa 104, 121
Aga Khan, the 161,
163
Agapius, Bishop 70–1,
74, 83
Agra, Red Fort
117–18
Ahmad, A. 44
Ahmed, A. 86, 150,
161, 170, 182, 184,
208, 220, 228, 233
Ahmed, L. 13, 61, 62,
106, 249
Ahsan, M.M. 85
'A'isha 58, 61, 62,
127, 144, 146, 215,
249–52
Akhbaris, the 165
Akhtar, S. 1, 13, 65,
222
alcohol 43
Alexander the Great 3
Alfonso 91
Ali, Ibn Abi Talib 30,
55, 144, 146, 147,
156, 157, 158, 159,
161, 162, 167, 169,
173, 245, 246
Ali, M. 34, 51, 119,
122, 223
Ali, Sayyid Ameer 59,
117, 124
allegory 49, 99
Almond, P. 70, 96,
102, 103, 125

al-Amin, Muhammad
as 30
Aminah 29, 52, 245
Anawati, G.C. 88
Andrae, T. 18, 83, 96,
125–8, 211
Annas ibn Malik 20,
46, 50, 62
anthropological
theology 11–12
anthropology 4, 7, 8,
12, 13, 129, 184,
194, 222
Antichrist, the 79, 81,
87, 97, 123
Aquinas, St Thomas
90
Arabian Nights 50, 86,
98, 209
Arabic 22, 35, 58, 71,
86, 88, 90, 91, 100,
106, 124, 128, 140,
152, 185, 195, 208
Aristotle 86, 106, 174
Arkoun, M. 241–2
Arnold, M. 103, 123
Arnold, T.W. 121
Arthur of Britain 84
Asad, M. 21, 32, 34,
45, 46, 47
al-Ashari 147, 178,
181, 185–6
Assassins, the 162,
246
Athir, Ibn 93
Averroës see Rushd, Ibn
Avicenna see Sina, Ibn
Ayotollahs, 166
Azami, M.M. 26, 59
al-Azhar University
154, 170
al-Azmeh 170, 191

Bacon, Roger 87, 88,
90
Badr, battle of 30, 34,
40, 49, 50, 51, 82,
245, 249
Baghdad 85, 152, 153,
161, 171, 181, 246,
247
Bahira 29, 77
legend 77, 79, 87,
91, 94
Bait-al-Mal 150, 238
Baksh, K. 106
Baldick, J. 135
Bangladesh 6, 14,
184, 195–200, 208,
248
baqa 173, 190
Barakah 176, 178,
179, 180
Barelvis 184, 201
Barthes, R. 233–4
batin-zahir 162,
170–1, 201
Bede, the Venerable
83
Bell, R. 21, 23, 185
Bennett, C. 1, 12, 51,
69, 104, 124, 160,
185, 200, 201, 203,
229, 234, 241

Bentall, J. 12
Bible 21, 75, 83, 87,
90, 104, 225
corruption of 22, 75
bida 152, 165, 183
bila kayfa 49
Bilal 216
Birmingham 6, 79,
182, 184
Bishr-al-Hafi 171
Bismillahi 36
al-Bistami 53, 174
Blake, W. 211–12
blasphemy 217,
218–19, 223
Blyden, E.W. 124
Bosworth, C.E. 20,
34, 94, 95
Boulainvilliers, Count
95–6, 100, 104, 108
Bowen, D. 184
Bradley, R. 86, 228
breast, cleaning of
Prophet's 46–8
Brians, P. 207, 208
British Empire 112,
207, 212
Buaben, Jabal 1, 11,
29, 31, 39, 70, 77,
82, 91, 102, 110,
116, 124, 127, 131,
132, 238
Buddha, the 45, 228
Bukhari, Imam 25, 27,
30, 31, 32, 33, 34,
41, 43, 46, 50, 57,
62, 64, 118, 178,
215, 246
Burton, J. 43, 63
Buyids, the 153, 156

Caesar 3, 236
Cambridge 206, 211
Carlyle, T. 108–10,
123, 129, 133, 221
Caspar, R. 69, 97
Centre for the Study of
Islam and
Christian–Muslim
Relations
(Birmingham) 79
Chadwick, H. 79
charisma 134–5, 147,
236
Chittick, W.C. 39
Christ–Muhammad
comparison 78,
128, 202, 226–9,
236–9
Christians and Jews
29, 52, 74, 75, 104,
113, 115, 239
Companions (sahaba)
25, 33, 34, 40, 44,
114
Constantine the
African 85
Cook, M. 37, 38, 59,
63, 110, 119, 128,
139, 248
Cordoba 81, 133, 152
Cornwallis, Lord 112
cosmopolitan
anthropology 12

Coulson, N. 44, 54,
139, 152, 159
Cox, H. 237
Cox, J. 9, 11
Cragg, K. 1, 12, 123,
177, 202, 227
Cromer, Lord 60,
107–8, 112
Crone, P. 21, 25, 37,
38, 39, 40, 54, 56,
63, 65, 110, 119,
128, 135, 139, 145,
248
crucifixion denied 73,
76, 238–9
Crusades/Crusaders
21, 85, 86, 104,
246–7
Cundy, C. 206, 208,
209, 213, 214

Daftary, F. 162, 163
da'i 161, 162
Daniel, N. 5, 7, 70,
77, 81, 82, 84, 94,
95, 96, 99, 101, 112,
128, 129
Dante 89, 108, 247
al-Darimi 31, 57
D'Costa, G. 234
Daud, Abu 31, 32
da'wa 162
Deedat, A. 73
Deobandis 183–4, 201
Dhaka 195, 198
Dhikr 177, 182, 200,
202
Dhimmi (protected
minority) 70, 115
Ditch, battle of 30, 51,
116, 245
Dome of the Rock
150, 180, 246
Doner, F. 119
Dyson, A. 12

Edinburgh 130
Egypt 6, 72, 110, 154,
161, 228
Esack, F. 75, 178,
204, 224, 225, 237,
239–42
Esau 111
Esposito, J. 47, 48,
152, 163, 165, 166,
167
evolutionary theory
121
Eyre, R. 170, 181, 229

al-Farabi 53, 88, 152,
187, 246
fard (obligatory duty)
24
Fatimah 156, 157
Fatimids 156, 161,
162, 163, 246
fatwa (regarding
Rushdie) 209, 218,
219, 248
fatwas 188
Forster, C. 103–7,
108, 112, 115, 122,
132, 247

271

Forward, M. 25, 39, 82, 119, 224, 226
Foucault, M. 4, 7, 233
Fox, M. 125
Francis, Saint 87, 247
French, T.V. 118
Futuh-esh-Sham 98

Gabriel, Angel 2, 42, 47, 81, 213–17
Gagnier, J. 93, 94
Galland, A. 98, 108
Gandhi, I. 208
Gandhi, M.K. 203
Geertz, C. 4, 8, 10, 180, 194, 200–1
al-Ghazali 57, 152, 178, 181, 186, 246
Gibb, H.A.R. 32
Gibbon, E. 79, 99, 100, 105, 120, 122, 247
Gilsenan, M. 179, 182
Gladstone, W. 196, 247
Glasse, C. 20, 141, 148, 150, 156, 181, 249
God/Allah 2, 19, 20, 21, 22, 24, 36, 42, 45, 49, 52, 53, 55, 56, 60, 65, 72, 73, 74, 78, 79, 81, 82, 87, 94, 95, 107, 109, 111, 115, 118, 120, 123, 129, 130, 131, 134, 139, 140, 141, 142, 143, 144, 145, 147, 149, 151, 152, 157, 160, 161, 162, 166, 169, 171, 172, 173, 174, 175, 176, 179, 180, 181, 183, 185, 187, 189, 190, 192, 196, 202, 203, 205, 210, 211, 225, 226, 227, 229, 230, 231, 232, 234, 235, 237, 238, 239, 240, 241, 242
God's Attributes 78, 81, 172, 176, 177, 242
God's face 49
God's Throne 49
Goddard, H. 21, 110, 226–8
Goethe 108–9
Goldziher, I. 37, 54, 55, 139
Gordon, C.G., General 166, 247
Gospel/Gospels 2, 45, 52, 53, 64, 71, 75, 113, 235
Grotius, H. 91
Guibert of Nugent 84
Guillaume, A. 17, 26, 28, 29, 32, 34, 52, 54, 64, 86, 102, 131, 159
Gunny, A. 96

hadith 17, 20, 22, 24, 25, 26, 28, 30, 31–5, 40, 41, 43, 44, 45, 46, 47, 50, 51, 53–64, 76, 82, 87, 115, 122, 127, 141, 170, 175, 178, 179, 184, 197, 198, 199, 201, 223, 224, 253–4
  authenticity 27, 37, 43, 54, 56, 58, 59, 62, 115–16
  categories 23, 32–3
  recording 26, 31, 33, 34
  on women 61–2, 83–4, 215–16
hajj 182, 184, 246
halal/haram
  distinction 19, 24, 43, 141
al-Hallaj 181
Halliday, F. 43, 140, 191, 236
Halm, H. 157, 165, 166, 167, 168
Hanbal, ibn 24, 27, 55, 57, 158, 159
Hanifa, Imam 61, 159, 160, 186
Hasan ibn Ali 148, 156, 159
Hasan of Basra 170
Hebraeus, Bar 73, 77, 90, 93, 94, 100, 133
Henry Martyn Institute (Hyderabad) 215
Heraclius, Emperor 71, 72, 104, 123
Hick, J. 230–2, 241
Higgins, G. 102, 103, 106, 108
hijab 152, 196, 199, 201
hijrah (migration) 17, 18, 19, 30, 42, 100, 113, 126, 182, 245
Hind bint Utbah 216
Hinds, M. 38, 56, 145
Hira, Mt 40, 45, 101, 123, 125, 134, 245
Hisham, Ibn 28, 29, 102, 127
historical anthropology 7, 13, 129
historiography 4, 13, 39, 105
Hitti, P.K. 1
Hixon, L. 170, 179–80, 184
Hogg, A.G. 202, 203, 234
Holy Roman Empire 83, 247
Hourani, A. 5, 86, 109, 112
hubb (love) 171, 174, 176
Hudaybiyyah, affair of 50, 77, 246
hudud 166, 189
Hughes, T.P. 50, 52, 133, 249, 250, 251
Huntington, S.P. 233

Hurayra, Abu 25, 26, 46, 58, 61, 62
Hurgronje, S. 110–11
Husayn ibn Ali 148, 149, 156, 159, 167, 246
Husayn, Taha 190–1
Husserl, E. 7–8
Hyderabad 215

ijma 25, 31, 143, 159, 165
ijtihad 31, 164, 189
Imams (Shi'a) 159–70
India 6, 112, 133, 202, 206, 209, 212, 247
Indonesia 6, 200–1
insider–outsider
  polarity 3–5, 8, 10, 14, 48, 132, 133, 205, 210, 220, 221, 223, 225, 238, 253
inter-religious
  dialogue 9, 242
Iqbal, M. 88, 90, 189–90, 200, 247
Irving, W. 101, 122
Isaac 104, 105, 111
Ishaq, Ibn 19, 28, 29, 30, 32, 40, 41, 51, 52, 55, 72, 111, 127, 144, 195, 246
Ishiguro, K. 208
Ishmael 29, 51, 52, 72, 104, 105, 110, 111
Islamic art 35–6
Islamic calendar 17
Islamic Computer Centre (London) 29, 32
Ismail, Shah 166–77, 247
Ismailis 161–3, 172
isnad 30, 32–5, 59, 60, 170

al-Jafar 159–61, 164, 183, 246
jahilia 216
Jama, Ibn 153
Jamaati-i-Islam 183, 248
Jerusalem 19, 47, 70, 79, 110, 150, 180, 246, 247
Jesus 2, 52, 73, 74, 81, 102, 130, 131, 139, 160, 202, 226, 227, 236, 240, 241
jihad (striving) 1, 86, 150,166
John of Damascus 74, 76, 79, 80, 81, 83, 89, 91, 133
Jomier, J. 236
Jones, L.B. 226, 242
al-Jilani 173, 202
Jinnah, M.A. 191, 248

ka'abah, 30, 51, 115, 245
Ka'b ibn Ashraf 117–18, 126, 222
Ka'b ibn Malik 116

Kabbalah 163
Kabbani, R. 196, 220
Kabbani, Shaikh 155, 180, 184
Kamali, M.H. 23, 44, 164
Kant, E. 108–9
al-Karaki 167
Karbala 149, 160, 161, 167, 246
al-Karim Jili 175
al-Kaysi 23, 179
Khadijah 21, 29, 61, 134, 245, 249, 252
Khaibar 71, 77, 238, 246, 250
Khaldun, Ibn 150, 154, 159, 247
khalifs
  authority of 38, 56, 57, 144, 145, 180
  office of 143, 145–9, 151, 153, 155, 156, 157, 159
Khalili collection 35
Khan, Ahmed Riza 184
Khan, M.M. 31, 32, 47, 50, 73, 76, 156
Khan, Sayyid Ahmed 45, 48, 51, 58, 60, 75, 102, 117, 127, 191, 199, 247
Kharijites 147, 150, 163, 188
al-Khayr 176
khilafat 139, 140, 142
Khodr, G. 235
Khomeini, Imam 167–9, 218–9, 248
al-Kindi 76, 80, 87, 89, 96, 114, 122
King, J. 212
Kipling, R. 212
Knitter, P. 235, 239, 242
knowledge 27, 122, 158, 172, 174, 180, 181, 183, 188
Kraemer, H. 203
Kufa 147, 148
Küng, H. 225, 232, 236, 239–41
Kuper, A. 12, 222
Kurtz, P. 49

Lammens, H. 1–2, 37
Lane, E.W. 179, 182
Lane-Poole, S. 98, 124
Leaman, O. 226
Lebanon 43
Leeuw, G van der 7
Leibnitz, G.W. von 108–9
Leicester 9
Lewis, B. 5, 102
Lindholm, C. 7, 140, 155, 167, 168, 171, 176, 180
Lings, M. 31, 46, 47, 48, 51, 111, 117, 170, 171, 175, 177, 249, 250, 251
Lott, E. 9, 12

Lull, R.   87, 88, 89, 247
Luther, M.   97, 247

Macauley, T.B.   208–9
Madinah   17, 19, 28, 113, 122, 123, 146, 182, 187, 191, 192, 245, 246, 249
  constitution   25, 116
Mahdi, the   166, 247
al-Mahdi, Khalif   74
Makkah   17, 19, 28, 29, 30, 37, 51, 79, 80, 110, 111, 113, 116, 122, 126, 177, 245, 246, 250
Makruh   24, 197
Malaysia   6
Malik, Imam   159, 160
Ma'mun   55, 57
Mar Timothy, Catholicos   74, 75, 76, 79, 83, 89
Marco Polo   82
Margoliouth, D.S.   24, 35
Markham, I.   168, 218
Mary the Copt   113, 133, 251
Mary, the Virgin   77, 114, 115, 232
Marques, G.C.   214
Massignon, L.   170
Mathews, A.N.   34, 100
Maududi, A.   21, 65, 140, 141, 142, 248
Maurice, F.D.   109, 237
Mawardi   143
Mawdu'at   58
Meadows, P.   9–11
Menzel, T.   127–8
Mernissi, F.   13, 44, 58, 61–2, 153, 156, 216
Midnight's Children   206, 208, 209, 210, 214, 216, 221
Milad-al-Nabi (Prophet's birthday)   182, 183
Mingana, A.   74, 75, 79
miracles   2, 29, 45–53, 64, 76, 77, 101, 179, 198, 199, 201, 204, 224, 254
Mishkat-al-Masabih   34, 43, 50, 55, 100, 104, 184
Mo, T.   208
Moore's Last Sigh, The   208, 210, 212, 213, 216, 218, 220, 201
Morocco, 156, 200–1, 228, 247
Moses   29, 49, 72, 75, 82, 105, 123
Mozaffari, M.   218
Mu'awiyah, Khalif   54, 71, 147, 148, 149, 150, 246
Muhammad

and animals   51, 52, 58
birth   29, 51, 245
  as cardinal   84
  chronology disputed   18, 37, 38, 40, 110, 135
cloak/mantle   41, 151, 155
death and death legends   18, 30, 79, 80, 84, 91, 94, 143, 246
description of   36
epilepsy alleged/denied   80, 94, 97, 98, 99, 100, 101, 102, 107, 134
as exemplar   1, 3, 18, 23, 65, 128, 140, 143, 175, 186, 192, 222, 228
genealogy   29, 52, 72, 111, 114
as heretic   76, 80, 81, 89, 91, 97, 99, 114
as hero   102, 108–10
as idol   82, 84
as intercessor   178, 198, 202, 255
letters and treaties   25, 116
on lying   56, 60–1, 118
love of   3, 65, 177, 179, 190
as magician   52, 83, 91, 215
marriages   18, 77, 79, 99, 113, 122, 224, 249–52
nurse   29, 134
as Perfect Man   128, 140, 172, 175, 190
as Prophet   6, 123, 130, 134, 139, 141, 142, 222, 225
as pseudo-prophet   76, 79, 135
revelatory experience   41–2, 98, 101, 109, 123, 125, 131, 133, 134, 205, 221, 225, 231–2, 254
ring   42, 148
satanic inspiration alleged   79, 83, 87, 91, 107, 113, 114, 123, 205, 211, 221
self-delusion alleged/defended   79, 96, 98, 100, 102, 107, 120, 123, 133, 135, 221
sexuality   76–7, 78, 81, 82, 84, 97, 98, 122, 215, 216, 238
sinlessness   20, 21, 128, 131, 159, 186, 204, 225
unletteredness   21, 77, 232, 254
visions of   27, 178–9, 186

and war/the sword   76, 77, 79, 91, 94, 100, 104, 113, 114, 119, 221, 237
  see also names used for Muhammad
Muhammad–Christ comparison see Christ–Muhammad comparison
Muir, W.   26, 28, 30, 35, 36, 42–4, 48, 55, 60, 63, 64, 105, 111–20, 122, 124, 130, 133, 134, 161, 211, 222, 228, 238, 247, 249, 252
mujtahid/mujtahidun   164, 165, 166, 167, 168
murid   176, 183, 223
Murji'ites   150
Muslim, Abu'l Hussain   31, 32, 33, 50, 56, 144, 152, 178
Musnad   24, 27, 57
mustad'afun   134, 169, 237
mu'tah   251
Mu'tazalites   55, 185

nafs   173, 180
Nahjul Balaagah   30, 158
Najran   22, 71
names used for Muhammad   83, 84, 91, 95, 210, 214
Naipaul, V.S.   210–11
Napoleon, Emperor   3
Naqshbandi   174, 184
Nasi   74
Nasr, S.H.   23, 41, 60, 77, 143, 170, 175, 183, 232
Nestorians   70, 74, 94
Neuman, L.   10
Newbigin, L.   203–4, 230, 232
Nicholson, R.A.   60, 172, 176, 177, 180
Night Journey and Ascension   47, 48, 49, 64, 91, 94, 133, 180
Ninety-nine Names of God   24, 82, 242
Noble Scribes   22, 26
Nur (light)   48, 160, 172, 255

Ockley, S.   91, 98
Orientalism   4, 5, 6
Oxford   88, 91, 93, 98, 101, 103, 247
Oxford Centre for Islamic Studies   6, 14
Otto, R.   125
Ottomans, 90, 148, 155, 156, 247

Padwick, C.   140, 176, 177, 202
Pahlavis   167–8

Pakistan   184, 191, 199, 200, 206, 207, 209, 220, 248
Palmer, E.H.   124
Paraclete, Muhammad as   76
Paradise   34, 48, 62, 71, 77, 78, 91, 99, 171, 180, 211, 215, 216, 239
Parekh, B.   207
Parrinder, G.   122, 226
Patai, R.   93, 101
Persinger, M.   134
Peter the Venerable   87, 89
Peters, F.E.   18, 29, 39, 40, 52, 153, 157, 182, 183, 187
Pettifer, J.   86, 228
Pfander, K.G.   229
phenomenology   7–9, 11
Phipps, W.E.   43, 120, 226, 238
Pickthall, M.M.   99, 127, 249, 250, 251, 252
pir/pirs   173, 183, 184, 199, 204, 223, 255
Plato   141, 187
Pocock, E.   91, 93, 94
polygamy   113, 122, 198, 223–4
postmodernism   8, 208, 223, 232, 233, 234, 240
Prideaux, H.   91, 96, 97, 100
prophets   21, 141–2
psychology   109, 125, 129, 133–5, 222

qadi   57, 152
Qadir, C.A.   173, 187
Qajars   167
qiblah   19, 61, 177, 178
qiyas   25, 49
qudsi hadith   24, 197, 198
Qur'an   2, 3, 18, 19–26, 27, 33, 36, 38–49, 52–4, 57–8, 62–3, 65, 74–7, 79, 84, 87, 89, 90, 96, 98–100, 110, 119, 120, 122, 123, 127, 129–31, 140–3, 145, 147, 157–60, 171, 176, 178, 183, 185, 186, 189, 190, 191, 192, 195–9, 201, 205, 223–7, 237, 238–42, 246, 249–52, 254
  created/uncreated   22, 78, 185–6
  incoherency alleged   76, 86, 90, 96
  Muhammad as author   3, 77, 79, 81, 84, 91, 93, 101, 111, 113, 123, 127, 131, 196, 211, 225, 232, 254

recension of 22, 110
rendered into
    English 98, 99
rendered into
    French 99
rendered into Latin
    87, 90
Quraysh 49, 117, 144,
    156, 245
Qurayzah, bani 116,
    245, 252
Qutb 180
Qutb, M. 11
Qutb, S. 248

Rabi'a 171, 179
racism/race relations
    207, 219
Rahman, A. 119
Rahman, F. 240
al-Raziq, A.A. 191
Reat, R. 8
reflexivity 11
Reland, A. 94, 104
religious studies 7, 11
Renaissance 13, 92,
    93
Renan, E. 103, 105,
    106, 211, 247
Richard, Y. 157, 160,
    161, 169
Ricoeur, P. 241
Ricoldo 87, 88, 90,
    91, 133
Rippin, A. 38, 56, 145
Risalah 76, 82, 87, 90,
    114, 133
Robinson, N. 22, 38,
    41, 46, 47, 73, 215
Robson, J. 24, 33, 34,
    63
Rodinson, M. 1,
    37–40, 44, 70, 90,
    94, 96, 98, 100, 109,
    125, 134, 216
Roland of France 84
Ross, A. 99
Roy, A. 200
Rumi 172, 176
Rushd, Ibn
    (Averroës) 49, 86,
    88, 89, 90, 106, 152,
    187, 211, 247
Rushdie, S. 1, 2, 13,
    14, 23, 83, 91, 127,
    196, 205–23, 248
Rushdie affair 1, 14,
    205–23
Ruthven, M. 206, 213
Ryer, du A. 99

Sa'd, Ibn 29, 30, 34,
    40, 46, 127
Safavids, the 166, 167,
    247
Sahas, S. 71, 78, 80
Said, E. 4–7, 107,
    108, 110, 111, 113,
    220, 223, 233, 241
Saladin 85, 87, 89
salatu'ala al-Nabi 176
Sale, G. 94, 96, 98,
    99, 100, 103, 104,
    122, 247
Saljuks 153, 162, 246

Sardar, Z. 188, 192–3
Satanic Verses, The 1,
    83, 205–20, 248
Satanic Verses affair,
    the 91, 113, 127,
    129, 216–17, 254
Schacht, J. 28, 43, 54,
    55, 139, 152, 153,
    188
Schimmel, A. 125,
    140, 190, 191, 192
Schuon, F. 52, 170,
    173, 175, 177, 201,
    227
Scott, W. 84, 85
Shafi'i, Imam 28, 54,
    159, 246
shahadah 140, 150,
    160, 171, 173, 236
Shahrastani 20
Shaikhs, Sufi 53, 173,
    175, 179, 180
Shamanism 125
Shame 208, 220
Shari'ah 23, 25, 142,
    143, 152, 153, 165,
    188, 189, 191, 192,
    229, 248
Shepard, W. 190, 191
Shi'a 30, 31, 40, 55,
    57, 140, 142, 143,
    149, 150, 157–70,
    173, 246, 247, 251
shirk 76, 199
shura 142–3
Siddiqi, M.S. 249,
    251
Siddiqi, M.Z. 25, 26,
    27, 57, 58, 61, 135,
    150
Siffin, battle of 147
silsilah 173, 175
Sina, Ibn (Avicenna)
    88, 152, 174, 187,
    246, 247
sira 17, 28–31, 40, 41,
    53, 71, 81, 93, 110,
    111, 114, 116, 253–4
Smith, J. 91, 95
Smith, M. 53, 171,
    174, 176, 179
Smith, R.B. 84,
    120–5, 128, 129,
    130, 247
Smith, W.C. 3, 5, 6,
    11, 108, 154, 192,
    223, 224, 241
Soderblom, N. 125
Southern, R.W. 70,
    83, 84, 85, 87, 88, 89
Spain 81, 82, 83, 86,
    88, 90, 93, 101, 152,
    246, 247
SPCK 99
splitting of the moon
    45–6, 198
Sprenger, A. 102, 114,
    122
Stanley, A.P. 123
Storr, A. 134
Stubbe, H. 94, 95, 96,
    100, 106, 122

Sufism 53, 140,
    154–5, 170–84, 190,
    199, 200–2, 208,
    210, 255
sunnah 19, 20, 23, 24,
    28, 54, 56, 57, 60,
    65, 117, 139, 142,
    143, 145, 147, 158,
    163, 168, 169, 183,
    188, 189, 200, 227,
    228, 236, 237, 238,
    243
    authority of 25, 56,
    57, 145, 186
Sunnis 31, 40, 55,
    140, 142, 143, 144,
    147, 148, 152, 154,
    156, 169–70, 173,
    181, 184, 188
Sweetman, J.W. 70,
    71, 72, 73, 75, 76,
    77, 78, 84, 85, 87,
    88, 89, 90, 91

al-Tabari 26, 28, 40,
    127, 149
tafsir 27, 46, 49
Taha, M. 190–1
Talhah, 146–7, 158
Taliban, the 188, 196,
    197, 199, 201, 248
Talmud, the 21
taqiyah 60, 161, 181
taqlid 152, 165
Taragona, Council of
    89
Tariqah 173, 174, 175,
    180
tasliya 174, 177, 182,
    202
tawhid 19, 171, 173,
    185, 242
Theophanes 80–1
Thousand and One
    Nights, The 50, 86,
    98, 209
Tibawi, A.L. 101
Tillich, P. 237
Tirmidhi 31, 144
Tisdall, W.St C. 21,
    47, 222
Tours, battle of 81,
    246
Tracy, D. 10, 223
Trench/Ditch, battle
    of 30, 51, 116, 245
Trinity, the 11, 74, 81,
    82, 88, 89, 114, 130,
    234–5, 240–2
Troll, C. 20, 33, 45,
    48, 51, 58, 60, 117,
    127, 183, 191
Tufayl, Ibn 86
Turkey 6, 43, 155
Twelvers 164–9

Uhud, defeat of 30,
    82, 245, 250
'Umar I 25, 26, 59,
    64, 73, 143, 144,
    145, 146, 147, 158,
    182, 247, 249
'Umar II 27, 150

Umayyads 43, 54, 56,
    74, 148, 150, 151,
    152, 246
ummah 19, 31, 143,
    149, 168, 169
ummi (unlettered) 21,
    77, 232, 254
Unitarians 234, 241,
    247
'urf 44
ur-Rahman, M.'A. 72,
    73
Usulis 165
'Uthman 22, 55, 59,
    146, 147, 148, 158,
    247

Vahiuddin, S. 31
virtual insidership
    8–11
Voltaire 96–7, 99, 120

Wali Allah, Shah 58
Wansbrough, J. 21–2
al-Waqidi 30, 55, 64,
    98
Warraq, Ibn 21, 54,
    55, 95, 105, 110,
    118–20
Watkins, Lord Justice
    219
Watt, W.M. 1, 2, 21,
    23, 39, 40, 51, 53,
    55, 75, 86, 100, 108,
    119–20, 128–32,
    141, 145, 146, 147,
    148, 149, 153, 155,
    160, 185, 186, 225,
    227, 241
Weber, M. 147, 149
Weil, G. 101–2
Wesley, C. 204
Westminster College
    6, 14, 200
Whaling, F. 7–8
White, J. 103, 120
William of Tripoli 85
William of Tyre 85–6
women 61–3, 83–4,
    196–7, 198–9, 213,
    215–16, 249–52

Yachnes, P. 170, 184
Yazid, Khalif 80, 148,
    149, 161, 246

Zaehner, R.C. 173,
    181
Zahiri school 49
Zaid/Zainab affair 77,
    81, 82, 91, 113,
    126–7, 129, 133,
    250, 254
Zakaria, R. 42, 52,
    116, 140, 146, 147,
    148, 150, 151, 154,
    155, 186, 191, 241,
    249, 251
Zaydis 163–4
Ziyad, ibn 149
Zwemer, S.W. 119
Zubayr, az 146–7,
    148, 158
Zubayr, ibn 148, 246

Index of Qur'anic References

2. Al Baqarah
(The Cow)
2.2   142, 198
2.23   45
2.30   140
2.37   140
2.59   22, 75
2.62   239
2.75   75
2.111   239
2.121   75
2.140   75
2.142   19
2.143   19
2.135   141
2.148   239
2.165   171
2.185   225
2.219   43
2.255   242
2.256   241
2.285   141

3. Al 'Imran
(The Family of Imran)
3.3   22, 142
3.7   49
3.31   177
3.59   81
3.63   75
3.85   239
3.104   19
3.113   75
3.124   49
3.135   58
3.144   21
3.159   142
3.199   239

4. Al Nisa
(The Women)
4.1   223–4
4.3   223–4, 250, 251
4.24   251
4.43   43
4.44   75
4.59   18, 141
4.113   239
4.152   141
4.157   73, 76, 238
4.159   178
4.171   71, 74, 237

5. Al Ma'idah
(The Repast)
5.3   19, 142
5.15   160
5.39   58
5.48   130, 239, 242
5.54   171
5.68   239
5.90   43
5.117   178

6. Al An'am
(The Cattle)
6.51   178
6.70   178

8. Al Anfal
(The Spoils of War)
8.17   49

9. Al Tawbah
(The Repentance)
9   36
9.5   119
9.29   70
9.40   42

10. Yunus (Jonah)
10.19   178
10.48   21

11. Hud
(The Prophet Hud)
11.114   24

12. Yusuf (Joseph)
12.2   22

13. Al Ra'd
(The Thunder)
13.37   22
13.38   52

16 Al Nahl (The Bee)
16.125   52

17. Al Isra'
(Night Journey)
17.1   47
17.33   58

22. Al Hajj
(The Pilgrimage)
22.40   237
22.52   127

24. Al Nur
(The Light)
24.2   43
24.6–8   43
24.11–20   249
24.35   48
24.58   24

25. Al Furqan
(The Criteria)
25.33   49

26. Al Shu'ara
(The Poets)
26.15   49
26.63   49

29. Al 'Ankabut (The Spider)
29.50   45, 52

33. Al Ahzab
(The Clans)
33.4–5   81, 250
33.21   18
33.30   251
33.33   157
33.37   81, 250
33.40   21, 134, 142
33.50   250
33.53   251
33.56   176

42. Al Shura
(Consultation)
42.38   143
42.40   58

43. Al Zukhruf
(The Gold Ornaments)
43.3   185
43.86   178

47. Muhammad
47.15   48

48. Al Fath
(The Victory)
48.2   128

53. Al Najm
(The Star)
53.1–12   47
53.19–23   127

54. Al Qamar
(The Moon)
54.1   45–6

55. Al Rahman
(The Merciful)
55.7   180

57. Al Hadid (Iron)
57.4   48

59. Al Hashr
(The Mustering)
59.7   18, 20

66. Al Tahrim
(The Prohibition)
66.1   251

68. Al Qalam
(The Pen)
68   41

74. Al Muddaththir
(The Cloaked)
74   40

75. Al Qiyamah (The Resurrection)
75.16   41
75.23   49

80. 'Abasa
(He Frowned)
80.15–16   22

85. Al Buruj
(The Constellations)
85.21–2   22, 185

93. Al Duha
(The Morning Hours)
93   41
93.9–10   19

96. Al'Alaq
(The Clot)
96   40

112 Al Tawhid
(The Unity)
112   19

Index of Hadith References

From Bukhari's Sahih (Khan, 1987)

B1.1   41, 42
B2.1   24
B2.6   64
B2.7   64
B2.8   3
B3.8   65
B3.20   27
B3.35   27
B3.39   46
B3.40   26
B3.43   26
B5.13   82
B9.13   62
B30.13   182
B34.16   198
B34.17   64
B39   23
B39.1   23
B39.15   23

B43.14   23
B52.157   118
B52.156   118
B52.160   118
B52.174   73
B55.46   58
B56.24   50
B56.26   45
B57.6   144, 158
B58.27   18, 52
B58.35   45–6
B59.6   40
B59.14   126
B59.81   157
B59.83   18
B59.84   36
B60.332   22
B72.41   171
B72.43   61
B74.29   157
B75.4   64

B76.13   64
B76.16   61
B76.51   61
B81.5   43
B81.6   43
B82.24   43
B85.4   64
B87.3   178
B87.10   179
B89.1   149
B89.3   156
B89.4   149
B92.2   38
B92.12   24
B92.13   38
B92.23   24
B92.26   142
B93.12   24
B93.43   42

From the Mishkat-al-Masabih (Robson, 1990)

MM,1,39   152
MM,1,42   56
MM,1,43   20
MM,1,45–46   31, 191
MM,1,47   45
MM,1,49   22, 27
MM,1,50   33

MM,1,658   62
MM,1,691   61
MM,1,693   61
MM,1,762   43
MM,1,772   43
MM,2,1091   62
MM,2,1230   34, 175
MM,2,1231   142, 178
MM,2,1271f   50
MM,2,1320   34
MM,2,1322   59, 144
MM,2,1323   144
MM,2,1351   149
MM,2,1358   149
MM,2,1361   61
MM,2,1362   61

From Tirmidhi's Jami (as cited in Ali, 1977)

Tir.   39.2   27
Tir.   39.12   26

From Muslim's Sahih (Siddiqi, 1975)

M4.1259   22